Complete Czech

David Short

First published in Great Britain in 1993 as Teach Yourself Czech by Hodder Education. An Hachette UK company.

This edition published in 2015 by John Murray Learning

British Library Cataloguing in Publication Data: a catalogue record for this title is available from the British Library.

Library of Congress Catalogue Card Number: on file

ISBN: 9781444106916

10

Cover image © wrangle/iStockphoto.com

Typeset by Cenveo® Publisher Services.

Printed and bound in Great Britain by CPI Group (UK) Ltd., Croydon, CR0 4YY.

John Murray Learning policy is to use papers that are natural, renewable and recyclable products and made from wood grown in sustainable forests. The logging and manufacturing processes are expected to conform to the environmental regulations of the country of origin.

Carmelite House
50 Victoria Embankment
London EC4Y 0DZ
www.hodder.co.uk

Contents

Credits

Front cover: © wrangle/iStockphoto.com

Back cover and pack: © Jakub Semeniuk/iStockphoto.com, © Royalty-Free/Corbis, © agencyby/iStockphoto.com, © Andy Cook/iStockphoto.com, © Christopher Ewing/iStockphoto.com, © zebicho – Fotolia.com, © Geoffrey Holman/iStockphoto.com, © Photodisc/Getty Images,© James C. Pruitt/iStockphoto.com, © Mohamed Saber – Fotolia.com

Meet the author

I have taught Czech since 1973, at the School of Slavonic and East European Studies, University of London, now a department of University College London. Previously I had studied a related language, Russian, at Birmingham University, after which I spent six years in Prague, studying Czech in particular and life in general.

I teach at all levels for both undergraduate and postgraduate students from a wide variety of language backgrounds. In the course of my teaching career, which has included occasional private tuition, I have prepared a wide range of learning materials besides the present textbook. Moreover, I have cooperated on a variety of dictionaries (four volumes of the Czech dictionary of idioms and the revision of the largest English–Czech dictionary currently available, amongst others); dictionaries are, obviously, a major tool for the language-learner. I am a founding member of the International Association of Teachers of Czech.

I have written widely on aspects of the Czech language and, to a lesser extent, Czech literature, and in recent years I have become a translator from the literature; it is my quiet wish that as more literature appears in translation, more people will be drawn to that which has not been translated. This is just one reason for learning Czech, but I believe my book will act as a good springboard, whatever your particular reason for learning this fascinating language.

David Short

Only got a minute?

Czech is the state language of the Czech Republic (capital Prague, in central Europe) and is spoken by most of its c. 10 million citizens. Some Slovaks, largely post-independence immigrants, get by quite happily with their own language, as the two are largely mutually intelligible. Czech, like Slovak, Polish, and Upper and Lower Sorbian (the latter spoken in the south-east corner of eastern Germany) is a West Slavonic language. These quite closely-related languages are more distantly related to the South Slavonic languages (Bosnian/ Croatian/Montenegrin/Serbian [i.e. the offshoots of Serbo-Croatian as used in former Yugoslavia], Bulgarian, Macedonian and Slovene) and the East Slavonic languages (Russian, Ukrainian, Belarusian). Czech has been influenced in the past by German, Germany being its closest neighbour geographically, but today very visibly by English, from which it borrows almost daily – in business, administration, IT, popular culture, sport, leisure and other areas.

Czech is also spoken by small, generally rural, communities elsewhere in eastern Europe, larger communities in North America and scattered populations worldwide, owing to several waves of emigration during the late 19th and 20th centuries.

Czech uses the Latin alphabet, with diacritics ('accents') to denote sounds for which the Latin alphabet is unsuited. This convention has been gradually refined since its first introduction by the religious reformer Jan Hus in the 14th century and has been adopted by several other languages since.

The language's main characteristic is inflection: relations among the parts of a sentence are largely expressed by the endings of words.

Only got ten minutes?

So who speaks Czech? There are about 10 million people in the Czech Republic and a million or so others beyond its frontiers. Following waves of emigration in the late 19th and 20th centuries some live in close-knit rural communities in eastern Europe, others in bigger, compact or quite diffuse, areas in North America in particular, but plenty more scattered worldwide. Except in the old outlying communities in Europe, generally static and retaining the archaic dialect version of the language with which they arrived, other extraterritorial Czechs lose touch with their language through increasing contamination in their host community and – especially with second and later generations – through questioning the real need to sustain the language at all. The other side of this is the modern trend to 'find one's roots' and many young non-Czech-speaking expatriates are now meeting, especially in the larger US cities but elsewhere too, and learning or re-learning their ancestral language.

There are plenty of reasons why non-Czechs should learn the language. Anyone for whom doing business in the post-Communist Czech Republic is an appropriate proposition (and there have been plenty) would be well advised to learn Czech and not rely on Czechs' knowledge of English or rely forever on interpreters and translators. Likewise, while there is a growing body of translations from Czech literature, making more Czech poets and writers better known and appreciated, there is much more that has not been translated – whether by previously-translated authors or others – but will undoubtedly reward the reader for whom it will inevitably be eye-opening. It goes without saying that as the language is the key to the literature, the reverse can also be true – the more you read, even if with the aid of a dictionary, the broader your language will become.

Beyond literature, the Czechs have a rich cultural heritage in art and architecture and the country has scores of magnificent stately homes, many housing impressive libraries or collections of native or foreign artworks, and magnificent old ruined castles. Many of its towns have fine historic centres with impressive, often baroque, squares, beautiful churches and the great townhouses of the erstwhile aristocracy. True, some suffered neglect under the previous regime, and many fine old houses were used as sanatoria or potato stores but many have been or are being restored to their former glory.

Geographically, the main appeal lies in the mountains and rivers, much neglected by outsiders, but offering both excellent sport (rock climbing, downhill and cross-country skiing, kayaking, white-water rafting) and more leisurely recreation in the form of hiking or cyclotouring (excellent maps are widely available with footpaths and long-distance trails all marked; most have the key in English and other languages). The Czechs have a long tradition in sport, recreation and tourism, being among the first to have had national hiking and cycling clubs. The Prague Cycling Club even maintained collections of memorabilia, autographs and the like, and sometimes published under their own rubric within the popular weeklies. Here, just for fun, is a poem by Josef Šváb Malostranský (1860–1930):

Má píseň na kole

Já sjezdit chtěl bych celý svět,

mne žádná cesta neleká,

ani ten vítr k Roudnici –

ptejte se jenom Koenecka...!

Já sjezdit chtěl bych celý svět,

jak rytíř, co má panoše,

jenom nebýt těch vrchů moc,

ptejte se tuhle – Jaroše...!

Já sjezdit chtěl bych celý svět

a třeba byl by na zámce;

jenom nebýt těch pádů moc –

ptejte se pana – Adamce...!

My Song on my Bicycle

I'd like to ride the whole world o'er,

no road could ever put me off,

nor even the wind t'wards Roudnice –

Ask friend Koeneck – he caught a cough!

I'd like to ride the whole world o'er,

but like a knight with a squire around,

as long as there aren't too many hills –

Ask Jaroš here – hills got him down!

I'd like to ride the whole world o'er,

but live in style and free of woes

and not keep falling off my bike –

Ask Mr Adamec – he knows!

Translation from Czech © David Short 2003

It appeared in the magazine *Švanda dudák*, Vol.5/12, December 1886, p. 711. One must assume that Messrs Koeneck, Jaroš and Adamec were actual club members with reputations that have to be deduced; my deductions are encapsulated in the last line of each verse, which are more explicit than the original (as you will appreciate once you have learned Czech and can test the translation for accuracy). The author wrote prose, plays, songs and jingles, acted in revues and films, and was a publisher and bookseller.

Czechs frequently point out that of all the things a foreign visitor would like to do or see in a new place, the only thing their country lacks is the seaside. Traditionally, the Czechs and Slovaks have made up for being landlocked by holidaying on the Black Sea and Adriatic coasts, less so in the colder Baltic, but since the crumbling of Communism and the complete freedom of movement this brought, they have ventured to every corner of the earth – as long as the money was available.

The country has long been renowned for its spas, especially in West Bohemia but found all over the country, each one noted for this or that particular therapy; these inland resorts compensate in part for the lack of a coast. King Edward VII used to visit. Under Communism spas were integrated into the national health service, but were also enjoyed by bigwigs from 'fraternal' countries and Arab sheiks the Czechoslovak Communist authorities were particularly interested in cultivating.

There is plenty for the visitor to enjoy and there are many reasons why a good basic knowledge of the language is worth acquiring.

The Czech Republic as presently constituted is of course a young country, coming into being only on 1 January 1993, along with its previous partner, Slovakia. Together they had made up Czechoslovakia, which was also a creation of the 20th century, emerging out of the ruins of Imperial Austria after the First World War. During the Second World War, the country's boundaries were trimmed back, with many borderlands ceded to Nazi Germany. Slovakia then became a quasi-independent client of Germany, the western two-thirds of the country becoming Germany's Protectorate of Bohemia and Moravia. The present Czech Republic comprises these two ancient provinces, Bohemia in the west, Moravia in the east, plus a part of southern Silesia (the rest is in Poland) tacked onto northern Moravia, but more or less within their pre-war frontiers.

Let's look briefly at some of these names and some of the matters they raise. First: the Czech Republic, in Czech **Česká republika** (note the small **r-** in the second word). There exists a strong urge to find the country a one-word name and **Česko** has been generally adopted, though against some fierce opposition. Its merit is in not overlapping with **Čechy** 'Bohemia', so its use can embrace Moravia without offence. **Čechy** used colloquially for the whole country (and in neighbouring Polish the equivalent word does have both meanings) is offensive. So, **Čechy** it shall be for the province that surrounds Prague, and **Česko** for the whole country. The problem then arises of what single expression might be adopted in English. It was proposed in the 1990s, but not implemented, that this should be *Czechia*. I hear of people going to '*Czech*', but I see no merit in the general adoption of this (despite the English-language labelling of Pilsner Urquell crates), when the word already serves as a noun – to denote a Czech person *and* his/her language, and as an adjective. English really lacks an acceptable one-word name; I believe *Czechia* is feasible, but somehow it cannot find more general acceptability. Where English does have an edge, however, is in having two adjectives, *Czech* and *Bohemian* (*bohemian* is a different matter altogether) where Czech itself has just one, **český**. The distinction between the two in English is by no means dead, but the greater frequency of **Czech** can lead to its inappropriate use in certain historical contexts. One very clear distinction would be in the phrases *the Bohemian crown*, that is, the royal headgear from the time when Bohemia was indeed a kingdom (hence too 'the Lands of the Bohemian Crown', in contrast to the more recent 'Czech lands'), and *the Czech crown*, the modern currency. In Czech, both of these are **česká koruna**, only the latter can be more formally **koruna česká**, indeed that reverse order is the source of the standard abbreviation of the currency, **Kč**. The other misuse of *Czech* in modern times, up to 1989, was when it acted as a false shorthand for *Czechoslovak(ian)*; in those days it was Slovaks more than Moravians who might quite properly take offence.

And so to *Moravia*, in Czech **Morava**. The Czech name applies both to the more easterly of the two main provinces that make up the country, Moravia, and to the great river, a tributary of the Danube, which runs through it in the north and round it on the east, known as the March, though this name is little used outside historical geography. If we recall the English usage that speaks of the 'Welsh marches' for the border strip between Wales and England, we appreciate that this really is in some sense a border river, indeed the **mor-/mar-** element has precisely this meaning, and the -**ava** ending in the name of many Czech rivers is part of what is called the Celtic substrate and related to our own *Avon*, once meaning simply 'river' (cf. *afon* in Welsh). The river Morava/March thus once marked the limit of civilized Europe viewed from further west. The association between the river and provincial names in part also explains why Czech uses different prepositions to express 'in': Primarily *in* is expressed by **v**, hence **v české republice** *'in the Czech Republic'*, **v čechách** *'in Bohemia'*, but with *Moravia/***Morava** usage requires **na**, which means primarily 'on'. This is the same 'on' as in *'on the Thames/Rhine, [Stratford] on Avon'*, so **na Moravě** is *'on the March/Morava'* first, but also 'in Moravia'. (Another explanation is that **na** is used in Czech for 'in' in the case of flat areas, e.g. plains and deserts, and areas that project out of flat areas, e.g. mountains and islands. Hence it is the preposition that must be used with the Czech words meaning 'plain', 'desert', 'island', 'mountain', and geographical names of these kinds of terrain, such as *Ukraine* – **na Ukrajině**, *Sahara* – **na Sahaře**, *Cyprus* – **na Kypru**, *Caucasus* – **na Kavkaze**. However, Moravia is by no means one great plain, nor is it notoriously mountainous, though it has elements of both. I prefer to think that the necessary use of **na Moravě** is to do with the overlap between province and river name.)

As you learn more of the language, you will appreciate not only how many borrowed words Czech has absorbed, but also how many names it has for non-Czech places. Some remain recognizable, such as **Londýn**-*London*, **Paříž**-*Paris*, **Atény**-*Athens*, **Moskva**-*Moscow*, while others may be less transparent, such as **Drážďany**-*Dresden*, **Řím**-*Rome* or **Vídeň**-*Vienna*. Yet others may be beyond instant recognition, most notoriously in the case of **Kodaň**-*Copenhagen* or **Rakousko**-*Austria*. There are many historical reasons for each of these, but much can be attributed to the power and importance of the medieval Bohemian kingdom and perhaps also to the Czechs' **touha cestovatelská**, or *longing to travel*, which has deep and ancient roots and is to this day a key part of their self-image; in addition to their 'natural' democratism, their 'dove-like' (i.e. peace-loving) nature, their hospitality, their ownership of the best hops and beer in the world, and their pride in a language that is unique in having the sound **ř**, and one which may create the odd sentence 'with no vowels'. Most self-images are best taken with a grain, if not a pinch of salt...

Introduction

The Czech Republic and its language

The Czech Republic is, since 1 January 1993, one of the two daughter states of Czechoslovakia (the other is Slovakia to the east). Its unforgettable capital, Prague, lies halfway down a line drawn from Stockholm to Rome, at roughly the same latitude as the Scilly Isles, which places the country in the very heart of Europe.

The Czech Republic consists of the lands of Bohemia (Čechy), Moravia (Morava) and part of Silesia (Slezsko; the rest is in Poland), and is inhabited by Czechs, the westernmost members of the Slav family of nations. There are small pockets inhabited by German and Polish minorities, and a fairly large number of Slovaks – the nearest relatives of the Czechs – and even more Roms (Gypsies) scattered throughout the republic. The provincial capital of Moravia–Silesia is the industrial city of Brno.

What you will be learning

The language you will be learning in this course is an informal version of standard Czech, which perhaps needs explaining. The standard language has some features which are rarely, if ever, used in speech, and many more that are only used in such formal contexts as schools or the courts. While you would never be wrong using such features, you could sound rather stuffy. On the other hand, much of the everyday speech of most Czechs is different from the standard language; it has no normally written version, nor any absolutely rigid rules. If you were to try to learn this colloquial version first, you would expose yourself to the risk of sounding funny – a bit like a foreigner attempting Cockney and failing. The solution adopted in this book is to keep to forms from the 'lower end' of the range that is currently accepted within standard Czech. Some guidance will be given at the end of the course on the main features which separate the two extreme versions of the language.

Why learn Czech?

People, whether as tourists or businesspeople and industrialists, have become increasingly aware of the potential of all the countries of eastern and central Europe thanks to the huge political, and increasing social, changes since the mid 1980s – or since November 1989 in the case of former Czechoslovakia. Those who already knew the area have sometimes been frustrated by the alleged intractability of the languages. This new version of *Complete Czech* aims to meet the first needs of the leisure, and in some measure the business, traveller in the Czech Republic, equipping them with the practical skills to cope with everyday situations. Grammatical terms are introduced, where necessary, as simply and painlessly as possible, to aid which a **Glossary of grammatical terms** is included.

The course should help you to communicate, perhaps not in an error-free manner, but adequately enough to show your Czech hosts that you have made an honest effort. They will often have a good command of English or German, especially in the cities, but if you want to make your basic wishes or needs known in some of the remoter parts of this beautiful country, having some Czech of your own will serve you well. Within simple 'domestic' contexts, we mean to help you make requests, seek information, apologize, even complain, and describe simply events that have happened, will or may happen; all of this can be applied in any context or environment.

The Czechs are apt to think of theirs as a 'minor' language, one that foreigners do not bother with, so the greater your success with learning, the warmer the response you will receive. One added bonus of knowing Czech is that you should be able, though not quite so freely, to communicate with Slovaks too (for the native, the two languages have traditionally been about ninety-nine per cent mutually intelligible, though since the break-up the distance between the languages is increasing and the man in the street's familiarity with the other language has begun to decline). Thus, if your interests lie mainly in Slovakia, common sense and courtesy make it vital to learn Slovak first.

The course

Each unit is based on simple dialogues between two or more people discussing everyday matters. In addition to the material in the dialogue you will be given snippets of background information on the language itself and on the society that uses it.

Words and phrases will appear in manageable quotas, in readily reuseable formats. Your skill with these will be tested by various means after each unit, and only when you are confident that you have mastered one unit should you proceed to the next.

Each unit contains two dialogues. These build up to give you a command of many essential phrases and, especially in the earlier units, much of the basic language you will need on first arriving in the Czech Republic. First there is a simple dialogue derived from the unit's theme – hinted at in the unit's title – with explanations and exercises to practise what you have learnt. The second dialogue usually expands this introduction with more phrases in the same domain, but also brings in some new material. Each unit also contains a Cultural Information passage, giving additional information about the Czech people, life or language. Scattered here and there you will find additional 'Insight' boxes giving all manner of additional information about the language and country.

HOW TO PROCEED

Read each section separately, practising the dialogue by imitation of the recording if you have it, or learn together with a friend. All the material that is recorded is indicated with a recording icon. Once you are confident, tackle the exercises. Some of the exercises help you with examples to follow; others require you merely to follow a simple instruction. By referring back you can easily verify that you have got them right: the book's primary aim is, after all, to be your teacher, so going back is no worse than having to ask a teacher to go through something again. If you are still uncertain about your answer, you can check with the **Key to the exercises** at the back of the book.

You should aim to master all new words as they arise in the dialogues and Quick vocabs. It is time-wasting to have to go back and retrieve them if you don't do this properly. Each of us eventually finds his or her own most satisfactory method of vocabulary-learning – some people learn their words by rote, as laid out in the book, others by creating their own alphabetized list, perhaps on cards, or simply by copying everything out, along with any words acquired from elsewhere, into a notebook. You could assemble them by word-class (nouns, verbs, adjectives, adverbs), by the general topic in which you first encounter them, or roughly alphabetically. Whatever method you use, make sure you know the words in both directions – Czech to English and English to Czech.

How difficult is Czech?

Relative difficulty is hard to measure, but Czech is a European language, which means that it must be nearer to English and French, for example, than an oriental or African language. Two major areas with which the learner has to come to terms are how nouns and adjectives change their form to serve different functions (within a system of *cases*), and how most verbs, which also change according to who, and how many people are doing the action, and sometimes even their sex, have to be learned in two sets of forms, representing the two *aspects* – the means by which Czech compensates for having a simple tense system.

One huge advantage of Czech is that, unlike English or French, the spelling is remarkably consistent with the pronunciation, although to convey all the sounds required the normal Roman alphabet is supplemented by letters with diacritics (you may call them 'accents'). And if you were put off French at school, do not worry. Here you will be guided along in easy stages, and it is you who sets the pace. The accompanying recording contains most of the dialogues, a few of the exercises in the course, and some extra material. So get used to hearing the language, and if possible enlist the help of Czechs in the neighbourhood so that you may hear more types of voice. Get them to let you practise your dialogue skills on them to give your achievements an airing before you even travel. And before long you will realize it can be done. Then when you get to your hotel or your business negotiations in **Praha, Plzeň** or **Mariánské Lázně** (*Prague, Pilsen* or *Marienbad*) and your hosts compliment you on your skills, you can say with pride: **A naučil jsem se to sám** (*And I taught myself*).

The Czech alphabet and pronunciation

🔊 **TRS 1–4**

The Czech alphabet, for dictionary purposes:

a	h	o	u
b	ch	p	v
c	i	q	w
č	j	r	x
d	k	ř	y
e	l	s	z
f	m	š	ž
g	n	t	

Of these note the letters that are absent from the English alphabet:

č, ch, ř, š, ž (in particular **ch**, which counts as a single letter and always comes after **h**).

In addition, there are several more letters, which have to be observed in spelling, but which are not alphabetized, that is, they are treated, for dictionary purposes, as variants. These are:

á	ě	ó	ů
ď	í	ť	ý
é	ň	ú	

VOWELS

There are just five vowel sounds: **a**, **e**, **i**, **o** and **u** pronounced consistently:

> **a** is pronounced roughly like the *u* in *but*: try **a** (*and*), **pan** (*Mr*), **mapa** (*map*).
>
> **e** is pronounced like the *e* in *bed*: try **flek** (*stain*), **nese** (*is carrying*), **Havel** (*a surname*).
>
> **i** is pronounced short like the *i* in *bit*, but with more of the quality of *ee* in *beet*; **i** and **y** are different letters for the same sound: try **byli** (*they were*), **bili** (*they struck*), **styl** (*style*), **syn** (*son*), **emigrant** (*émigré*).
>
> **o** is pronounced like *o* in *hot*: try **dole** (*downstairs*), **oko** (*eye*), **revidovat** (*to revise*).
>
> **u** is pronounced roughly like *oo* in *good*: try **sud** (*barrel*), **mluvit** (*to speak*), **uniforma** (*uniform*).

These short vowels are matched by a set of long vowels, which are marked by the 'acute accent' ´ and are about 1¾ times as long as the short vowels. Compare **dal** (*gave*) and **dál** (*further* – also *Come in!*), **mile** (*kindly*) and **míle** (*mile*), **byt** (*apartment*) and **být** (*to be*), **rychle** (*quickly*) and **rychlé** (*quick*), and **uhel** (*a coal*) and **úhel** (*corner*). Long **u** is also represented, in set circumstances, by the symbol **ů**; here too we may find contrasting words with the short and long vowel respectively, e.g. **domu** (*of the house*) and **domů** (*of the houses; homewards*).

Sequences of vowels that make up a single sound are called diphthongs. Czech has one native diphthong, **ou**, combining **o** and **u** in roughly equal proportions: try **soud** (*court*), **nesou** (*they are carrying*), **doufat** (*to hope*). (Warning: Avoid any use of the English diphthongs as heard in *hope* or *now*.) Two foreign diphthongs **au** and **eu** are found in such words as **auto** (*car*), **pneumatika** (*tyre*).

CONSONANTS

Among the letters denoting consonants, many represent sounds quite like the values of the equivalent English letters; these are:

b	**f**	**l**	**s**	**x** (only in foreign words)
d	**v**	**m**	**z**	
g		**n**		

Some others are slightly less close to the English ones:

Czech **p**, **t** and **k** represent unaspirated sounds, that is, they are not followed, except at the end of a word, by the puff of breath that follows their English counterparts (Czech **p** is always like that in English *spin*, never like that in *pin*) – try pronouncing **kabelka** (*handbag*), **pán** (*gentleman*), **tuna** (*tonne*); all three occur in **katapult**. At the end of a word some breath is heard, as in **pot** (*sweat*), **mop** (*mop*), **kluk** (*boy*).

Czech **r** is rolled as in Scottish English – try **ragby** (*rugby*), **pero** (*pen*).

Czech **h** is more than the outgoing breath of English *h*, since it is accompanied by resonance in the vocal chords, an effect sometimes achieved in English with *h* between vowels (as in *ahead*); the common informal greeting **ahoj** (*hello*, also *goodbye*) contains it.

The letters **q** and **w** only occur in a few foreign words and are pronounced like **kv** and **v** respectively.

Some sounds are present in both languages, but represented by different letters:

Czech **š** is English *sh*, try **šok** (*shock*), **šek** (*cheque*).

Czech **ž** is English *s* in *leisure*, try **garáže** (*garages*), **žurnalista** (*journalist*).

Czech **č** is English *ch*, try **čokoláda** (*chocolate*), **čip** (*microchip*).

Czech **c** is English *ts*, hence **noc** (*night*) rhymes with *knots*; **ocet** (*vinegar*).

Czech **j** is (roughly) like English *y* before or after vowels (never like English *j*), hence **já** (*I*), **je** (*is*), **ji** (*her*), **jogurt** (*yoghurt*); **tramvaj** (*tram*), **dej!** (*give!*), **bij!** (*hit!*), **můj**, **moje**, **moji** (forms of *my*).

Two sounds for special attention

Be particularly careful with:

▶ the compound letter **ch**, pronounced as the *ch* in Scots *loch*, try **charakter** (*character*), **chudý** (*poor*), **bych** (*I would*);

▶ **ř** – familiar from the composer's name **Dvořák** – it may be treated as a rolled *r* with a simultaneous *sh* or *zh* – try **řada** (*line, row, series*), **doktoři** (*doctors*), **tři** (*three*), **hřmí** (*it is thundering*).

Three more sounds to watch out for

You should also be very careful with the sounds **ť**, **ď** and **ň**. They are formed with the front half of the tongue pressed firmly against the back of the upper gum and above the front teeth to produce sounds somewhat like those represented by the bold letters in **t**une, **d**une, o**n**ion. The main problem is learning to recognize their presence: they are only represented by the letters **ť**, **ď** and **ň** before **a**, **u** or **o** or at the end of words or syllables.

šťáva	*juice*	buďme	*let's be*
chuť	*appetite*	umožňovat	*to make possible*
ďábel	*devil*	jabloň	*apple tree*

Before **e** the presence of these same sounds is marked by a ˇ (called a **háček**) on the **e**:

tetě	*to the aunt* (only the second **t** is **ť**)
dělat	*to do, to make*
něco	*something*

and before an *i*-sound by the presence of an **i** in the spelling (as opposed to **y**):

ti	*to you* (fam.) (contrast **ty** = *you*)
divné	*strange*
nic	*nothing*

Capital **ť** and **ď** use the **háček**: **Ť** and **Ď**, and it is also used in the handwritten versions of the small letters, hence **t˘** and **d˘**.

Other uses of the letter ě

You will also meet the letter **ě** after **b**, **p**, **f**, **v** and **m**. After the first four it represents the pronunciation of a *j* between the consonant and *e*, e.g. **obědy** (pron. objedy) (*lunches*), **koupě** (pron. koupje) (*purchase*), **o katastrofě** (pron. -fje) (*about the disaster*), and **Věra** (pron. vje-) (*Vera*), while after **m** it represents an intervening *ň*, as in **mě** (pron. mně) (*me*), **město** (pron. mňesto) (*town*).

You will find more details on pronunciation and spelling in **Appendix 2**, which you should consult from time to time.

Abbreviations used in the book are: acc. = accusative case, advb. = adverb, anim. = animate, comp. = comparative, dat. = dative case, f. = feminine, gen. = genitive case, impfv. = imperfective, inan. = inanimate, infin. = infinitive, inst. = instrumental case, Lit. = literal translation, loc. = locative case, m. = masculine, n. = neuter, pfv. = perfective, pl. = plural, pron. = pronunciation, sg. = singular.

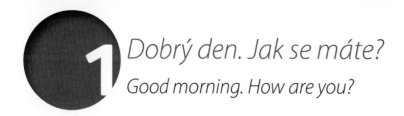

1 Dobrý den. Jak se máte?

Good morning. How are you?

In this unit you will learn

▶ *How to handle first encounters with greetings and responses*
▶ *How to spot some words that are common to Czech and English*
▶ *How to say I (first person singular)*

Dialogue 1

Alan Smith has just arrived in Prague to be met by Zdeněk Navrátil. It is evening.

🔊 **TR 5**

Zdeněk	Dobrý večer. Navrátil.
Alan	Dobrý večer. Alan Smith.
Zdeněk	Jak se máte?
Alan	Velmi dobře, děkuji. A jak se máte vy?
Zdeněk	Děkuju, dobře.

Alan is taken to his hotel, where they part for the night.

Alan	Na shledanou.
Zdeněk	Dobrou noc.

Zdeněk collects Alan from the hotel the next morning.

Zdeněk	Dobré ráno. Jak se máte?
Alan	Dobrý den. Děkuju, dobře.

 Quick vocab

dobrý večer *good evening*
jak se máte? *how are you?*
velmi dobře, děkuji *very well, thank you*
velmi *very*
a *and*
vy *you*

na shledanou *goodbye* (pron. nas**ch**ledanou)
dobrou noc *goodnight*
dobré ráno *good morning*
dobrý den *good morning, good day, good afternoon*

1 *DOBRÉ RÁNO* AND OTHER GREETINGS

This is only used to greet someone first thing in the morning, say up to 8 a.m.; an alternative is **dobré jitro**. After 8 a.m. and through the day use **dobrý den** (Lit. *good day*). **Dobrý večer** is used to greet someone in the evening; **dobrou noc** on parting for the night or before bedtime. **Na shledanou** (Lit. 'au revoir') can be used at any parting.

2 *DOBRÝ, DOBRÉ, DOBROU* – 'GOOD'

These are all forms of the same adjective *good*, which is in dictionaries in the form of **dobrý**. Note that the various forms of such an adjective end in a long vowel or the two-vowel sound **ou**. Contrast this with the related adverb **dobře** (*well*), which ends in a short vowel. You may remember meeting, in the section on pronunciation, a similar pair **rychlé** (*quick*), **rychle** (*quickly*).

3 *VELMI* – 'VERY'

As in English, **velmi** (*very*) is an adverb that qualifies adjectives or other adverbs.

4 *DĚKUJU* – 'THANK YOU'

You may also hear a more formal version of this: **děkuji**.

5 *JAK SE MÁTE?* – 'HOW ARE YOU?'

This expression is an idiom which has to be learned as a piece; the word *you* does not actually occur, though in the return question it does, as **vy**. You will understand the whole structure better in later units.

Exercises

1 **Respond in kind to the following greetings:**
   a Dobré ráno.
   b Dobrý den.
   c Dobrý večer.

2 a **You have just met someone; it is 11 a.m. How would you greet him/her? Fill in the gaps: D.... d.. J.. .. m...?**
   b You are asked how you are: **Jak se máte?** and you respond positively: **V.... d...., d.....**
   c You are asked how you are and you have replied: (**Jak se máte? Dobře, děkuju.**) It is now your turn to ask: **A ... . v.?**
   d On parting, you say goodnight to your host and say you hope to meet again: **D..... n.. a n. s........**

Dialogue 2

Zdeněk is meeting Alan on his second visit to Prague.

 TR 6

Zdeněk	Dobré jitro. Vítám vás znova v Praze.
Alan	Děkuju. Jak se máte?
Zdeněk	Jde to. A jak se máte vy?
Alan	Dnes špatně, bolí mě v krku, ale jsem rád, že jsem tady v Praze.
At the hotel.	
Zdeněk	Dobrou noc.
Alan	Na shledanou zítra.

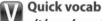 **Quick vocab**

vítám vás *welcome* (Lit. *I welcome you*)
znova *again*
jde to *so, so* (Lit. *goes it*)
dnes *today*
špatně *badly*
krk *throat*
Praha *Prague*
v Praze *in Prague* (pron. **fp**raze)

ale *but*
že *that*
tady *here*
zítra *tomorrow*
bolí mě v krku *I've got a sore throat* (Lit. *it hurts me in the throat*) (pron. f*krku*)
jsem rád, že jsem tady *I'm glad that I'm here* (**ráda** *for female speaker*)

6 MORE ON SPELLING AND PRONUNCIATION

 TR 6, 0:36

Most Czech words are stressed (given more forceful pronunciation) on the first syllable, irrespective of the length of the vowels in the word. This means that, among the words that you now know, **dobrý** is stressed on the first half of the word, though with the short vowel **o**, and the second syllable is unstressed but has a long **ý**. This is a stress pattern matched by such English words as "blackbird' (as opposed to 'black 'bird'), or some people's pronunciation of "garage', as opposed to the American pronunciation 'ga'rage'. Try to imitate some of the contrasting patterns using the following words:

mile	*kindly*
milé	*kind*
míle	*mile*
nakládat	*to load*
náklady	*loads; costs*
domu	*of the house*
dómu	*of the cathedral*
domů	*of the houses* and *home(-wards)*

Clearly, mispronunciation can lead to a breakdown in communication.

If you have the recording you will have noticed that there are some exceptions to the basic stress rule. The little word **a** (*and*) is stressless; **se** is also stressless, but needs something to 'lean back on' to form a stress-group, hence **jak se** and **máte**; while **na** (roughly *to*), in **na shledanou**, attracts the stress from the following word. These patterns will recur.

7 THE SPECIAL QUALITY OF *L* AND *R*

 TR 6, 2:41

A peculiarity of Czech is that **l** and **r** may have the same function as a vowel (they can be syllabic). They may occur between other consonants, as in **krk** (*throat*), **vlna** (*wave, wool*), or at the end of a word after a consonant, as in the name **Petr** (*Peter*) or **smysl** (*sense*). An **r** in these circumstances has a very prominent roll, as when we might make a threatening *grrr*, while syllabic **l** is similar to that in, say, *fiddlesticks*. Practise these sounds using the words:

prst	*finger*	**vlk**	*wolf*
vítr	*wind*	**blbý**	*stupid*
cukr	*sugar*	**nesl**	*was carrying*
mysl	*mind*	**singl**	*single (record)*

8 VERB-FORMS ENDING IN *-M* OR *-U/-I*

Note that **vítám** (*I welcome*) ends in **-m**, like **jsem** (*I am*). In **děkuju** (*I thank*), used for *thank you*, however, *I*, which is the 1st person singular, is expressed by the final **-u**, or by the **-i** in the **děkuji** version of the word. Sometimes, for emphasis, the word for *I* (**já**) is used as well. You will see this in Unit 2.

9 BIDDING WELCOME

Welcome to ... is expressed as '*Welcome in ...*', so in **Vítám vás v Praze** Zdeněk is saying *I welcome you in Prague*.

10 EXPANDING A FAREWELL

You may follow **Na shledanou** with a word to suggest when you hope next to meet the person in question, so **Na shledanou zítra** means *Goodbye until tomorrow* or *See you tomorrow*; similarly **Na shledanou večer** (*Till we meet this evening*).

11 THE IDEA OF CASE

Czech words change according to their function in the sentence. Each form represents a different *case*, and each case has a number of different functions, as you will gradually see. In this second dialogue **Praha** (*Prague*), which is a noun, appears in the form **Praze**. This is because it comes after the preposition **v** (*in*); all prepositions bring about changes of ending (case-endings) in the nouns which follow them, and here the form **Praze** is the *locative case* of **Praha**. Similarly, when Zdeněk visits Alan in London (**Londýn**), he will doubtless be welcomed with the words: **Vítám vás v Londýně**. This also accounts for the difference between **krk** (*neck, throat*), and **v krku** (*in the throat*). The word **dům** (*house*), mentioned earlier, has the locative **domě**, as in **v domě** (*in the house*). Full details of the locative case will be learned in due course. The dictionary form of nouns is their *nominative case*.

12 INTRODUCING GENDER

You have also seen the changing form of words in the alternations between **dobrý den** (*good day*), **dobrou noc** (*goodnight*) and **dobré ráno** (*good morning*). This is your first encounter with the way adjectives must agree with the nouns that they are describing: Czech nouns are randomly divided into three main groups – masculine, feminine and neuter. These are grammatical genders. Adjectives change according to the gender of the noun they are qualifying. The dictionary form of adjectives, e.g. **dobrý**, is their nominative case in the masculine.

> ● **INSIGHT**
>
> Grammatical gender has little to do with sex, though the words **býk** *bull*, **muž** *man*, **sněhulák** *snowman* denoting males are, unsurprisingly, masculine, just as **kráva** *cow*, **žena** *woman*, **víla** *fairy* are feminine. For the rest, classification of Czech words by gender may appear arbitrary. Thus the noun **den** *day* is a masculine word, **noc** *night* is feminine, and **ráno** (*early morning*) is neuter; there will be more on this in the next unit.

13 USE OF THE COMMA

ale means *but* and in writing it is often preceded by a comma; **že** (*that*) is always preceded by a comma, unless it is preceded by **a** (*and*).

Exercises

Answer the following questions out loud first. Then try writing down the answers, making sure you know exactly where the accents go. Check your answers with the **Key to the exercises** at the back of the book.

3 **a** It is evening in Prague. You are to greet someone, then extend a welcome. Fill in the gaps.
   D.... v.... V.... v.. v P....
   b If someone asks you how you are, what will they say?
   J.. s. m...?

4 **Reply to the question:**
   a positively: **V.... d...., d.....**
   b non-commitally: **J.. t.**
   c negatively: **Š.....**

5 **Using the words you already know, indicate when you next expect to meet someone:**
   a in the evening: **N. s........ v....**
   b in the morning: **N. s........ r...**

    c tomorrow: **N. s........ z....**

    d tomorrow evening: **N. s........ z.... v....**

6 **Indicate your pleasure at being somewhere (say** *'here',* **then** *'in Prague'*)**:**

    J... r.., ž. j... t... / v P....

7 **Practise all the greetings out loud, paying particular attention to the length of the syllables.**

🔊 **TR 7**

Notice how the basic intonation pattern is very similar whatever the length of the phrase. If you have the recording, listen to this unit again and then say the following with the correct stress.

dobrý den	jsem rád, že jsem tady
vítám vás v Praze	na shledanou večer

FOREIGN WORDS USED IN CZECH

Czech has adopted and adapted very many words that you recognize because they, or some very like them, are English as well. Some are technical and likely to be similar in many languages:

šek *cheque* **chróm** *chrome* **žirafa** *giraffe*

Others are everyday words:

> mop   tramvaj   uniforma   auto
> jogurt   turista   banka   šok

Some have been in Czech a long time (**ďábel** *devil*, think of 'diabolical' in English), others are obviously relatively recent acquisitions (**ragby**, **autobus**). Several appeared in the introductory section; take a second look at them, train yourself to 'see through' the uncustomary spelling. How such words are adapted into Czech will help reinforce your sense of the value of letters in native words. You could start with **ahoj**, the common greeting used among friends, like *hi* or *hello*, or *'bye* or *cheerio*.

Then try to guess what the following imports from English mean:

a	sendvič	**e**	víkend	**i**	trénink
b	šejkr	**f**	tým	**j**	gól
c	lančmít	**g**	šoumen	**k**	kombajn
d	džem	**h**	svetr	**l**	chuligán

The answers are in the **Key to the exercises** at the back of the book.

Summary

PRONUNCIATION REMINDER

If you have made full use of the introductory sections, Appendix 2, and the pronunciation section in this unit you should:

a know all the Czech letters, how they are ordered alphabetically and where special caution is needed – with **ch**, with **ď, ť** and **ň**, and with **ě**.

Remember that **č, ř, š, ž** and **ch** are alphabetized – they affect how words are ordered in the dictionary. This means that, for example, taking words you already know, **zítra** comes before **že**. On the other hand the letters **á, ď, é, ě, í, ň, ó, ť, ú, ů, ý** – the vowel symbols with accents and the 'soft' consonants when marked with a *háček* or 'apostrophe' – have no effect on ordering, so **děkuju** comes before **den**. Remembering these principles will help you save time when using the vocabulary lists at the back of the book.

b not forget the value of the letter **ě** in the sequences spelled **tě, dě, ně** (= **ťe, ďe, ňe**), and in **bě, pě, fě, vě, mě** (= **bje, pje, fje, vje, mně**).

c not forget the value of the sequences **ti, di, ni** (= **ťi, ďi, ňi**) in contrast to **ty, dy, ny** (= **ti, di, ni**).

Jak se jmenujete?

What's your name?

In this unit you will learn
- ▶ *How to make introductions*
- ▶ *How to ask where someone comes from*
- ▶ *How to form verbs in the present tense*

Dialogue 1

A group of people, Štěpán Bělohlávek, Jan Novák and Hilary Smith, meet in their hotel lobby. They have seen each other before, but do not all know each other yet.

🔊 **TR 8**

Štěpán	Dobrý den. Smím se vám konečně představit?
Jan	Samozřejmě.
Štěpán	Jmenuji se Štěpán Bělohlávek.
Jan	Těší mě.
Štěpán	Mimochodem, ještě nevím, jak se jmenujete vy.
Jan	Jan Novák. A smím vás představit? To je Hilary Smithová. Z Anglie. Těší mě.
Hilary	Těší mě.
Štěpán	*(to Jan)* A odkud jste vy?
Jan	Z Prahy, a vy?
Štěpán	Z Manchestru. Slečno Smithová, odkud pocházíte vy?
Hilary	Z Edinburghu. Omlouvám se, ale já moc nemluvím česky.
Štěpán	Tak vy jste vlastně Skotka, ne Angličanka. Já taky nejsem Angličan, ale Čech, emigrant.
A fourth person joins them.	
Pavel	Promiňte, že ruším. Jsem taky český emigrant, ale z Německa, z Berlína. Jmenuji se Pavel Lenoch a pocházím původně z Brna.
Jan	Tedy Moravan.
Pavel	Ano.

Quick vocab

Smím se vám představit? *May I introduce myself (to you)?*

vám *to you*

konečně *at last*

samozřejmě *of course*

Jmenuji se ... *My name is ...*

Těší mě *Pleased to meet you* (Lit. *it consoles me*)

mě *me*

mimochodem *by the way*

ještě nevím *I still don't know/I don't know yet*

Jak se jmenujete? *What is your name?*

Smím vás představit? *May I introduce you?*

To je *This is*

to *this*

z *from*

z Anglie *from England*

Odkud jste? *Where are you from?*

odkud *where from*

jste *you are*

slečno Smithová *Miss Smith* (when addressing her)

slečna *Miss*

odkud pocházíte? *Where do you come from?*

Omlouvám se *I apologize, I'm sorry*

Nemluvím česky *I don't speak Czech*

česky (in) *Czech*

moc *much, a lot*

Mluvím jenom anglicky *I only speak English*

anglicky (in) *English*

tak *so*

vy jste vlastně X, ne Y *you are really an X, not a Y*

já taky nejsem Angličan *I'm not English either*

Čech *Czech*

emigrant *émigré*

Promiňte, že ruším *Forgive me for intruding*

český *Czech* (adjective)

ale z Německa *but from Germany*

původně *originally*

z Brna *from Brno*

tedy Moravan *a Moravian then*

ano *yes*

Dictionary forms of some of the other words you have met:

představit (se)	*to introduce (oneself)*	**mluvit**	*to speak*
jmenovat se	*to be called*	**prominout**	*to forgive*
omlouvat se	*to apologize*	**rušit**	*to intrude, interrupt*
pocházet	*to come from*		

1 INTRODUCING YOURSELF

To say *My name is ...* use **Jmenuji se ...** . Sometimes, in less formal circumstances, you might also hear, and say, **jmenuju** – compare **děkuju/děkuji** in Unit 1.

2 SURNAMES

Surnames in Czech vary by sex. Generally, a female's surname is formed by the addition of the ending **-ová** to the male form, even in the case of foreign surnames, hence **Novák-Nováková**, **Smith-Smithová**. Native surnames ending in **-ek**, **-ec** or **-el** lose the **-e-** in the process, hence **Bělohlávek-Bělohlávková**, **Němec-Němcová**, **Havel-Havlová**. The feminist movement and the influence of increasing numbers of foreign women in the Czech Republic who do not wish to see their surname in any other form than what they are used to at home has meant some decline in the once strict use of the **-ová** ending. True feminine surname forms change according to their function in the sentence in the same way as adjectives do. Note also **pan** (*Mr*) and **paní** (*Mrs*).

3 OTHER MALE/FEMALE EQUIVALENTS

Czech has hardly any nouns of common gender, that is, applicable to persons of either sex. You will usually know from the noun used to refer to them whether a doctor, a German or a worker, for example, is a man or a woman. For females the word will usually have a distinctive feminine suffix which is either added to the masculine word, replaces a masculine ending or alters the masculine stem.

doktor-doktorka	*doctor*
dělník-dělnice	*worker*
Čech-Češka	*a Czech*
cizinec-cizinka	*foreigner*
průvodce-průvodkyně	*guide*

The first type, simple addition of **-ka**, is the most widespread: **student-ka** (*student*), **občanka** (*citizen*) (and others you can identify among the nationalities listed below). The second type is also very frequent: **úředník–úřednice** (*office-worker*), **tlumočník–tlumočnice** (*interpreter*).

4 MAKING APOLOGIES

Promiňte means *Excuse me, I'm sorry* (Lit. *Forgive!*) when you have committed a minor error, to apologize in advance of an intrusion, or when asking to be let past. The borrowed expression **pardon** has a generally similar function. **Omlouvám se** means *I'm sorry, I apologize* for a state of affairs.

5 SAYING WHERE YOU ARE FROM

To say where you are from you may use either **jsem** (*I am*) or **pocházím** (*I come/hail*) with the preposition **z** (*from*), which always takes the *genitive case*, more details of which are given in Unit 7. The following table gives you a few samples of origins and nationalities.

The nominative (dictionary) forms of these place names are:

Amerika	**Brno, Morava**	**Irsko**	**Skotsko**
Anglie, Manchester	**Čechy, Česko**	**Kanada**	**Slovensko**
Berlín, Německo	**Francie, Paříž**	**Praha**	**Wales**

Remember that **Čechy**, *Bohemia*, is the name of only the western province of **Česká republika**, *Czech Republic*; the latter may be replaced by the approved one-word alternative **Česko**, which the Czech authorities vainly hoped would become *Czechia* in English.

z Ameriky	jsem Američan/-ka	*I'm American*
z Anglie, z Manchestru	jsem Angličan/-ka	*I'm English*
z Berlína, z Německa	jsem Němec/Němka	*I'm German*
z Brna, z Moravy	jsem Moravan/-ka	*I'm Moravian*

z Čech, Česka	jsem Čech/Češka	*I'm Bohemian, Czech*
z Francie, z Paříže	jsem Francouz/-ka	*I'm French*
z Irska	jsem Ir/-ka	*I'm Irish*
z Kanady	jsem Kanaďan/-ka	*I'm Canadian*
z Prahy	jsem Pražan/-ka	*I'm a Praguer*
ze Skotska	jsem Skot/-ka	*I'm Scottish*
ze Slovenska	jsem Slovák/Slovenka	*I'm Slovak*
z Walesu	jsem Velšan/-ka	*I'm Welsh*

6 *ŽE* – 'THAT'

že means *that* and introduces clauses that state a fact (as opposed to a circumstance of time, manner, place, condition and so on), e.g. *She thinks **that**..., I think **that** ..., Would you believe **that** ..., It's hard to imagine **that** ... .*

7 SOME VERB FORMS

In Unit 1 you met some of the parts (*I, you*) of some verbs. Here are some forms of the 3rd person singular (*he, she, it*), namely **je** (*is*), **těší**, in **těší mě** (*pleases*, Lit. *consoles*). For the time being note that they end in a vowel. Note again the previous variety in forms for the 1st person singular (*I*): in **-m**, as in **omlouvám se**, **nemluvím**, **pocházím**, and in **-u** as in the everyday **děkuju**, or **-i** as in **jmenuji se**.

Note how all 2nd person (*you*) forms met so far end in **-te**: **jste** (*you are*), **jmenujete se** (*you are called*), **pocházíte** (*you come from*), **promiňte** ([*you*] *forgive!*). **Vy** (*you*) itself also appears in several utterances.

8 NEGATION

A number of the verb forms met so far have begun with the prefix **ne-** – **nejste** (*you are not*), **nevím** (*I don't know*), **nemluvím** (*I don't speak*). The translations show these to be negative forms; indeed, **ne-** is the universal negative prefix in Czech verbs. It is written as one word with the verb which it negates, and therefore it attracts the stress (listen out for this as you play back the dialogue on your recording). **Ne** on its own is *not* or *no*, the opposite of **ano** (*yes*).

● **INSIGHT**

In fact, **ne-** is not only the universal negative prefix in verbs, but equally universally negates other word-classes as well. Hence, for example, the adjective **neanglick´y** *non-English* or such nouns as **nestudent** *a non-student* or **Nečech** *a non-Czech*. You will see that it regularly replaces the English prefixes *un-* (as in *unlikely*), *in-* (as in *inedible*, or its mutation in *illegible*) and others. In all types the stress shifts to the **ne-**, as the new first syllable.

Exercises

1 **a** You are at a reception. Ask someone if you may introduce yourself, then give your name:

  S... s. v.. p.........? J...... s. X.Y.

  b Now ask Jane Williams if you may introduce her: (To Jane:) **S... v.. p.........?** (to a third party:) **T. j. J.W.** (Did you remember how to treat Jane's surname?)

  c That person wishes to convey his/her pleasure, so will say: **T... m.**

2 **a** You wish to convey that, despite appearances, you are actually English, not Czech (choose forms appropriate to your sex): **J... v...... A......./-.., n. Č.../Č.... .**

  b or that John is actually Scots, not English: **John j. v...... S..., n. A....... .**

  c or that Sabine is actually French, not German: **Sabine j. v...... F........., n. N.... .**

3 **a** Having cleared that up, now ask Miss Schmidt where she is from: **S..... S., o.... j...?**

  b Her reply, in impeccable Czech, that she is from New York **(z New Yorku)** puzzles you, so ask where she comes from originally: **Ale o.... p....... p......?**

4 **Slečna Schmidtová je Američanka. Je studentka.** Make up more sentences on this pattern using the following:

  a Patrick   Irish   student
  b Mrs Evans   Welsh   guide
  c Mária Slobodová Slovak   doctor
  d Heinz Bayer   German   interpreter

5 **Slečna Schmidtová je studentka. Je z Ameriky.**

  Taking the same four names as in 4, invert the information.

Dialogue 2

Various people are getting to know each other in a hotel lobby (Zdeněk Navrátil, Petr Dlouhý and Mr Smith).

 TR 9

Zdeněk	Dobrý den. Neznám vás z letadla?
Petr	Dobrý den. Ano. Můžu se vám představit? Petr Dlouhý.
Zdeněk	Zdeněk Navrátil. Těší mě.
Petr	Mě taky.
Zdeněk	Já jsem tady na konferenci. Vy taky?
Petr	Ne, já v Praze studuju, normálně bydlím v Londýně.
Zdeněk	Kdo je ten pán, a ta paní?

Petr	To jsou Smithovi, z Londýna. (*to the Smiths*) Dobrý den. (*to Zdeněk*) Známe se taky z letadla.
Mr Smith	Dobrý den. My jdeme ven. Bohužel musíme spěchat. Mimochodem, co je to tam naproti?
Petr	To je hotel Jalta.
Mr Smith	Aha, děkuju. A na shledanou.
Zdeněk	Ti ale mají naspěch! Já musím taky jít. Konference začíná.

Ti ale mají naspěch!

 Quick vocab

Neznám vás z letadla? *Don't I know you from the plane?*

letadlo *aeroplane*

Můžu se vám představit? *May I introduce myself (to you)?*

(Já) jsem tady na konferenci *I'm here for a conference*

konference *conference*

studuju *I study, I am studying*

bydlím *I live (dwell)*

normálně *normally*

Kdo je ten pán? *Who is that (gentle)man?*

pán *(gentle)man*

ta paní *that lady*

paní *lady*

To jsou Smithovi *it's the Smiths, those/these/they are the Smiths*

Známe se z letadla *We know each other from the plane*

(My) jdeme ven *We're going out*

bohužel *unfortunately*

Musíme spěchat *We must hurry*

Co je to? *What is it/this/that?*

tam *there*

naproti *opposite*

To je hotel Jalta *That/This/It is the Hotel Jalta*

Ti ale mají naspěch! *My, they're in a hurry!*

Musím jít *I must go*

konference začíná *the conference is beginning*

9 MORE ABOUT NAMES

a When you wish to refer to a couple, or all the members of a family, such as the Smiths or the Nováks, you have to use another form of the name, with the suffix **-ovi**: **Smithovi**, **Novákovi**.

b Some surnames look like adjectives, here **Dlouhý** (= *long*); compare this with **dobrý**, the masculine form for *good*. Mrs Dlouhý would be called **paní Dlouhá**, the feminine form. (Saying *the Dlouhýs* is too complex a matter; ignore it!)

10 WHAT IS ..? WHAT ARE ..? WHO IS ..? WHO ARE ..?

To ask *What is ..?*, *Who is ..?*, use **Co** (*what*) and **Kdo** (*who*) with **je** (*is*):

Co je to?	*What is that?*
Kdo je ten pán?	*Who is that man?*

To reply to either use **To je ...** (*it is* or *that/this is*).

To je pan Smith.   *That is Mr Smith.*

To is a demonstrative ('pointing') pronoun. If the item to be introduced is plural, use the same **kdo**, **co** or **to**, but with the verb form **jsou** (*are*):

To jsou Smithovi.   *They are/Those are the Smiths.*

11 WHAT ABOUT ..?

Such questions are expressed by a simple formula equivalent to *And what ..?* e.g. **A co Praha?** (*And what about Prague?*), whether the phrase is used as the basis of an inquiry, a suggestion or in amazement.

12 HERE AND THERE

Notice the opposition between **tady** (*here*) and **tam** (*there*). You may also meet **zde** and **tu** for here.

13 THE REFLEXIVE PRONOUN: *SE*, 'SELF'

This vital little word has many uses in Czech. So far you have met it in its two primary uses: in forms of the verbs **představit se** (*to introduce oneself*) and **znát se** (*to know one another* – its reciprocal use). Notice that **se** is the same form for all persons:

Smím **se** představit?   *May I introduce **my**self?*
Smíme **se** představit?   *May we introduce **our**selves?*
Známe **se** z letadla.   *We know **each other** from the plane.*

14 IDENTIFYING VERBS

Verbs are quoted in the dictionary in the infinitive (equivalent to English forms with *to*, e.g. *to know*). In Czech all infinitives end in **-t**. So far you have met **představit** (*to introduce*), **jít** (*to go*), **spěchat** (*to hurry*) and, in 13 above, **znát** (*to know*).

The forms **jsou** (*they are*) and **mají** (*they have*) are your first encounter with the 3rd person plural (*they* form) of verbs – of **být** (*to be*) and **mít** (*to have*). All 3rd person plural forms end in either **-ou** or **-í**.

15 ADDING INFORMALITY TO REQUESTS

Můžu in, say, **Můžu se vám představit** means *can I* and is an informal alternative to **smím** (*may I*), met previously.

16 MORE ABOUT VERBS

You have now met various verb endings with a common function, such as **-ou** or **-í** both meaning *they*. There are four main verb classes in Czech. Each verb class is associated with a particular vowel or other marker: **-a-**, **-i-**, **-e-** and **-uje-** (though these may not appear in all the forms of a particular class).

You should now familiarize yourself with the verb classes, or *conjugations*, in full.

	a-conjugation **znát** *(know)*	**i**-conjugation **mluvit** *(speak)*	**e**-conjugation **moct/moci** *(can)*	**uje**-conjugation **jmenovat** *(name)*
I	znám	mluvím	můžu/mohu	jmenuju/jmenuji
you	znáš	mluvíš	můžeš	jmenuješ
he/she/it	zná	mluví	může	jmenuje
we	známe	mluvíme	můžeme	jmenujeme
you	znáte	mluvíte	můžete	jmenujete
they	znají	mluví	můžou/mohou	jmenujou/jmenují

Note: where two equivalent forms of a verb appear in the tables, the right-hand ones are the more formal – largely, though not exclusively, restricted to written language. Infinitives of the **moci** type are the only survivors, when used, of infinitives not ending in **-t**.

> ●**INSIGHT**
>
> As a learning strategy, familiarize yourself with the infinitive and the *he/she/it* (3rd person singular) form of any verb where you are given it. This will usually enable you to predict the other forms. The need for this applies particularly to members of the **e**-conjugation, of which the example used, **moct**, is typical in the apparent lack of correlation between the two crucial parts.

The *uje*-conjugation

This class is entirely predictable: any infinitive ending in **-ovat** (see **jmenovat** above) will follow this pattern, that is it will exchange the **-ova-** for **-uj-** before adding the endings. Similarly, most verbs ending in **-it** or **-at** (but not **-ovat**!) can safely be predicted to follow **mluvit** and **znát** respectively.

Like most other languages, Czech has the odd irregularity, and due warning of these will be given as they arise.

Infinitives ending in *-et* or *-ět*

With these it is essential also to learn the *they*-form (the 3rd person plural). Some are members of the same class as **mluvit**; others, while generally similar, have a different *they* form, e.g. **pocházet** (*come from*), hence **Pocházejí z Brna** (*They come from Brno*).

When you begin to learn new verbs in their dictionary forms, rather than as parts of phrases, the *they*-form will be indicated until you learn how to predict which one will apply. The issue is complicated by a number of verbs which have competing, but equally accepted forms, such as **muset**: **musí** *he, she, it must*, **musí** or **musejí** *they must*. Similarly with **večeřet** *to dine* (that is, take one's evening meal).

Watch for the -š ending

The first *you*-form (2nd person singular) always ends in **-š**; it is reserved for addressing children, animals, God and, in certain contexts, social equals. It will therefore be usual, at the outset, for you to employ the *you* forms ending in **-te** (2nd person plural), which it is polite to use even when addressing one person.

17 THE VERB *BÝT* ('TO BE')

This is an irregular verb.

jsem	*I am*	**nejsem**	*I am not*
jsi	*you are*	**nejsi**	*you are not* (familiar singular)
je	*he/she/it is*	**není (!!)**	*he/she/it isn't*
jsme	*we are*	**nejsme**	*we aren't*
jste	*you are*	**nejste**	*you aren't* (plural or polite singular)
jsou	*they are*	**nejsou**	*they aren't*

On the other hand, **mít** (*to have*) is entirely regular, like **znát** (3rd person singular **má**), though its infinitive would not predict this. Thus **mít**, like **moct**, may serve as a warning to take particular care when learning how to assign monosyllabic verbs to their conjugational class.

Exercises

6 **Imagine yourself at a party, where few people know each other. This exercise will help you to cope with several things you might hear asked or need to ask yourself. First say the answers out loud then write them down checking you know exactly which accents go where.**

  a Reply to the question **Odkud jste?**, suggesting Prague, London, England, Wales: **J... z P..../L......./A....../W...... .**

  b In what two ways would you expect to hear someone proposing to introduce himself to you? **S.../M... s. v.. p.........?**

  c Remind them that you met in the plane: **Z.... s. z l...... .**

  d You have been asked to identify the person(s) opposite, who you know as Mr Smith/Mrs Smith/the Smiths: **N......, t. j. p.. S..../p... S........ . T. j... S........ .**

  e Now someone wants to know who this person is (i) here, (ii) there; what will you expect to hear? (i) **K.. j. t. t...? (ii) ... . t..?**

  f Explain that he/she is a student from Edinburgh: **J. t. s....../.. z E........ .**

  g You will frequently need to find out what something is; what will you say? **C. j. t.?**

  h Now make your first excuses: apologize for having to hurry to the conference: **P .... (or: O....... s.), a.. m.... s...... n. k......... .**

7 Unscramble the following sentences:

a máte jak se

b Brna profesor z pochází

c tady jsem jsem že v rád Praze

d Londýně vítám v vás

e představit slečno vás můžu Navrátilová

f představit vám smím se

 TR 10

8   You should now be able to pronounce most things you read in Czech. Rehearse the various sections on pronunciation and make sure you understand and remember them, and then read out loud the following passage. If you have the recording, check your pronunciation with what you hear.

Manželé Brabcovi bydlí v hotelu Jalta. Jejich kufr je ještě v taxíku, protože taxikář chce deset dolarů a Brabcovi mají jenom kreditní karty a koruny. Honem hledají směnárnu, protože už jsou unavení a mají taky hlad.

Quick vocab

v taxíku (pron. **ft**axíku) *in the taxi*
jejich kufr *their suitcase*
protože *because*
chce *he wants*
deset *ten*
honem *in a hurry*
hlad (pron. hla**t**) *hunger*

mají hlad *they are hungry*
manželé Brabcovi (pron. bra**pts**ovi)
  Mr and Mrs Brabec
hledají směnárnu (pron. s**mňe**nárnu) *they are looking for a bureau de change*
už (pron. **uš**) **jsou unavení** (pron. unave**ňí**)
  they're tired by now

SOME FREE TIME

You will find Czechs out shopping, having done their day's work, relatively early in the afternoon because the working day starts as early as six or seven in the morning (a custom blamed on the 19th-century Austrian Emperor Francis Joseph, within whose territories the Czech Lands fell).

Without having to keep their shopping to the weekends, many Czechs use the weekend to get away from the towns and spend time at the second homes which many are fortunate enough to possess. These **chalupa**s and **chata**s (*cottages* or *purpose-built chalets* – though the terms can apply to almost any building used for weekend recreation) are an important institution, but one which has declined slightly, since the market economy has made their upkeep, and the petrol needed to reach them, more costly. For the time being, you may still, if you acquire personal contacts in the Czech Republic, look forward to a weekend in the country with your hosts and their family. The Czechs are very hospitable, and this is one of the best ways to see the country's beautiful landscapes.

 Test yourself

Revise the forms of the verbs, then make up sentences in Czech based on the following:

  a He is looking for the hotel.

  b I must hurry.

  c We don't know you.

  d They come from London.

  e She is staying at Hotel Jalta.

  f You are Mr Smith.

  g We haven't got a suitcase.

  h She's Irish and he's American.

  i Do you speak Czech?

  j May I interrupt?

  k We must introduce ourselves.

Kde pracujete?
Where do you work?

In this unit you will learn
▶ *How to ask where someone works*
▶ *How to ask what their job is*
▶ *How to use basic kinship terms*
▶ *How to ask about the work of others in the family*
▶ *How to express more complex things about work*

Dialogue 1

A number of people meet and quickly become acquainted.

 TR 11

Navrátil	Dobrý den. Vy jste ten pán z letadla, že?
Smith	Dobrý den. Ne, my se neznáme, já jsem cizinec.
Navrátil	Promiňte. A odkud jste?
Smith	Z New Yorku. Jsem tu na konferenci. To je moje žena a syn.
Navrátil	Těší mě. Navrátil.
Mrs Smith	Mě také. Alice Smith. Bohužel nemluvím česky.
Navrátil	*(to Mr Smith)* Kde pracujete?
Smith	Jsem inženýr. Pracuju v továrně. A vy?
Navrátil	Pracuju ve školství. Jsem učitel. Vaše žena taky pracuje?
Smith	Ano, je úřednice, pracuje v bance.
Navrátil	A co dělá váš syn?
Smith	Je také úředník. Pracuje v pojišťovně v Manhattanu.
Navrátil	Moje žena pracuje v divadle. Je herečka.
Smith	To je zajímavé. Můj otec je také herec. A matka pracuje v kanceláři. V návrhářství.
The hotel porter approaches.	
Porter	Promiňte, že ruším. Pane Smith, máte telefon.

Quick vocab

Vy jste ten pán z letadla, že? *You're that (gentle)man from the plane, aren't you?*

My se neznáme *We haven't met (Lit. We don't know each other)*

cizinec *foreigner*

moje žena a (můj) syn *my wife and (my) son*

Kde pracujete? *Where do you work?*

kde *where*

pracovat *to work*

inženýr *engineer (f.* **inženýrka***)*

v továrně *in a factory*

ve školství *in education*

učitel *teacher (f.* **učitelka***)*

Vaše žena taky pracuje? *Does your wife work as well?*

úřednice *office worker (f)*

v bance *in a bank*

A co dělá váš syn? *And what does your son do?*

dělat *to do*

Je také úředník *He's a clerk (office worker) too*

také *also (a more formal version of* **taky***)*

v pojišťovně *in an insurance office*

v divadle *in the theatre (at a theatre)*

herec/herečka *actor/actress*

To je zajímavé. *That's interesting.*

můj otec *my father*

matka *mother*

v kanceláři *in an office*

v návrhářství *in design*

Máte telefon *You have a phone-call*

telefon *telephone (-call)*

1 STATING YOUR JOB

One basic way of stating your employment (or other characteristics) is, as in English, to use the verb *to be* and the noun denoting the profession. Remember, the form of that noun will usually differ according to the sex of the speaker. You have already met such pairs as **úředník/úřednice** (*office worker*) and **cizinec/cizinka** (*foreigner*). Note some others:

Male	herec	inženýr	učitel	novinář	doktor
Female	herečka	inženýrka	učitelka	novinářka	doktorka

Another way is to use the preposition **v** (*in, at*) plus either

a the physical place of employment:

 Quick vocab

továrna *factory:*	**v továrně** *in a factory*
banka *bank:*	**v bance** *in a bank*
kancelář *office:*	**v kanceláři** *in an office*
pojišťovna *insurance office:*	**v pojišťovně** *in an insurance office*
divadlo *theatre:*	**v divadle** *in a/the theatre*
škola *school:*	**ve škole** *in (a) school*

or **b** the abstract noun denoting the general area of employment:

 Quick vocab

školství *education:*	**ve školství** *in education*
dráha *course, track, railway:*	**na dráze** *on the railways*
doprava *transport:*	**v dopravě** *in transport*
pojišťovnictví *insurance:*	**v pojišťovnictví** *in insurance*
návrhářství *design(ing):* also **dizajn – v dizajnu**	**v návrhářství** *in design*
novinářství *journalism:*	**v novinářství** *in journalism*

The two ways do not necessarily mean the same thing, any more than in English: not everyone in journalism is a journalist. Of, say, a journalist or designer proper the more likely description will be to use the nouns: **Jsem novinář/-ka, Jsem návrhář/-ka, dizajnér/-ka.**

2 KINSHIP TERMS

 Quick vocab

otec *father*	**dcera** *daughter*
matka *mother*	**syn** *son*

The word **muž** means man as well as husband; **žena** means woman as well as wife. There are more specific words for *husband* and *wife*, namely **manžel** and **manželka** (remember **manželé** *married couple* or *Mr* and *Mrs* from the last unit, and note again the feminine suffix **-ka**), but these are less likely to occur in more informal situations.

3 *MŮJ, VÁŠ* – 'MY, YOUR', AND SO ON

These are *possessive pronouns* and they change according to the gender of the noun which they are specifying. For the time being, all you need to remember is that you must use the form **můj** (*my*) and **váš** (*your*) to accompany nouns in the singular denoting males, e.g. **můj/ váš otec** (*my/your father*), and all other grammatically masculine nouns (see below), and **moje** and **vaše** for females, e.g. **vaše matka** (*your mother*) and feminine nouns. The same pattern of distribution applies to **náš** and **naše** (*our*), e.g. **náš syn** (*our son*), **naše dcera** (*our daughter*).

In practice, kinship terms very often dispense with the possessive pronoun, especially if it is apparent from the context whose relation is meant:

Otec je bankéř.	*My father is a banker.*
Žena pracuje?	*Does your wife work?*

4 SUCH ECONOMICAL VERB FORMS!

You may have noticed (if not, look back at some phrases) that the forms of the verb correspond to a variety of forms in English.

žena pracuje is entirely adequate both to *my/your wife works* (or *is working* or *has a job*), and, as a question, *Does your wife work?* (or *Is your wife working?*). Similarly, for example, **Co dělá Jan?** means *What does Jan do?* (permanently) or *What is Jan doing?* (here and now).

Also, since Czech often does not use the *I, you* and so on as the subject of the verb (**pracuju** is *I work*, even without putting in **já** for *I*), notice that the third person singular form, e.g. **pracuje**, will mean variously *he* or *she* (even *it*) *works/is working* according to context. To avoid ambiguity, or for emphasis (or simply as a feature of more informal speech patterns) the pronouns **on** (*he*) and **ona** (*she*) may be inserted.

Sometimes a choice of a particular verb-form, depending on context, may dictate which verb should be used in Czech. When, in the dialogue, Mrs Smith claims not to speak much Czech, she says **Moc neumím česky**. She might equally have said **Moc nemluvím česky**, despite speaking it at the moment of utterance. Like **pracuje** above, **mluví** may mean *s/he speaks* or *is speaking*, so **Mluví česky** is either *S/he speaks Czech* (regularly etc.) or *S/he is speaking Czech* (here and now). When *actual use* of the language is not referred to, but merely the capacity to use it, **umět** is the sensible alternative. Hence **Umí česky** means *S/he speaks Czech = She can speak Czech* (as required). In general **umět** is used for acquired skills and is usually followed by an infinitive, as in **Umí vařit** *He can* [knows how to] *cook*, **Umí plavat** *She can swim*, so expressions with the language adverbs like **Umí česky/anglicky** etc. are really short for **Umí mluvit česky**, though the infinitive **mluvit** is regularly omitted. Because of this special sense, *She is speaking Czech* can only be translated using **mluví**, never **umí**.

5 PERSONAL PRONOUNS

já	*I*	**on**	*he*	**my**	*we*		
ty	*you* (singular familiar)	**ona**	*she*	**vy**	*you* (plural or formal singular)		
		ono	*it*	**oni**	*they*		

Note that **oni** is only one of three forms for *they*, the others being **ony** and **ona** (this too is explained later). **Ono** (*it*) is often replaced by **to**.

6 ADDRESSING A PERSON

Addressing someone requires a special case form – the vocative. In a previous unit Miss Smith was addressed as **slečno Smithová**, where **slečno** is the vocative case of the noun **slečna** (*young/unmarried woman*). And in Dialogue 1 of this unit the porter addresses Mr Smith (**pan Smith**) as **pane Smith**. Here **pane** is also the vocative form. Most types of noun have a distinctive form in this function (see Unit 14).

7 A SMALL MATTER OF SPELLING

Related words can vary in the length of syllables, which affects the spelling and pronunciation. In this unit this applies to such pairs as **váš** (m.) and **vaše** (f.) (*your*), and **pán** (*gentleman*) and **pan** (*Mr, sir*).

This is not a trivial matter since the meaning may change considerably:

Chceme **byt** v Londýně.	*We want a flat in London.*
Chceme **být** v Londýně.	*We want to be in London.*

Remember that the same difference of long or short syllables may also apply to totally unrelated words (see Introduction, 'Vowels' above).

Experience shows that many learners whose first language has different relationships between long and short vowels or syllables from the situation in Czech need to focus on this fundamentally simple opposition. That same learner is also apt to neglect the Czech requirement by which words are generally stressed on the first syllable. Thus in the example, the phrase **v Londýně** is stressed on [vlon], not on [dýn], though learners may be all too easily seduced into stressing the latter, long syllable.

8 WHEN DOES *V* BECOME *VE*?

If the preposition **v** stands before a word beginning with **v-**, **f-** or certain groups of consonants, it acquires the support of the vowel **-e**, hence **ve vodě** (**voda** = *water*), **ve farmacii** (**farmacie** = *pharmacy*) and **ve škole** (**škola** = *school*).

The different endings of the various expressions you have met with **v/ve** will be explained later in the course.

9 MORE ABOUT *ŽE*

Another of the functions of **že** is that, informally, it is an adequate equivalent to any of the vast number of English question tags (e.g. *will she, wouldn't you, did they, mightn't he*):

Vy mě neznáte, že?	*You don't know me, do you?*
Petr pracuje, že?	*Peter's working, isn't he?*

This makes it even more economical than the verb forms above!

Exercises

1 **You're still getting to know people. Now you can be a bit inquisitive as to their families and jobs:**
   a Ask a man where he works, then what his wife does:
      K.. p........? A c. d... v... ž...?
   b Then they ask what you do: **Co děláte vy?**; reply that you are: **i** a journalist; **ii** a doctor; **iii** a teacher; **iv** an office worker. (Give the male then the female versions.)

     i J... n......./-..   iii u...../-..

     ii d...../-..   iv ú......./ú.......

2 **You'll then be asked 'Kde pracujete?' Reply, substituting the items suggested after the samples, according to: a place, b place of work, c field.**
   a Pracuju v Brně (London, New York, Prague, Edinburgh)
   b Pracuju v hotelu (factory, office, theatre, a school)
   c Pracuju v pojišťovnictví (education, design, banking, transport) (Did you remember when to replace **v** by **ve**?)

3 a Now you ask where the other person's wife works:

   K.. p...... v... ž...?

   b And what their son does:

   A c. d... v.. s..?

   c Indicate that your own son works in the theatre, and why:

   M.. s.. p...... v d......, j. h.... .

   d The conversation is interrupted by the telephone; excuse yourself for breaking off the conversation, explaining why: **P......, m.. t......** . (There are of course two other possibilities for the apology: **O....... s.**, and **P.....**)

4 Now try to create sentences of your own similar to some of the questions above, about members of your family and their jobs. You can compile, from a dictionary, a list of jobs and workplaces that would be useful to talk about your own circumstances. Be sure to check for female equivalents where relevant.

5 Je to pravda nebo ne? (*Is it true or not?*) **Reply: Ano, je to pravda** (*Yes, it is true*)**, or Ne, není to pravda** (*No, it isn't true*) **to the following statements based on the dialogue:**

   a Pan Smith a pan Navrátil se už znají.

   b Pan Smith je z New Yorku.

   c Paní Smithová umí česky.

   d Pan Smith je v Praze na konferenci.

   e Paní Navrátilová je bankéřka.

   f Paní Smithová je učitelka.

6 Where you answered 'Ne, není to pravda', in 5, supply a short true statement.

Dialogue 2

The Smiths are on holiday in Prague. Mr Smith and a new acquaintance, Dr Jiří Švejda, are getting to know more about each other's background.

 TR 12

Švejda	Dobré ráno, pane Smith.
Smith	Dobrý den. Jak se máte?
Švejda	Děkuju, dobře. Co dělá paní Smithová?
Smith	Ještě spí.
Švejda	A co vlastně dělá doma?
Smith	Máme vlastní podnik, tak mi někdy pomáhá v práci. Jinak je v domácnosti.
Švejda	A máte děti?
Smith	Ano, syn je nezaměstnaný, ale dcera je zaměstnaná v hotelu. Má docela dobré místo, v kanceláři.

Jestěže paní Smithová spí!

Švejda	Co dělá váš podnik?
Smith	Naše továrna vyrábí koberce. A co vy a vaše rodina?
Švejda	Já přednáším na univerzitě, ale bohužel jsem svobodný.
Smith	Bohužel nebo bohudík?… Ještěže žena spí a neslyší mě!

 Quick vocab

ještě spí *he/she is still asleep*
spát (spí) *to sleep*
co vlastně dělá doma? *What does she actually do at home?*
doma *at home*
máme vlastní podnik *we have our own business*
vlastní *one's own*
podnik *enterprise, firm, business*
tak *so*
někdy *sometimes*
v práci *at work*
práce *work*
pomáhat (pomáhá) *to help*
jinak *otherwise*
je v domácnosti *she is a housewife*
domácnost *household*
máte děti? *have you got children?*
syn je nezaměstnaný *my/our son is unemployed*
dcera je zaměstnaná v hotelu *my/our daughter is employed at a hotel*
má dobré zaměstnání (or místo), má dobrou práci *he/she has a good job*

zaměstnání *employment*
místo *place, job*
naše továrna vyrábí koberce *our factory makes carpets*
továrna *factory*
vyrábět (he/she/it **vyrábí,** they **vyrábějí)** *to make, manufacture*
koberec *carpet*
rodina *family*
přednáším na univerzitě *I lecture at the university*
přednášet (he/she/it **přednáší,** they **přednášejí)** *to lecture*
univerzita *university*
jsem svobodný *I am single*
bohudík *fortunately*
ještěže žena spí a neslyší mě *It's a good thing my wife's asleep and can't hear me*
ještěže *it's a good thing*
slyšet (slyší) *to hear*
tak mi někdy pomáhá v práci *so she sometimes helps me at work*

10 GETTING TO GRIPS WITH GENDER

In Unit 2 you saw the variety of verb forms. Now we must begin to clarify the situation with nouns and their gender.

All Czech nouns belong to one of three genders: masculine, feminine or neuter. This has consequences not only for how they change, but also for how other words, such as adjectives and some parts of verbs, show agreement with them. Some of these patterns have already appeared, for example the differences between **náš** and **naše**, or now between **nezaměstnaný**, referring, as it does in the dialogue, to a male, as opposed to **zaměstnaná**, referring to a female.

Gender has nothing to do with the sexes. Thus **Londýn**, **hotel**, **podnik** are masculine; **Praha**, **továrna**, **univerzita** are feminine; and **Brno**, **divadlo** and **letadlo** are neuter.

The gender of very many such nouns – which we shall call 'hard' nouns, since they have hard stems (the part of the word without the ending) – can be predicted easily from these examples.

Unless they denote a male human, all nouns ending in **-a** are feminine; all nouns ending in **-o** are neuter. Nouns ending in a 'hard' consonant are masculine. But which consonants are hard? It is actually easier to exclude those which are 'soft' – there are fewer 'soft' consonants. Soft consonants are those that carry the háček (or its equivalent 'apostrophe' – in ť and ď), and **c** and **j**. Thus **zub** (*tooth*), **oběd** (*lunch*), **dialog** (*dialogue*) and **oděv** (*clothing*) are 'hard', while **muž**, **novinář**, **koberec** are 'soft' masculine nouns. Here predictions are less easy, since many feminine nouns end in the same range of 'soft' consonants, e.g. **garáž**, **kancelář** or **tramvaj**.

Moreover, there are numerous types of noun which have an ending, typically **-e**, on a soft stem and could be members of any gender, for example:

masculine **průvodce** *guide*

neuter **vejce** *egg*

feminine **práce** *work*

It is essential that each word whose gender cannot be predicted from the dictionary form should be learnt with its gender.

In future vocabulary boxes gender will be marked by the simple abbreviations (m), (f) and (n). Various tips for identifying certain gender sub-groups will be given as the opportunity arises. For example, the word **domácnost** from the dialogue is one representative of a vast class of feminine nouns with their own typical set of endings. They are recognized by the suffix **-ost**. Or again, almost any noun ending in **-í** will belong to a special (and huge!) neuter class. The exceptions are **paní** (f, *Mrs, lady*) and items denoting male humans, such as **Jiří** (*George*), **krejčí** (*tailor*).

Throughout this section we have been referring to the form in which you will find nouns in the dictionary. It represents the nominative case of these nouns, the main function of which is to express the subject of the sentence: **Učitel spí** (*The teacher's asleep*). You have also seen such forms after the verb **být** (*be*): **Je učitel** (*He's a teacher*).

11 HOW TO SAY WHERE THINGS ARE

The simplest ways of saying where something is are by means of *in* and *on*. You have already seen many such expressions, mostly containing **v** (*in*, sometimes *at*). The various forms of words following **v** have been the *locative case* forms of the various noun classes. The locative case is also required after **na** (*on*, *at*) and a few other prepositions, including **o** (*about*, *concerning*), **po** (*up*, *down*, *along*, *all over* and *after*). In fact *the locative case never occurs without a preposition*. You will have seen that there are four endings for the word classes encountered so far, namely, **-ě**, **-u**, **-i** and **-í**.

-ě and -u endings

The ending **-ě** is for most 'hard' stem nouns of any gender, except masculines and neuters whose stems end in **-g**, **-h**, **-ch**, **-k**, or **-r**, which will usually have **-u**. Hence:

masculine	**v Londýně**, but: **v dialogu**
feminine	**na univerzitě**
neuter	**v autě** (*in the car*), **ve Skotsku**

The ending **-ě** only shows in this form after stems ending in **-b**, **-p**, **-f**, **-v** and **-m**, and **-d**, **-t** and **-n**, with the consequent changes in pronunciation (if you are uncertain about this, revise **The Czech alphabet and pronunciation** section). After other consonants the **-ě** appears as **-e**.

v pase *in the passport*   **ve váze** *in the vase*   **na kole** *on/by bicycle*

 Quick vocab

pas *passport*   **váza** *vase*   **kolo** *wheel, bicycle*

Feminine nouns ending in **-g**, **-h**, **-ch**, **-k** or **-r** entail major consonant alternations, caused by the **-ě** ending:

k → c	as in **banka**, hence	**v bance**	(*in the bank*)
h → z	as in **kniha** (*book*), hence	**v knize**	(*in a/the book*)
g → z	as in **Olga**, hence	**o Olze**	(*about Olga*)
ch → š	as in **střecha** (*roof*), hence	**na střeše**	(*on the roof*)
r → ř	as in **fara** (*vicarage*), hence	**na faře**	(*at the vicarage*)

● INSIGHT

In the distant past, **g** disappeared from Czech and was replaced by **h**. This explains why very few words need to be treated like **Olga** above, being borrowings from elsewhere, e.g. **synagoga** *synagogue*, **liga** *league*, **sfinga** *sphinx*, or the non-Czech names of people and places, e.g. **Helga**, **Volga**, **Riga**, and also why **Olga** and **kniha** both produce **z** in the procedures above, hence, for example, **v synagoze** *in the synagogue*, **na Volze** *on the Volga*, **o sfinze** *about a sphinx*.

Similar alternations before **-ě** apply to a small number of masculines and neuters (which therefore have not adopted the **-u** ending); such words will be duly indicated as they occur. Some words may show both possibilities, but in different senses: from **jazyk** *language, tongue* you will meet **na jazyku** *on the tip of one's tongue* but **v jazyce** *in [such and such a] language*.

Two advance warnings: the above rules do not apply to most masculine names of people and animals, which will be dealt with separately. And many more 'hard' masculine nouns take the locative ending **-u** than the text above might suggest. They will include cases such as **ve Walesu** and **v hotelu**.

-i ending

The ending **-i** is general for soft noun types, irrespective of gender:

masculine	**koberec** (carpet)	**na koberci**	(on the carpet)
feminine	**kancelář** (office)	**v kanceláři**	(in a/the office)
masc. in **-e**	**správce** (caretaker)	**o správci**	(about the caretaker)
neut. in **-e**	**moře** (sea)	**v/na moři**	(in/on the sea)

Even the special class of feminine nouns to which **domácnost** belongs uses the **-i** ending, as you saw in the dialogue.

-í ending

One of the largest noun classes overall are the neuters ending in **-í**. You have seen several already as the abstract nouns denoting various callings and disciplines (**novinářství** *journalism*). This class has relatively few distinct forms, indeed you have seen that their locative forms are like the nominative, ending in the same long **-í** (**v novinářství**). Not all items in the class share the abstract suffix **-ství** or -**ctví**; other examples include, say, **zelí** (*cabbage*), **nádraží** (*station*), **umění** (*art*) – the last two represent large sub-classes of neuter nouns.

12 FUNCTIONS OF *NA* WITH THE LOCATIVE CASE

While **na** literally means *on*, as in **na židli** (**židle** [f]) *on the chair*, **na Temži** (**Temže** [f]) *on the Thames*, it is widespread in many names of locations where English uses *at*.

na univerzitě (univerzita)	*at (a/the) university*
na této poště (pošta)	*at this post office*
na tom koncertě (koncert)	*at that concert*
na přednášce (přednáška)	*at a lecture*
na trhu (trh)	*at (or on) the market*

Sometimes the opposite is true; English uses *at* and Czech **v**:

v kině (kino)	*at/in the cinema*
ve škole (škola)	*at/in (the) school*
v práci (práce)	*at work*

Sometimes, especially with highland and island place names, **na** replaces English *in*:

na Slovensku	*in Slovakia*
na Kypru (Kypr)	*in Cyprus*

13 FLEETING *-E-*

Notice that in the word **koberec** (*carpet*) the **-e-** before the final consonant is lost in **na koberci**.

14 WAYS OF EXPRESSING RELIEF

Ještěže, also spelled **ještě že** or **ještě, že** (*it's a good thing that* or *thank goodness that*) conveys a particular attitude for which there is no convenient one-word device in English. Unlike the more neutral **bohudík** (*fortunately*), **ještěže** must stand at the head of the sentence.

15 GENDER IN ADJECTIVES

Had **Jiří** (*George*) been **Jiřina** (*Georgina*) – both are common names – and had she too been single, she would have said: **Jsem svobodná**, using the feminine adjectival ending.

The form of the adjective **zajímavý** (*interesting*) appearing in the dialogue – **zajímavé** – contains the basic neuter singular ending, previously met in **dobré ráno**. There will be more on adjectives in the next unit. Meanwhile, remember that the nominative singular of the main class of adjectives is:

-ý (masculine)   **-á** (feminine)   **-é** (neuter)

● INSIGHT

In the first Insight in Unit 2 you learnt about **ne-** negation of other items besides the verbs. In this unit contrast the positive adjective **zaměstnaný** *employed* and its negative **nezaměstnaný** *unemployed,* but also *a jobless person*; in the latter sense we call this an 'adjectival noun' – a noun by meaning, but an adjective in form; Czech has many of these. (An *employed person*, *employee*, is the true noun **zaměstnanec**.) From the adjective **zajímavý** in the paragraph above we can easily form **nezajímavý** *uninteresting*. And from **vlastní** *one's own* (in the dialogue) Czech has produced the negative **nevlastní** '*not one's own*', used with simple logic in such kinship terms as **nevlastní syn** *stepson*.

Exercises

7 You are still finding out about the people round you.
  a Ask Mr Navrátil what job he does: **C. d....., p... N.......?**
  b You may have been misunderstood to be inquiring what he happens to be doing here and now, so ask him instead where he works: **K.. p........?**
  c Ask if he has a good job: **M... d.... m....?**

8 He has now asked you to state your own job; tell him, but bear in mind your sex (you may be a doctor, engineer, journalist, teacher, or you may use a dictionary to find an expression for your actual job):
  J... d...../-.. / i......./-.. / n......./-.. / u....../-..

9 a Now ask about Mr Navrátil's children's jobs (he has a son and a daughter): **C. d... v.. s..?**
      A c. d... v... d....?
  d Conjecture that his wife also has a good job:
      V... ž... m. t... d.... m...., ž.?

10 **Mr Navrátil now conjectures that you have no children; what do you expect to hear: V. n..... d..., ž.?**

11 **Express regret that you have no children: B....... n.... d... .**

🔊 **TR 13**

12 **You have been asked where you met someone. According to the pattern 'Bylo to (*it was*) ... na konferenci', reply in turn: at the post office, in school, in Brno, at home, at the university, at work, at the bank, in the plane.**

A FEW CZECH CONVENTIONS ON TITLING

One of this unit's new words has been **inženýr**, which is used differently from its English apparent equivalent. Chiefly it is associated with a level of education roughly equivalent to any non-arts master's degree. Hence anyone comparable to an Englishman with M.Sc. after his name will write **Ing**. before the name in Czech. (The spelling **Ing**., unofficially 'abbreviated' further to **ing**., reflects an earlier spelling of the whole word from the time when it was borrowed into Czech from French.) Moreover since this is a title which precedes the name, it often enters into how you address people: in courteous usage, Czechs frequently employ, as in German, academic or functional titles instead of names, such as **pane doktore, pane profesore, paní profesorko, pane inženýre**, also **pane starosto** (*Mr Mayor*), **pane správce** (*Mr Caretaker*). These terms are in the vocative (see Unit 14).

Note that, outside direct address, all titles, from **pan** and **paní** (abbreviated p., pí) to **ing**., **prof**. or even **král** (*king*, no abbreviation), and the alien **sir** and **lord**, are traditionally written with small letters, though increasingly **Dr**, **Lord**, **Prof**. and **Sir** are to be seen capitalized (wrongly according to Czech rules, but probably under the influence of English or German).

However, abbreviations of the Latin designations of academic degrees do use capitals, and they customarily stand before the name, in contrast to English usage: thus **PhDr**. Jan Moudrý, **RNDr**. Josef Ptáčník, **JUDr**. Václav Pravec, and **MUDr** Bedřich Stavinoha have doctorates in, respectively, philosophy (or arts), natural sciences, law and medicine. Note also the titles **Mgr**. (**magistr**, f **magistra** *master*) written before the name and used by arts graduates after a full five-year course, and **Bc**. (**bakalář** *bachelor*) for those who have completed three years of undergraduate study; these came into use only in the 1990s.

Summary

You could now increase your active vocabulary by returning to the start of the course, retrieving all the nouns you have met and assigning them a gender – this really is an exercise in teaching yourself! In most cases it will be obvious; for the rest you may need to use the list of vocabulary at the back of the book.

4 Jak bydlíte?
What is your house like?

In this unit you will learn
▶ *How to talk about how people live*
▶ *How to say numbers*
▶ *How to talk about going visiting*
▶ *How to express possession*
▶ *How to use can and must*
▶ *How to express the 'direct object'*

Dialogue 1

Here is a conversation between pan Navrátil and his English friend Mr Smith, who are comparing notes on their respective homes.

 TR 14

Smith	A jak bydlíte?
Navrátil	Bydlíme v bytě, ve věžáku. A vy?
Smith	My bydlíme v domě, máme svůj vlastní.
Navrátil	Bydlí někdo v Anglii v bytě?
Smith	Samozřejmě – v činžáku, nebo ve věžáku, jako u vás.
Navrátil	Kolik máte v domě místností?
Smith	Pět, jestliže počítáme kuchyň. A vy?
Navrátil	Náš byt je malý. Zato bratr má pěkný dům na české poměry. Má čtyři velké pokoje a příslušenství, dílnu, sklep a zahradu.
Smith	A váš byt?
Navrátil	Máme byt tři plus jedna.
Smith	Co to znamená?
Navrátil	Že máme tři pokoje – obývací pokoj a dvě ložnice – a kuchyň.
Smith	A co koupelna?
Navrátil	Ovšemže máme koupelnu a záchod, ale ty se nepočítají.
Smith	Váš byt tedy není zvlášť malý?
Navrátil	Asi ne, ale my máme pocit, že v tom velkém věžáku je malý.

Quick vocab

Jak bydlíte? *How do you live?* (in the sense *What is your home like?*)

Bydlíme v bytě *We live in a flat*

ve věžáku *in a tower block*

v domě *in a house*

v činžáku *in a tenement block*

byt *flat*

bydlet (bydlí) *live (= dwell)*, also stay, *as in a hotel*

činžák *tenement block*

věžák *tower block*

dům *house*

někdo *someone*

Máme svůj byt/dům *We have our own flat/house*

Kolik máte místností

(or **pokojů)?** *How many rooms do you have?*

kolik *how much, how many*

místnost (f) *room* (this word behaves like **domácnost** in Unit 3)

pokoj (m) *room*

u vás *in your house, country, street, class, case, etc.*

u nás *in our house, etc.*

jestliže počítáme kuchyň *if we count the kitchen*

jestliže *if*

počítat *count*

kuchyň or kuchyně (f) *kitchen*

Náš byt je malý *Our flat is small*

malý *small*

zato *on the other hand*

bratr má pěkný dům *my brother has a nice house*

bratr *brother*

pěkný *nice*

na české poměry *by Czech standards*

poměry *conditions* (**poměr** *relation(ship), ratio, attitude*)

čtyři velké pokoje *four big rooms*

velký *big, large, great*

příslušenství (n) *bathroom and lavatory*

dílna *workshop*

sklep *cellar*

zahrada *garden*

(my) máme byt 3 + 1 (read as **tři plus jedna**) *we have a three-room flat*

Co to znamená? *What does that mean?*

obývací pokoj (colloquial **obývák**) *living room* (from **obývat** *to inhabit*)

ložnice (f) *bedroom*

koupelna *bathroom*

záchod *lavatory*

ovšemže (also **ovšem že**) *of course* (conjunction, = *it goes without saying that*)

ty se nepočítají *they don't count*

váš byt tedy není zvlášť malý *so your flat isn't particularly small*

zvlášť *particularly*

asi ne *perhaps not*

máme pocit, že ... *we have a/the feeling that ...*

pocit *feeling*

v tom velkém věžáku *in that great tower block*

1 NUMERALS

You cannot progress far without numbers in any language. *One* is **jeden**, which has three forms according to the three genders:

jeden dům/pokoj	*one house/room*
jedna koupelna/ložnice	*one bathroom/bedroom*
jedno okno/zelí	*one window/cabbage*

Sometimes, where there is no direct reference to any item of a particular gender, the feminine form, **jedna**, is used as the neutral form. This will become more significant later, but note the conventional way in which Czech flat sizes are given (3 + 1 – **tři plus jedna** meaning a living room, two bedrooms and a kitchen).

Two has two forms, **dva** for masculine and **dvě** for feminine and neuter; they are followed by nouns in the plural, which you have not learnt yet, so for the time being learn these as phrases.

dva pokoje	*two rooms*
dvě ložnice	*two bedrooms*
dvě okna	*two windows*

Three, **tři**, and *four*, **čtyři**, are also followed by plurals, but there is only one form, irrespective of gender:

tři pokoje	*three rooms*
čtyři ložnice	*four bedrooms*
tři/čtyři okna	*three/four windows*

Five, **pět**, and all numbers above five are subject to special rules which will be dealt with in a later unit. The same applies to indefinite numerals like *several, many,* and interrogative *how many* (the only one met so far: **kolik**).

2 'HARD' AND 'SOFT' ADJECTIVES

You will recall the important division of nouns into 'hard' and 'soft' types (see Unit 3). There are 'hard' and 'soft' adjectives too: all those discussed so far, with distinct gender forms, have been of the 'hard' type. The 'soft' adjectives are much simpler to handle; they are instantly recognizable, irrespective of the nature of the stem-final consonant, by their ending **-í**, which is the same for all genders in the nominative.

obývací pokoj (m)	*living room*
vlastní ložnice (f)	*one's own bedroom*
cizí město (n)	*strange city*

3 HOW TO EXPRESS POSSESSION

Possession may be expressed in the same two basic ways as in English, with **mít** (*to have*): **Máme nové auto** (*We have a new car*), and using the possessive pronouns, such as **můj** (*my*), **náš** (*our*) and **váš** (*your*). Later in this unit you will meet most other possessive words, but so far you have met **svůj** (*one's own*): **Máme svůj byt** *We have our own flat*.

This translation of **svůj** is deceptive, since the word lacks the emphasis of *own*, which is properly expressed by **vlastní**. The function of **svůj** is to express *my, your, his, her, our,* or *their*, wherever *I, you, he, she, we* or *they* respectively is the subject of the sentence.

Therefore, you cannot properly say **Miluju můj dům** (*I love my house*), **Milujete váš dům** (*You love your house*), but only:

Miluju ⎫			*I*		*(my)* own house.
Milujete ⎭	svůj dům.		*You*	*love*	*(your)*

If subject and possessor are not the same, then the normal possessive adjectives are used, as in: **Milujeme váš starý dům** (*We love your old house*).

> ● **INSIGHT**
>
> One of the consequences of the fall of the Berlin Wall and the 'liberations' that came to all the countries of Central and Eastern Europe was that Western companies, advisers and such like spread throughout the area like wildfire, bringing with them their own languages and usages. Possibly due to sloppy translating by Czechs themselves as to the use of possessive pronouns in West-European languages, versions of English in particular, the proper use of **svůj**, cross-referring to the subject as possessor, has suffered a serious decline, being often replaced, within few constraints, by the person-specific pronouns **můj**, **náš**, **váš** etc., that is in a distribution matching *my*, *our*, *your* etc. My advice is to stick to the traditional usage described above, which will never be wrong, rather than slipping into the modern patterns, which may – surprisingly, you might think – lead to unfortunate ambiguities.

4 ANOTHER USE OF *SE*

Notice how the reflexive pronoun **se** can be used to form passive sentences:

Ty se nepočítají. *They do not count./They are not counted.* (Lit. *Those do not count (them) selves*)

This is a very common feature of Czech, especially in various kinds of instructions, prohibitions and similar: **To se nedělá!** *That's not done!* = a rebuke to cover 'Stop it!', 'Don't do that!' and such like.

5 ALTERNATING VOWELS: *Ů* AND *O*

The word **dům** (*house*) has a **-ů-** in the nominative, but the other form in the dialogue – the locative after **v** (*in*), **v domě** – has **-o-**. Alternation of **ů** and **o** is particularly common between short and longer versions of the same item. Another word where it occurs is **svůj**: **Miluje svůj byt** (*She loves her (own) flat*), but **Miluje svoje auto** (*She loves her car*). Compare also **stůl** *table* and **na stole** *on the table* or **stolek** *small table*.

6 A PAIR OF NEAR-SYNONYMS

The two words for *room*, **místnost** and **pokoj**, are not interchangeable. **Místnost** is the more general word, **pokoj** being confined to 'habitable' rooms, such as bedrooms or sitting rooms in the home, or hotel rooms. So if the question asked has been **Kolik máte pokojů?**, the answer would probably be the same, but there would be no need to exclude explicitly the kitchen and bathroom.

Another pair of synonyms is **příslušenství** (only one word but much commoner than *appurtenances*) and **záchod a koupelna**.

The Czechs, like the Germanic, Celtic and other Slavonic peoples make great use of *diminutives*. These words denote primarily an item that is genuinely small as such items go. Hence, from **noc** *night* and **stolek** (in Section 5 above) we have the expression **noční stolek** *bedside table*, any **stolek** being small compared to the typical **stůl**, the neutral word for 'table'. Diminutive forms of words may also convey some notion of attachment, liking, for a thing. Thus from **kniha** *book* the diminutive is **knížka**, which is not only used of necessity in **šeková knížka** *cheque-book* (small as books go), but can be used of almost any book of any size in one's private collection, but especially one of which one is particularly fond – even one's big, fat, reliable friend the probably quite un-small dictionary.

Perversely, the principle of diminutivisation for small things can go wrong. In this unit we have met the important word **záchod** *lavatory, toilet*. Its diminutive **záchodek** is what you will often see in the plural expression **veřejné záchodky** (though also the neutral **záchody**) *public toilets*, which on the whole are larger, not smaller than the 'smallest room in the house'. Also, a 'window' is **okno**, but the window, service point or till in a bank or post office, which may be of any size, including quite large, is often expressed by the diminutive form **okénko**.

Finally on this subject for now, note that **stolek**, **knížka** and **okénko** all have a **k** to mark out the diminutive forms.

7 *V TOM VELKÉM VĚŽÁKU ... – 'IN THAT GREAT TOWER BLOCK ...'*

Tom is the locative masculine singular of **ten** (*that*) after **v** (*in*); **ty**, as in **ty se nepočítají**, is one of the plural forms. Fuller details are given in Unit 6.

Exercises

1 **Familiarity with your new Prague friends leads you to enquire about their home.**
   a First ask the daughter Jana where she lives.
   Her reply (**v Brně**) suggests she has left home, so ask about the kind of accommodation she lives in.
   b You are then asked a similar question. Say that at home you (as a family, i.e. we) live in a house; a flat in a tenement block; a flat in a tower block.
   c But you happen to be in Prague, where you are alone and in a hotel. Reply accordingly.

2 **a** Now ask your Czech friend Ivan about his home: ask about the number of rooms.
   b You are impressed by his answer (**Máme čtyři pokoje**), so complain that your flat is small, but that your daughter has a big house.
   c Add that she has four large rooms, kitchen and bathroom. (There is a special Czech way of saying this. Can you remember it?)

3 **Question words: you have already met some of these in this and previous units, and since they are central to several sets of related words, we may begin to systematize them, including one or two new ones:**

kdo	*who*	**někdo**	*someone*
co	*what*	**něco**	*something*
kde	*where*	**někde**	*somewhere*
kdy	*when*	**někdy**	*sometime(s)*
jak	*how*	**nějak**	*somehow*
jaký	*what ... like, what kind of*	**nějaký**	*some, a*
který	*which*	**některý**	*a certain*
kolik	*how many/much*	**několik**	*several*
odkud	*where from*	**odněkud**	*from somewhere*
kam	*where to*	**někam**	*(to) somewhere*

Using this table, attempt to:

a ask someone when s/he is in (use: *at home*).

b say you sometimes live in London.

c ask someone what their flat is like.

d say that the phone is somewhere in the office.

e ask which room is yours (i.e. asking *mine* or *ours*), or

f ask which is your (i.e. using *my* or *our*) room.

g regret that you have to go somewhere.

h ask Miss Brabec what she is doing.

Dialogue 2

The Smiths' Czech friend, Ivan, is inviting them to visit his flat.

 TR 15

Ivan	Chceme vás pozvat k nám na návštěvu.
Smith	Děkuju, to je od vás milé.
Ivan	Přijďte tedy zítra v poledne.
Mrs Smith	Už se těšíme.
The Smiths are getting ready to go (and practising their Czech!).	
Smith	Máme něco vzít?
Mrs Smith	Snad bonboniéru nebo kytici?
Smith	Ano, to je dobrý nápad.
They arrive and are met at the door.	
Ivan	Dobrý den, vítám vás u nás!
Smith	Dobrý den. *(He begins to remove his shoes.)*
Ivan	Nemusíte se zouvat. My se sice zouváme, ale návštěvy rozhodně nemusí.
Mrs Smith	Ale ano. My se doma zouváme taky.
Ivan	Tak dobře. Tady máte bačkory. Pojďte dál!

Smith	Děkujeme.
Ivan	*(whose wife has appeared)* Můžu vás představit? To je moje žena, Marie.
Marie	Těší mě.
Smith	Smith.
Mrs Smith	Smithová.
Marie	Paní Smithová, vítám vás. Ó, to je krásná kytice! Děkuju pěkně. Omlouvám se, ale já moc neumím anglicky.
Mrs Smith	A já jenom trochu česky.
Ivan	Ale dvě ženy se vždycky domluví! A my dva taky, že? Máme na to čas. Večeříme až v sedm.

 Quick vocab

chceme vás pozvat k nám na návštěvu
  we want to invite you to our house
  (Lit. *we want to invite you to us on visit*)
chtít (see Section 8) *to want*
pozvat (pozve) *to invite*
k nám *to us, to our place*
na návštěvu *on a visit*
návštěva *visit (also visitor(s), as in*
Máme návštěvu *We've got visitors)*
přijďte *come*
v poledne *at noon*
poledne (n) *noon, midday*
už se těšíme *we're looking forward to it*
máme něco vzít? *should we take something?*
máme *here: should we*
vzít (vezme) *to take*
bonboniéra *box of chocolates*
kytice (f) *bunch of flowers*
snad *perhaps*
nápad *(sudden) idea*
nemusíte se zouvat *you needn't take your shoes off*

muset (or **musit**) **(-í; -í/-ejí)** *must, have to*
nemuset *need not, not have to*
zouvat se *remove one's shoes*
zouvat *remove (of footwear)*
sice (see Section 11) *though*
my se sice zouváme, ale návštěvy nemusí
  while we do change our shoes, visitors needn't
rozhodně *definitely*
bačkory (f pl) *slippers*
krásný *beautiful*
pojďte dál *come in*
děkuju pěkně *thank you very much*
pěkně *nicely*
domluvit se *make oneself understood, come to an agreement*
večeříme až v sedm *we don't eat until seven*
večeřet (-í; í/-ejí) *have dinner (i.e. evening meal, remember* **večer** *evening)*
až *not until, as late as*
v sedm *at seven*

8 CAN, MAY, MUST, SHOULD, MUSTN'T, NEEDN'T

Modal verbs are those verbs which add a dimension beyond the statement of a fact or a question about a fact; these added dimensions are chiefly to do with necessity, possibility, desirability and so on, and are expressed in English by such verbs as *can, may, must, need not, ought, should,* and some others. You have previously met **moct** (*can*) and **smět** (*may*); **chtít** (*to want*) is sometimes included in the same general group. Not only **moct** (Unit 2, Section

16), but also **smět** and **chtít** have certain peculiarities in their various forms, but since they are extremely common the deviant forms must be mastered.

	moct (can)	smět (may)	chtít (want)
I	můžu (mohu)	smím	chci
you (singular)	můžeš	smíš	chceš
he/she	může	smí	chce
we	můžeme	smíme	chceme
you (plural)	můžete	smíte	chcete
they	můžou (mohou)	smějí	chtějí

Another common pair are **muset** (alternatively **musit**) (*must, have to*) and **mít** (*should, be supposed/expected/due to*) – most definitely not 'have to', even though it looks like the ordinary **mít** *have*, denoting possession. Compare the sentences:

Musím být doma v sedm.   *I have to (must) be home at seven* (otherwise I'll be in trouble).

Mám být doma v sedm.   *I'm supposed to be at home at seven* (that's what I promised).

or *I should be home at seven* (that's when the train should get me there).

Another important verb **umět** (with endings like **smět**) which also means *can*, but in the case of 'acquired skills', may sometimes need to be translated in other ways:

Neumíš počítat?   *Can't you count?*

Umí pracovat.   *He knows how to work (is a good worker).*

It is also widely used, like **mluvit**, with words ending in **-y** to denote a language known or spoken:

Umějí česky a anglicky.   *They speak Czech and English.*

Rusky neumí.   *He doesn't know any Russian.*

An important factor about some of these modal verbs is their behaviour with negation; it is the modal itself which is negated in such oppositions as:

Musí být doma v sedm.   *He must (has to) be at home at seven.*

but

Nemusí být doma v sedm.   *He needn't (doesn't have to) be at home at seven.*

and

Smí tady být ráno.   *He may (is permitted to) be here in the morning(s).*

but

Nesmí tady být ráno.   *He must not (is not permitted to) be here in the morning(s).*

and

Může tady být ráno.   *He may be here in the morning.* (i.e. it is possible or permissible)

but

Nemůže tady být ráno.   *He cannot be here in the morning.* (i.e. it is impossible; also meaning he is not allowed)

9 EXPRESSING THE OBJECT (ACCUSATIVE CASE)

You have already met the nominative (see Unit 1, Section 11), vocative (see Unit 3, Section 6) and locative cases (see Unit 1, Section 11 and Unit 3, Section 11). Here is the *accusative case*. Its main function is to express the person or thing to whom or to which an action is done – this is called the direct object. Thus in:

Vidím auto/stůl/ženu/   *I (can) see the car/table/woman/Mary.*
Marii.

the words **auto**, **stůl**, **ženu** and **Marii** are in the accusative.

a   The good news is that several types of nouns are unchanged in the accusative: all neuters (**auto**, **nádraží**), all 'inanimate' masculines – those which do not refer to people or animals (**stůl**, **večer**), and those feminines that end in a consonant (**kuchyň**; **noc**, **domácnost**).

b   Other types of feminine noun undergo a change:

▷ 'hard' feminine nouns drop the final **-a** and replace it by **-u**:

Praha becomes **Prahu**: **Petr zná dobře Prahu** (*Peter knows Prague well*).

▷ 'soft' feminine nouns drop the final **-e** and replace it by **-i**:

Anglie becomes **Anglii**: **Ivan miluje Anglii** (*Ivan loves England*).
In the dialogue the words **bonboniéru** and **kytici** are feminine accusatives, direct objects of the verb *to take* understood from the previous utterance.

c   'Hard' masculine nouns denoting male beings and living creatures ('masculine animate nouns') add, in the accusative, the ending **-a**: **Petr má syna/psa** (*Peter has a son/a dog*) (from **pes**, which loses the **-e-**); 'soft' masculine animate nouns add **-ě/-e** (subject to the spelling rules):

Neznám bankéře.   *I don't know a banker.*
Má koně.   *He has a horse.* (from **kůň** – note also the alternation **ů/o** in **kůň**)

Many masculine nouns end in **-ek** or **-ec**, which, like **pes** above, contain a 'fleeting **-e-**', lost when the accusative case ending is added.

potomek/potomka   *descendant, offspring*
chlapec/chlapce   *boy*

Masculine animate nouns that end in **-e** in the nominative remain unchanged in the accusative:

Nemáme průvodce.   *We have no guide.*

The distinction between animate and inanimate, or between 'living' and 'non-living', is a crucial subdivision within the masculine gender only.

To summarize the main accusative endings of nouns:

	Nominative	Accusative
Masculine 'hard' inanimate	dům	**dům**
Masculine 'soft' inanimate	koberec	**koberec**
Masculine 'hard' animate	pán	**pána**
Masculine 'soft' animate	muž	**muže**
	průvodce	**průvodce**
Feminine 'hard'	žena	**ženu**
Feminine 'soft'	práce	**práci**
Other feminine types	kuchyň	**kuchyň**
	domácnost	**domácnost**
Neuter 'hard'	letadlo	**letadlo**
Neuter 'soft'	moře	**moře**
Neuter ending in **-í**	zelí	**zelí**

Some nouns will have to be learnt as 'soft' in their behaviour despite their final consonant. These will be marked when necessary. Those whose stem ends in **l** are common, such as feminine **židle** (*chair*) (where the nominative ending **-e** gives a hint) and masculine animate **učitel** (*teacher*) – accusative **učitele**.

> **● INSIGHT**
>
> Although the division in the animacy category between living and non-living is essentially absolute (within the animal kingdom; plants may live, but do not apply), and a maggot – **červ** – is therefore just as animate as a student, the principle also extends to cover such entities as gods, spirits, Martians, snowmen and other 'humanoids' as well as such formerly-living items as the deceased and sometimes even kippers. Thus **Amorek** *Cupid*, **šotek** *imp*, **Marťan** *Martian*, **sněhulák** *snowman*, **strašák** *scarecrow*, **nebožtík** *the deceased* and **uzenáč** *kipper* have the relevant (i.e. hard or soft) animate accusative endings: **Amorka**, **šotka** (both of which lose the fleeting **-e-** when the ending is added), **Marťana**, **sněhuláka**, **strašáka**, **nebožtíka** and **uzenáče**. One word in this general class that is of huge importance in Czech culture and folklore is the **vodník** or water-sprite, a distant cousin of the leprechaun.

10 PLACE VERSUS MOTION

You may have noticed the use of different prepositions, and with them different cases, in phrases expressing place as opposed to motion, such as **u nás** (**nás** happens to be genitive) *at our house* and **k nám** (**nám** is dative) *to our house*. The same type of opposition may also be expressed by different forms of related adverbs, such as **doma** (*at home*) and **domů** (*home(wards)*). The full pattern of place/motion oppositions will have to be developed gradually. Meanwhile, another type is the opposition between different cases after one and the same preposition, as happens with **na**. Compare for example:

(být) na návštěvě (někde)	*(be) on a visit (somewhere)*
(jít) na návštěvu (někam)	*(go) on a visit ('to' somewhere)*

The different case forms after the preposition **na** – locative (to express location, place, i.e. *on, at*) and accusative (for destination, direction or goal, i.e. *onto, on, to*) respectively, express this opposition regularly.

Auto stojí na mostě.	*The car is standing on the bridge.*
Jsme na koncertě.	*We're at a concert.*
Auto jede na most.	*The car is driving onto the bridge.*
Jdeme na koncert.	*We're going to a concert.*

A related use is that of **na** with just the accusative to denote purpose – a 'goal' of a slightly different sort:

blok na poznámky	*notepad (pad for notes)*
otvírák na konzervy	*tin-opener (opener for tins)*

11 *SICE ... ALE* – 'THOUGH'

The word **sice**, which is always paired with **ale** in the next clause, has its nearest equivalent in English in *admittedly* or in the insertion of forms of *do* in the verb-phrase; it may also be rendered by the conjunction *while* or *though* (which do not need *but* to start the second clause):

Doma sice pije čaj, ale v Praze **ho odmítá (odmítat** *to refuse***).**	*He does drink/Admittedly he drinks tea at home, but in Prague he declines it.*
Doma sice pije jenom čaj, ale v Praze pije také pivo (pít *to drink***).**	*While/Though at home he drinks only tea, in Prague he also drinks beer.*

12 *AŽ* – 'AS MUCH AS'

The word **až** is combined with phrases expressing quantity or time to suggest relative lateness, distance and so on.

 **Quick vocab**

v sedm *at seven*	**čtyři míle** *four miles*
až v sedm *as late as at seven i.e. not until seven*	**až čtyři míle** *as much as four miles*

13 BIDDING 'COME!'

The full details of how to make commands will be introduced later. For now, simply note that when *Come!* means here and now, as in *Come in* in the dialogue, you should use **Pojďte**

(**Pojď** if addressing someone with whom you are on familiar terms). If the invitation is for the person to come at a later time or date, use **Přijďte** (or **Přijď**).

Pojďte sem!	*Come here.*
Přijďte zítra!	*Come tomorrow.*

 Quick vocab

milovat *to love*	**jet (jede)** *to go (involving vehicles)*
pes (psa) *dog*	**most** *bridge*
kůň (koně) *horse*	**blok** *notepad*
potomek *descendant*	**otvírák** *opener*
chlapec *boy*	**čaj** (m) *tea*
domů *home(wards)*	**pivo** *beer*
stát (stojí) *to stand; cost*	**pít (pije)** *to drink*
jít (jde) *to go (on foot)*	**odmítat** *to decline, refuse*
poznámka *note*	**konzerva** *tin, can, jar (of foods)*

Exercises

Practise these phrases, which you will need if you wish to arrange a visit.

🔊 **TR 16**

4 a Tell the person you are talking to that you wish to invite him to your home. Try two versions, one speaking for yourself (*I*), and one speaking for yourself and your spouse (*we*). In either case you may refer to their visiting *us*.

  b Tell him not to come before seven.

  c Later on, when he arrives, bid him come in and say he needn't change his shoes.

  d He may well indicate that it is normal for him to change his shoes at home as well; what will he probably say – speaking for himself (*I*), or of the whole family (*we*)?

5 a Now you are the visitor: remark what a beautiful flat your hosts have.

  b Ask where the toilet is in their flat.

  c You have been asked the size of your own flat; reply

   i you have two bedrooms (the English response),

   ii you have four main rooms (in the Czech manner).

  d Finally, apologize for having to rush home.

THE FOOTWEAR RITUAL

You may have been perplexed about the issue of footwear. Whenever a Czech arrives home he will automatically and immediately, in the doorway, change his outdoor shoes for house shoes or slippers. Equally, it is almost unknown for someone to pop out without changing his indoor shoes. All this may even happen outside the front door, where the shoe box or shelf (**botník**; **boty** = *shoes*) may be located, though more usually it will be just inside the door.

Instead of **bačkory** for *slippers* you may meet another word, **pantofle** – a rare instance of a word with variable gender, from either masculine **pantofel** or feminine **pantofle**.

Czechs visiting friends will equally automatically kick off their outdoor shoes before entering the flat and be prepared to wander round in their stockinged feet or, more probably, accept the use of a spare pair of indoor shoes from the shoe-shelf. In some households an explicit exception is made for visitors, hence the line taken in the dialogue in this unit. The Czechs are immensely houseproud and the footwear ritual is just one of the manifestations.

Test yourself

If you have coped well with the exercises in this unit, you are ready to move on. Optionally, however, you may use the diagram on the next page to describe the apartment as if it were **a** your host or hostess's; and **b** your own; you may need the assistance of a native speaker. You will also need the words for *his*, *her* and/or *their*. You are advised to learn the new words below the diagram; they have their obvious utility in real-life situations, and they may crop up at later stages in the book, in anticipation of which their gender is given where it cannot be guessed at first sight.

Unlike, say, **můj** or **náš**, which change their forms according to the nouns they qualify, the words **jeho** (*his*) and **jejich** (*their*) never change at all! Thus you can say not only **jeho byt** and **jeho auto** or **jejich ložnice** and **jejich dům**, but also, for example, **v jeho bytě** (*in his flat*), or **v jejich ložnici** (*in their bedroom*).

To say *her* use **její**, which does change according to function, but in the same way as the 'soft' adjectives – like them it ends in **-í**.

Begin your sentences variously with **Můj/náš/jeho byt** (etc.) **má...** or **V pokoji** (etc.) **má/ mají/mám/máme**, according to sense. Remember that any words following will have to be in the accusative.

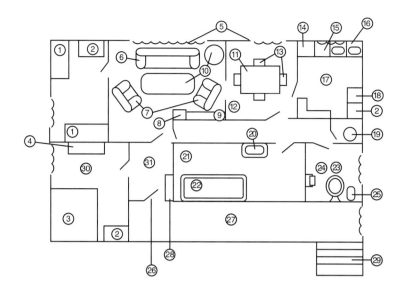

1 **postel** (f) *bed*
2 **skříň** (f) *cupboard, wardrobe*
3 **manželská postel** *double bed*
4 **prádelník** *chest of drawers*
5 **okna (sg. okno)** *windows*
6 **gauč** (m) *settee*
7 **křesla (**sg. **křeslo)** *armchairs*
8 **televizor** *television*
17 **kuchyň** (f) *kitchen*
18 **sporák** *stove*
19 **bojler** *boiler*
20 **umyvadlo** *wash basin*
21 **koupelna** *bathroom*
22 **vana** *bath*
23 **záchod** *lavatory*
24 **toaletní papír** *toilet paper*

9 **knihovna** *bookcase*
10 **stolek** *(coffee-) table*
11 **jídelní stůl** *dining table*
12 **jídelna** *dining room*
13 **židle** (f) *chair(s)*
14 **pračka** *washing machine*
15 **myčka** *dishwasher*
16 **dřez** *sink*
25 **košík** *bin, basket*
26 **hlavní dveře** (f pl)* *front door*
27 **chodba** *corridor*
28 **botník** *shoe rack*
29 **schody (**sg. **schod** *step, stair) stairs*
30 **podlaha** *floor*
31 **předsíň** *hall*

*In Czech 'door' is always plural, like, say, 'scissors' or 'pants'.

5 Je tu někde knihkupectví?

Is there a bookshop near here?

In this unit you will learn

▶ *How to watch your Ps and Qs*
▶ *How to ask questions politely*
▶ *How to say there is, there are*
▶ *How to say that you like something*
▶ *How to form and use adjectives in the accusative*

Dialogue 1

Mr Smith is lost in a strange town and turns to a passer-by, pan Novák, for help.

🔊 **TR 17**

Smith	Promiňte, prosím. Jsem tu cizí a nevím, kde jsem.
Novák	To se u nás stává. Nemáte mapu? Mapu potřebujete.
Smith	Nemám. Je tu někde knihkupectví?
Novák	Ano, velmi blízko. Vidíte, tam na rohu je hotel.
Smith	Ta velká budova?
Novák	Ano. Potom vidíte tu benzínovou pumpu, že? Dále jsou tři obchody a hned první je knihkupectví.
Smith	Děkuju. A prosím vás ještě…

Novák	Ano?
Smith	Nevíte náhodou, jak daleko je odsud hotel Jadran? Musím si nejdříve odpočinout. Mám tenhle velký kufr a malou, ale těžkou tašku.
Novák	Hotel Jadran přece vidíte tam na rohu.
Smith	Ach ano, jsem slepý.
Novák	Ale ne, jenom unavený.
Smith	Máte pravdu. Děkuju ještě jednou za pomoc.
Novák	Nemáte zač. Určitě se zastavte v tom knihkupectví. Mají tam dobré mapy.
Smith	Jak to víte?
Novák	Já jsem jeho majitel. Na shledanou!

 Quick vocab

Promiňte, prosím *Excuse me, please*
Jsem tu cizí *I'm a stranger here*
cizí *strange, foreign, alien; someone else's*
nevím, kde jsem *I don't know where I am*
nevím from **vědět** *know* (see the next page)
To se u nás stává *that happens here* (**u nás here** = *in our town*)
stávat se *to happen*
mapa *map*
potřebovat *to need*
Je tu někde knihkupectví? *Is there a bookshop near here?*
knihkupectví *bookshop*
blízko *near*
vidět (-í) *to see*
tam na rohu je hotel *there is a hotel there on the corner*
roh *corner*
ta velká budova *that big building*
ta *that* (f)
budova *building*
benzínová pumpa *petrol station, petrol pump*
dále jsou tři obchody *further on there are three shops*
dále *further on*
obchod *shop*
hned první je knihkupectví *the very first one is a/the bookshop*
hned *immediately*

a prosím vás ještě *and one more thing ('and please again')*
nevíte náhodou, jak… *do you happen to know how ('don't you know by chance how…')*
náhoda *chance, coincidence*
daleko *far*
Jadran *Adriatic*
odsud *from here* (remember **odkud** *from where*)
musím si nejdříve odpočinout *I must have a rest first*
nejdříve *first (adverb)*
odpočinout si (-ne) *to have a rest*
tenhle *this* (m)
kufr *suitcase*
těžký *heavy*
taška *bag*
Hotel přece vidíte na rohu *Surely you can see the hotel on the corner*
přece *surely* (used in mild protestation)
slepý *blind*
jenom (also **jen**) *only*
unavený *tired*
máte pravdu *you're right*
pravda *truth*
děkuju ještě jednou *thank you once again*
děkovat za (+ accusative) *to say thank you for something*
pomoc (f) *help* (although not ending in **-ost**, **pomoc** behaves like **domácnost**)

nemáte zač *don't mention it*

určitě se zastavte v tom knihkupectví
  be sure to call in that bookshop

určitě *definitely*

zastavte se *call in (imperative)*

mají tam dobré mapy *they have (some) good maps there*

Jak to víte? *How do you know?*

jeho *its*

majitel (-e) *owner*

vědět (*know***)** vím víš ví víme víte vědí

Vědět (see above) is one of the commonest verbs in Czech. It is, as you see, rather irregular, but you cannot go far without needing it, so familiarize yourself with it quickly!

1 SAYING 'PLEASE'

The basic word for *please* is **prosím** (**prosit** = *to ask, beg*). Usually it is tacked on to the end of the request or intrusion.

Promiňte, prosím.   *Excuse me, please.*

If it precedes a request, it is often, though not necessarily, accompanied by **vás** (*you*, accusative after 'I beg').

Prosím vás, ještě něco.   *Please, (there's) something else* (a variant of
                                                   the expression in the dialogue).

Very commonly, **prosím** and **prosím vás** are followed, almost redundantly, by the adverb **pěkně** (*nicely*). This is really a mark of deference.

Prosím is also used in these contexts:

  a   when waiters or shop assistants indicate their readiness to take your order or serve you, or when an official is ready to deal with your enquiry, etc.; they may simply say **Prosím?** (said with various rising or falling intonations), in place of English *Yes, please* or *Can I help you?*

  b   when you stand back to let someone else through a door first, again say simply **Prosím** (on a falling intonation; you will hear the same version after someone has done you a service – brought your meal, handed you your purchase, etc.). This version is also the almost automatic, neutral response to **Děkuju.**

  c   and it is more polite than **Co?** (*What?*) to use **Prosím?** (with a rising intonation) if you failed to catch what someone has said.

● **INSIGHT**

Those of you with a prior knowledge of German will appreciate how the source of **prosím** (a verb in the sense of 'request') and its usages described above are a perfect parallel to the way German uses *bitte*, even to the extent that **pěkně** matches German *schön*. While Czech exhibits numerous foreign influences (German and English in particular), the German element is in parts very old and parallels between German and Czech are never hard to find.

2 SAYING 'THANK YOU'

You met the basic **děkuju** in Unit 1. It too can be enhanced to **děkuju pěkně** or **velmi pěkně**, to give rough equivalents to *thank you very much* or *thank you very much indeed*.

To thank *for* something, use the preposition **za** and the accusative case:

Děkuju za krásný večer.   *Thank you for a wonderful evening.*

If someone has thanked you for a minor service, you can dismiss it with **Nemáte zač** or **Není zač** (*Don't mention it*, Lit. You do not have what [to thank] for). An alternative, with the same function, is **Za málo** (Lit. for little).

3 SAYING 'THERE IS/THERE ARE'

This is a very simple matter; there is no element in Czech for *there* in this sense. You simply use **je** and **jsou**. Typically these expressions are used to indicate the presence of something somewhere, and in Czech the giveaway to the *there is/are* meaning will usually be mention of *the place* first:

Na rohu **je hotel.**   *There is a hotel on the corner.*

or

Dále **jsou tři obchody.**   *Further on there are three shops.*

These are distinct from:

Hotel je na rohu.   *The hotel is on the corner.*

and

Obchody jsou dále.   *The shops are further on.*

Notice how in the second type of English sentence *hotel* and *shops* are accompanied by *the*; they are already 'known'.

4 HOW TO MAKE A POLITE ENQUIRY

As you saw earlier, a verb form, e.g. **máte**, may mean not only *you have*, but also *have you?* or *do you have?* If you express a question as an enquiry or request, there are several degrees of politeness. The simplest is to ask the question in the negative.

Nevíte, kde je hotel Jadran?   *Do you (not) know where the Jadran is?*

This tells the person asked that *you* want to know. The positive form of the question, **Víte, kde...** is more appropriate to, say, quizzes – I already know the answer and am checking whether you do. A (slightly) more deferential enquiry includes the word **náhodou** (*by chance*), and is a good counterpart to the English formula based on *happen* (and similar):

Nevíte náhodou, kde je   *Do you happen to know where*
  Jadran?   *the Jadran is?*

Similarly:

Nemáte náhodou sirky?   *Do you happen to have a light? (***sirky**
                                   = matches)
Nejste náhodou pan Novák? *Aren't you Mr Novák?*

Not every negative question expresses a polite enquiry or request. They can be neutral and based on the same assumptions as an English negative question. Look at the other one in the dialogue:

Nemáte mapu?   *Haven't you got a map (I assume not)?*

This is also one type of utterance where it is (also) appropriate to use the subject pronoun, hence the alternative form of the last question: **Vy nemáte mapu?**

5 TWO KINDS OF KNOWING: *VĚDĚT* VERSUS *ZNÁT*

When you met **znát** earlier, it involved acquaintance: **známe se z letadla** (*We know each other from the plane*). Use this verb for other types of acquaintance too, with places or books, as well as people:

Neznám Prahu.   *I don't know Prague.*
Eva nezná Češtinu pro   *Eva doesn't know Teach Yourself*
  samouky.   *Czech.*

For knowing facts, use **vědět**. This means that in most cases it will be followed by clauses beginning with **že**:

Pan Novák ví, že tam mají *Mr Novák knows that they have good*
  dobré mapy.   *maps there.*

or with question words, like **kde** (*where*) or **jestli** (*if*):

Víme, kde mají dobré mapy. *We know where they have good maps.*
Nevědí, jestli je hotel daleko. *They don't know if the hotel is far away.*

> ● **INSIGHT**
> Mindful of what was said in the previous **Insight** about Czech/German parallels, note that the above opposition between **vědět** and **znát** matches that between *wissen* and *kennen*, not to mention French *savoir* and *connaître* and their equivalents in Spanish, Dutch or Italian. Russian and English almost alone in Europe have found one verb 'know' to be sufficient.

Notice how, in written Czech, all conjunctions – such words as **jestli**, **kdy** or **že**, words that introduce a special type of clause and 'conjoin' it to the main clause – are preceded by a comma when they are not at the beginning of the sentence. This is a grammatical convention; the comma has no association with a pause – as is commonly the case in English.

6 RIGHT AND WRONG

Pravda means *truth*. It combines with **mít** to give the basic meaning of 'being right' or 'wrong' of persons:

Paní Nováková má pravdu.	*Mrs Novák is right.*
Pan Novák nemá pravdu.	*Mr Novák is wrong.*

and with **být** to express that something is true (as in an earlier exercise):

To je pravda.	*That's true/That's right.*
To není pravda.	*That isn't true/That's wrong.*

As answers to questions you are possibly more likely to hear **Ano, je to pravda** and **Ne, není to pravda**, but the two word-orders are largely interchangeable.

7 ADJECTIVES IN THE ACCUSATIVE

Two new 'hard' adjective endings now need to be learnt:

a the feminine singular, which ends in **-ou**, hence Mr Smith's complaint:
Mám těžkou tašku.
a pattern repeated in the expression (**vidíte**) **benzínovou pumpu**;

b the special ending to match animate masculine nouns (i.e. a living being such as a person, animal), which is not illustrated in the dialogue. This is the ending **-ého**:

Eva má hodného muže.	*Eva has a kind husband.*
Vidím nového studenta.	*I (can) see a new student.*

For the 'soft' adjectives the only new ending is also for agreement with animate masculine nouns – all other forms have simply **-í**. The special form is **-ího**, as in:

Známe prvního pacienta.	*We know the first patient.*

8 'MY': MŮJ (M), MOJE/MÁ (F), MOJE/MÉ (N); 'OUR': NÁŠ (M), NAŠE (F), NAŠE (N)

The possessives (*my* etc.) must also change according to case. **Můj** *my* shows some similarity – where there are long endings – to the above adjective forms:

Vidí mého nového pacienta.	*He can see my new patient.*
Pije mou studenou kávu.	*He is drinking my cold coffee.*

The same forms apply to **tvůj** *your* (familiar) and **svůj** (the reflexive possessive, see Unit 4, Section 3), though **svůj** has no nominative forms (it refers *back* to the subject, so cannot be part of the subject). The longer forms **moje**, **moji** are less formal and therefore more likely to be encountered in conversation.

The possessive **náš** *our* only has short endings, which it shares with **moje**, **moji**. The forms of **náš** are shared by **váš** *your* (plural or polite). Remember that the long **-á-** of **náš** and **váš** shortens in all forms with an ending.

For **jeho** (*his*), **jejich** (*their*) and **její** (*her*) see Unit 4.

	Masculine inanimate	Masculine animate	Feminine	Neuter
Nominative	můj dům	můj pacient	moje/má taška	moje/mé auto
Accusative	můj dům	mého pacienta	moji/mou tašku	moje/mé auto
Nominative	náš dům	náš pacient	naše taška	naše auto
Accusative	náš dům	našeho pacienta	naši tašku	naše auto

9 POINTING THINGS OUT: *TEN* (M), *TA* (F), *TO* (N)

These are the words used to point to things (*demonstrative pronouns*), usually translated as *that*, but occasionally as *this*:

ta benzínová pumpa   *that petrol station*

It has a special form **tu** for agreement with nouns in the accusative:

Vidíte tu benzínovou pumpu?   *Can you see that petrol station?*

It also has a special form for agreement with masculine animate nouns in the accusative:

ten první pacient   *that first patient*

Neznáme toho prvního   *We don't know that first patient.*
   pacienta.

To specify *this* as opposed to *that*, add **-hle** to the appropriate form of **ten**, hence Mr Smith points to:

tenhle velký kufr   *this big suitcase*

or you might say:

Neznám tohohle pacienta.   *I don't know this patient.*

To say *that* of something further away, or directly contrasted to *this*, put **tam-** in front of the forms of **ten**:

Tenhle kufr je jeho, můj je   *This case is his, mine's that one.*
   tamten.

Here is a summary table for nominative and accusative of **ten** and adjectives.

	Masculine inanimate	Masculine animate	Feminine	Neuter
Nom.	ten nový dům	ten nový pacient	ta nová taška	to nové auto
Acc.	ten nový dům	t**oho** nov**ého** pacienta	t**u** nov**ou** tašku	to nové auto
Nom.	ten cizí kufr	ten cizí pacient	ta cizí taška	to cizí auto
Acc.	ten cizí kufr	t**oho** ciz**ího** pacienta	t**u** cizí tašku	to cizí auto

(See Unit 4, Section 9 for an explanation of inanimate and animate nouns.)

 Quick vocab

hodný *kind*
nový *new*
byznysmen *businessman*
pacient *patient*

samouk *self-taught person*
sirka *match*
studený *cold*

Exercises

1 Looking back at Dialogue 1, say whether these are *true* **(Ano, je to pravda) or** *false* **(Ne, není to pravda).**

  a Je pravda, že pan Novák má knihkupectví?
  b Je pravda, že pan Smith ví, kde je?
  c Je pravda, že na rohu je benzínová pumpa?
  d Je pravda, že pan Smith nemá mapu?
  e Je pravda, že pan Smith je slepý?
  f Je pravda, že pan Smith nemluví česky?
  g Je pravda, že pan Novák je dobrý byznysmen?

2 Attempt true statements for those sentences where you answered 'Ne, není to pravda'.

3 In the following sentences, which form is correct?

a Ivan má (pravda/pravdu).

b (Ta taška/Tu tašku) je těžká.

c Pan Smith nevidí (benzínová pumpa/benzínovou pumpu).

d Paní Navrátilová vítá (pana Čermáka a paní Čermákovou/pan Čermák a paní Čermáková).

e Spěchám tam na (ta pošta/tu poštu).

f Neznáme (ten starý cizinec/toho starého cizince).

g Neví, kde je (moje židle/moji židli).

h Zná (vaši matku/vaše matka) a (váš otec/vašeho otce).

4 Complete your part of this conversation:

You	*Excuse me, I need help.*
Čech	Ano?
You	*Do you happen to know where the Hotel Forum is?*
Čech	Mm, Forum je odsud daleko.
You	*How far exactly?*
Čech	Dva kilometry.
You	*That's not far – I haven't got a suitcase.*

Dialogue 2

The Smiths have just rung the Navrátils' door bell again and Mr Navrátil has opened the door.

 TR 18

Smith	Dobrý večer, Zdeňku, tak jsme zase tady.
Navrátil	Dobrý večer, Alane, vítám vás. Pojďte dál. Dobrý večer, paní Smithová.
Mrs Smith	Dobrý večer. Už se těším, že si sednu. Máme za sebou dlouhý den.
Smith	Ano, je to tak. Mám rád Prahu, ale někdy mě hodně unavuje.
Navrátil	Tak pojďte, pojďte – ne, nezouvejte se. Manželka se na vás těší.
Mrs Smith	Já se taky těším. Velmi ráda poslouchám její historky o rodině.
Navrátil	To nerad slyším, to určitě znamená nějakou kritiku na můj účet!

> **Mrs Smith** Kdepak! Vás jenom chválí… většinou. Má vás ráda.
>
> *While they're still chatting Mrs Navrátil comes towards them.*
>
> **Navrátilová** Dobrý večer, Heleno. Dobrý večer, pane Smith. Co tady
> děláte tak dlouho? Slyším zvonek, slyším dveře, čekám,
> čekám – a nic. Ale jsem velmi ráda, že jste tady. Pojďte.
> Večeře bude hned.
>
> **Smith** (*šeptem*) Ta tvoje kamarádka opravdu mluví hodně.

 Quick vocab

Zdeňku, Alane (vocative case-forms of
  Zdeněk and *Alan*)
tak jsme zase tady *here we are again*
zase *again*
už se těším, že si sednu *I can't wait to sit down*
těšit se, že … *look forward (to the prospect)
  that …*
máme za sebou dlouhý den *we've had a
  long day*
mít (něco) za sebou *to have (something)
  behind one*
dlouhý *long*
je to tak *that's so, that's right*
tak *so, thus*
mám rád Prahu *I like Prague*
mít rád *to like, to love*
někdy mě hodně unavuje *sometimes it tires
  me a lot*
hodně *a lot, a great deal, greatly* (adverb)
unavovat *to tire* (think of **unavený** *tired* in
  Dialogue I)
nezouvejte se *don't take your shoes off*
  (a simpler command used instead of
  nemusíte se zouvat)
manželka se na vás těší *my wife's looking
  forward to (seeing) you*
těšit se na (+ acc.) *to look forward to something*
ráda poslouchám její historky *I like listening
  to her tales*
o rodině *about the family*
poslouchat *to listen; obey*
historky *tales, stories, anecdotes*

to nerad slyším *I don't like the sound of that*
to určitě znamená *that's bound to mean*
nějakou kritiku *some (sort of) criticism*
znamenat *to mean*
nějaký *some (kind of);*
it often means little more than *a*
kritika *criticism*
na můj účet *to my account* (here, *at my
  expense*)
účet *account, bill*
kdepak! *not a bit of it! oh no!*
vás jenom chválí *she only praises you*
chválit *praise*
většinou *mostly*
má vás ráda *she loves you*
co tady děláte tak dlouho? *what's taking you
  so long?*
dlouho (for) *a long time*
zvonek *bell*
dveře (f pl) *door*
čekám, čekám – a nic *I wait and wait – and
  nothing (happens)*
čekat *to wait*
nic *nothing*
jsem ráda, že … *I'm glad that …*
večeře (f) *dinner (main evening meal)*
bude *will be*
hned *at once*
šeptem *in a whisper*
ta tvoje kamarádka *that friend of yours*
opravdu *really*

10 EXPRESSING 'LIKE'

The crucial word here is **rád**, which means *glad*, as in **jsem rád, že ...** (*I'm glad that ...*). In combination with **mít** it means both *like* and *love*:

Má rád Helenu.	*He loves Helena.*
Nemám rád politiku.	*I don't like politics.*
Má rád zlatou Prahu.	*He likes golden Prague.*

> ● **INSIGHT**
>
> Note that **zlatý** *golden* has become an automatic epithet for Prague. Another is **stověžatá** *hundred-spired* (**věž** *tower, spire*, **sto** *hundred*) – the fitness of which will be appreciated on your first visit. Sentimentally the city is also known as **matička Praha** *little mother Prague*; most sentimentally by a combination of this with one of the previous epithets: **stověžatá matička Praha**. The Latin motto on the city arms reads **Praga caput regni** *Prague capital of the Kingdom* (that is, the historic Kingdom of Bohemia), which is jocularly interpreted in one old chestnut as 'Prague destroyed by rain'.

The structure of the *like/love* phrase is something like 'x has y gladly'. It is the nature of the object that determines the English interpretation of what is being said.

An extension of the use of **rád** with **mít** (which you can now think of as 'like having') is to combine **rád** with almost any other verb, when it means *like ...-ing*. Mrs Smith *likes listening* to Mrs Navrátil's family gossip; Mr Navrátil doesn't *like hearing* that she does; you may or may not *like learning* Czech.

This vital little word **rád** is a new kind of adjective (what makes it special is that it only combines with verbs, not nouns). And as an adjective it will change form to agree with the subject of the sentence, in any of its functions. Hence Mrs Smith will require feminine agreement and so she **ráda poslouchá** family gossip, while her husband is masculine and so **nerad slyší** about it. With a neuter word, such as **dítě** (*child*), the ending would be **-o**:

Dítě rádo hraje fotbal.	*The child likes playing football.*

(Note the coincidence between the endings of **rád** and those of the main, 'hard' noun types.)

Negating 'like'

Note that negative sentences with *like ...-ing* usually attach the negative prefix **ne-** to **rád**, NOT to the verb (except in the case of **mít rád**, as can be seen in the second example above), and the middle **-á-** shortens. Thus

Pan Navrátil to nerad slyší.	*Mr Navrátil doesn't like hearing that.*
Paní Navrátilová nerada čeká.	*Mrs Navrátil doesn't like waiting.*
To dítě nerado hraje fotbal.	*That child doesn't like playing football.*

Apart from plurals, there are no other forms (case-endings) of **rád** to be learnt.

11 MORE EXPRESSIONS WITH *TĚŠIT*

In Unit 2 you met **těší mě** (Lit. *it consoles me*), as the idiom for *pleased to meet you*. There are two uses of **těšit se**, a reflexive verb (it must have **se** in these senses). The commoner construction contains the preposition **na** (+ accusative) denoting the direction, goal or target of your hopes, for **těšit se** means *to look forward to* ('console oneself at the prospect of something').

Jiří se těší na večeři.	*George is looking forward to dinner.*
Ivan se těší na Olgu.	*Ivan is looking forward to (seeing) Olga.*

Other expressions denoting 'goal' besides **na** may also be used.

Těším se k vám.	*I'm looking forward to (coming to see) you.*
Těší se do Prahy.	*She's looking forward to (going to) Prague.*
Těšíme se domů.	*We're looking forward to (going) home.*

The other use of **těšit se** is with the conjunction **že**, as in **Těším se, že si sednu.** You may meet more instances of it after you learn the future tense. (The **sednu si** = *I'll sit down* in Dialogue 2 is in the future.)

12 HOW MANY DOORS DO CZECHS KNOCK ON AT ONCE?

In the next unit you will look at plurals. One or two plural forms (mostly ending in **-y**) have already crept into some of the dialogues and were left without comment. But they did denote 'proper' plurals – like the *tales* (**historky**) that Mrs Navrátil is said to tell. But Czech, like English, has several plural words – such as *trousers* or *scissors* – that refer to single items. But there are other odd plurals as well, like *oats* in English or **dveře** (*door*) in Czech, without any obvious reason. Watch out for others.

13 WORD ORDER WITH *SE* AND *SI*

These little words, forms of the reflexive pronoun (see Unit 2, Section 13), cannot stand at the beginning of the sentence. In fact they must stand in the second grammatical 'slot' (i.e. not necessarily second word) in the sentence. This is why they always follow the word they go with in the vocabulary boxes (**těšit se, odpočinout si**), although the order may easily be reversed in actual sentences: **manželka se na vás těší, musím si nejdříve odpočinout**. Many pronouns are subject to a similar rule.

14 WORD ORDER GENERALLY

In Czech, a general principle applies that items in a sentence referring to information already mentioned – or otherwise 'known' – stand at the front; new, or more important, information stands at the end. This can frequently mean that the object (accusative) may stand first.

Vás jenom chválí.	*You (acc.) (she) only praises.*

You is known from the situation, the praise being the substantially new information. Do not worry about the finer issues governing word order just yet; you will learn things that are subject to strong rules when they arise (as with **se/si** above).

Remember that word order matters in two contrasting types of statements:

Na stole je kniha.   *There is a book on the table.*
Kniha je na stole.   *The book is on the table.*

(see Section 3), but in the questions *Where is the book*? or *Where is there a book*? you have little to worry about: **Kde je kniha?** is used for either, but for the second version it would be better to add a form of **nějaký** – **Kde je nějaká kniha?** – an instance where, as noted in the third last item of the Quick vocab after Dialogue 2 above, it is close to the English *a*.

Exercises

5 Read and reply in Czech, using full sentences:
   a Hrajete fotbal?
   b Kdo chválí pana Navrátila?
   c Mluví váš muž/vaše žena hodně?

Note that there is more to play (**hrát**, **hraje**) than football:

   hrát is just *to play* (non-human subject)

   hrát si *to play* (human subject)

   hrát na + acc. *to play* an instrument

   hrát na + acc. for some children's games

   hrát + acc. *to play* cards, games that are sports, music and theatre parts

rozhlas hraje	*the radio is on*
my si jenom hrajeme	*we're just playing*
hrát na klavír	*to play the piano*
hrát na slepou bábu	*to play blindman's buff*
hrát karty/fotbal/valčík/Hamleta	*to play cards/football/a waltz/Hamlet*

6 See if you can ask the following questions (as politely as circumstances may require):
   a Do you have a light?
   b Do you happen to know where Mrs Navrátil is?
   c Do you like hearing criticism?
   d Are you looking forward to lunch?
   e Is she tired?
   f Does she want to rest first?
   g Isn't that Mrs Smith?

7 Read the following text and answer the questions in English:

 TR 19

Pan Smith je v Praze. Doma v Anglii bydlí v bytě v činžáku, ale tady v Praze má luxusní pokoj v hotelu. Je bankovní úředník, svobodný a každý rok tráví měsíc někde v cizině. Takhle si může krásně odpočinout. Rád poznává osobně každé město, které zná jen z obrázků. Všude kupuje pohlednice, ale zásadně nikomu nepíše. Je rád, že může být chvíli sám.

 Quick vocab

luxus (noun)**, luxusní** (adj.) *luxury*	**město** *town, city*
banka (noun)**, bankovní** (adj.) *bank*	**z obrázků** *from pictures*
každý *each, every*	**obrázek** *picture*
rok *year*	**všude** *everywhere*
trávit *to spend (time)*	**kupovat** *to buy*
měsíc (m) *month; moon*	**pohlednice picture** *postcard*
v cizině *abroad*	**zásadně** *on principle*
cizina *foreign parts*	**nikomu nepíše** *he doesn't write to anyone*
takhle *like this*	**chvíli** *for a while*
poznávat *to get to know; recognize*	**sám** *alone*
osobně *personally*	

a What is Mr Smith's job?
b How often does he go abroad?
c For how long?
d Find two reasons why.
e Compare his home and holiday accommodation.

CZECHS AND THEIR STOMACHS

Czechs are great eaters. The national dish is commonly known as **vepřoknedlozelo**, a jocular combination of **vepřové** (*pork* – roast or braised), **knedlíky** (*dumplings* – large fat sausage-shaped things, made of flour, yeast, eggs and croutons, boiled, then sliced into rounds on a special slicer) and **zelí** (*cabbage*, the drumhead kinds, white or red – either sweet or as sauerkraut). They also eat a lot of **hovězí** (*beef*), **drůbež** (f) (*poultry*) and many kinds of **salám** (*salami*), but little or no lamb. Cooked vegetables are not very varied, though **brambory** (*potatoes*) are plentiful. There is much more variety in those served as mixed cold garnishes out of a tin. In season **rajčata** (*tomatoes*), **okurek** (*cucumber*) and **zelená** and **červená paprika** (*green* and *red peppers*), including some very hot ones, are widely used; the elongated ones are called **kápie**. At any time of year, **okurky** (*pickled gherkins*) are delicious (and widely exported). Many types of **salát** (*salad*) are eaten; however, if not further qualified, **salát** just means *lettuce*. As well as potatoes or dumplings, **rýže** (f) (*rice*) and **těstoviny** (f. pl) (*pasta*) are common accompaniments to meat.

The eating day begins with **snídaně** (f) (*breakfast*), usually fairly light in the continental manner. Many people have a second breakfast, **přesnídavka**, mid-morning. The midday meal, **oběd**, may, according to family practice or such considerations as subsidized lunches in the workplace, be more substantial than the evening meal, **večeře** (f), while for many the latter is *the* big meal of the day. This may in part depend on whether a teatime snack, **svačina**, has been taken; the latter word may also apply mid-morning, and it is used for 'packed lunch'.

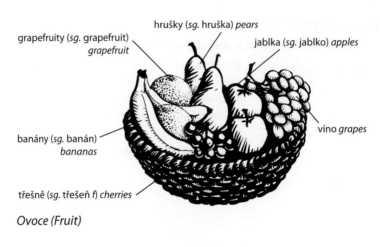

hrušky (*sg.* hruška) *pears*

grapefruity (*sg.* grapefruit) *grapefruit*

jablka (*sg.* jablko) *apples*

banány (*sg.* banán) *bananas*

víno *grapes*

třešně (*sg.* třešeň f) *cherries*

Ovoce (Fruit)

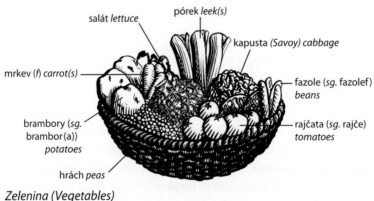

salát *lettuce*

pórek *leek(s)*

kapusta *(Savoy) cabbage*

mrkev (f) *carrot(s)*

fazole (*sg.* fazolef) *beans*

brambory (*sg.* brambor(a)) *potatoes*

rajčata (*sg.* rajče) *tomatoes*

hrách *peas*

Zelenina (Vegetables)

Before people start eating it is customary to wish them **Dobrou chuť** (*Good appetite*) – **chuť** (f) = *appetite, taste*. You will eat well – so learn this bit of Czech etiquette for use from the first moment you sit down to table. Even if you are sitting on a park bench munching a burger or sandwich, it is quite likely some of the Czech passers-by will likewise wish you **Dobrou chuť.**

Also, at meals or just out for a drink, you will find plenty of **pivo** (*beer*) and **víno** (*wine*), so it's vital to know **Na zdraví!** (*Cheers!*) as well – **zdraví** (n) = *health*.

? Test yourself

Read and reply in Czech, using full sentences.

1 Jak se jmenujete?

2 Bydlíte v Londýně?

3 Čekáte rád?

4 Paní Smithová ráda poslouchá historky?

Ask the following questions in Czech.

5 Are you looking forward to seeing Prague?

6 Are they looking forward to going to Prague?

7 Is he outside (**venku**) playing football?

6 Na celnici
At customs

In this unit you will learn
▸ *How to understand questions about your person*
▸ *How to answer in an appropriate manner*
▸ *How to begin to use plurals*
▸ *How to use some means of expressing reason and purpose*

Dialogue 1

Mr Smith is going through customs.

 TR 20

Celník	Dobrý den. Toto jsou vaše zavazadla?
Smith	Ano, prosím. Tenhle kufr a taška.
Celník	Máte nějaké zboží na prodej v České republice?
Smith	Ne, v kufru mám jenom osobní věci – oblečení, fotoaparát a podobně.
Celník	A v tašce?
Smith	Tam mám jenom věci na cestu – mycí potřeby, nějaké jídlo, knihu.
Celník	Tak proč je ta taška tak těžká?
Smith	Protože tam mám kameny.
Celník	Cože? Jaké kameny?
Smith	Různé. Budu je v Praze potřebovat.
Celník	*(to his colleague)* Hele, Honzo, tady ten pán si myslí, že v Praze potřebuje kameny!
Honza	Není sám.
Celník	Jak to?
Honza	Tento týden se přece v Praze koná geologická konference. Jsou to vědci, geologové.
Smith	To je pravda, jsem geolog. Proto mám ty kameny a proto je moje taška tak těžká. Hrozně těžká.
Celník	Tak můžete jít. Hezkou konferenci přeju!

Pan Smith je geolog. V tašce má kameny, proto je taška tak těžká.

Quick vocab

zavazadla *luggage* (**zavazadlo** *a piece of luggage*)

ano, prosím *yes* (the **prosím** adds a degree of deference)

celník *customs officer*

zboží na prodej *goods for sale*

zboží *goods* (a neuter singular collective word)

v České republice *in the Czech Republic*

republika *republic*

osobní věci *personal items, belongings*

věc (f) *thing, object* (a word in the same class as **domácnost**)

oblečení *clothing*

fotoaparát *camera* (colloquially, and so frequently, also **foťák**, and beware: **kamera** means *cine-camera*, hence also **videokamera**)

a podobně *and such like* (in printed texts often abbreviated to **apod.**)

v tašce *in the bag*

věci na cestu *things for the journey*

cesta *journey, trip, way, path, track*

mycí potřeby *washing things* (toiletries)

mycí *adjective from* **mýt (myje)** *to wash*

potřeba *need,* (item of) *necessity*

jídlo *food; also meal, dish*

kniha *book*

proč *why*

protože *because*

kameny *stones* (singular = **kámen**)

cože! *what!*

jaký *what kind (of)*

různý *various, different*

budu je potřebovat *I will need them*

hele *hey!, I say!*

Honzo *vocative of* **Honza**, *familiar form of* **Jan** *John*

tady ten pán *this chap here*

myslet si (-í) *to think*

jak to? *how come?, what do you mean?*

není sám *he's not alone, he's not the only one*

tento týden se přece koná geologická konference *after all, there's a geological conference going on this week*

týden *week*

přece *after all* (remember its previous use as *surely*; here it amounts to *surely you know*)

konat se *to be held, to be going on*

geologický *geological*

vědci *scientists* (singular = **vědec**)

geologové *geologists* (singular = **geolog**)

proto *that's why, therefore*

hrozně *terribly, awfully, dreadfully* (from **hrozný** *terrible, awful, dreadful*)

tak můžete jít *all right, you can go*

hezký *nice*

přát (přeje) *to wish*

1 FORMING THE PLURAL

You cannot get far without the plural. How do you form it?

a 'Hard' nouns: feminines, like **žena**, **historka** or **potřeba**, replace their final **-a** by **-y**.

ženy	*women*
historky	*tales, anecdotes*
potřeby	*requisites*

The same ending is simply added to such 'hard' masculine inanimate nouns as **hotel**, **obchod**, **kámen** or **stůl**.

hotely	*hotels*	**kameny**	*stones*
obchody	*shops*	**stoly**	*tables*

Notice how sometimes there may be a change in the vowel: k**á**men-k**a**meny; st**ů**l-st**o**ly.

'Hard' neuter nouns, such as **zavazadlo**, **slovo** (*word*), **kolo** (*wheel, bicycle*) replace the ending **-o** by **-a**.

zavazadla	*items of luggage*
slova	*words*
kola	*wheels*

b All the 'soft' matching types of any gender, such as **pokoj** (m) (*room*), **kancelář** (f) (*office*), or **kuchyně** (f) (*kitchen*), and a few neuters such as **moře** (*sea*) end in **-e** or **-ě** – subject to the spelling rules (if in doubt about these still, see the **Introduction**).

pokoje	*rooms*	**kuchyně**	*kitchens*
kanceláře	*offices*	**moře**	*seas*

Note: most feminines and neuters that already end in **-e/-ě** in the singular appear not to change. You will soon see that there can rarely be any ambiguity.

c The other feminine nouns, like **domácnost** or **věc**, form their plural by adding **-i**, just like their locative singular (remember **žena v domácnosti** to describe a housewife) (see Unit 3, Section 10):

domácnosti	*households*	**věci**	*things*

Many case-forms of these words end in **-i**, which is why they are commonly referred to as **i**-declension words. (For an explanation of 'declension', see the **Glossary of grammatical terms**.)

d The many neuter nouns that end in long **-í** retain this in the plural, as in their locative singular.

zelí	*cabbage(s)*
knihkupectví	*bookshop(s)*
nádraží	*station(s)*

The same applies to the only such feminine noun, **paní** (*lady/ladies*).

2 NOMINATIVE/VOCATIVE/ACCUSATIVE PLURALS

For all the words in **a–d** above, the nominative, vocative and accusative plural forms are the same.

3 MASCULINE ANIMATE NOUNS

In the *accusative* the endings are as for the inanimate (see **1 a** and **b** above) – **-y** for 'hard' nouns and **-e** for 'soft' nouns.

studenty	*students*	**geology**	*geologists*
vědce	*scientists*	**majitele**	*owners*
Angličany	*Englishmen*		

(Note that nouns ending in **-tel** behave as 'soft', although **l** itself is not normally a 'soft' consonant.) However, in the *nominative* plural of masculine animate nouns there are three endings.

a **-i** is used for most whether 'hard' or 'soft'.

'hard'

student → student**i** (and remember that **-ti** at the end will be pronounced **ťi**)

'soft'

vědec → vědc**i** (remember 'fleeting **-e-**'; see Unit 4, Section 9c)

Just as final **t** is pronounced **ť** before **-i**, so a final **d** is pronounced **ď**, and a final **n** is pronounced **ň**.

kamarád (*pal*) → kamарád**i**   had (*snake*) → had**i**

vegetarián (*vegetarian*) → vegetarián**i**   rabín (*rabbi*) → rabín**i**

Also final **k**, **h**, **ch** and **r** change, but far more conspicuously, to **c**, **z**, **š** and **ř** respectively.

celník → (*customs officer*) celníci   Slovák → (*Slovak*) Slováci

vrah → (*murderer*) vrazi   pstruh → (*trout*) pstruzi

Čech → (*Czech*) Češi   mnich → (*monk*) mniši

manažer → (*manager*) manažeři   doktor → (*doctor*) doktoři

The changes of **k** to **c**, and **r** to **ř** are particularly common because many words end in **-ek, -ník, -er, -ér, -or** and **-ýr**.

b **-ové**, rather easier to handle, is chiefly used with polysyllabic 'international' words for professions and other human conditions.

biolog-ové	*biologist(s)*	ekonom-ové	*economist(s)*
fotograf-ové	*photographer(s)*	politik-ové	*politician(s)*
pedofil-ové	*paedophile(s)*	(**also** politici)	

● **INSIGHT**

The 'competition' between **-i** and **-ové** in the nominative plural of masculine animate nouns is actually a far more complex issue and often depends on the final consonant, irrespective of whether a word is native or international. Thus final **-j** prefers **-ové**, as in **zpravodaj|ové** (*reporter*), **kovboj|ové** (*cowboy*), **samuraj|ové** (*samurai*), while **-r, -n** or **-k** are generally happy with **-i**, even though this entails a consonant change: **pediatr-pediatři** (*paediatrician*), **megaloman|-i** (*megalomaniac*), **matematik-matematici/matematikové** (*mathematician*). Monolingual dictionaries generally indicate the correct, or approved form, and for the foreign learner the widely available dictionaries by Josef Fronek offer a reliable guide to this and other formal peculiarities of individual words.

The ending **-ové** is also widely used to form the plural of one-syllable words, including many names of nationalities.

syn-ové	*son*	Švéd-ové	*Swede(s)*
pán-ové	*gentleman/-men*	Skot-ové	*Scot(s)*
Ir-ové	*Irishman/-men*	Dán-ové	*Dane(s)*

(**Pán** has an alternative plural in **-i**: pán**i**.)

   c **-é** is mainly confined to readily identifiable groups of words.

Nouns ending in **-tel**:	majitel-**é** *owner(s)*	učitel-**é** *teacher(s)*
Nouns with **-(č)an**:	Angličan-**é** *Englishman/(men)*	Velšan-**é** *Welshman/(men)*
	Kanaďan-**é** *Canadian(s)*	občan-**é** *citizen(s)*
Nouns with **-at**:	demokrat-**é** *democrat(s)*	byrokrat-**é** *bureaucrat(s)*

And a few common oddments:

soused-é	*neighbour(s)*	host-é	*guest(s)*
žid-é	*Jew(s)*	Španěl-é	*Spaniard(s)*

It is also used for **manželé** (*Mr* and *Mrs*, *husband* and *wife*), plural of **manžel** (*husband*).

> ● **INSIGHT**
>
> Colloquially, many words, especially those ending in **-(č)an**, **-at** and the 'common oddments' above, may also take **-i** instead of **-ové**.

These endings, and any changes they entail, apply solely to the nominative plural, so note the contrast with the accusative plural:

Nominative	Accusative	Nominative	Accusative
celníci	**celníky**	**vrazi**	**vrahy**
Češi	**Čechy**	**inženýři**	**inženýry**
geologové	**geology**	**Irové**	**Iry**
Angličané	**Angličany**	**učitelé**	**učitele (!!'soft')**

Remember, animacy only applies to masculine nouns, that is, it affects all masculine nouns denoting living creatures. It is an important factor in the nominative plural and the accusative singular, as you have seen.

4 MORE USES OF *NA*

In an early unit you met the preposition **na** with the accusative of **konference**, namely **konferenci**, and it means *for a conference* (that is, the *reason* or *purpose* for being somewhere). In this unit you have two related expressions (like those in Unit 4, Section 10):

(zboži) na prodej	*goods for (the purpose of) sale*
(věci) na cestu	*things for the journey*

There are countless other possibilities, which will not be commented on separately, but you could need:

prášek na prádlo   *washing powder*
místo na kufry   *room for the suitcases*

5 HOW TO ASK 'WHY?'

Why is expressed by **proč**, from **pro co** (*for what*). To explain his heavy bag Mr Smith says he is a geologist and **proto** (*that is why*) (from **pro to** *for that [reason]*) he needs his stones. He could have said:

Mám kameny, protože jsem   *I have the stones because I am*
   geolog.   *a geologist.*

This includes **protože** (from **pro to že** = *for the fact that*), which is the ordinary way of saying *because*.

Pan Novák ví, že v knihkupectví mají mapy, protože je jeho majitel. Remember the rule about commas before clauses – Unit 5, Section 5.

6 *HEZKOU KONFERENCI PŘEJU* – 'I WISH YOU A PLEASANT CONFERENCE'

Přát means *to wish* (somebody something) and takes the accusative for the 'something' (here *a pleasant conference*). Very often **přeju** (*I wish you*) is dropped. This explains why *good night* in Unit 1 took the form **dobrou noc** (**noc** is a feminine **i-**declension noun). And why *bon appétit* has the form it does – see the end of Unit 5. *Bon voyage*, another wish, is expressed by **Šťastnou cestu!** (**šťastný** = *happy, lucky*).

Exercises

1 **Convert the verbs and nouns in these sentences to the plural. Be sure you understand both versions of each sentence.**

   a Jsem cizinec.
   b Dívka (*the girl*) je Velšanka.
   c Chci knihu.
   d Má tašku a kufr.
   e Kanaďan si myslí, že vidí celníka.
   f Pan Smith je v Praze týden.
   g Fotografa neznám, je to Ir.
   h Syn nemá zavazadlo.
   i Host neví, kde je záchod.

2 **Using na, make sensible expressions out of the following pairs of words (the order in which they are given is not necessarily a guide). Example: šaty (*dress, clothes*) and ramínko (*hanger*) → ramínko na šaty**
   a **pneumatika** (*tyre*) and **škodovka** (*Škoda*)
   b **dopis** (*letter*) and **papír** (*paper*)
   c **hadr** (*cloth*) and **podlaha** (*floor*)
   d **zub** (*tooth*) and **kartáček** (*brush*)

e **asfalt** and **silnice** (*road*)

f **dřevo** (*wood*) and **pila** (*saw*)

g **růže** (f. *rose*) and **váza** (*vase*)

h **nůžky** (*scissors*) and **papír**

i **dveře** and **nový zámek** (*new lock*)

3 **In Dialogue 1 of this unit Mr Smith talks to the customs official; now answer the following questions for him. Your answers may not be as detailed as Mr Smith's own.**

 TR 21

a To jsou jeho zavazadla?

b Má nějaké zboží na prodej v České republice?

c Co má v tašce?

d Proč je taška tak těžká?

e Na co potřebuje kameny?

Dialogue 2

Mr Smith has now moved on from customs to immigration.

 TR 22

Pasový úředník	Pasová kontrola. Dobrý den. Váš pas, prosím.
Smith	Prosím.
Úředník	Vaše jméno a příjmení.
Smith	Alan Smith.
Úředník	Kde máte trvalé bydliště? – To tu v pase není.
Smith	V Maidenheadu.
Úředník	Přesná adresa?
Smith	17, Fountain Gardens, Maidenhead, Berkshire.
Úředník	Znáte svoje PSČ?
Smith	PSČ?
Úředník	Poštovní směrovací číslo – poštovní kód.
Smith	Ach, ano. SL6 9DX
Úředník	Tak je to v pořádku. Nezlobte se, že Vás takhle obtěžuji.
Smith	To nic. Jistě máte své důvody!
Úředník	Ano, očekáváme jiného pana Smithe, známého pašeráka drog a mí kolegové na celnici trošku podezřívají vaše těžká zavazadla.
Smith	Už chápu. Mám moc běžné příjmení, ale je opravdu moje.
Úředník	Jsme na tom stejně – já se jmenuji Novák.

Quick vocab

úředník *official*

pasový úředník *immigration official*

pasový *adjective from* **pas** *passport*

kontrola *control, check(-ing)*

jméno *name = first name, sometimes = whole name* (remember **jmenovat se**)

příjmení (n) *surname*

trvalý *permanent*

bydliště (n) *abode* (remember **bydlet**)

to tu v pase není *it isn't here in the passport*

přesný *exact*

adresa *address*

poštovní směrovací číslo (PSČ) *postcode*

poštovní *adj. from* **pošta** *post, post office*

směrovací *adj. from* **směrovat** *to direct*

číslo *number, also size*

kód *code*

tak je to v pořádku *so that's all right then*

v pořádku *in order, all right*

pořádek *order; tidiness*

nezlobte se, že vás takhle obtěžuji *forgive me for pestering you like this*

nezlobte se (a common apology) *don't be angry, forgive me*

takhle *like this* (remember **tak** *thus, so* and **-hle** *after* to *to express 'this' in pointing*)

obtěžovat *to pester, annoy, intrude, harass*

to nic *never mind, not to worry*

jistě máte své důvody *I expect you've got your reasons*

jistě *surely, I expect* (conveys the idea of a conjecture)

důvod *reason*

očekávat *to expect; be waiting for*

známý *well-known, familiar, notorious*

pašerák drog *drug-smuggler*

pašerák *smuggler*

droga *drug*

kolega (m!) *colleague*

trošku podezřívají *they're a bit suspicious about*

podezřívat *to suspect*

už chápu *I see now*

chápat (chápe) *see as in grasp, understand*

mám moc běžné příjmení *my surname's too common*

moc *too, very* (in informal use)

běžný *common, ordinary*

ale je opravdu moje *but it really is mine!*

jsme na tom stejně (idiom) *we're both in the same boat* (Lit. *we are on it the same*)

7 STATING YOUR PERSONAL DETAILS

Many of the details you could be asked, by an official or on a form, are taken care of in the dialogue. The slightly simplified mock-up of a form (**formulář**) shown on the next page adds a few more – study the vocabulary list before trying to fill it in.

 Quick vocab

dřívější *previous*

m = muž *i.e. male*

ž = žena *i.e. female*

datum *date*

místo *place*

narození *birth*

povolání *profession*

tel. = telefonní (adj. from **telefon**)

název *name, title* (e.g. of *company, book,* etc., not personal name)

zaměstnavatel *employer*

nehodící se škrtněte *delete where inapplicable*

hodit se *to be suitable, applicable*

škrtnout *to cross out*

pohlaví *sex*

Note: the forms **manžela, manželky, vašeho** and **zaměstnavatele** are in the genitive case (translate *as of*), which you have not yet learned fully.

```
Příjmení _____        Jméno        _____
dřívější příjmení _____    M/Ž*         _____
jméno a příjmení manžela/-ky _____
datum a místo narození – vaše  _____    manžela/-ky  _____
                                                       _____
děti: _____
   jména _____        data narození _____
          _____                      _____
adresa _____
       _____
                                     PSČ _____ tel.č. _____
povolání – vaše _____   manžela/-ky _____
název a adresa zaměstnavatele – vašeho _____

                    manžela/-ky _____

*Nehodící se skrtněte
```

8 PLURAL ADJECTIVES AND POSSESSIVES

As you have already seen, adjectives have 'long' endings. So too in the plural. The great thing about their nominative, vocative and accusative plural is that there are relatively few forms to worry about. The basic ending for 'hard' adjectives for agreement with masculine inaminate or feminine nouns is **-é**.

různé kameny   *various stones*   **různé věci**   *various things*

Two special forms are:

(i) those ending in **-á** for agreement with neuters.

   těžká zavazadla *heavy luggage*   **běžná příjmení** *common surnames*

(ii) those ending in **-í** for the *nominative* and *vocative* of adjectives agreeing with masculine animate nouns. As in the case of the **-i** ending of masculine animate nouns, this **-í** causes changes to final consonants, some more 'visible' than others, as in the nouns.

t + í	(pron. **t'í**)	**bohatí cizinci**	*rich foreigners* (from **bohatý cizinec**)
d + í	(pron. **d'i**)	**mladí kluci**	*young lads* (from **mladý kluk**)
n + í	(pron. **ňí**)	**hodní celníci**	*kind customs men* (from **hodný celník**)
k + í	→ **cí**	**nějací studenti**	*some students* (from **nějaký student**)
h + í	→ **zí**	**drazí přátelé**	*dear friends* (from **drahý přítel**)
ch + í	→ **ší**	**hluší staříci**	*deaf old men* (from **hluchý stařík**)
r + í	→ **ří**	**staří sousedé**	*old neighbours* (from **starý soused**)

Adjectives ending in **-ský** and **-cký** are treated differently.

| sk + í | → **ští** | **čeští studenti** | *Czech students* (from **český student**) |
| ck + í | → **čtí** | **američtí turisté** | *American tourists* (from **americký turista**) |

'Soft' adjectives show no new changes at all: the ending is **-í** for nominative, vocative and accusative plural of all three genders. Thus in Dialogue 1, **osobní věci** was feminine accusative plural, no different formally from **směrovací číslo** – neuter accusative singular.

Patterns of endings similar to those now seen in nouns and adjectives in the nominative (and the vocative) and accusative plural also apply to the possessive and demonstrative pronouns:

můj *(my)*, **tvůj** *(your)* (fam.) and **svůj** *(own)*

Masculine animate	Nominative / Vocative	mí	tví		moji	tvoji	
	Accusative	mé	tvé	*své	moje	tvoje	*svoje
Masculine inanimate and feminine	Nominative / Vocative / Accusative	mé	tvé	*své	moje	tvoje	*svoje
Neuter	Nominative / Vocative / Accusative	má	tvá	*svá	moje	tvoje	*svoje

The shorter forms, ending in long vowels, are just like the 'hard' adjectives. The longer, more colloquial, forms, containing **-j-**, show a soft pattern of endings, which, as usual, is more economical to learn; only the masculine animate nominative is distinct.

*Note: No form of **svůj** can ever occur in the nominative, that is, the subject position, since it can only cross-refer to whatever is the subject:

Má rád svou sestru.   *He (x) loves his (x's) sister.*

náš *(our)*, **váš** *(your)*

Masculine animate	Nominative / Vocative	naši	vaši
	Accusative	naše	vaše
Masculine inanimate, feminine and neuter	Nominative / Vocative / Accusative	naše	vaše

These two items, ending in **-š**, take 'soft' endings, hence they are just like the longer versions of 'my', etc. (only the masculine animate nominative plural is distinctive).

ten, ta, to (*that/this*)			
Masculine animate	Nominative	}	ti
	Vocative		
	Accusative		ty
Masculine inanimate	Nominative		
and feminine	Vocative	}	ty
	Accusative		
Neuter	Nominative		
	Vocative	}	ta
	Accusative		

These endings reflect those of 'hard' nouns, so you might combine:

Ti studenti jsou Češi./Ty studentky jsou Češky.	*Those students are Czech.*
Vidíme ty studenty/studentky.	*We can see those students* (m/f).

9 ANOTHER WAY OF APOLOGIZING

Inviting somebody to *avoid getting enraged* may seem a bit much to say *I'm sorry*, but **nezlobte se** is a very common formula for this. It comes from **zlobit se** (*to be/get angry*) which in turn comes from **zlobit** (*to annoy*).

10 MASCULINE NOUNS THAT END IN -A

There is no shortage of such words, but many are names and many have identifiable meanings, having been borrowed from other languages. In the singular they have many case forms like the feminines (accusative ends in **-u**, for example) but in the plural they are like 'hard' masculine nouns. Most, like **kolega**, however, have the nominative plural ending **-ové** – **kolegové**, but the accusative is just like any other 'hard' masculine noun: **kolegy**. A large group of these words end in **-ista** and take the other secondary masculine animate nominative plural ending, **-é**, hence **turisté** (*tourists*), from **turista**, though **-i** may also be met in colloquial usage. All masculine nouns ending in **-a** are animate.

> ● INSIGHT
>
> Native words of this kind include **sluha** (*man)servant*, **vévoda** *duke* and some other stylistically neutral words, but by far the most common are names of people with, usually, some unfortunate characteristic, such as **neposeda** *fidget*, **ožrala** *drunkard*, **vejtaha** *braggart* or **brepta** *chatterbox* – they often come from verbs (here from **sedět** *sit*, **ožrat se** *get drunk*, **vytahovat se** *boast* and **breptat** *chatter*) or adjectives, like **neruda** *grouch* or **nezbeda** *scallywag* (from **nerudný** *grumpy* and **nezbedný** *rascally*). Some come about from a 'change of use' of otherwise innocent words; thus **trouba**, a feminine noun meaning *oven*, becomes the masculine pejorative *twit, imbecile*. This is a very rich and colourful field.

11 *PŘÁTELÉ!* – 'FRIENDS!'

The word **přítel** (*friend*) is one of the many that end in **-tel** (and are 'soft' in their behaviour) and so it has **-é** in the nominative plural. It is an oddity in having the extra change of **-í-** to **-á-** in the middle, hence **Přátelé!** (*Friends!*), **Nepodezříváme své přátele** (*We do not suspect our friends*).

Exercises

4 Complete your part of the following dialogue with a hotel receptionist.

Vy	*Say 'Excuse me, please.'*
Recepční	Ano, co si přejete?
Vy	*Ask if this is Hotel Jalta.*
Recepční	Ano. Máte tady objednávku?
Vy	*Say you do have a booking.*
Recepční	Vaše jméno, prosím.
Vy	*Give your name (remember what to do if you're female).*
Recepční	Váš cestovní pas, prosím. ... Děkuju (she hands it back).
Vy	*(respond appropriately)*
Recepční	Mohu se Vás zeptat, kde v Anglii bydlíte?
Vy	*You live in Manchester. Say so.*
Recepční	Já tam mám přátele. Jmenují se Wimpenny. Neznáte je náhodou.
Vy	*Say unfortunately not. Manchester is a big city.*
Recepční	Nezlobte se, že vás tak obtěžuju.
Vy	*Say that's all right (adding that you must hurry and you still need your key),* **klíč** (m).
Recepční	Tady je. Číslo 53 (padesát tři).
Vy	*Thank her and say goodbye.*

5 To what questions might you give these answers?

- **a** Tašku mám v hotelu.
- **b** Protože toto město neznám.
- **c** M znamená 'muž', ž znamená 'žena'.
- **d** Mám jen malý byt.
- **e** V kufru mám jenom osobní věci.
- **f** Tento papír je na dopisy.
- **g** To jsou Novákovi.

MORE QUIRKS ABOUT SINGULAR AND PLURAL WORDS

In the last unit you learnt that the singular English *door* happens to be a plural word in Czech – **dveře**. Now you have met the English word *luggage*, which has no plural, while its strict Czech equivalent is a countable word, **zavazadlo**, plural **zavazadla**, so you must think of it as meaning *item(s) of luggage*. **Informace** (f) *(piece of) information* and **rada** *(piece of) advice* behave in the same way.

Then we have the English plural word *goods*, which normally has no singular, while its Czech equivalent **zboží** is a singular word with no plural.

Another related problem is where one word in one language may mean two things and you have to be alert to the difference: English *hair* meaning a single hair is Czech **vlas**; but the Czech plural **vlasy** is hair in the mass, that is, on the head: **Má černé vlasy** *(He has black hair)*. At least there's some logic to that one! Then again, while the Czech plural word **šaty** has, as one equivalent, an English plural *clothes*, its first meaning is *a dress*!

Test yourself

1 Identify from both dialogues in this unit all the nominative and accusative plural forms. Separate nouns from adjectives and pronouns, and accusative forms from nominative forms.

2 What basic fact follows from the immigration officer's final sentence in the dialogue?

7 Kde jste vlastně studoval?
Where exactly did you study?

In this unit you will learn
▶ *How to say something about past events*
▶ *How to say more about going places*
▶ *How to use numbers above four*

Dialogue 1

Mr Smith and his Czech colleague, Mr Navrátil, are finding out about each other's past during a break at the geological conference.

 TR 23

Smith	Ještěže si můžeme během konference občas odpočinout.
Navrátil	Jsem také rád, protože jsem se vás chtěl na pár věcí zeptat.
Smith	Já také, pojďte někam na kávu.
	They go off to the coffee place outside the conference hall.
Navrátil	Dáte si kafe nebo čaj?
Smith	Radši čaj. Kávu jsem pil dřív, ale teď mi nedělá dobře.
Navrátil	Kde jste vlastně studoval? Na které univerzitě?
Smith	Původně jsem studoval v Edinburghu, ale na doktorát jsem se připravoval nejprve v Londýně a potom v Praze. Proto mluvím trochu česky.
Navrátil	Neznal jste náhodou doktora Stuarta v Edinburghu, nebo profesora Williamse v Londýně?
Smith	Ano, znal, ale doktor Stuart je teď v New Yorku a profesor Williams zemřel.
Navrátil	Já jsem vlastně věděl, že doktor Stuart je v New Yorku, ale tu smutnou zprávu o profesoru Williamsovi jsem ještě neslyšel. Kdy se to stalo?
Smith	Minulý týden. Měl tady být na konferenci, ale bohužel není. Bylo to velmi nečekané a velmi jsme jeho odchodu litovali.

Quick vocab

během konference *during the conference*

během (preposition + genitive) *during*

občas *sometimes, from time to time*

chtěl jsem se vás na pár věcí zeptat
I wanted to ask you about a few things

chtěl past tense of **chtít** *(to want)*

zeptat se a form of **ptát se** + genitive *to ask (someone)*

pár *pair, couple, a few*

pojďte někam na kávu *come somewhere for a coffee*

káva *coffee*

dáte si kafe nebo čaj *will you have coffee or tea*

kafe (n) (colloquial) *coffee*

čaj (m) *tea*

radši *preferably*

kávu jsem pil dřív *I used to drink coffee*

dřív *earlier, before*

teď mi nedělá dobře *now it makes me ill* (idiom Lit. *it doesn't do me well*)

mi *to me*

kde jste vlastně studoval? *where did you actually study?*

na které univerzitě *at which university*

nejprve *first of all*

na doktorát jsem se připravoval
I prepared for my doctorate

připravovat se *prepare (oneself), get ready, train, study*

neznal jste náhodou doktora Stuarta?
did you happen to know Dr Stuart?

doktor Stuart je teď v New Yorku
Dr Stuart's in New York now

profesor Williams zemřel *Professor Williams has died*

zemřel past tense of **zemřít (zemře)** *die*

já jsem vlastně věděl, že ... *I actually knew that ...*

tu smutnou zprávu jsem ještě neslyšel
I hadn't heard that sad news yet

smutný *sad*

zpráva *report,* (item of) *news* (plural **zprávy** *the news*)

kdy se to stalo? *when did it happen?*

stalo se past tense of **stát se (stane se)** *to happen*

minulý *past, last*

měl tady být na konferenci *he was to have been at the conference*

měl past tense of **mít** (here **mít** is in the special meaning of *'be supposed to'*)

nečekaný *unexpected*

velmi jsme jeho odchodu litovali *we much regretted his passing*

velmi *very* (with adjectives); *(very) much* (with verbs)

odchod *departure, leaving*

litovat (lituje) + genitive *to regret*

1 FORMING THE PAST TENSE

To form the past tense of a verb, first find the infinitive. Remove the final **-t** and replace it with **-l**. This gives the form for *he* (masculine singular): **dělat → dělal** (*he was doing*).

Now, because past tense forms *must* agree with the gender of the subject, add **-a** for *she* (or any feminine subject) and **-o** for *it* (or any neuter subject).

Marie dělala snídani.	*Mary was making breakfast.*
Cesta byla dlouhá.	*The trip was (a) long (one).*
To bylo nečekané.	*It was unexpected.*
Na rohu stálo kino.	*At the corner stood a cinema.*

In the plural (*they* forms), gender matters more in writing than speaking. The strict written endings are **-i** for masculine animate plural (muži chtě**li** *the men wanted*), **-y** for masculine inanimate and feminine plural (stoly/ženy byl**y** *the tables/women were*), and **-a** for neuter plural (města byl**a** *the cities were*), but normally you will hear (and may use) a general **i**-ending in speech. Notice how the past-tense endings match the ends of the basic types of noun you have met:

	Masculine animate	Masculine inanimate	Feminine	Neuter
Singular	student byl	kámen byl	studentka byla	město bylo
Plural	studenti byli	kameny byly	studentky byly	města byla

To form the other persons you must use an auxiliary verb (like English *have* or *was* in, for example, *I have done it, I was doing it*).

However, you have not much new to learn here: the Czech auxiliary verb in the past tense is the 1st and 2nd person forms of the verb **být**, which you already know. This explains the following forms in the dialogue: **chtěl jsem, pil jsem, studoval jsem, připravoval jsem se, neslyšel jsem** (all *I* – male speaker); **studoval jste, neznal jste** (*you*: on **vy**-terms; the person addressed is male); **litovali jsme** (*we* – at least one of whom is male).

The full past tense, based on **být**, appears below:

byl jsem	*I was* (or **byla** for female *I*)
byl jsi	*you* (*thou*) *were* (or **byla** [f])
byl	*he* (or other masculine) *was*
byla	*she* (or other feminine) *was*
bylo	*it* (or other neuter) *was*
byli jsme	*we* (at least one of us is male) *were*
byly jsme	*we* (who are all female) *were*
byli jste	*you* (at least one of whom is male) *were*
byly jste	*you* (who are all female) *were*
byl jste	*you* (one male, non-familiar) *were*
byla jste	*you* (one female, non-familiar) *were*
byli	*they* (of whom at least one is masculine animate) *were*
byly	*they* (of whom none is masculine animate) *were*
byla	*they* (neuter) *were*

Note the important variety of *you* forms:

a singular past-tense forms (ending in **-l** or **-la**) with singular auxiliary **jsi** for informal address, e.g. among children and close friends, by adults to children, among students or soldiers – people who address one another as **ty**;

b plural past-tense forms (ending in **-li** or **-ly**) with plural auxiliary **jste** for any group of persons being addressed;

c the version you are most likely to need first: singular past-tense forms with plural auxiliary **jste** to address those with whom you are still on **vy** terms. There are social niceties to be observed here and you should wait until your Czech friends suggest you switch from **vy** to **ty** forms.

Past tense and word order

You will notice that the past-tense forms in the table have the auxiliary verb in second place although in the dialogue you might have noticed that the two parts were sometimes inverted or not even next to one another. This is because the auxiliary verb must be in the second grammatical slot in the sentence or clause. Auxiliaries are, like **se** and **si**, stressless words (Unit 5, Section 12). This means that Mr Smith might have said not only **Původně / jsem / studoval / v Edinburghu** (/ separates the slots in the sentence) but also **Studoval / jsem / původně / v Edinburghu**. **Studoval** moves, but **jsem** (the auxiliary verb) remains firmly in the second slot.

Where there are several stressless items fighting for this second slot, the past-tense auxiliary always wins, followed by the reflexives **se** and **si**, followed by other pronouns, hence Dr Novák's: ..., **protože / jsem se vás / chtěl / zeptat**. The same sentence without *because* would be: **Chtěl / jsem se vás / zeptat**. Similarly, **velmi / jsme / jeho odchodu / litovali** could be converted to **jeho odchodu / jsme / velmi / litovali**. The difference in emphasis brought about by this change of word order is relatively slight. In other circumstances the change of emphasis could be much greater.

An important Czech–English contrast

In English, you can respond to what someone else has said using the relevant auxiliary part, e.g. *'Has she been?' 'Yes she **has**'*, and *'Did she go?' 'No she **didn't**'*. If a remark eliciting a response has no auxiliary, you use one anyway, e.g. *'She went on Tuesday.' 'Oh no she **didn't**!'*

In Czech, auxiliaries are weak words and aren't even used in the third persons, so it is the main part of the verb that is used in replies. In the dialogue Mr Smith is asked whether he had known Dr Stuart. His reply omits the auxiliary and so is simply **znal** for *I had (known)* or *I did (know)*; because this is a dialogue it would not be misunderstood to be the sort of **znal** that would mean *he knew*.

The Czech past tense is simple!

There is only one form of the past tense in Czech to translate all the formal variety of the English *I wanted*, *did you study*, *I used to drink*, *I haven't* or *hadn't heard*.

Negation is also a simple matter: just add **ne-** to the main verb (not to the auxiliary): **ne**slyšel jsem.

Watch out for verbs of one syllable

One-syllable verbs tend to be very common and you won't get far without them. So not only must you learn their 3rd-person singular form, you must also learn any oddities there may be in their past-tense forms. Basically, the rule is that their long vowel is shortened: **být → byl**; **znát → znal**; **pít → pil**.

But if the infinitive contains **-í-**, shortening it may change the vowel: **mít → měl**; **chtít → chtěl**.

This may also happen with some other verbs: **zemřít → zemřel**. All such verbs must be specially noted. Some verbs with **-á-** keep the long vowel: **stát** (*stand, cost*) → **stál**; **hrát** (*play*) → **hrál**.

There is a simple test for this: length is not lost if the present tense contains a **-j-**, as in **stojí** *he/she is standing, it costs*, **hraje** *he/she is playing*.

> ● INSIGHT
>
> The above is a rule to relish – it has only one common exception: **zdát se** *to seem* has no **-j-** in its conjugation (**zdá se**), yet the vowel stays long in the past – **zdálo se, že...** *it seemed that...* A rarer one is **přistát** (**přistane, přistál**) *to land*.

The verb **jít** has a totally irregular past tense (but then so does *go [went, has gone, has been]*):

	Singular		Plural
Masculine	šel	Masculine animate	šli
Feminine	šla	Masculine inanimate	šly
Neuter	šlo	Feminine	šly
		Neuter	šla

2 ANIMATE MASCULINES AND THE LOCATIVE SINGULAR

The locative singular ending for masculine animate nouns is **-ovi**, but if more than one word is involved **-u** is used except for the last word:

Mluvíme o profesorovi.	*We are talking about the professor.*
Mluvíme o profesoru Novákovi.	*We are talking about Prof. Novák.*

'Soft' masculine nouns use just the ordinary soft locative ending **-i**: **o muži** (*about the man*), except in the case of proper names, when **-ovi** is used: **o Milošovi** (*about Miloš*).

> ● INSIGHT
>
> Notice that English names ending in **-s**, however they may be pronounced at home (in *Harris* it is as **-s**, in *Williams* as **-z**, though never as **-sh**, are usually pronounced in Czech with final **-s** and follow the Czech soft declension, hence **znám profesora Williamse** ('soft' animate accusative). Many Czechs (perhaps proportionately more than English people) can claim: **Znám dobře Charlese Dickense.**

3 ADJECTIVES AND THE LOCATIVE SINGULAR

'Hard' masculine and neuter:	-ém	'Hard' feminine:	-é
'Soft' masculine and neuter:	-ím	'Soft' feminine:	-í

na starém hradě *at the old castle*
ve starém městě *in an old city*
o staré univerzitě *about an old university*

v cizím kufru *in someone else's suitcase*
v cizím autě *in someone else's car*
na cizí univerzitě *at a foreign university*

Possessive **můj**, **tvůj**, **svůj** share the 'hard' adjective endings:

v mém kufru *in my suitcase*; **na tvém stole** *on your desk*;

v tvé knize *in your book*

while **náš**, **váš** have the endings **-em** (masculine and neuter) and **-í** (feminine); remember the vowel will shorten:

v našem hotelu   *in our hotel*
ve vaší ložnici   *in your bedroom*

The demonstrative pronoun **ten**, **ta**, **to** has the forms **tom** (masculine and neuter) and **té** (feminine):

v tom případě   *in that case* (**případ** = *case, event*)
v této situaci   *in this situation* (**situace** = *situation*)

This has now fully explained the expression **v tom velkém věžáku**, which you had to learn in one piece and take on trust back in Dialogue 1 of Unit 4.

Exercises

1 **Read the dialogue and answer the questions. Přečtěte rozhovor a odpovězte na otázky.**
   a Kde studoval pan Smith?
   b Proč mluví pan Smith česky?
   c Kde teď pracuje doktor Stuart a kde pracoval dřív?
   d Co víme o profesoru Williamsovi?
   e Na jaké konferenci se setkali (**setkat se** = *meet*) pan Smith a doktor Navrátil?

2 **Put in the past. Převeďte do minulého času.**
   a Nemají mapu.
   b Jsme na návštěvě u pana Navrátila.
   c Mluví celý den česky.
   d Chcete si večer odpočinout?
   e Doma se zouváme.
   f Konference nás velmi unavuje.
   g Co to znamená?
      (Before checking your answers, make sure you've got the word order right!)
   h Translate your answers into English in writing, check them, set them aside, and then, after a suitable interval (at least an hour), put them back into Czech without reference to the book.

3 **What questions might you have asked to get the following answers?**
   a Studoval jsem na univerzitě v Berlíně.
   b Protože mi káva nedělá dobře.
   c O jeho smrti (**smrt**, **i**-declension = *death*) jsem neslyšel.

d Stalo se to včera (**včera** = *yesterday*).

e Ano, Prahu máme velmi rádi.

f V tašce mají jenom pár věcí.

Dialogue 2

The conference is over for the day and Mr Smith wants to go somewhere interesting for the evening. He asks his colleague, Mr Navrátil, for some help.

 TR 24

Smith	Řekněte mi, kam můžu jít večer?
Navrátil	Můžete jít do divadla – ve městě je osm různých divadel, nebo na koncert. Můžete jít samozřejmě do kina, běží alespoň šest anglických filmů, pokud se chcete cítit jako doma.
Smith	Radši ne. Chci něco, co je typicky pražské.
Navrátil	Aha. Většina cizinců jde při první návštěvě Prahy do hospody u Fleků. Je to odsud jenom pět minut pěšky.
Smith	Co tam mají?
Navrátil	Unikátní černé pivo. Víte, že máme hodně dobrých piv.
Smith	Ale já nechci jenom sedět u piva. A taky potřebuju být v hotelu ve slušnou hodinu a střízlivý. Chci do rána přepsat několik pasáží ve svém zítřejším referátu.
Navrátil	Váš referát není zítra, ale pozítří. Víte co, pojďte do mé laboratoře. Mám klíč a je tam pár zdejších kuriozit, které jste určitě nikdy neviděl.

 Quick vocab

řekněte mi *tell me*

kam můžu jít večer? *where can I go this evening?*

můžete jít do divadla *you can go to the theatre*

divadlo *theatre*

ve městě je osm různých divadel *there are eight different theatres in the city*

osm *eight*

samozřejmě *of course, obviously*

do kina *to the cinema*

kino *cinema*

běží alespoň šest anglických filmů *there are at least six English films on*

běžet (-í) *to run*

alespoň (colloquial also **aspoň**) *at least*

šest *six*

pokud se chcete cítit jako doma *if you want to feel at home*

pokud *if, in so far as*

cítit se *to feel*

jako *as, like*

chci něco, co je typicky pražské *I want something that is typically (of) Prague*

něco, co *something that/which*

typicky (adverb from **typický** *typical*) *typically*

pražský (adjective from **Praha**) *of Prague*

většina cizinců *most foreigners* **většina** *the majority (of)*

při první návštěvě *on their first visit*

do hospody *to a/the pub*

u Fleků *at Fleks' (a well-known Prague pub)*

pět minut pěšky *five minutes on foot*

minuta *minute*
pěšky *on foot*
unikátní *unique*
černý *black*
sedět u piva *to sit around drinking beer*
sedět (-í) *to sit*
u *at (preposition + genitive)*
ve slušnou hodinu *at a respectable hour*
slušný *decent, respectable*
hodina *hour*
střízlivý *sober*
do rána *by morning*

přepsat *(compound of* **psát – piše** *write)*
   to re-write
několik *several*
pasáž (f) *passage*
zítřejší *(adjective from* **zítra**) *tomorrow's*
referát *(conference, seminar, etc.) paper, report*
pozítří *the day after tomorrow*
laboratoř (f) *laboratory*
zdejší *(adjective from* **zde** *here) local*
kuriozita *(item of) curiosity*
nikdy *never*

4 HOW TO EXPRESS 'TO SOMEWHERE'

The main preposition for *to*, or *into* is **do**, which is followed by the *genitive case*. You will almost always need it where the goal is an enclosed space, hence, in the dialogue, the items **divadlo**, **kino**, **hospoda**, **hotel**, **laboratoř**. (Also in the dialogue, **do rána**, where **do** means *by*, also *until*, in time expressions.)

The tables below summarize the genitive case endings of the main types of nouns and adjectives/pronouns. You will see some familiar endings from the various phrases you have already met containing **z** (*from*), which also takes the genitive.

	Nominative singular	Genitive singular	Genitive plural
Hard masculine animate	student	studenta	studentů
Hard masculine inanimate	stůl	stolu	stolů
Masculine ending in **-a**	kolega	kolegy	kolegů
Soft masculine animate	muž	muže	mužů
Soft masculine inanimate	klíč	klíče	klíčů
Hard feminine	hospoda	hospody	hospod
Soft feminine	pasáž	pasáže	pasáží
	kuchyně	kuchyně	kuchyní
Hard neuter	město	města	měst
Soft neuter	moře	moře	moří
Feminine **i**-declension	věc	věci	věcí
Neuters ending in **-í**	nádraží	nádraží	nádraží

Some other points to note:
   a if a hard feminine or neuter noun would end in a group of consonants in the genitive plural, which has a 'zero' ending, they will be separated by **-e-**: **studentka-studentek**, **divadlo-divadel**. This does not happen with final **-st**: **město-měst.**
   b 'soft' feminine nouns ending in **-ice** and a small number of others also have no ending in the genitive plural: **ulice-ulic** (*street*), **košile-košil** (*shirt*). 'Soft' neuters ending in **-iště** have the same feature: **letiště-letišť** (*airport*).
   c some feminine and neuter words of two syllables with a long vowel or diphthong in the first syllable shorten this in the genitive plural: **dílo-děl** (*work*), **kráva-krav** (*cow*), **moucha-much** (*fly*), **míle-mil** (f) (*mile*). Shortening, as you see, may, as with the past tense, change the vowel.

7 Kde jste vlastně studoval? Where exactly did you study?   **85**

Study the the three tables in this section at length, noting how the available endings are distributed (for example, in the *nouns* genitive singular masculine animate = accusative singular masculine animate; *all* soft genitive singulars end in **-e/-ě**; 'hard' feminine and neuter genitive plural both end in zero; *all* genitive plurals in *adjectives* and *pronouns* are the same, irrespective of gender).

Using the models: **do těch malých hospod** or **z toho malého města** or **během té nudné** (*boring*) **konference**, write down phrases of your own until you begin to be more spontaneous in achieving the right combinations. The table below is followed by more prepositions which require the genitive case:

		Nominative singular	Genitive singular	Genitive plural
Hard adjective	masculine	dobr**ý**	dobr**ého**	dobr**ých**
	feminine	dobr**á**	dobr**é**	dobr**ých**
	neuter	dobr**é**	dobr**ého**	dobr**ých**
Soft adjective	masculine	ciz**í**	ciz**ího**	ciz**ích**
	feminine	ciz**í**	ciz**í**	ciz**ích**
	neuter	ciz**í**	ciz**ího**	ciz**ích**
This, that	masculine	**ten**	**toho**	**těch**
	feminine	t**a**	t**é**	**těch**
	neuter	t**o**	**toho**	**těch**
My	masculine	m**ůj**	m**ého**	m**ých**
	feminine	m**á/moje**	m**é**	m**ých**
	neuter	m**é/moje**	m**ého**	m**ých**
Our	masculine	n**áš**	naš**eho**	naš**ich**
	feminine	n**aše**	naš**í**	naš**ich**
	neuter	n**aše**	naš**eho**	naš**ich**

 Quick vocab

bez *without*

blízko *near*

kolem *round, past*

kromě *besides, except*

od *(away) from*

podle *according to*

vedle *beside*

u *at, by, near*

To go from place to place you need to learn the formula: **Jak se dostanu do ..?** (or **na ..?** if the name of the destination warrants it – remember the kind of words that used **na** with the locative, Unit 3, Section 12) meaning *How do I get to..?* Also learn the version: **Nevím, jak se dostat do ... (na ...)** *I don't know how to get to...*

In the next unit you will meet some of the advice you might get in response to these.

5 NUMBERS 5 TO 10

pět	*5*	**sedm**	*7*	**devět**	*9*
šest	*6*	**osm**	*8*	**deset**	*10*

Higher numbers will be dealt with later. They are all followed by the genitive plural, e.g. **osm divadel**, **šest anglických filmů**, **pět minut**.

Other expressions denoting quantity also require the genitive plural, as in **několik pasáží** (*several passages*), and you've already seen **pár věcí** (*a few things*). Other 'quantifiers' of the same type include:

 Quick vocab

kolik *how many*	**nemnoho** *not many*
tolik *so many*	**hodně** *a lot of*
mnoho *many*	**dost** *enough*
málo *few*	

Note: unlike **několik** and **pár**, the above words may also combine with the genitive singular, in the senses 'much' and 'little': **mnoho času** (*plenty of time*), **kolik práce?** (*how much work?*), **málo piva** (*little (not much) beer*).

Some quantifiers such as **většina**, as in **většina cizinců** (*most foreigners*), also **řada** (*many, several*), behave entirely like the nouns from which they have come: **většina** (*the majority*), **řada** (*line, row, series, queue*).

6 VERB AGREEMENT WITH COUNTED EXPRESSIONS

Numbers above five, and most of the other quantifying words, behave as neuter singular nouns, so when any phrase containing them is the subject of the sentence the verb is singular:

ve městě je osm divadel	v laboratoři je pár kuriozit
sedm koncertů se **koná**	většina cizinců **jde**

Note what happens in the past tense:

ve městě **bylo** osm divadel	v laboratoři **bylo** pár kuriozit
sedm koncertů se **konalo**	

These verbs, above, are in the neuter singular, but in

> **většina cizinců šla**

the verb agrees with the feminine noun **většina.**

7 'ONE/ONES': AVOID NOUN REPETITION

The pattern of agreement with adjectives and pronouns means there is never any doubt about what is referred to.

Petr má nové auto, já mám jen staré.	*Peter has a new car, I only have an old (one).*
Můžete jít do divadla – máme tu sedm různých.	*You can go to the theatre – we have seven different (ones) here.*
Tamta hospoda je dobrá, tahle není.	*That pub is (a) good (one), this (one) isn't.*

8 DOUBLE NEGATIVES

If you combine in English, 'not ... anyone/anywhere', or use 'nobody', 'nowhere', etc. in a sentence, you must use the Czech forms beginning with **ni-** and reinforce the negation in the verb:

Nikdo nešel do divadla. *No one went to the theatre.*

Nepotřebuji nic. *I don't need anything.*

Triple (and higher) negation is also obligatory where applicable:

Nikdy nikde nikomu nic *I never buy anything for anyone*
nekupuju. *anywhere.*

Exercises

4 Read the dialogue and answer the questions.

    a Kolik divadel je ve městě?

    b Jak je daleko do hospody u Fleků?

    c Jaké pivo mají u Fleků?

    d Proč se chce pan Smith vrátit do hotelu střízlivý?

    e Co má doktor Navrátil ve své laboratoři?

5   **a** Tell a friend: you have two daughters and five sons; it is only ten minutes' walk to work; you have several types (**druh** = *type, sort*) of beer at home.

    b Ask him if they have: a lot of foreigners in the town; enough time; six suitcases.

    c Tell him there were: two sad items of news yesterday; five different keys on the table; seven English geologists on (in) the plane besides that German colleague.

PUBS AND BEERS

The Czechs and their beers are renowned the world over. Pils, Pilsen and Pilsner are all variants on one of the few Czech words borrowed by other languages. It comes from the name of the city of **Plzeň** (*Pilsen*). It is not the only beer, though most others are of the same general **ležák** (*lager*) type. To recognize what beers are on sale you need to spot the name of the town that is home to the particular **pivovar** (*brewery*) or the adjectival form of the name: **plzeňský** in the Pilsen case, or **velkopopovický** from Velké Popovice, **vratislavický** from Vratislavice nad Nisou, **budějovický** from České Budějovice, home of the original Budweiser–Budvar, and so on. Some brands have a name: **Prazdroj**, the local name for Pilsner Urquell, **Staropramen** (*Old Spring*), the well-known Prague brew, **Kozel** (*Goat*) from Velké Popovice, and countless others.

There are three common strengths, described as **desítka** (ten per cent gravity), **jedenáctka** (eleven per cent) and **dvanáctka** (twelve per cent), though you may find a **čtrnáctka** (fourteen per cent).

Pubs themselves are easily recognized by the words **hostinec** or **pivnice**; the word you have learned, **hospoda**, usually doesn't figure on signs. Pub names are of two main types, based on a surname in the genitive plural, as in **U Fleků**, or on the name of an animal, plant or other object, as in **U Supa** (*The Vulture*), **U Dvou koček** (*The Two Cats*), **U Kalicha** (*The Chalice*), etc. Very widespread is **U Lípy** (*The Linden Tree*), the Czech national tree. Common to both types is the use of the preposition **u**, here meaning *at the place of* or *at the sign of*. Occasionally you may meet plain names referring to places, such as **Port Artur** (*Port Arthur*) or **Na Bojišti** (*On the Battlefield*).

● INSIGHT

This seems a good point to consider the Czech internet, if you haven't done so already. While there are several good Czech search engines, I suggest you first try www.seznam.cz (**seznam** means *list*). Type any of the words, phrases or names in bold in the section above, and see where it takes you. For a particular search, type in **U Fleku** (you generally needn't worry about the accents when doing Czech searches; the sites 'know' what you mean) and see whether you would fancy any of the traditional Czech dishes Mr Smith missed out on. If you find it hard going, you will eventually find a Union Jack flag to click on for an English version of the site – and it's in better English than many you will meet, if still some way off perfection.

? Test yourself

Make the following suggestions to a friend:

a Come for a beer/a coffee.

b Come and see us this evening.

c Where do you feel more (**víc**) at home: at the office or in the pub?

d Can we go to the theatre or the cinema together?

f Do you want to rest first?

g Come into the kitchen for (some) tea.

8 Nemůžu najít klíč
I can't find the key

In this unit you will learn
▶ *How to use the past tense*
▶ *How to complain about this and that*
▶ *How to ask what something costs*
▶ *How to use higher numbers*
▶ *How to give and understand simple directions*

Dialogue 1

Mr and Mrs Navrátil are having a discussion at home, Mr Navrátil having just pronounced himself a **smolař**, one dogged by misfortune (**smůla**).

 TR 25

Ona	Proč si myslíš, že jsi smolař?
On	Jestli to chceš opravdu vědět, tak nemůžu najít klíče od kanceláře, hodinky mi nejdou, rozhlas v pracovně nefunguje, celou noc jsem nespal, protože tramvaje dělaly hluk, a teď mě už dvě hodiny bolí hlava.
Ona	Ale, broučku, klíče byly včera na televizi, musels je tam vidět. Hodinky zlobí delší dobu, proto ti právě dnes kupuju nové. Rozhlas při práci nepotřebuješ. Tramvaje dělají stejný hluk každou noc, tak nevím, proč jsi nespal zrovna dnes, a na tu hlavu sis mohl něco vzít dávno.
On	Děkuju za útěchu! Víš, že mi prášky nepomáhají. Ještě mi řekni, jak mám celý den pracovat.
Ona	Ty si pořád na něco stěžuješ. Mě také někdy budí tramvaje, ale dnes jsem se náhodou vyspala krásně.

proč si myslíš, že ... *why do you think that ...*

jestli to chceš opravdu vědět *if you really want to know*

nemůžu najít klíče od kanceláře *I cannot find the office keys*

najít *to find*

od *Lit. from (i.e. the keys belong to the office)*

hodinky mi nejdou *my watch isn't working*

hodinky *(f pl) watch*

mi *dative of I (denoting either possessor of the watch or the victim of its refusal to work)*

rozhlas *radio*

pracovna *study, private office*

fungovat *to work, function*

celou noc *all night*

hluk *noise*

bolí mě hlava *I've got a headache*

bolet (bolí) *to hurt, ache*

mě *me*

hlava *head*

broučku *vocative of* **brouček** *little beetle (a common term of endearment)*

musels je tam vidět *you must have seen them there*

je *them*

zlobit *to annoy, be naughty, cause trouble*

delší dobu *for some time*

delší *(comparative of* **dlouhý** *long) longish*

doba *time*

ti *to/for you*

právě dnes *this very day*

právě *just, exactly, precisely*

při práci *at work = while you're working*

stejný *the same*

každou noc *every night*

zrovna dnes *today of all days*

zrovna = právě (*see above***)**

na tu hlavu sis mohl něco vzít

dávno *you could have taken something for that head long ago*

vzít (si) *to take*

mohl *past tense of* **moct**

dávno *long ago*

děkuju za útěchu *thanks for the consolation*

za *(preposition + accusative) for, in exchange for*

útěcha *consolation*

prášek *powder, pill*

ještě mi řekni *now tell me*

pořád *all the time*

stěžovat si + na *(+ acc.) to complain (about)*

budit *to wake*

vyspat se (vyspí se) *to have a good night's sleep*

1 COMPLAINING

If something doesn't work, use negative forms of **jít** (*go*) or **fungovat** (*function*). **Pracovat** (*work*) is usually limited to people. Other useful expressions are **zlobit** (*give trouble*), **mít poruchu** (*have something wrong*), **být rozbitý** (*be broken*).

Aches and pains are all expressed by **bolet** (*hurt*), either with the offending body part as the subject and the sufferer as the object:

Bolí mě hlava. *I've got a headache.* **Bolí ji noha.** *She's got a sore leg.* **Bolí ho ucho.** *He's got earache.* **Bolely mě zuby.** *I had toothache.*

or by saying where the pain is:

Bolí mě v krku. *I've got a sore throat.* **Bolí ho v kříži.** *He's got lumbago.*

Note: Ji (*her*), **ho** (*him*). Like **se**, **si** and **mě**, **mi** these are stressless words and go in the second slot in the sentence.

Here are more words that could be useful.

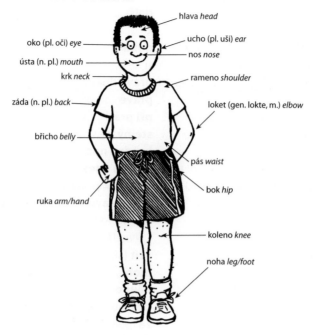

Diagram labels:
- hlava *head*
- oko (pl. oči) *eye*
- ucho (pl. uši) *ear*
- ústa (n. pl.) *mouth*
- nos *nose*
- krk *neck*
- rameno *shoulder*
- záda (n. pl.) *back*
- loket (gen. lokte, m.) *elbow*
- břicho *belly*
- pás *waist*
- bok *hip*
- ruka *arm/hand*
- koleno *knee*
- noha *leg/foot*

OTHER USEFUL BODY PARTS

 Quick vocab

jazyk *tongue*
kotník *ankle, knuckle*
kříž (m) *small of the back* (Lit. *cross*)
nehet (gen. **nehtu**) *nail*
obočí *eyebrow(s)*
palec (gen. **palce**, m) *thumb, big toe*
pata *heel*

prst *finger, toe*
ret (pl. **rty**) *lip*
srdce (n) *heart*
střevo *intestine*
zadek (gen. **zadku**) *bottom*
zápěstí *wrist*
žaludek (gen. **žaludku**) *stomach*

SOME EXTRA EVERYDAY ITEMS

rozhlas, radio *radio*
televize (f) *TV*
vypínač (m) *switch*
lampa *lamp*
světlo *light*
kohoutek *tap*
voda *water*
fax *fax*
mobil *mobile (phone)*
holicí strojek *shaver*

zásuvka *socket, plug; drawer*
počítač (m) *computer*
zámek *lock*
stroj (m) *machine*
hodiny (f pl) *clock*
pračka *washing machine*
sprcha *shower*
přehrávač *player (mp3/dvd)*
esemeska *text (message)*
notebook *laptop*

Note that in **kohoutek**, **strojek** and **zámek** the **-e-** disappears before endings, e.g. gen. **kohoutku**. And remember that **notebook** is necessarily pronounced [noudbuk].

You are not expected to learn all these words at once, but they may be used in exercises, etc., and of course the sooner you do learn them, the less you'll have to use dictionaries.

2 USING THE PAST TENSE WHEN ADDRESSING OTHER PEOPLE

In Unit 7 Mr Navrátil asked Mr Smith whether he knew certain people, and he used the form **neznal jste**. He is using **vykání**, saying **vy**, the polite plural *you* to him. Had he been speaking on the same terms with a woman he would have said, following the rules given in Unit 7, Section 1, **neznal*a* jste**.

In this unit, in the informal dialogue of a married couple, who use **tykání**, saying **ty** to each other, **nespal jsi** is the masculine singular form addressed to Mr Navrátil. Had *he* been speaking to *her* he would have said **nespala jsi**, the feminine equivalent. Thus it is vital to appreciate the degree of intimacy between yourself and the other speaker. If, however, *you* refers to a group of people, at any degree of (in)formality, then the true plural of the past tense is used, for example, **byli jste** (*you were*), where at least one of those addressed is male, or **byly jste**, where all the addressees are female. Of course, you cannot hear the difference, but it must be observed in writing.

You are less likely to need the informal singular forms of **tykání**, but you should note what may happen to the auxiliary verb **jsi**. If the verb stands at the beginning of a sentence, **jsi** may be reduced to **-s**, as in **musels** for **musel jsi** in the dialogue. Moreover, if the verb is accompanied by **si**, which should follow **jsi** in past-tense phrases, the two items merge as **sis**, as in **na tu hlavu sis mohl něco vzít**.

A similar situation applies in verbs accompanied by **se**, so for **nepředstavil jsi se panu Novákovi** (*you didn't introduce yourself to Mr Novák*), you will normally hear: **nepředstavil ses …**

Jsi is commonly reduced to **-s** after question words:

Cos viděl?	*What did you see?*
Kdes byl?	*Where have you been?*

3 TIME/DURATION

Many common time notions are expressed by the simple accusative case. With masculine expressions like **celý den** (*all day*) or **dnes večer** (*this evening*), or plurals like **dvě hodiny** (*two hours*), you cannot tell that this is accusative, but with feminines in the singular, thanks to agreement with any adjectives, it becomes obvious: **celou noc** and **každou noc**. It is even more obvious with nouns that show a distinct accusative case form, such as in **celou dobu** (*all the time*), **každou sobotu** (*every Saturday*), **čekal hodinu** (*he waited an hour*) and others.

4 *ZA* FOLLOWED BY THE ACCUSATIVE

The preposition **za** has various meanings and takes various cases. The most important is to express *for*, denoting in some sense 'exchange'. Hence it follows **děkovat** *to thank* (my thanks are in exchange for some gift, kindness, etc.), or after verbs of giving, selling, offering, etc. for a price: **nabízím mu** (*to him*) **za jeho auto svou chatu** (*I'm offering him my cottage for his car*) (**nabízet**, **nabízí**, 3rd pl. **nabízejí** *to offer*).

It is also used when you do something for someone, in that person's stead:

Já to dělám za Petra, on   *I'm doing it for Peter, he cannot (do it)*
  sám nemůže.   *himself* (**sám**, **sama**, etc. *-self* m, f).

5 PAST TENSE: VERBS ENDING IN A CONSONANT + *T*

Several Czech infinitives have a consonant before the final **-t**. You have so far met **moct** (*to be able*). Some others are **číst** (*to read*), **nést** (*to carry*), **vést** (*to lead*), **krást** (*to steal*), **téct** (*to flow*, *run of water*). Their past tenses usually have to be learnt separately, since there will be a consonant before the **-l** that indicates past, but it may not be the same as that in the infinitive, or indeed that of the present tense. Exact forms will be indicated as required, but note the ones quoted:

moct-může-mohl **číst-čte-četl**   **nést-nese-nesl**
vést-vede-vedl   **krást-krade-kradl** **téct-teče-tekl**

It is appropriate here to remind yourself how important it is to pay close attention to the peculiarities of monosyllabic verbs.

Exercises

1 Answer according to the dialogue.
  a Myslíte, že pan Navrátil je opravdu smolař? (Give a positive and a negative answer.)
  b Kde má pan Navrátil klíče? Jaké klíče to jsou?
  c Proč nemohl pan Navrátil spát?
  d Proč kupuje paní Navrátilová nové hodinky?
  e Kde má pan Navrátil rozhlas?
  f Bolí pana Navrátila zub?
  g Kdo si u Navrátilů stěžuje?

2 Answer as appropriate: Co ho/ji bolí?

3 Replace the English responses with suitable Czech expressions.

Přítel	Co ti je? *(What's the matter with you?)*
You	*I've got a headache.*
Přítel	Musíš si vzít aspirín.
You	*It doesn't help.*
Přítel	Nespals?
You	*Not much. The trams kept waking me (say: woke me all the time).*
Přítel	Zrovna dnes mě taky bolí hlava.
You	*So that makes two of us (say: So we are two).*

4 Ask the hotel porter:

  a how to get to the cinema;
  b whether he has seen your keys;
  c whether he has a watch; yours isn't working;
  d how many aspirins he has; you need two because you have a headache and one isn't enough (use **stačit** *to suffice*);
  e if the receptionist (**recepční** – an adjectival noun, m or f) can wake you;
  f if he happens to know where the post office (station) is.

Dialogue 2

Dr Navrátil has arrived to collect Mr Smith from his hotel.

 TR 26

Smith	Dobrý den.
Navrátil	Dobrý den. Vyspal jste se?
Smith	Děkuju. Velmi dobře.
Navrátil	Promiňte, že jdu pozdě. Měl jsem na křižovatce nehodu.
Smith	Kudy jste jel?
Navrátil	Z domova doleva, potom doprava a rovně až na křižovatku u obchodního domu. Tam se to stalo, u semaforu, když jsem odbočoval sem.
Smith	Co se vlastně stalo?
Navrátil	Nic moc. Mám jenom trochu pomačkaný blatník.
Smith	Kolik tu stojí oprava blatníku?
Navrátil	Asi pět set korun, ale ten druhý řidič to zaplatí – prý. Jsem na to zvědav – ale mám jeho adresu.
Smith	Aspoň nemusíte mít nový blatník.
Navrátil	Zaplaťpánbůh! Tak pojďte, jedeme na ten fotbal nebo ne!?
Smith	Tak dobře, když auto máte jakžtakž v pořádku. Jen pozor na křižovatky!

 Quick vocab

promiňte, že jdu pozdě *sorry I'm late*
pozdě (adverb, not adjective) *late*
křižovatka *crossroads*
nehoda *accident*
kudy jste jel *which way did you come/go*
kudy *which way* (contrast **kam** *where to*)
jet (jede) *to go* (by some means of transport)
z domova *from home* (goes with **doma** *at home* and **domů** *home (wards)*)
domov (gen. **domova**) *home*
doleva *to the left*
potom *then*
doprava *to the right*
rovně *straight on*
až na *all the way to*
až intensifying particle; compare Unit 4, Section 12

obchodní dům *department store* (Lit. *commercial house*)
obchodní *commercial, business from* **obchod** *trade, business, shop*
semafor *traffic light(s)*
když jsem odbočoval sem *as I was turning (to come) here*
když *as, when*
odbočovat *to turn off; to digress*
sem *(to) here* (opposite of **tam** *(to) there*; used for motion, direction, goal, not location)
nic moc *not(hing) much*
nic *nothing*
moc *much, a lot*
pomačkaný *dented*
blatník *mudguard, wing* (from **bláto** *mud*)
kolik tu stojí oprava *how much does a/the repair cost here*

oprava *repair*
asi pět set korun *about five hundred crowns*
pět set *five hundred*
druhý *second, the other*
řidič *driver*
zaplatí *will pay*
prý *here, he says*

jsem na to zvědav *I wonder ... (I'm curious about it)*
zaplaťpánbůh *thank God!*
když auto máte jakžtakž v pořádku *if/since your car's more or less okay*
když *here, if, since*
jakžtakž *(colloquial) more or less, also so-so*
pozor na *(+ acc.) watch out for*

6 GIVING DIRECTIONS

The three main items you will need are in the dialogue:

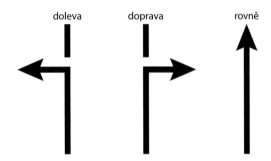

doleva   doprava   rovně

Related words are **vlevo**, **nalevo** (*on the left*) and **vpravo**, **napravo** (*on the right*).

You may also need to use and/or recognize such expressions as *first/second*, etc. *street/ building*, etc. *on the left/right*. This is done by combining the ordinal numerals given below with **ulice** (*street*), **budova** (*building*), etc. and those adverbs denoting *on the left/right* – **třetí ulice vpravo** = *third street on the right*. Places at which you might be told to turn will take the prepositions **na** (+ locative) and **u** (+ genitive) basically according to whether they are open spaces (like a crossroads) or three-dimensional objects (like traffic-lights or a department store, as in the dialogue). If you ask the way somewhere, expect the answer to contain **jděte** (*go – if on foot*), **jeďte** (*go – if driving*), **zahněte** (*turn*), **pokračujte** (*continue, carry on*). These are all imperative (command) forms. Further commands are explained in a later unit.

první	1st	**třetí**	3rd	**pátá**	5th
druhá	2nd	**čtvrtá**	4th	**šestá**	6th

Ordinal numerals are adjectives and therefore agree with the noun. These forms are feminine to agree with **ulice** and **budova**.

7 HOW TO ASK WHAT SOMETHING COSTS

The ordinary question is **Kolik to stojí?** (*How much does it cost?*) This uses one of those verbs with no obvious direct relationship between the infinitive and the personal forms. The infinitive is **stát**, and because the present tense forms contain **-j-**, the past tense keeps the vowel long (see the note in Unit 7, Section 1, 'Watch out for words of one syllable'):

Kolik stál váš nový dům?   *How much did your new house cost?*

Statements of cost are numerical or general, so in addition to actual prices you will often hear utterances like:

Stálo to majlant.   *It cost a fortune.* (Lit. *It cost Milan!*)

Hostina stála fůru peněz.   *The reception cost a packet.* (Lit. *a (wagon) load of money*).

● INSIGHT

And then there is the wonderful adjective **nekřesťanský** lit. *un-Christian*, but matching anything on a scale from *ludicrous* to *crippling*, which can qualify all manner of money words, from **peníze** (m.pl. gen. **peněz**) *money* itself to **poplatek** *charge, fee*, **cena** *price*, **úroky** *interest*, or the names of currencies, as in **nekřesťanské dolary** *a ridiculous cost/ outlay* etc. *in dollars*. The adverb from it, **nekřesťansky**, frequently qualifies relevant adjectives, most obviously **drahý** *expensive*. Although the word is felt nowadays as just a synonym of other, less colourful, words that may have the English meanings suggested, e.g. **hrozný** *dreadful*, its origin surely lies in medieval and early modern Bohemia, where Christians could not engage in financial services, a realm left perforce to the non-Christian Jews, who often combined their role as publicans with that of money-lending. That historical reality is, of course, not unique to Bohemia.

To state real costs you now need the rest of the Czech numerals (Unit 4, Section 1 (numbers 1–4); Unit 7, Section 5 (numbers 5–10)).

8 MORE NUMBERS

jedenáct	11	dvacet	20	dvacet jedna	21
dvanáct	12	třicet	30	třicet dva	32
třináct	13	čtyřicet	40	čtyřicet tři	43
čtrnáct	14	padesát	50	padesát čtyři	54
patnáct	15	šedesát	60	šedesát pět	65
šestnáct	16	sedmdesát	70	sedmdesát šest	76
sedmnáct	17	osmdesát	80	osmdesát sedm	87
osmnáct	18	devadesát	90	devadesát osm	98
devatenáct	19				

sto	100	sto jedna	101	tisíc	1,000
dvě stě	200	sto dva	102	dva tisíce	2,000
tři sta	300	dvě stě tři	203	tři tisíce	3,000
čtyři sta	400	dvě stě sedm	207	pět tisíc	5,000
pět set	500	tři sta osm	308	šest tisíc	6,000
šest set	600	tři sta dvacet	320	sto tisíc	100,000
sedm set	700	čtyři sta devadesát šest	496		
osm set	800	pět set sedmdesát čtyři	574		
devět set	900	šest set třicet sedm	637		
milion pět set padesát osm tisíc tři sta sedm			1,558,307		

Use this table for reference. Note how the form for the digits 4, 5, 6 and 9 varies in the teens and tens. Notice too that the words for *hundred* and *thousand* behave like nouns and change their form according to the digit to the left (note irregular genitive plural of **tisíc**, also **tisíc**, with no ending). And finally notice how the parts of compound numbers are just listed in sequence: there is no '*and*'.

In real life you will sometimes hear two-digit numerals inverted, as in '*four-and-twenty blackbirds*'. Expect this in reference to prices: **pětadvacet korun** (*25 crowns*), and ages: **je mu pětačtyřicet** (*he's 45*).

9 HOW TO USE *PRÝ*

Prý is a useful little particle; it enables the speaker to avoid responsibility for the truth of what he is saying. It can translate as *I've heard*, *it is said*, *apparently*, *allegedly*, or sometimes *he/she says/said*, where the source of the statement is actually known, as in the dialogue.

10 *JSEM NA TO ZVĚDAV* – 'I WONDER ...'

Zvědav is a short adjective, rather like **rád**: it changes only according to gender and number. There are only a handful of surviving short adjectives of this kind in Czech.

The two main facts about them are:
- **a** they only come after the verb **být**, and so only exist in the nominative case;
- **b** they generally have a narrower meaning than their corresponding long forms (**rád** does not have a long form). The long forms behave like any other adjective. Thus, **zvědavý** means *curious*, *inquisitive* by nature, while **být zvědav** means *to be curious* about one single fact. It is particularly common with 'if'-clauses: **Jsem zvědav, jestli ...**, in which case it translates as *wonder (whether)*.

Short adjectives

Quick vocab

spokojen (**s** + inst.) *satisfied (with something)*   **schopný** *able*
spokojený *contented (by nature)*   **hoden** (+ gen.) *worthy of*
schopen (+ gen.) *capable of*   **hodný** *good, kind*

laskav *(momentarily) kind*	**hotov** *ready (with something)*
laskavý *kind (by nature)*	**hotový** *ready-made, finished*
nemocen *(momentarily) ill*	**živ** *alive (not dead)*
nemocný *ill, sick (long-term)*	**živý** *living, lively, vivid*
zdráv *well (having been ill)*	**mrtev** *dead (suddenly)*
zdravý *fit, healthy*	**mrtvý** *dead, deceased*

Some occur in special phrases:

jsem si jist, že ... * I'm certain that ... but:
úspěch je jistý *success is certain*
jistý pan Novotný *a certain Mr Novotný*
byl si vědom, že ... * *he was aware that ... but:*
vědomá chyba *a conscious mistake*

živ a zdráv *alive and well, safe and sound*
Buď zdráv!, Buďte zdráv(i)! *Goodbye!*
Buďte tak laskav a ... * *Be so kind as to ...* (thus
often the equivalent of *Would you mind ...ing*)

*Informally you may also hear in these instances the equivalent long forms **jistý, vědomý** and **laskavý**.

Others you might meet are **šťasten/šťastný** (*happy*) and **nápomocen/nápomocný** (+ dat.) (*helpful, of assistance to*). Only one, **bos/ý** (*barefoot*), occurs with a verb other than **být**, the obvious candidates being verbs denoting movement on foot: **dívka chodila bosa** (*the girl was walking barefoot*).

Exercises

5 You wish to know how much the following items cost to buy, in the present tense and the past tense. Example: This book. Kolik stojí/stála tato kniha?

a That new suitcase.
b The watch.
c An hour's work.
d Two beers.
e Five teas.
f The concert.
g The beautiful bunch of flowers.
h That tin-opener.
i A new roof.
j That English shaver.

6 You, Mr Smith, are at the theatre box office. (Prices have of course risen considerably since this exchange was recorded!)

 TR 27

a Ask if they have tickets (**lístek** *ticket* – note the **-e-**). You're told **'Ano, máme'**.
b Ask how much they cost. The cashier says **'Čtyřicet korun'**.
c Say that's a lot. The cashier replies **'Máme lístky taky za třicet'** – which is more acceptable.
d Say: I need three, please. The cashier says **'Devadesát korun'**.
e Say: Unfortunately I've only got a 500-crown note (**pětistovka**). She replies **'To nevadí'** (*It doesn't matter*).
f Ask 'Tell me please, where are the toilets?' She says **'Zahněte tady vlevo, třetí dveře'.**
g You thank her saying 'You're very kind. Thank you'.
h Then you turn right. Why did the woman you met coming out of the third door giggle?

MONEY

The word for money is **peníze** (m.pl. genitive **peněz**), from a little-used singular word **peníz** (*coin*), related to German *pfennig* and English *penny*. The Czech currency is the **koruna** (*crown*), abbreviated **kč**, internationally CZK. The smaller unit (*1/100 crown*) used to be the **haléř** or **halíř** (m.) (*heller*), which you will now only encounter in literature or historical contexts. Besides being known by their value, the various coins and notes are usually identified by single-word names: **padesátník** (*a 50-heller coin*; even smaller coins previously in circulation had similar names, e.g. **desetník**, which you might meet in texts appropriate to the period before November 2003 when, with **dvacetník**, it was withdrawn); **dvoukoruna** (*a 2-crown coin*), similarly **pětikoruna** and **desetikoruna**, **stovka** (*a 100-crown note*), similarly **dvoustovka**, **pětistovka** and **tisícovka**. Curiously, for historical reasons going back to the 19th century, ten crowns – once a reasonable sum – is known colloquially as **pětka** (*a fiver*)! Other most frequently needed currency units are the self-evident **dolar** and **euro**; the latter is often left unchanged in form outside the nominative plural (hence **tři eura** but **sedm euro** – not 'eur'), and the less obvious **libra** *pound* (also the unit of weight), especially the **libra šterlingů** (GBP).

? Test yourself

Using the map below, explain to someone how to get from the hotel to the railway station, and then from the station to the post office. There are at least two possible routes. Then you might be prepared to advise if he decides to do things the other way round!

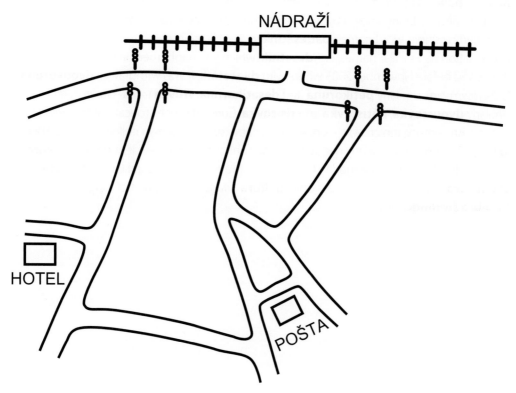

Kolik je hodin?
What's the time?

In this unit you will learn
▶ *How to ask the time*
▶ *How to ask at what time something happens*
▶ *How to say what time it is*
▶ *How to talk about the future*

Dialogue 1

Once more the Navrátils are having a domestic discussion.

 TR 28

Ona	Podívej se, kolik je hodin!
On	No, a kolik je?
Ona	Jsou tři hodiny, ne, tři pryč. Kde jsi byl tak dlouho?
On	Po práci jsme byli chvíli v hospodě. Ivan má narozeniny.
Ona	Chvíli! Čekala jsem tě v poledne. Doufám, že jste moc nepili.
On	Já jsem měl jenom tři piva. Kolik měli ostatní, nevím. Nepočítám, kolik kdo pije. A stejně platil Ivan, dostal dnes zvláštní odměnu.
Ona	Nevím, co tomu bude říkat Maruška. O té odměně věděla a chtěla za to kupovat nový gauč.
On	Ivan to dobře ví a peníze na gauč má stranou. Maruška nebude zklamaná. Navíc půjdou dnes večer v osm do vzorkovny nábytku. Ivan zná ředitele a ten sliboval, že ji bude provádět on sám.
Ona	Maruška se má! Kdy budeš ty tak spolupracovat v domácnosti?
On	Přece každý den myju nádobí!

podívej se, kolik je hodin! *look at the time!*

podívej se (2nd person singular imperative) *look!*

no *hmm, well*

jsou tři hodiny *it's three o'clock*

tři pryč *gone three*

pryč *gone, past, away*

po práci *after work*

po (preposition + locative) *after*

chvíli *for a while* (accusative, meaning *duration*, **of chvíle** (f) *while, moment*)

Ivan má narozeniny *it's Ivan's birthday*

narozeniny (f pl) *birthday*

čekat *to wait, expect*

tě accusative of **ty**

v poledne *at midday*

poledne (n) *midday*

doufat *to hope*

ostatní *the rest of, the other(s)*

nepočítám, kolik kdo pije *I don't count who drinks how much*

a stejně platil Ivan *and anyway, it was Ivan who paid*

stejně *anyway*

dostal dnes zvláštní odměna *he got a bonus today*

dostat *to get (something)*, compare **dostat se** *get = reach (somewhere)*

zvláštní odměna *bonus*

zvláštní *special*

odměna *remuneration, reward*

nevím, co tomu bude říkat Maruška *I don't know what Maruška will say about that*

bude říkat future of říkat *say*

Maruška *familiar affectionate form of Marie*

peníze na gauč má stranou *he's got the money for the couch set aside*

stranou *to one side*

nebude zklamaná *she won't be disappointed*

zklamaný *disappointed*

navíc *moreover, on top of that; extra*

půjdou future tense of **jdou**, from **jít** *go*

vzorkovna *showroom* (from **vzorek** *sample*)

nábytek *furniture*

ředitel (m. animate soft) *manager, director*

ten sliboval, zě *he promised that*

slibovat *to promise*

provádět *to show round*

Maruška se má (idiom) *Maruška doesn't know how lucky she is*

kdy budeš ty tak spolupracovat *when are you going to co-operate like that*

tak *so, thus, like this/that*

spolupracovat *co-operate, collaborate*

přece myju nádobí *but I wash the dishes*

nádobí (singular collective) *the dishes, the washing up*

1 ASKING THE TIME

The common formula for this is **Kolik je hodin?** (Lit. *how many is there of hours*). You may also hear: **Kolik máte hodin?** (Lit. *how many do you have of hours*), in practice equivalent to *What time do you make it?*, and exactly the same structure as, say, **Kolik máte času?** (*How much time have you got?*) or **Kolik máte peněz?** (*How much money do you have?*)

2 TELLING THE TIME

The answer to the question in **1** above for whole hours consists of the relevant numeral plus the word **hodina** in the appropriate case, with the verb *to be* in the singular for 1, and for 5 upwards, and, in the plural for 2, 3 and 4.

Je jedna hodina.	*It's one o'clock.*	**Je pět hodin.**	*It's five o'clock.*
Jsou dvě hodiny.	*It's two o'clock.*	**Je jedenáct hodin.**	*It's eleven o'clock.*
Jsou tři hodiny.	*It's three o'clock.*	**Je poledne.**	*It's midday.*

With reference not only to timetables, but to the working day generally, Czechs often use the 24-hour clock, so you may hear **Je čtrnáct hodin** (*It's 2 p.m.*), as an alternative to **Jsou dvě hodiny**, which avoids having to specify **ráno** (*in the*) *morning* or **odpoledne** (*in the*) *afternoon* – **odpoledne** (n) (*afternoon*).

3 SAYING/ASKING 'AT WHAT TIME?'

This is done by simple addition of the preposition **v** at the beginning of the 'o'clock' expressions: **v jednu hodinu** (*at one o'clock*; this time alone shows that **v** requires the *accusative case* in this function), **ve čtrnáct hodin** (*at 2 p.m.*). **Poledne** (*midday*) also counts as an exact time by the clock, so you can say **v poledne** as well as **ve dvanáct hodin** for *at 12 o'clock*.

In both types of time expressions the word **hodina/hodiny/hodin** can be dropped, as the dialogue shows.

Ne, (jsou) tři pryč.	*No, it's gone three.*
V osm.	*At eight.*

Note how some of the numerals beginning with 'awkward' groups of consonants, e.g. **dvě**, **tři** and **čtyři**, and the teens that begin with them, cause **v** to become **ve**.

4 THE FUTURE

The simplest future tense to form is that of **být** (*to be*). It has its own conjugation:

budu	*I will be*	**budeme**	*we will be*
budeš	*you (familiar) will be*	**budete**	*you will be*
bude	*he/she/it will be*	**budou**	*they will be*

As an example look at the expression in the dialogue:

Maruška nebude zklamaná.	*Maruška won't be disappointed.*

As you can see, **budu**, etc. are negated in the ordinary way.

Almost all the verbs you have met so far form their future tense by combining the future of **být** (**budu**, etc.) with the infinitive. Examples from the dialogue are:

Co … bude říkat Maruška?	*What will Maruška say?*
bude provádět	*he will show round*
budeš spolupracovat	*you will co-operate*

A small number of verbs you already know are different:

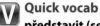
Quick vocab

představit (se) *introduce (oneself)*		**přepsat** *rewrite, overwrite*
stát se *happen* (also *become*)		**dostat (se)** *get*

vzít (si) *take*

setkat se *meet*

najít *find*

říct *say, tell* (of which you have only had the imperative **řekněte**)

podívat se *look* (of which you have only seen the singular imperative **podívej se**)

zemřít *die*

zeptat se *ask*

Do not worry about these for the time being, but do not try to use them in the future yet. For all the other verbs that you have met there is no problem.

Budu psát domů.	*I shall write home.*
Nebudeme sedět v hospodě dlouho.	*We aren't going to sit around in the pub long.*
Zítra bude kupovat nové auto.	*Tomorrow he'll be buying a new car.*

Forms like **budu** are then 'future auxiliary verbs' when combined with another verb. Unlike the past-tense auxiliaries they are not fixed in the sentence, that is, they are mobile like the other main elements. For example they may shift to the end to carry emphasis.

Nádobí mýt budu.	*I shall wash the dishes!*

5 THE SPECIAL CASE OF *JÍT* AND *JET* IN THE FUTURE

Jít *to go (on foot)* and **jet** *to go (by some means of transport, or said of a vehicle)* are two of a small family of verbs called *verbs of motion*. In passing you have already met **běžet** *to run*, **nést** *to carry* and **vést** *to lead*. The other main ones are **vézt** *to convey, carry (by vehicle)*, **letět** *to fly*, **táhnout** *to pull* and **hnát (žene)** *to chase*. Their future forms are different from other verbs in that you merely add **pů-** or **po-** to the present tense.

jdu	*I am going*	**půjdu**	*I will go*
jedu	*I am going*	**pojedu**	*I will go*
běžím	*I am running*	**poběžím**	*I will run*
nesu	*I am carrying*	**ponesu**	*I will carry*
vedu	*I am leading*	**povedu**	*I will lead*
vezu	*I am carrying (e.g. by lorry)*	**povezu**	*I will carry*
letím	*I am flying*	**poletím**	*I will fly*
táhnu	*I am pulling*	**potáhnu**	*I will pull*
ženu	*I am chasing*	**poženu**	*I will chase*

What is special about this narrow group of verbs is that they refer to single events – *here and now* or *there and then* – and there will always be a goal of the action stated or implied; in **Šel na nádraží** (*He was going to the station*) the goal is given: but in **Šla po ulici** (*She was going down the street*) she was clearly, or presumably, going somewhere, though the observer need not know where. These verbs of motion are said to be determinate because there is a *terminus*, or end point.

They stand in contrast to a set of indeterminate verbs of motion, so called because there is *no one terminus* involved, or *no terminus* at all. In the first case you might be using the context: 'She goes to school', which implies repeated regular journeys to and fro, which means that school is a *repeated terminus*, but so is home. In the second case you could be talking about random motion, as in 'We spent all day walking in the woods' or 'She chased him everywhere'.

The determinate-indeterminate pairs look like this:

jít	**chodit**	**nést**	**nosit**	**letět**	**létat**
jet	**jezdit**	**vést**	**vodit**	**táhnout**	**tahat**
běžet	**běhat**	**vézt**	**vozit**	**hnát**	**honit**

You can now express the contrast:

Jde do školy.   *She is going to school (this minute).*

with:

Chodí do školy.   *She goes to school (is of school age).*

and the directionless:

Chodili jsme celý den po lese.   *We walked in the woods all day.*

(Here **po** itself implies random direction.)

Similarly:

Tento naklad'ák veze nábytek do prodejny.
This lorry is taking furniture to the shop (now).

Toto auto vozí nábytek.
This lorry carries furniture (irrespective of when or where to).

Hnala ho domů z hospody.
She chased him home from the pub.

Honila je všude.
She chased them everywhere.

This pattern continues for the other persons of the verb. There is one example in the dialogue:

půjdou ... do vzorkovny   *they will be going to the showroom*

The **pů-/po-** prefix never occurs with either the infinitive or the past tense.

Vedu syna do školy.   *I am taking (leading) my son to school.*
Vedl jsem syna do školy.   *I took (led) my son to school.*
Nechci vést syna do školy.   *I don't want to take my son to school.*

but

Povedu syna do školy.   *I will take my son to school.*

The other verbs in this family behave in the same way. There will be more on the verbs of motion later.

● **INSIGHT**

The difference between **jít|chodit** and **jet|jezdit** was presented above basically as the opposition between feet and wheels. It's actually better to think in terms of 'assisted locomotion': we need the assistance of the car's or the train's wheels in order to **jet**; equally, without its wheels a car can have the best engine in the world and go nowhere. Our own locomotion may also be assisted, however, not just by the wheels of a vehicle, but the feet/legs of some quadruped, hence we use **jet** also if we go somewhere on horseback (**na koni**) or by donkey (**osel**) or camel (**velbloud**).

Also among the verbs of motion, notice that **nesu**, **vedu** and **vezu** might all be translated by 'I'm taking' in addition to the translations offered in the table, which makes it essential to think, when proceeding from English to Czech, about the exact nature of the 'taking': thus *He's taking his son away*: = 1. **Nese syna pryč** (that is, in his arms); = 2. **Vede syna pryč** (that is, leading him by the hand); = 3. **Veze syna pryč** (for example, by car).

6 *SÁM* – 'SELF' AND 'ALONE'

This little word has two basic meanings: -*self* (as a semi-emphatic expression), reinforcing the subject:

Bude ji provádět on sám.   *He'll show her round himself.*

and *alone, on one's own*:

Sedí v hospodě sám.   *He's sitting in the pub alone.*

Like **rád**, or the **l**-form of the past tense, it changes form according to the subject of the sentence:

Maruška nemusí mýt nádobí **sama.**   *Maruška doesn't have to wash the dishes **herself.***

Česky se učíte **sami.**   *You (readers) are learning Czech **on your own.***

Dívky to četly **samy.**   *The girls read it **on their own.***

Dítě se obléká **samo.**   *The child gets dressed by **itself.***

 Quick vocab

oblékat *to dress (someone)*   **oblékat se** *to get dressed*

The forms of **sám** are:

Singular		Plural	
Masculine	sám	Masculine animate	sami
Feminine	sama	Masculine inanimate	samy
Neuter	samo	Feminine	samy
		Neuter	sama

7 WAITING AND EXPECTING

There are two main uses of **čekat**:

   a with a direct object, when it means *expect*:

     Čekal jsem syna.   *I was expecting my son.*

   b with **na** + the accusative, when it means *wait for*:

     Čekal jsem na syna.   *I was waiting for my son.*

In Unit 5, Dialogue 2, you met it used on its own, also meaning *wait*: **Čekám, čekám, a nic.**

Expect may also be expressed by **očekávat**:

Zvláštní odměnu jsme neočekávali.   *We weren't expecting a bonus.*

8 SOME EXTRA WORDS

At the end of the dialogue, Mr Navrátil claims to wash the dishes every day. Here are some of the items he handles:

šálek   talíř (*m*)   nůž (*m*)   vidlička

lžíce (*f*)   sklenice   půllitr   sklenička

Exercises

1 Supply the questions to which the following might be answers:

   a Budu tady v šest.

   b Teď je sedm pryč.

   c Bohužel nevím, nemám hodinky.

   d Koncert začíná v devatenáct hodin.

   e Poledne znamená dvanáct hodin.

   f Mám jenom deset korun.

   g Pojedeme tam večer.

   h Máme jenom dvacet minut.

2 Answer the questions along the lines suggested:

🔊 **TR 29**

   a Kolik je hodin? *It's gone five.*

   b V kolik jste mě čekali? *We were expecting you at eight.*

   c V kolik večeříte? *We don't dine until nine.*

d Kolik máte v pracovně počítačů? *Only the new one, the old one doesn't work.*

e V kolik půjdete ráno do práce? *I'm going* (**future**) *at seven.*

f Kde a kdy budete čekat? *At the station at 3 p.m.*

3 Reread the dialogue and answer the questions in Czech:

  a Proč se paní Navrátilová zlobí?

  b Proč byl pan Navrátil v hospodě?

  c Kolik měl pan Navrátil piv?

  d Kdo platil? A proč?

  e Paní Navrátilová si myslí, Že se Maruška bude zlobit. Proč?

  f Kam půjdou večer Ivan a Maruška?

  g Jak pan Navrátil spolupracuje v domácnosti?

  h Kdo myje nádobí u vás doma?

4 Convert the following to the future and make sure the resulting sentences make sense (some might not work in the future) (adjust any adverbs as required):

  a Dnes má moje Žena narozeniny.

  b Kolik peněz nesete do banky?

  c Ve tři hodiny dávají krásný film.

  d Otec dnes vede naši dceru do školy.

  e Zuzano, kde vidíš moje klíče?

  f Promiňte, paní, čtete tyto noviny? (**noviny** [f pl] *newspaper*)

  g Co si o tom myslí?

  h V Praze nikoho neznáme.

  i Vy se máte!

5 Now go through the sentences in 4 above putting them into the past tense, again adjusting any adverbs to the sense.

Dialogue 2

Messrs Smith and Navrátil are trying to arrange a meeting to go and see Navrátil's workplace.

 TR 30

Navrátil	Budu na vás čekat v hotelu ve tři. Hodí se vám to?
Smith	Nevím, jestli se mi to bude hodit. Manželka si kupuje šaty a neví, kdy bude zpátky. Musím tu na ni čekat.
Navrátil	Tak v půl čtvrté? Můžu si mezitím něco číst.
Smith	Dobře. V půl čtvrté. Do té doby bude určitě zpátky.
Navrátil	To znamená, že můžeme jet asi ve tři čtvrtě na čtyři, pojedeme půl hodiny a na pracovišti budeme ve čtvrt na pět.
Smith	Dobře. Budu se těšit.

Navrátil	Hodina a půl nám stačí, budete tedy zpátky v hotelu ve tři čtvrtě na šest. Pokud vím, v hotelu se podává večeře v šest, takže času máme dost.
Smith	Ano, takhle bude všechno v nejlepším pořádku a žena se nebude moct zlobit, že jdu pozdě na večeři.
Navrátil	Tak na shledanou v půl čtvrté. Mimochodem, kolik je hodin teď?
Smith	Přesně půl jedné. Půjdu si na chvíli odpočinout.

 Quick vocab

hodí se vám to? *does it suit you?*
hodit se *to suit*
vám (a form of **vy**)
vás (accusative of **vy**)
zpátky *back*
čekat na ni *to wait for her*
tak v půl čtvrté *at 3.30 then*
můžu si mezitím něco číst *I can read something in the meantime*
mezitím *meanwhile, while I wait (etc.)*
do té doby *by then*
můžeme jet asi ve tři čtvrtě na čtyři *we can go about 3.45*
čtvrt (f) *quarter*
pojedeme půl hodiny *it will take us half an hour (Lit. we will be going/travelling for half an hour)*
půl *half*
na pracovišti *in/at (my) workplace*

pracoviště (n) *workplace*
hodina a půl nám stačí *an hour and a half is enough for us*
pokud vím *as far as I know, to the best of my knowledge*
večeře se podává v šest *dinner is served at six*
podávat *to serve; also offer, pass;* **podávat se** *to be served*
takže *so (that), therefore*
takhle bude všechno v nejlepším pořádku *that way everything will be perfectly all right*
všechno *everything*
v nejlepším pořádku a strong form of **v pořádku** (Lit. *in the best order*)
Žena se nebude moct zlobit *my wife won't be able to be cross*
přesně půl jedné *12.30 exactly*
půjdu si na chvíli odpočinout *I'll go and have a rest for a moment*

9 MORE ON TELLING THE TIME

The quarters

While you can always imitate the 'timetable' style of giving the quarter hours such as **tři patnáct** (*3.15*), you will still need to recognize the ordinary Czech way of telling them.

Crucially, they use the next whole hour as a point of reference. For example, 'quarter past two' and 'quarter to three' are interpreted as 'quarter (on the way) to three', and 'three-quarters (on the way) to three' respectively. The word for quarter in this context is **čtvrt**, plural **čtvrtě** (or **čtvrti**) hence: **čtvrt na tři** (*2.15*) and **tři čtvrtě na tři** (*2.45*). Since this **na** implies, like so many, goal or direction, it is followed by the accusative, but you will only see this in **čtvrt na jednu** (*12.15*). The word for *hour* never appears in these constructions, but it does explain the feminine accusative form **jednu**, and also why we use **dvě**, not **dva**, in, say, **tři čtvrtě na dvě** (*1.45*). This type of telling the quarters uses only the 12-hour clock.

The half-hour

This too uses the next whole hour as the reference point, but the construction amounts to 'half of the x-th (hour)'. Thus 3.30 is expressed as 'half of the fourth', **půl čtvrté**. So to say half-past something you need the word **půl** (*half*) and the ordinal numerals (see Section 10). The only exception is 12.30, which is expressed as 'half of one' (not 'of the first'), **půl jedné**. **Jedné** is the feminine genitive singular of **jeden**, that is, **jeden** behaves like **ten**.

At quarter past, half-past, quarter to

Nothing could be simpler: use **v/ve** as with the whole hours, hence: **ve čtvrt na tři**, **v půl třetí**, **ve tři čtvrtě na tři** (*at 2.15*, *2.30*, *2.45*). Note again the expansion of **v** to **ve** before the awkward groups of consonants.

Adding information about the time

You have met **pryč** (*gone*, *past*). In the second dialogue you have **asi** (*about*), and **přesně** (*exactly*). Other words to add are **skoro** and **téměř**, both meaning *almost*.

10 ORDINAL NUMERALS

The table below shows the ordinal numerals. Note that they are by their nature adjectives: three of them, *1st*, *3rd* and *1,000th*, are 'soft'.

první	1st	**dvacátý**	20th
druhý	2nd	**dvacátý první** or	
třetí	3rd	**jednadvacátý**	21st
čtvrtý	4th	**třicátý**	30th
pátý	5th	**třicátý druhý** or	
šestý	6th	**dvaatřicátý**	32nd
sedmý	7th	**čtyřicátý**	40th
osmý	8th	**padesátý**	50th
devátý	9th	**padesátý třetí** or	
desátý	10th	**třiapadesátý**	53rd
jedenáctý	11th	**šedesátý**	60th
dvanáctý	12th	**sedmdesátý**	70th
třináctý	13th	**osmdesátý**	80th
čtrnáctý	14th	**devadesátý**	90th
patnáctý	15th	**stý**	100th
šestnáctý	16th	**dvoustý**	200th
sedmnáctý	17th	**třístý**	300th
osmnáctý	18th	**tisící**	1,000th
devatenáctý	19th		

1st to *5th* are slightly irregular; the others all have the adjectival ending tacked on to the cardinal numerals, or their stem: **šest → šestý**, **sto → stý**. The only other change is that if a cardinal ends in **-et**, it has to change into **-át**: **deset → desátý**, **třicet → třicátý**.

Two-digit ordinals are often inverted, especially when referring to dates: **osmašedesátý rok** (*1968*) – remember what you learnt about the inversion of cardinal numerals in Unit 8, Section 8.

11 'UNTIL'

Until in English is both a preposition and a conjunction (it can stand before nouns or clauses – sentences). In the first case it is translated by **do** + genitive, just as '*by*' is. The context is what governs the different translations of say, **do té doby**:

Bude do té doby zpátky.	*She will be back by then ('by that time').*
Bude do té doby číst.	*She will read until then.*

The conjunction *until* in Czech is **dokud** with **ne-** attached to the verb. It expresses 'for as long as something is not the case'.

Musím tady čekat, dokud nebude	*Lit. I must wait here for as long as she*
zpátky.	*will not be back.*

You can also expect to meet **dokud** with a positive verb.

Bude ho mít ráda, dokud bude žít.	*She will love him as long as she lives.*

Notice that **dokud** in either sense is followed by future tense forms in Czech, but the simple present in English.

Exercises

6 Tell an acquaintance he or she can:
   a wait for you at work at 12.15.
   b read until you are back at 3.30.
   c go to the bank, where you will be waiting, at 9.00.
   d expect you at 4.45 exactly.
   e co-operate and wash the car at midday

   Ask if he or she:
   f can take your son and daughter to school this week at 8.15.
   g can go for you to the shop. It's late – gone 4.30 – and you have no time yourself (bear in mind your own gender).
   h can pass you (**mi** *to me*) the books from the table.
   i can find Unit 4 and read Dialogue 1 to you slowly (**pomalu**).

   Now ask if he or she:
   j knows what time it is.

PET NAMES

Like the rest of the Slavs, the Czechs use a rich system of pet names within the family or among groups of close friends. Some definitely come from diminutives and are still widely used to address children, but otherwise they merely denote a close, affectionate or simply familiar relationship between speaker and addressee of any age. In the dialogue at the beginning of this unit, Ivan's wife Marie is referred to as **Maruška**. Depending on age, the period, local or regional preference or even individual family use, she might also have been called **Mája**, **Madla**, **Máňa**, **Maruš**, **Márinka**.

The commonest male name is **Josef**, which yields **Jožka**, **Jóža**, **Jozífek**, **Pepa**, **Pepi**, **Pepík**, **Pepíček** (a twin set reminiscent of Spanish *José* and *Pepe*). **Jan** (*John*) gives **Jeník**, **Jeníček**, **Jenda**, **Honza**, **Honzík**, **Honzíček**.

Some pet names come from more than one name, so a **Mirek** could have either **Miroslav** or **Vladimír** on his birth certificate, and **Jarka** could be **Jaroslava** or **Jaroslav**, **Jaromíra** or **Jaromír** – it can be masculine or feminine. Some people go through life having adopted one of the (original) pet names as the form of their name by which they are generally known. Note that in the type **Jožka**, **Pepa**, **Jenda**, **Honza** and **Jarka** (m) we have another source of masculine animate nouns ending in **-a**. Yet another set are surnames that began life as feminine nouns, hence **procházka** (*walk*) features as the common male, so masculine, surname **Procházka**, or **červinka** (*robin*, the bird) as the surname **Červinka**. Females of families with such surnames carry the regularly feminised form, hence, here, **Procházková** and **Červinková**.

Test yourself

State the time shown on the following clock-faces:

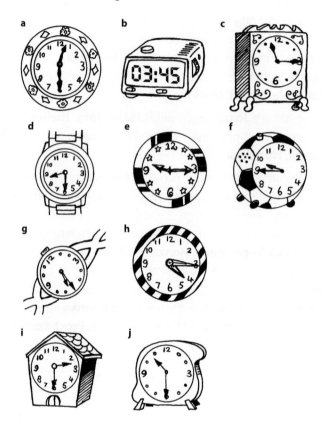

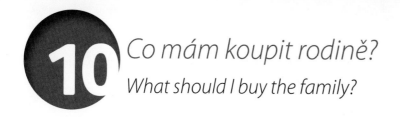

Co mám koupit rodině?

What should I buy the family?

In this unit you will learn

▶ *How to talk about the person(s) to whom something is given/said*
▶ *How to use place expressions in the plural*
▶ *How to say all*

Dialogue 1

Mr Navrátil is helping Mr Smith, alone in Prague on this trip, to choose presents to take back home to his family.

 TR 31

Navrátil	Zítra už jedete domů, že?
Smith	Bohužel ano. Ale mám velký problém.
Navrátil	Ano? Jaký? Mohu vám být nějak nápomocen?
Smith	Jestli máte čas, budu velmi rád.
Navrátil	Tak co? V čem je ten váš problém?
Smith	Nevím, co mám koupit rodině jako dárek z cesty.
Navrátil	To znamená – jestli se nemýlím – manželce, synovi a dceři. Nebo musíte něco shánět ještě někomu jinému?
Smith	Ano. Otci a matce, sousedům a snad sekretářce.
Navrátil	Ach, tolika lidem! Musí to být?
Smith	To víte, většina z nich něco čeká, to už je zvyk. Sousedům a sekretářce chci koupit nějaké drobnosti jako pozornost za všechny jejich laskavosti při přípravě mé cesty.
Navrátil	Vím, že vám sekretářka musela třikrát přepsat referát, ale co dělali sousedé?
Smith	Rodina je totiž taky pryč, na dovolené, a sousedé nám zalévají kytky a starají se o psa.

Quick vocab

zítra už jedete domů, že *you're going home tomorrow, aren't you*

čas *time*

v čem je ten váš problém *what is this problem of yours*

v čem *in what* (**v** + locative of **co**)

co mám koupit rodině *what I should buy my family*

dárek *present*

jestli se nemýlím *if I'm not mistaken*

mýlit se *to be mistaken*

manželce, synovi, dceři *for your wife, son, daughter*

nebo *or*

musíte něco shánět ještě někomu? *do you have to find something for anybody else?*

shánět (**-í**, 3rd pl. **-ějí**) *to try to get (to chase up)*

ještě *here, else, yet*

někomu jinému *dative case of* **někdo jiný**

jiný *other, another, different*

otci a matce *for my father and mother*

sousedům *for the neighbours*

sekretářce *for my secretary*

tolika lidem! *(for) so many people!*

musí to být? *does it have to be? do you have to?*

to víte *you know (how it is)*

většina z nich něco čeká *most of them expect something*

z nich *preposition* **z** *+ genitive plural of* **oni** *they*

to už je zvyk *it's customary, normal*

zvyk *custom, habit*

drobnosti *small things (from* **drobný** *small, tiny)*

drobnost (gen. **-i**) *something small*

pozornost (gen. **-i**) *small gift, token (of gratitude, etc.) (from* **pozorný** *attentive)*

za všechny jejich laskavosti *for all their kindnesses*

laskavost (gen. **-i**) *kindness*

při přípravě *during the preparation*

příprava *preparation*

třikrát *three times*

rodina je totiž taky pryč *the family, you see, is also away*

totiž *(an explanatory word that often defies exact translation, but if implied explanation is also apologetic,* actually *at the start of the sentence will usually serve)*

na dovolené *on holiday*

dovolená *holiday (has the form of a feminine adjective)*

zalévat *to water*

kytky *flowers, house-plants*

kytka *colloquial for* **květina** *flower and for* **kytice** *bouquet*

starají se o psa *they're looking after the dog*

starat se + o (+ acc.) *to look after*

1 THE PERSON TO WHOM YOU GIVE/SAY SOMETHING

Czech **dávat**, like English *to give* will normally be followed by two expressions, one denoting the thing given (direct object), and one denoting the recipient (indirect object). The direct object is what you have met so far, after numerous verbs, and it has been expressed in Czech by the accusative case. The indirect object is expressed by the dative case. The phrases below are given in the standard Czech manner using **někomu** (dative of **někdo**) to represent the recipient (or beneficiary) slot, and **něco**, to denote the direct object. (Other new words appearing in this section are in the Quick vocab after Dialogue 1, above.)

kupovat někomu něco	*buy something for someone*
nabízet někomu něco	*offer somebody something*
prodávat někomu něco	*sell something to someone*
doporučovat někomu něco	*recommend something to someone*

shánět někomu něco	*try to get something for someone*
přepsat někomu něco	*rewrite something for someone*
zalévat někomu kytky	*water the flowers for someone*

Notice how the 'beneficiary' in English may be introduced by *to, for* or indeed nothing at all. A beneficiary may be expressed even if the other chunk connected with the verb is not just a direct object in the accusative:

starat se někomu o něco	*to look after something for someone*

An indirect object also accompanies verbs meaning *tell* or *say*:

říkat někomu něco	*to tell someone something*

which includes **doporučovat** (*to recommend*) above and such verbs of speaking as **navrhovat** (*to suggest*).

2 FORMS OF THE DATIVE CASE

Most nouns have dative case endings similar to the locative case endings already learnt (see Unit 3, Section 11 and Unit 7, Section 2), including any changes to final consonants, as in **sekretářce** (*for my secretary*). Compare:

Locative

Mluví o Petrovi.	*He's talking about Peter.* (masculine animate)

Dative

Dává knihu Petrovi.	*He's giving the book to Peter.*

With compound masculine animate expressions the rule about the two endings **-u** and **-ovi** in the locative (Unit 7, Section 2) also applies in the dative:

Dává knihu profesoru Novákovi.	*He's giving the book to Prof. Novák.*

Locative

Mluví o ženě.	*He's talking about his wife.* (feminine)

Dative

Kupuje dárek ženě.	*He's buying a present for his wife.*

Locative

Mluví o muži.	*She's talking about her husband.* (masculine 'soft')

Dative

Posílá dopis muži.	*She's sending a letter to her husband.*

Locative

Mluví o pomocnici.	*He's talking about his assistant.* (feminine 'soft')

Dative

Dává pomocnici volno.	*He's giving his assistant time off.*

The dative of several classes of words denoting things or abstracts (masculine inanimates, neuters, **i**-declensions) are not given in this section – they cannot function as beneficiaries.

3 PREPOSITIONS: DATIVE CASE

The dative case must be used with certain prepositions. Here are the most common.

k (or **ke** before another **k-** and some groups of consonants) *to* (with people), *towards, up to* (with people or things), and some idiomatic uses:

Šel ke stolu.	*He went towards the table.*
Běžel k řezníkovi.	*He ran to the butcher's.*
To není k jídlu.	*That's not fit to eat.*

proti *against, opposite*

Pavel hlasoval proti návrhu.	*Paul voted against the motion.*
Dům stojí proti kostelu.	*The house stands opposite a church.*

kvůli *for the sake of, because of*

Dělala to kvůli rodině.	*She did it for the family's sake.*
Zavírá okno kvůli větru.	*She shuts the window because of the wind.*

díky *thanks to*

Díky jeho péči pes žije.	*Thanks to his care the dog is alive.*

So now you can tell that the dative of 'hard' masculine inanimate nouns end in **-u** (e.g. **návrhu, větru, kostelu**), as does that of 'hard' neuters (**jídlu**).

Most 'soft' nouns of any gender end in **-i** in the dative (that is, like their locatives), e.g. the feminines **pomocnici, péči**; masculine **muži**; neuter **srdci** (*heart*). The same ending applies to **i**-declension nouns, e.g. **kvůli drobnosti** (*because of a trifle*) and, as an exception, to **dcera** (*daughter*) (**dceři** not 'dceře'). Neuters ending in **-í**, and the feminine **paní**, are unchanged in the dative, e.g. **šel k nádraží** (*he walked towards the station*). 'Soft' masculine animate nouns that are proper names take **-ovi**, e.g. **Dává to Milošovi** (*He's giving it to Miloš*).

4 INDIVIDUAL VERBS: DATIVE CASE

A few verbs have to be followed by the dative case. They include: **pomáhat** (*to help*), **věřit** (*to believe*), **rozumět** (*to understand*), **důvěřovat** (*to trust*), **radit** (*to advise*), **vyhýbat se** (*to avoid*):

Pomáhá **mu** kupovat dárky.	*He helps him to buy presents.*
Nerozuměl **té větě.**	*He didn't understand that sentence.*
Petr **tomu** nebude věřit.	*Peter won't believe that.*
Nedůvěřujeme **svému instinktu.**	*We don't trust our instinct.*
Radí **našemu sousedovi.**	*He's advising our neighbour.*
Vyhýbáme se **velkým městům.**	*We avoid large cities.*

5 PRONOUNS/ADJECTIVES: DATIVE FORMS

You have already seen **(ně)komu** from **(ně)kdo**. **Ten**, **ta**, **to** have the forms **tomu**, **té**, **tomu**.

Similarly **náš** and **váš** have **našemu** (m), **naší** (f), **našemu** (n) while **co**, **něco** and **nic** have **čemu**, **něčemu** and **ničemu**.

'Hard' adjectives, and **můj**, **tvůj**, **svůj**, have **-ému**, **-é**, **-ému**, and 'soft' adjectives have **-ímu**, **-í**, **-ímu**.

kvůli tomu našemu velkému prvnímu problému/autu	*because of that first big problem/car of ours*

or

díky té vaší první velké laskavosti	*thanks to that first great kindness of yours*

(Notice the relative position in the sequence of *'that'* and *'our'* or *'your'* in the whole phrase.)

6 DATIVE PLURAL

Masculine	Nominative singular	Dative singular	Dative plural
animate 'hard'	student	studentovi	studentům
animate 'soft'	muž	muži	mužům
ending in **-a**	kolega	kolegovi	kolegům
inanimate 'hard'	stůl	stolu	stolům
inanimate 'soft'	klíč	klíči	klíčům
Neuter			
'hard'	okno	oknu	oknům
'soft'	srdce	srdci	srdcím
ending in **-í**	nádraží	nádraží	nádražím
Feminine			
'hard'	žena	ženě	ženám
'soft'	kuchyně	kuchyni	kuchyním
i-declension	věc	věci	věcem
náš, váš	náš / naše / naše	našemu / naší / našemu	našim
ten	ten / ta / to	tomu / té / tomu	těm
'Hard' adjective	velký / velká / velké	velkému / velké / velkému	velkým
'Soft' adjective	cizí / cizí / cizí	cizímu / cizí / cizímu	cizím

The great thing about the dative plural is that it always ends in **-m**, though the vowel before it may vary. The table above summarizes what has gone before, but adds the plurals.

7 OTHER DATIVES

For the time being just note the plural dative pronoun forms **vám** and **nám** (*to/for you and us*). The forms **mi** (*to/for me*) and **mu** (*to/for him*), met occasionally in earlier units and in some of the examples above, are also dative. In the dialogue there is the form **tolika**, from **tolik** (*so many*); the other expressions in the same family, e.g. **mnoho** (*many*), **několik** (*several*), **kolik** (*how many*) also attract **-a** in the dative, singular or plural. **Málo** (*little, few*) remains unchanged.

8 'IF'-CLAUSES

The word **jestli** (or **jestliže**) introduces ordinary *if*-clauses. Referring to the future you may also use **když** or **pokud**:

Jestli/Když/Pokud budete mít čas, ...   *If you (will) have time ...*

Jestli is also useful to express the *if* that introduces the indirect version of 'yes-no' questions:

Direct question: Je na dovolené? *Is he on holiday?*

Indirect question: Nevím, jestli je na dovolené. *I don't know if/whether he is on holiday.*

9 *LIDÉ* – 'PEOPLE'

Lidé (*people*) is the plural of **člověk** (*man, person, one*). It is the only masculine **i**-declension noun, hence its dative **lidem** in the dialogue. Its other peculiarity is to have **-é** as the nominative plural ending: **slušní lidé** (*decent people*), although in fairly recent times the once sub-colloquial form **lidi** has been admitted into the colloquial version of the standard language. This form is then nominative, vocative and accusative plural.

10 SAYING 'TIMES'

Adding the little word **krát** to a numeral expresses **kolikrát?** (*how many times?*) something happens, e.g. **dvakrát** (*twice*), **třikrát** (*three times*). Writing it separately, then following it with another numeral gives the multiplication sense: **dva krát sedm je čtrnáct** (2×7 *is 14*), **a krát b je c** ($a \times b = c$).

 Quick vocab

nabízet (**-í**, 3rd pl. **-ejí**) *to offer*
prodávat *to sell*
dárek (dárku) *present*
posílat *to send*
pomocnice (f) *assistant*
volno *time off*
řezník *butcher*
jídlo *food, dish, meal*
hlasovat *to vote*
návrh *suggestion, proposal, motion*

kostel (gen. **-a**) *church*
zavírat *to close, to shut*
vítr (gen. **větru**) *wind*
péče (f) *care*
věřit (+ dat.) *to believe*
důvěřovat (+ dat.) *to trust*
radit (+ dat.) *to advise*
vyhýbat se (+ dat.) *to avoid*
když (+ future) *if*
slušný *decent*

Exercises

1 **Find all the dative forms in the dialogue and try to explain their function.**

2 **Use the reference table (Section 6) and Sections 7 and 9 to supply appropriate forms for the words in brackets:**

a Petr a Jarmila nerozumějí (cizinci).

b Půjdeme k (Věra) na večeři.

c Kvůli (vy) jsme ještě nevečeřeli.

d Starali jsme se (sousedé) o kytky.

e Doporučujeme (sví studenti) měsíční pobyt v Praze.

f Kupuje (sekretářka) suvenýr z cesty.

g (Naši lidé) budou vydávat pasy zítra.

h Proti (hotel) a proti (nádraží) jsou nové obchody.

i Díky (krásné počasí) hrajeme dnes venku.

j Dáváme (studentky) málo cvičení.

k As a supplementary exercise, translate the resulting sentences to make doubly sure you understand them.

3 Many types of phrases involving the dative can come in handy. Put the following into Czech.

a I have to go to the butcher's/the doctor's/my aunt's/to see the professor.

b What have you got against the new proposal/English weather/Czech food/those people/his wife/us?

c It's because of the train/the cars/the customs people/the weather/my watch.

d It was thanks to our friends/the Slovaks/their neighbours/your old dog.

e We couldn't understand Petr/Marie/the old professor/the first word/his long letter (*didn't understand* will normally suffice here).

4 You are in the post office and need to say the following.

a I am sending this letter to a friend in England. How much will it cost?

b Must I go to another window? (**přepážka** in this sense)

c Can you lend (**půjčit**) this lady a biro, please?

d I'm trying to get some Czech stamps (**známka** *stamp*) for my daughter.

e I don't understand these regulations (**předpis** *regulation*).

f Do you close at five or at six?

g Do you have a Prague phonebook? (**telefonní seznam**)

Dialogue 2

The Navrátils are getting ready for some guests.

On	V kolik hodin tu mají být?
Ona	Přece v půl osmé, kolikrát ti to musím říkat?
On	A máš pro ně všechno připravené, všechny dárky, všechno jídlo?
Ona	Ano, dárky jsou v těch krabicích u dveří. Studená jídla jsou na talířích v ledničce. A teplá jsou v kastrolech, budu je dodělávat, až budou všichni tady.
On	A kdo vlastně přijde?

Ona	Smithovi a jejich pražští známí, Novákovi. Zvala jsem taky tvoji sestru, ale ta je někde na cestách.
On	To je celá ona!
Ona	A stále slibuju pozvání svým bratrům. Petrovi jsem to na dnešek vzkázala, ale nevím, jestli je vůbec v Praze. Ondřejovi jsem telefonovala několikrát, ale marně.
On	Škoda! Kdy jsme je všechny viděli naposled?
Ona	Loni o Vánocích, myslím.
On	Takže nás bude šest nebo sedm. Ještěže nemáme děti! Už takhle se sotva vejdeme do tohohle malého bytu!

 Quick vocab

v kolik hodin tu mají být *(at) what time are they due to be here*
přece v půl osmé *(at) half past seven of course*
máš všechno připravené *have you got everything ready*
připravený *ready, prepared*
krabice (f) *box*
u dveří *by the door*
studený *cold*
talíř (m) *plate*
lednička *fridge*
kastrol *(sauce-)pan*
budu je dodělávat, až budou všichni tady *I'll finish making them when everybody's here*
dodělávat *finish doing/making*
až *when* (with future meaning)
všichni *all, everybody*
kdo vlastně přijde *who's actually coming*
přijde (future tense) *will come*
jejich pražští známí *their Prague friends*
známý *friend, acquaintance* (behaves like an adjective)
zvát (zve) *to invite*
je někde na cestách *(she) is travelling somewhere* (Lit. *on trips*)
To je celá ona! *That's just like her! She would be!*
celý *whole*
stále slibuju bratrům *I keep promising my brothers*

stále *all the time, constantly*
pozvání *invitation*
vzkázala jsem to Petrovi *I sent a message to Peter about it*
vzkázat (future **vzkáže**) *to send a message (about something to somebody)*
na dnešek *for today*
dnešek (gen. **dneška**) *today* (as a noun)
nevím, jestli je vůbec v Praze *I don't know if he's even in Prague*
vůbec *at all*
několikrát *several times*
marně *in vain*
Škoda! *Pity!*
kdy jsme je všechny viděli naposled? *when did we last see them all?*
naposled *(for the) last (time)*
loni o Vánocích *last Christmas*
loni *last year*
o Vánocích *at Christmas* (**Vánoce** [pl] = *Christmas*)
takže nás bude šest nebo sedm *so there'll be six or seven of us*
už takhle *as it is*
sotva *hardly*
vejít se (vejde se) *to fit*

11 PLURALS AFTER *V* AND *NA*

The almost universal locative plural ending is **-ch**, but with different vowels before it:

-ách with 'hard' feminine nouns, e.g. **na cestách**

-ech with 'hard' masculine nouns, e.g. **v kastrolech**, also with 'hard' neuters, e.g. **na oknech** (*on the windows*)

-ích with most types of 'soft' nouns, e.g. **v krabicích** (f), **na talířích** (m), also **na polích** (n) (*in the fields*)

The **-ech** ending also occurs with **i**-declension nouns, e.g. **ve věcech** (*in matters*).

Any word ending in **-í**, including 'soft' adjectives, merely adds **-ch**:

na zdejších nádražích   *at the local stations*

'Hard' adjectives also just add **-ch** to the basic form:

na studených talířích   *on cold plates*

Points to watch: masculine nouns that end in **-k**, **-h**, **-g** and **-ch** usually take the ending **-ích** and the final consonants change according to the following pattern:

k → c	stolek	na stolcích	*on the little tables*
h → z	břeh	na březích	*on the (river) banks*
g → z	dialog	v dialozích	*in the dialogues*
ch → š	ořech	v ořeších	*in the nuts*

Neuter nouns ending in **-ko**, e.g. **kolečko** (*little wheel*), usually have **-ách**:

(kufr) na kolečkách   *(suitcase) on (little) wheels*

Náš and **váš** have **našich** and **vašich** for all genders; similarly **ten** has **těch**.

Remember that some other prepositions also require the locative case, hence *o* **bratrech** (*about the brothers*), *po* **hodinách** (*after the lessons*), *po* **zdech** (*all over the walls*), *při* **jeho kvalitách** (*given his qualities*). Note too some semi-idiomatic usages, such as **o** with plurals denoting holidays: **o Vánocích** (*at Christmas*), **o Velikonocích** (*at Easter*), **o prázdninách** (*during the holidays*), or such expressions as **při smyslech** (**smysl** = *sense*) *alert, conscious, with one's wits about one.*

12 OTHER LOCATIVE FORMS

Note the following pronoun forms, remembering that the locative case can never occur without a preposition (see Unit 3, Section 11).

já	**o mně** *about me*	ty	**o tobě** *about you* (familiar)
my	**o nás** *about us*	vy	**o vás** *about you* (polite or plural)
on	**o něm** *about him* or *it* (m)		
ona	**o ní** *about her* or *it* (f)	also:	
ono	**o něm** *about it* (n)	se	**o sobě** *about -self*

	Plural			
Masculine animate	oni		o nich	*about them*
Masculine inanimate	ony			
Feminine	ony			
Neuter	ona			

co?   **o čem?** *about what?*   **kdo?**   **o kom?** *about whom?*

13 EXPRESSING 'ALL'

To say *all* with singular mass names, like **cukr** (*sugar*), **mouka** (*flour*), **voda** (*water*), **kakao** (*cocoa*), the words **všechen**, **všechna**, **všechno** can be used. They have endings like **ten**, **ta**, **to** in the nominative and accusative.

(Vypotřebovali) všechnu mouku.   *(They used up) all the flour.*

Where *all the* means *the whole (quantity of)*, use **celý**:

(Vypotřebovali) celou mouku.   *(They used up) all the (the whole bag of) flour.*

According to the context, the same sentence may also mean *They used up a whole bag of flour*.

The nominative and accusative plural forms of **všechen**, etc., always translate as *all* and combine with countables. These plural forms have similar endings to **ten**, etc.

Note, however, that the nominative masculine animate mark **-i** occurs in both halves of the word. The remaining case forms are based on a shorter stem:

	Sing. masc.	Fem.	Neut.	Plural masc. animate	Masc. inanimate & fem.	Neut.
Nom.	všechen	všechna	všechno	všichni	všechny	všechna
Acc.	všechen	všechnu	všechno	všechny	všechny	všechna
Gen.	všeho	vší	všeho		všech	
Dat.	všemu	vší	všemu		všem	
Loc. (o)	všem	vší	všem		všech	
Inst.*	vším	vší	vším		všemi	

* The instrumental case forms are given here in advance, since this important table will not be repeated later

The neuter plural forms (**všechna**) are limited to written or very high-style spoken Czech. You will regularly hear them replaced by **všechny**.

14 'EVERYTHING' AND 'EVERYBODY'

The most common use of the neuter singular form **všechno** is as the general pronoun *everything*, while the plural form **všichni** means *everybody*, or *we/they/you all*.

Všichni jíme všechno.   *We all eat everything.*

15 *ZNÁMÍ* AND *PŘÁTELÉ* – 'FRIENDS' AND 'ACQUAINTANCES'

Any person you know is a **známý** (feminine = **známá**, plural = **známí**), a word which takes the forms of an adjective. It is a much more common word than the English *acquaintance*, and so is sensibly translated as *friend*, but it does not convey intimate friendship the way **přítel**, **přítelkyně** do. English *friend* therefore stands somewhere between the two.

Máme v Praze přátele.	*We have some good friends in Prague.*
Máme v Praze známé.	*We know some people in Prague.*

> ● **INSIGHT**
>
> The words **přítel** and **přítelkyně** are these days rather 'grand' in the neutral sense of *friend*. In quite recent times their meaning has (largely) narrowed to the sense of *boyfriend* and *girlfriend* and so they are typically preceded by **můj/moje** *my*. This has meant that the once much more colloquial **kamarád/-ka** (*pal, mate*) have taken on a heavier burden than in the past and so their standing has moved up from being simply colloquial to something closer to neutral. The latter have their own sub-colloquial counterparts in **kámoš/-ka**. The next stage up from **přítel/přítelkyně** is **snoubenec/snoubenka** *fiancé(e)*, who may wear a **snubní prsten** or **prstýnek** (*ring*).

16 SAYING 'TODAY'

So far you have used **dnes**, the adverb for *today*. As soon as this word begins to function as a noun, which it does if it has to follow a preposition, you need to replace **dnes** with **dnešek**. Prepositions require individual cases and nouns can show cases, adverbs cannot. Thus **do** + genitive gives **do dneška** (*by/until today*), also **na** + accusative gives: **na dnešek** (*for today*). Note these other 'conversions':

včera (*yesterday*)	**včerejšek** (gen. **včerejška**)
zítra (*tomorrow*)	**zítřek** (gen. **zítřka**)

17 USEFUL WORDS

  a **stále** means *all the time*, but, in combination with the verb, it is equivalent to *keep -ing*.

Stále slibuju.	*I keep promising.*
Stále padá.	*He/She/It keeps falling.*

  b **vůbec** is easy to handle after a negative: it always means *at all*.

Nemám vůbec peníze.	*I've no money at all.*

In positive questions it may also be *at all*.

Budou tam vůbec?	*Are they going to be there at all?*

Or *ever actually*.

Byli jste vůbec v Praze?	*Have you ever actually been to Prague* (with the subtext: *I somehow doubt it*)?

c **přece** is often *surely*.

To je přece Petr! *Surely/Why, that's Peter!*

The same sentence may, however, be a protestation at someone's ignorance, stupidity, forgetfulness, etc.: *It's Peter, silly!* Compare this with the rebuke contained in Mrs Navrátilová's first utterance in the dialogue.

d **takže** means *so* when someone is expressing a consequence of some foregoing facts.

Má rýmu a kašel, takže ven *He's got a cold and a cough, so he's not going out.*
nejde.

Look again at how it occurs in the dialogue.

e **celý** used with personal pronouns.

To je celá ona. *That's just like her/That's her all over.*

You may occasionally direct such gentle criticism towards yourself.

To jsem celý já! *That's me all over! Silly me!*

This last clearly shows how the verb must change according to the person concerned.

 Quick vocab

stolek *small table*	**smysl** *sense*
břeh *bank, shore*	**kakao** *cocoa*
ořech *(wal)nut (nut itself and tree)*	**mouka** *flour*
zeď (f gen. **zdi**) *wall*	**vypotřebovat** *to use up*
kvalita *quality*	**rýma** *a cold*
Velikonoce (pl) *Easter*	**kašel** (gen. **kašle**, i.e. 'soft') *cough*
prázdniny (pl) *holidays*	**při** (+ loc.) *at, by, with, during*

Exercises

5 Respond as suggested to the following enquiries:

  a Kdy budete v Praze? (At Christmas.)
  b Jak ponesete ty věci domů? (In these suitcases.)
  c O kom mluvíte? (We're talking about our neighbours.)
  d Proč jste rádi, že děti už nejsou doma? (Because there's little room in these small flats.)
  e Kde je stávka? (*strike*) (At all the stations.)

6 Replace the words in round brackets by forms appropriate to the context:

 TR 32

Včera o (Petr) mluvili na (konference) velmi pěkně. Všichni říkali, že když byl v (Praha) naposled, česky neuměl, ale teď mluví skoro bez (chyby). Trochu přehánějí, ale pro (většina) (příležitosti) to stačí. Umí v (hospody) objednávat (pivo), v (banka) vyměňovat (peníze) a na (ulice) se ptát na (cesta). Když něco nezná, používá (anglická) nebo (německá slova).

Kdekoli je na (cesty), všude se nakonec domluví, je dost talentovaný a od (zítřek) se bude učit dokonce slovensky.

 Quick vocab

přehánět *to exaggerate*
(-í, 3rd pl. **-její)**
příležitost *occasion*
objednávat *to order*
vyměňovat *to exchange*

dokonce *even*
používat *to use*
kdekoli *wherever*
nakonec *in the end*
talentovaný *talented*

7 Now check your answers to Exercise 6, not by looking at the back of the book, but by listening to the recording (if you have it). This should help you to verify that you are hearing the differences between long and short vowels.

DID YOU KNOW ...

England and Bohemia have twice been linked dynastically. In 1382, Richard II married Anne of Bohemia, granddaughter of the blind King of Bohemia, John of Luxembourg (died 1346 at the Battle of Crecy fighting against Edward II and the Black Prince), daughter of King Charles IV (founder of Prague University) and sister of Wenceslas (Václav) IV. She introduced riding side-saddle for ladies and various other new fashions to England, and she was a patron of Geoffrey Chaucer. On Whit Sunday, 7th June, 1394, Anne died of the plague at her favourite home, Shene Manor in Richmond on Thames, aged only 28. On 9th April the following year, Richard had the manor demolished.

Much later, in 1614, James I's daughter Elizabeth married Frederick of the Palatinate, who, in 1619, briefly became King of Bohemia, until driven out by the Habsburgs in 1620 after the Battle of the White Mountain (**Bílá hora** in Prague), early in the Thirty Years War. This event is sometimes compared for its significance in Czech history to the Battle of Hastings. English pubs formerly called *The Queen of Bohemia* referred to this Elizabeth, also known as the Winter Queen. Her husband Frederick gave rise to several pubs called *The King of Bohemia*, possibly the last of which survived on Hampstead High Street in London until 2005.

Did you also know … that the ancestry of the presidents Bush has been traced back to the earliest Bohemian prince or duke, Bořivoj I. Regrettably, the evidence – once at http://www.genea.cz/ruzne.htm – seems to have disappeared.

 Test yourself

Answer the following questions, following the prompts given.

1 Kdy jste byl naposled v Londýně? (*Last year during the holidays.*)

2 Kde je Praha? (*In Bohemia.*)

3 O čem mluvili o přestávce (*during the break*)? (*About Prague pubs.*)

4 Kdy máte narozeniny? (*After Easter.*)

5 O kom jste mluvili včera? (*About the Czechs and Slovaks and their problems.*)

11 Ve čtvrtek k nám přijde návštěva
We've got visitors coming on Thursday

In this unit you will learn
▶ *How to say more about future events*
▶ *How to compensate for Czech's simple tense system*
▶ *How to say the days of the week*
▶ *How to say the months of the year*
▶ *How to form dates*

Dialogue 1

Mr Navrátil is helping Mr Smith, back in Prague, to plan the week ahead.

 TR 33

Navrátil	Tak zítra je pondělí. Co budete dělat celý den?
Smith	Nejdřív půjdu do banky a vyměním si peníze.
Navrátil	A potom?
Smith	Myslím, že se podívám do nové galerie, o které jsem slyšel. To mi bude stačit na celý den. Někde se tam taky najím.
Navrátil	Chtěl jsem vás jeden den vzít na výlet, ale v úterý musím dát auto do opravny, půjde to tedy až v pátek, až ho dostanu zpátky. Ale co v úterý místo toho?
Smith	Na úterý i na středu mám program. Známí mi totiž nabídli, že mě vezmou někam do hor.
Navrátil	A ve čtvrtek k nám přijde návštěva, které se musím věnovat.
Smith	To přece nevadí. Já se o sebe postarám. Vymyslím si vlastní program a v pátek vám řeknu, jaký byl.
Navrátil	Dobře. Tak v pátek vycestujeme někam spolu. Ale kam?
Smith	Můžeme na Slapy? Slyšel jsem, že je tam hezky.
Navrátil	Samozřejmě, když chcete. Naši známí tam mají novou restauraci. Zkusíme Ji tedy. Můžeme u nich zůstat přes sobotu a neděli. Co vy na to?
Smith	Jsem pro! Takhle si důkladně před návratem odpočinu.

pondělí *Monday*

vyměním si (from **vyměnit si**) **peníze** *I'll change some money*

galerie (f) *(art) gallery*

to mi bude stačit na celý den *that will give me enough to do for the whole day*

najím se (from **najíst se**) *I'll eat, have a meal*

výlet *trip, day out*

(v) úterý *(on) Tuesday*

dát auto do opravny *to take the car to the garage*

dát (dá) *to give, to put*

opravna *repair shop*

půjde to tedy až v pátek *so it will have to wait until (on) Friday*

půjde to *it will go, work* (and similar)

pátek *Friday*

až ho dostanu zpátky *when I get it back*

místo toho *instead (of that)*

místo (+ gen.) *instead of*

na úterý a na středu mám program *I've got things to do for Tuesday and Wednesday*

středa *Wednesday*

nabídli past tense of **nabídnout (nabídne)** *to offer*

vezmou mě do hor *they'll take me to the mountains*

vzít (vezme) *to take*

hora *mountain*

(ve) čtvrtek *(on) Thursday*

věnovat (se) *to devote (oneself)*

to přece nevadí *but that doesn't matter*

vadit (+ dat.) *to matter; to be a nuisance to*

já se o sebe postarám *I'll look after myself*

sebe form of **se** (used after prepositions)

vymyslím si program *I'll think of a programme (for myself)*

vymyslet *to think up*

řeknu vám, jaký byl *I'll tell you what it was (like)*

říct (řekne) *to say, tell*

vycestujeme (from **vycestovat**) *we'll go off, travel out*

spolu *together*

Můžeme na Slapy? *Can we go to Slapy? (a weekend and holiday area by a dam south of Prague)*

je tam hezky *it's nice there*

samozřejmě *of course*

když chcete *if you wish, if you like*

zkusíme (from **zkusit**) *we shall/can try*

můžeme zůstat přes sobotu a neděli *we can stay over the weekend*

zůstat (zůstane) *to stay*

přes (+ acc.) *over, across*

sobota *Saturday*

neděle *Sunday; week*

co vy na to? *what do you say to that?*

jsem pro *I'm in favour*

důkladně *thoroughly*

před návratem *before (my) return*

odpočinu si (from **odpočinout si**) *I'll (have a) rest*

návrat *return*

1 MORE ABOUT EXPRESSING FUTURE EVENTS

In previous units you were advised against trying to use certain verbs in the future because they were not combinable with **budu**, etc., the future auxiliaries. In Dialogue 1 in this unit you have a number of verb forms which are clearly indicated as having future meaning, without any auxiliary: **vyměním si, podívám se, najím se, dám, dostanu, vezmou, přijde, postarám se, udělám, řeknu, vycestujeme, zkusíme, odpočinu si**. These are all verbs in the *perfective aspect*. The difference between this and the *imperfective* which you have used up to now is explained below.

2 WHAT IS 'ASPECT'?

As, say, a house, has different aspects according to how you view it, verbal aspect means the way in which you view the particular act or action. You may view it as ongoing, proceeding before your eyes, or as having been in progress at some time in the past, or due to proceed in the future. This is one use of the imperfective aspect ('imperfective' for short).

Zpívá.	*He is singing.*
Zpíval.	*He was singing.*
Bude zpívat.	*He will (be) sing(ing).*

The *-ing* form in English is a certain guarantee that the Czech equivalent will be imperfective. However, an action can be seen as ongoing, having duration, even if simple English tense forms are used, for example:

Zpíval při práci.	*He sang as he worked.*

The imperfective is also used if an action is expressed as being habitual, or regularly repeated.

Zpívá ve vaně.	*He sings in the bath.*
Zpíval ve vaně.	*He used to sing in the bath.*

And it is used if you are speaking merely about the action per se, or someone's ability to perform it.

Zpíváte?	*Do (or Can) you sing?*
Zpívala krásně.	*She sang beautifully.*

So one form has various functions, and it is the context alone that determines the equivalents in English: **zpíval** is merely the past tense of **zpívat**, but in context may be *he sang, he was singing, he could sing, he used to sing*, and some other possibilities, not to mention the question forms of the same: *did he sing, was he singing* etc.

Using **zpívat**, you have already seen how a verb denotes an *activity* more than an *act*. However, acts may also be ongoing, uncompleted, or indeed repeated processes.

Dělá krabici.	*He is making a box.*
Dělá chyby.	*He makes mistakes.*
Dělal krabici.	*He was making a box.*
Dělal chyby.	*He made/kept making/used to make mistakes.*

It is with acts, as opposed to activities, that the difference from the perfective is clear. With the perfective an act is seen as complete – often as a single or sudden event, and having had to be completed before other acts could follow.

Udělá krabici zítra.	*He'll make the box tomorrow.*
Udělal krabici a pak do ní dal knihy.	*He made the box then put the books in it.*

Very commonly an activity or ongoing process (imperfective) is interrupted by a different (perfective) event.

Večeřeli (impf.)**, když zazvonil** (pfv.) **telefon.**	*They were having dinner when the phone rang.*

According to context, the events could be reversed.

Když zazvonil (pfv.) **telefon, spali** (impfv.).	*When the phone rang they were asleep.*

It follows from all this that things going on simultaneously are expressed in the imperfective (various adverbs and conjunctions will often serve as indicators).

Když zalévala kytky, zpívala. *As (when) she watered the plants she sang.*

Sequences of consecutive events, however, are likely to be in the perfective.

Ráno vstal, umyl se, vyčistil si zuby, *In the morning, he got up, washed, cleaned*
   oblékl se a nasnídal se. *his teeth, got dressed and had his breakfast.*

If, however, the whole sequence is habitual, the imperfective is used:

Vstával v osm, myl se, čistil si *He would get up at eight, wash, clean his*
   zuby … *teeth …*

It also follows, from the above, that you would not normally use the perfective in the present tense. If an act is viewed as completed, either it has to have been completed (prior to the present), or be predicted to be going to be completed (later than the present). Note, though, that English frequently uses its present tense forms with a future meaning, especially after certain conjunctions, as in:

She'll be wearing pink pyjamas when she comes

[clear future]   [present tense form, future meaning]

Bude na sobě mít růžové pyžamo, až přijede.

[**bude mít** imperfective fut. of *have*, **přijede** perfective future of *arrive, come*]

Similarly:

Jestli se nás zeptá, … *If he asks us, …*
Jakmile dočteš noviny, … *As soon as you finish reading the paper, …*

in which **zeptá se** and **dočteš** are perfective future forms; English cannot have said (though foreign learners frequently do): 'If he will ask us…', 'When you will finish…'.

The two most common Czech verbs, **být** and **mít**, are, and only can be, imperfective. You may need to read this section again to grasp the principles of how the aspects are used.

3 HOW ARE ASPECTS FORMED?

Let's start with one of the basic verbs with which you are already familiar – **dělat** = *to make*. This is a typical example of a primary imperfective. It forms its perfective by adding the prefix **u-**.

	Imperfective	Perfective
Infinitive	dělat	udělat
Present	dělá	—
Past	dělal	udělal
Future	bude dělat	udělá

The conjugated form of a perfective verb is the perfective future. You cannot combine *bude*, etc. with a perfective infinitive.

There is no single way of forming perfectives, and each new verb should be learnt with its counterpart. The convention is to learn the imperfective first, followed by the perfective, usually in the form **'dělat/udělat** (*to make*)'; this is called an aspectual pair. You may also see **'dělat/u-'**. The imperfective is the more general in meaning so dictionaries tend to list it first and to include the perfective somewhere else in the entry, or separately.

Examples using other verbs you have met:

číst/přečíst	**pít/vypít**	**mýlit se/zmýlit se**	**ptát se/zeptat se**
mýt/umýt	**psát/napsat**	**dívat se/podívat se**	**zvonit/zazvonit**

None of these require a change of conjugation. If you can say 'I am reading the book' (**čtu**) you can predict 'I shall (have) read the book' (**přečtu**).

A *perfectivizing prefix*, e.g. here **pře-**, **vy-**, **z(e)-**, **u-**, **na-**, **po-**, **za-**, that goes with a particular verb may not be the only one to combine with that verb. So while **psát** uses **na-** as its perfective prefix, and **dělat** uses **u-**, there are also verbs **upsat** *to subscribe (shares)* and **nadělat** *to make a lot of something*. The verbs **psát** and **dělat** have many compounds. Here are some of them.

vypsat	*to write out*	**vydělat**	*to earn*
přepsat	*to rewrite*	**předělat**	*to redo*
připsat	*to add (writing)*	**přidělat**	*to make more* (e.g. cakes)
popsat	*to describe*	**podělat**	*to foul (something up)* (vulg.)

These verbs are all perfective – they represent combinations of an imperfective verb and a prefix (even if this is not the 'merely perfectivizing' prefix). These other prefixes have added considerably to the meaning. This leaves the problem of conveying that changed meaning for the purpose of imperfective contexts, that is, the problem of forming *secondary imperfective* verbs. Here the common method is to add an ending (suffixation), and it is here that a change of conjugation may take place (with compounds of **psát** it does, though not with compounds of **dělat**). The secondary imperfectives of the verbs in the last list are:

vypisovat	**vydělávat**
přepisovat	**předělávat**
připisovat	**přidělávat**
popisovat	**podělávat** (vulg.)

For learning purposes you would meet these as, say:

vypisovat/vypsat (*to write out*)   **předělávat/předělat** (*to redo*)

Verbs in the **i-**conjugation show typically two ways of forming their secondary imperfectives. One can be illustrated from **myslet**:

myslet/pomyslet (*to think*)

vymýšlet/vymyslet (*to think up/out, invent*)

This type typically shows:

    a the same number of syllables in both aspects;

    b different length or quality in the middle syllable (here **ý** and **y**);

    c and usually a different consonant or consonants at the end of the stem (here **šl** and **sl**).

Imperfectives of this kind always have **-ejí/-ějí** in the *they* form, as opposed to **-í**, the normal 3rd person plural ending:

Něco vymyslí.	*He'll think of something.*
Něco vymyslí.	*They'll think of something.*
Něco vymýšlí.	*He's trying to think something up.*
Něco vymýšlejí.	*They're trying to think something up.*

The other main pattern with **i**-class verbs may be illustrated by **měnit/změnit** (*to change*) and its compound **vyměňovat/vyměnit** *to exchange (money)*. Here too there is a change of conjugation: just remember that infinitives ending in **-ovat** conjugate **-uje**.

Kde můžu vyměnit tyto libry?	*Where can I change these pounds?*
Vyměňuje peníze jenom v bance.	*He changes money only in the bank.*

The aspectual pairings of some verbs are not fully predictable. However, if you make it a principle to learn both members together, along with any peculiarities of either member, they should not cause much bother. Here are some of the verbs, most of which you have already met, where you must learn the aspectual pairs:

pomáhat/pomoct	*to help*
říkat/říct (řekne, past řekl)	*to say, tell*
chápat/pochopit	*to grasp, understand*
kupovat/koupit	*to buy*
dávat/dát	*to give; to put*
nabízet/nabídnout	*to offer*
navštěvovat/navštívit	*to visit, attend*
brát (bere)/vzít (vezme, past vzal)	*to take*
krást (krade, past kradl)/ukrást (ukradne, past ukradl)	*to steal*
klást (klade, past kladl)/položit	*to put down, to lay*
překládat/přeložit	*to translate*
odpočívat/odpočinout si	*to have a rest*

Any verbs that you meet from now on will have their aspectual pairings indicated where relevant. Many will have no second member, since if they denote states or positions or activities, as opposed to acts, they cannot be perfectivized: you can merely stop performing an activity, or cease being in such and such a state – you cannot complete it in the way an act or action can be completed.

Now go back over these paragraphs again, just to make sure you understand the principles behind the formation of aspect pairs.

4 DAYS

 Quick vocab

pondělí *Monday*	**pátek** *Friday*
úterý *Tuesday*	**sobota** *Saturday*
středa *Wednesday*	**neděle** *Sunday* (also *week*)
čtvrtek *Thursday*	

Note a peculiarity of **pondělí** (*Monday*) and **úterý** (*Tuesday*): sometimes the names of the days follow prepositions, e.g. **do středy** (*by/until Wednesday*), but **pondělí and úterý** are replaced by the words **pondělek** and **úterek** after prepositions that take cases other than the accusative.

do pondělka	*by/until Monday*
od úterka	*from/since Tuesday*

You saw something similar with the noun forms of **zítra** and **dnes** in a previous unit. Note, too, that all the 'day' words ending in **-ek** have the genitive in **-ka** (except **pátek** which has the normal inanimate genitive ending **-u** – **do pátku** = *by Friday*).

To say *on* such and such a day, use **v** with the accusative:

v pondělí/sobotu   *on Monday/Saturday*

To say *for* such a day (or other period of time) in the sense of intending to spend it, use **na** and the accusative:

Jedeme tam na sobotu/na týden/	*We're going there for Saturday/*
na dva dny.	*a week/two days.*

Notice that with numerals from 5 upwards, the two meanings of **neděle** become more apparent (eg. **pět neděl** = *five weeks*, **pět nedělí** = *five Sundays*). The practice depending entirely on context, no serious ambiguity ever arises.

● INSIGHT

Just as in English we have certain 'special' days, with names of their own, like *Shrove Tuesday*, some of which may be variable (not fixed by the calendar), like a *black Monday*, so too does Czech. Understandably, many are associated with the Church calendar. Thus there is:

Pondělí svatodušní *Whit Monday*; **Pondělí velikonoční** *Easter Monday*; **modré** (*blue*) **pondělí**, any Monday when you elect not to go to work so as to recover from the weekend's excesses;

masopustní úterý *Shrove Tuesday*;

Popeleční středa *Ash Wednesday* (**popel** *ash*); **Škaredá** (*ugly*) **středa**, the Wednesday before Good Friday, known at least in Catholic Ireland as *Spy Wednesday*;

Tučný (*fat*) **čtvrtek** the Thursday following Shrove Tuesday and Ash Wednesday, the second day of Lent; **Zelený čtvrtek** *Maundy Thursday*, the old *Sheer* or *Shere Thursday*, before Good Friday;

Velký pátek *Good Friday*; Friday also figures in several proverbs as not a good day for many reasons, so there is a generalised **černý** (*black*) **pátek**;v

> **Bílá** (*white*) **sobota** *Holy Saturday* (before Easter Sunday); **anglická sobota** *'English' Saturday* was, at the height of Communist rule, a popular aspiration – a Saturday when you didn't/wouldn't have to go to work, or at least finished at lunchtime;
>
> **zlatá** (*gold*) **neděle** the last Sunday before Christmas; **stříbrná** (*silver*) **neděle** the last but one Sunday before Christmas; **Květná neděle** *Palm Sunday* (**květ** *blossom*); **Smrtná neděle** *Care, Judica* or *Passion Sunday*, the fifth in Lent (**smrt** *death*); **Družebná neděle** *Laetare Sunday*, fourth in Lent, hence also, in England, *Mothering Sunday* (**družba** *friendship*); **Křížová** or **Prosebná neděle** *Rogation Sunday* (**kříž** *cross*; **prosba** *request, beseeching*); **železná** (*iron*) **neděle** is a locally or regionally agreed Sunday when the populace may leave outside their homes any large scrap metal items to be collected for recycling. Perhaps unsurprisingly, this is also the name of a Czech heavy metal band.'

5 EATING AND DRINKING: VERBS

a Learn how to conjugate **jíst**. It is partially irregular (though very like **vědět** – see Unit 5, Quick vocab after Dialogue 1).

jím	*I eat*	**jíme**	*we eat*
jíš	*you eat* (i.e. singular, familiar)	**jíte**	*you eat* (i.e. plural or non-familiar)
jí	*he/she/it eats*	**jedí**	*they eat*
Past tense:	**jedl**		

b You need to discriminate between just eating or drinking and eating or drinking something, since each view of the action is perfectivized in different ways. Compare:

Pije mléko.	*He is drinking milk.*
Vypil mléko.	*He drank the milk.*
Pil.	*He was drinking.*
Napil se.	*He had a drink.*
Napil se mléka (gen.!)	*He had a drink of milk.*

Similarly

Jedl brambory.	*He was eating potatoes.*
Snědl brambory.	*He ate the potatoes.*
Jedl.	*He was eating.*
Najedl se.	*He had something to eat.*
Najedl se brambor (gen.!)	*He ate his fill of potatoes.*

c The verbs denoting meals also perfectivize by **na-** (+ **se**).

Quick vocab

snídat/nasnídat se	*to have breakfast*
obědvat/naobědvat se	*to have lunch*
večeřet/navečeřet se	*to dine/eat evening meal*
svačit/nasvačit se	*to have a snack*

d Human eating is expressed by **jíst**, etc. For animals use **žrát (žere)/sežrat (něco)** or **žrát/nažrat se**. Like many animal words, the latter can be applied to humans, but are necessarily insulting or jocular!

6 *AŽ* AND *KDYŽ*: TWO WORDS FOR 'WHEN'

You have already met **až** as a word giving intensity to prepositions. Combined with **v** it means *as late as* or *not until*. Another **až** stands at the beginning of clauses and is followed by the future tense and means *when*, or sometimes *until*:

Až zavolá, pozveme ho na večeři. *When he rings we'll invite him to dinner.*

Počkám tady, až zavolá. *I'll wait here until he phones.*

Both types of **až** occur in the dialogue.

Do not confuse **až** with **když**. **Když** also means *when*, but only in the past tense and present; with the future tense **když** means *if*.

Když jedli, zazvonil telefon. *When/While they were eating, the phone rang.*

Když je ve vaně, zpívá. *When he's in the bath he sings.*

Když přijde, dám mu váš vzkaz. *If he comes I'll give him your message.*

Exercises

1 Find all the verbs in this unit and Unit 10 and begin to make up aspect pairs using the vocabulary lists at the back of the book. (It is a good idea to do this for all the verbs you now know.)

2 The following are a set of predictions. Reformulate them as events that have already happened. For example: 'Budeme sedět v hospodě' becomes 'Seděli jsme v hospodě'. Do not try to change the aspect of the verbs. And think hard about word order!

   a Nabídnou nám výlet do hor.

   b Kde vyměníte peníze?

   c Bude vám to vadit?

   d Nejdřív se podíváme do galerie, potom se najíme.

   e Celý den nebudu dělat nic.

   f Bude pršet.

   g Marie udělá strašnou chybu, když si ho vezme. (**vzít si někoho** = *to marry someone*) (Appreciate the change of meaning in this one.)

   h Budou celý den kupovat suvenýry.

   i V neděli pojedeme domů.

   j Nekoupíte dceři něco k narozeninám?

3 Fill the gaps with appropriate verbs according to the sense; you may need to refer to the glossary:

a Normálně vydělávám 900 dolarů, ale minulý měsíc ____ ____ 975. (As an extra, write out the numerals in full!)

b Celý den kupovali nový gauč, ale nakonec ho ne____.

c Mluví česky velmi dobře, ale včera ____ strašnou chybu.

d Budeme poslouchat rozhlas. Snad ____ nějakou hezkou hudbu.

e Všem rád pomáhal, ale Petrovi ____ nechtěl.

f Až ____ ____, umyju po vás nádobí.

g Jsem strašně unavený, po večeři ____ půjdu od____t.

h Pane Nováku, ř____te mi, kolik je hodin?

i Dlouho jsem nechápal, co chce, až jsem konečně ____.

j N____ ____ v sedm, protože divadlo začíná v osm.

4 You are looking ahead. Tell someone what you plan to do this week (using the guidelines):

(*Monday*) You'll go to the bank where you'll change some pounds, post office where you'll buy stamps, railway station to collect (just say **pro** *for*) your luggage, and you'll spend the afternoon resting.

(*Tuesday*) You'll visit friends in Benešov; they'll bring you back at 7.30.

(*Wednesday*) You'll change your hotel, you'll try the one at the end (**na konci**) of the street; you don't like your room, and at the other hotel you'll have a nice view of the castle. You must not forget (**zapomínat/zapomenout**) to return (**vracet/vrátit**) the key. In the afternoon you will be buying books, but you don't know whether you'll get what you want. You won't have anything to do in the evening.

(*Thursday*) In the morning you'll be at the post office again, you'll wait there until your wife phones – she's in Cyprus on holiday, so you cannot call her (and neither of you uses a mobile!). In the afternoon you want to try at least three good Prague pubs, and in the evening you'll have to rest again.

(*Friday*) If you haven't got a hangover (**kocovina**) you will accept (**přijímat/přijmout** [**přijme**]) Mr Novák's invitation for the weekend and try life in the Bohemian countryside (**na českém venkově**). He has a country cottage. You won't be resting though – you and he will be clearing up (use **čistit**) the garden after the winter.

(*Sunday night*) You'll come back (**vracet se/vrátit se**) to Prague; you want to get a good night's sleep, because on Monday morning you're flying home.

Dialogue 2

Mr Smith has more or less got to grips with the days of the week. He's been having trouble with the months and asks his friend, Mr Navrátil, for help.

Smith Příteli, vysvětlíte mi, jak si mám zapamatovat názvy měsíců?

Navrátil Samozřejmě. Tak v lednu je tu ještě led. V únoru led taje a příroda se vynořuje zpod sněhu. Potom vidíme určitý logický postup, pokud znáte přírodopis: v březnu pučí bříza, v dubnu duby a v květnu už kvete leccos. Červen a červenec vám moc vysvětlit nedovedu, zato v srpnu český člověk asi vytahoval srp a kosil obilí. V říjnu probíhá říje jelenů, která začíná vlastně o měsíc dřív, v září. 'Listopad' se snad vysvětlí sám – padá listí, a v prosinci jsou Vánoce – slovo prosinec sice umím vysvětlit, ale je to moc složité a málo užitečné!

Smith Tak děkuju. Mohl jsem si ušetřit čas: leden a listopad jsou jasné, kvůli ostatním se musím jenom naučit ještě další zbytečná slova.

 Quick vocab

vysvětlovat/vysvětlit *to explain*
pamatovat si/za- *to remember, memorize*
leden (gen. **ledna**) *January*
led *ice*
únor (gen. **února**) *February*
tát/roztát (taje) *to melt*
příroda *nature*
vynořovat se/vynořit se *to emerge*
zpod preposition + gen. *from under*
sníh (gen. **sněhu**) *snow*
určitý *a certain*
logický postup *logical progression*
postup *progression, procedure*
přírodopis *natural history, biology*
březen (gen. **března**) *March*
pučet (-í) *to burst, come into bud*
bříza *birch*
duben (gen. **dubna**) *April*
dub *oak*
květen (gen. **května**) *May*
kvést/vykvést (kvete, past **kvetl)** *to bloom*

leccos *all manner of things*
červen (gen. **června**) *June*
červenec *July*
nedovedu vám vysvětlit *I can't explain to you*
dovést (only perfective, irrespective of tense) *be able, capable*
srpen (gen. **srpna**) *August*
asi *I expect, probably, perhaps*
vytahovat/vytáhnout *to pull out, get out*
srp *sickle*
kosit *to scythe*
obilí *corn*
říjen (gen. **října**) *October*
říje (f) *the rutting season* (!)
jelen *stag*
o měsíc dřív *a month earlier*
dřív *sooner, earlier*
září *September*
'listopad' se snad vysvětlí sám 'listopad' is perhaps self-explanatory
listopad *November*
snad *perhaps, probably*

padat/spadnout *to fall*
listí *leaves, foliage*
prosinec *December*
složitý *complicated*
užitečný *useful*

šetřit/u- *to save, spare*
jasný *bright, plain, obvious*
učit se/na- *to learn*
další (sg.) *another*, (pl) *other, more*
zbytečný *useless, superfluous*

Like Mr Smith you may be selective about the words you take the trouble to learn.

7 THE MONTHS

 TR 35

	LEDEN	ÚNOR	BŘEZEN		ČERVENEC	SRPEN	ZÁŘÍ
P	2 9 16 23 30	6 13 20 27	6 13 20 27	P	3 10 17 24 31	7 14 21 28	4 11 18 25
Ú	3 10 17 24 31	7 14 21 28	7 14 21 28	Ú	4 11 18 25	1 8 15 22 29	5 12 19 26
S	4 11 18 25	1 8 15 22	1 8 15 22 29	S	5 12 19 26	2 9 16 23 30	6 13 20 27
Č	5 12 19 26	2 9 16 23	2 9 16 23 30	Č	6 13 20 27	3 10 17 24 31	7 14 21 28
P	6 13 20 27	3 10 17 24	3 10 17 24 31	P	7 14 21 28	4 11 18 25	1 8 15 22 29
S	7 14 21 28	4 11 18 25	4 11 18 25	S	1 8 15 22 29	5 12 19 26	2 9 16 23 30
N	1 8 15 22 29	5 12 19 26	5 12 19 26	N	2 9 16 23 30	6 13 20 27	3 10 17 24

	DUBEN	KVĚTEN	ČERVEN		ŘÍJEN	LISTOPAD	PROSINEC
P	3 10 17 24	1 8 15 22 29	5 12 19 26	P	2 9 16 23 30	6 13 20 27	4 11 18 25
Ú	4 11 18 25	2 9 16 23 30	6 13 20 27	Ú	3 10 17 24 31	7 14 21 28	5 12 19 26
S	5 12 19 26	3 10 17 24 31	7 14 21 28	S	4 11 18 25	1 8 15 22 29	6 13 20 27
Č	6 13 20 27	4 11 18 25	1 8 15 22 29	Č	5 12 19 26	2 9 16 23 30	7 14 21 28
P	7 14 21 28	5 12 19 26	2 9 16 23 30	P	6 13 20 27	3 10 17 24	1 8 15 22 29
S	1 8 15 22 29	6 13 20 27	3 10 17 24	S	7 14 21 28	4 11 18 25	2 9 16 23 30
N	2 9 16 23 30	7 14 21 28	4 11 18 25	N	1 8 15 22 29	5 12 19 26	3 10 17 24 31

 Quick vocab

leden *January*
únor *February*
březen *March*
duben *April*
květen *May*
červen *June*

červenec *July*
srpen *August*
září *September*
říjen *October*
listopad *November*
prosinec *December*

There are just two rules:

a *In* a month is expressed by **v** with the locative (contrast *on* a day with **v** and the accusative). With the 'hard' masculine words this always ends in **-u**, the 'soft' ones in **-i**, while **září** in effect does not change.

b although inanimate, all the 'hard' names of the months have the genitive in **-a**, except **listopad**.

Like the days, certain months have special, particularly historical, associations, most notably:

únor, adorned by the Communist authorities with the adjective **vítězný** (victorious), refers to February 1948, when the Communists seized power in post-war Czechoslovakia;

březen frequently refers to March in the 'revolutionary year' of 1848, the period known as the 'Spring of Nations';

srpen is frequently used as shorthand for August 1968, when the Soviet Union and its Warsaw Pact allies occupied Czechoslovakia on the 21st;

říjen is also frequently used as shorthand for October 1917, and the Great October Socialist Revolution in Russia;

and **listopad** is used similarly elliptically for November 1989, when the Communist régime in Czechoslovakia was finally ousted.

8 TELLING AND ASKING THE DATE

To ask what the date is you need to combine the genitive singular of **kolikátý** (the how many-eth?) with **být** in the (neuter) singular:

Kolikátého je dnes?	*What's the date today?*
Kolikátého bylo ve čtvrtek?	*What was the date on Thursday?*

To reply, use the appropriate ordinal number with the name of the month, all in the genitive (dates above the 20th usually use the inverted form of ordinal):

Dnes je dvanáctého/dvaadvacátého   *Today is the 12th/22nd of April.*
  (or: **dvacátého druhého**) **dubna.**

To say something happened on such and such a date, use the same form:

Narodil jsem se třetího března.   *I was born on the 3rd of March.*

Dates expressed in figures use the numeral and a full stop:

26. srpna   *26th August*

And to add the year, use either **roku** (abbreviated **r.**) or **v roce** and the appropriate four-digit number, or, for events in the same century, **v roce** with the ordinal numeral between:

v roce (roku) tisíc devět set třicet osm   *in 1938*

and more commonly

v roce (roku) devatenáct set třicet osm

or

v osmatřicátém roce   *in '38*

9 THE SEASONS

| jaro | léto | podzim | zima |
| *spring* | *summer* | *autumn* | *winter* |

 **Quick vocab**

na jaře *in spring*   **na podzim** *in the autumn*
v létě *in summer*   **v zimě** *in winter*

Learn these with care, if only because of their inconsistency!

Compound time expressions, such as *this spring*, *last summer*, are expressed by combinations of the above with **loni** (*last year*) and **letos** (*this year*); **letos na jaře**, **loni v létě**. *Next year* is usually **napřesrok**, but, for example, *next summer* is more commonly expressed by **za rok v létě** or by using the adjective **příští** (*next*): **příští zimu** = *next winter* (accusative as in the time expressions learned earlier). Note that the plural **léta** is commonly used in the sense 'years' (as well as 'summers'):

Byli jsme tam léta   *We were there for years*
   pět let (or **roků)**   *five years*

10 MORE ABOUT TENSE

Aspect is not the only replacement for the English tense system. Another is what happens to tense in clauses following verbs of speaking and verbs of perception. You saw one following a verb of speaking in Dialogue 1:

Nabídli, že mě vezmou   *They offered to take me to the mountains./They*
   do hor.   *offered that they would take me to the mountains.*

There you have **vezmou** (*they **will** take*). At the time, '*they*' had actually said '*we will take*', that is, they used the future perfective. In the reported version of the same offer, all that changes is *we* to *they*: the future tense remains unaltered. Similarly,

Myslela, že manžel má rýmu. *She thought that her husband **had** a cold.*

What she thought at the time (*My husband **has** a cold*) was expressed in the present tense, so this tense stays even in the reported version. Conversely: **Myslela, že manžel měl rýmu** must mean (since her thought now is: **'Manžel měl rýmu'**) *She thought her husband had had a cold.* As an example of a 'verb of perception' causing the same thing compare:

Petr si čistil zuby. *Peter was cleaning his teeth.*

Viděla, jak si Petr čistí zuby. *She saw (how) Peter (was = is) cleaning his teeth.*

Thus you can see that Czech has no need of all the complexities of 'future in the past', 'pluperfect' and other refinements of the English verb system. The Czech learner of English has a much harder time!

The daily newspaper MFDnes.

Exercises

5 Select acceptable answers to the questions from among those suggested (more than one may work).

   a Co jste dělali v sedm hodin? (Seděli jsme v hospodě. / Umyli jsme nádobí. / Četli jsme noviny. / Přečetli jsme noviny. / Šli jsme do divadla.)

   b Umíte rusky? (Neumím, ale učím se. / Neumím, ale naučím se. / Neumím, ale budu se učit. / Umím, rusky jsem se naučil ve škole.)

   c Kdy přijdete domů? (Celou noc. / V půl dvanácté. / Hned po představení. / Až zavoláš. / Dokud ji nekoupí. / Z nádraží. / Pátého ledna. / Zítra večer, jestli se nemýlím. / Na dvě hodiny.)

   d Kde jsou klíče? (V září. / Nevím. / Na televizoru. / Byly v téhle kapse. / Zůstaly v kanceláři. / Klíče si vzal Petr. / Které? / Leží u dveří. / Zapomenu.)

   e Jak dlouho budete v Praze? (Čtyři dny. / Dokud budou stačit peníze. / Ve dvě hodiny. / Dvě hodiny. / V červnu. / Celý příští měsíc. / Dokud nám nenapíšeš, že se máme vrátit. / Zítra večer. / Do čtvrtka. / Do března.)

Go back over these questions and satisfy yourself that you have really understood each alternative in each question. It is a good idea to re-read the section on aspects and the various types of time expression (some came earlier than this unit), have a break of at least half an hour, and then re-do all this unit's exercises as revision.

SOME EDUCATIONAL HISTORY

▶ The first university in Central Europe was founded at Prague, in 1348.

▶ The first grammar school in the Habsburg monarchy was founded in Prague, in 1556.

▶ The first civilian technical college in the world was founded in Prague, in 1707.

▶ The world's first college of mining was founded in Jáchymov (N. Bohemia) in 1716.

▶ The great Czech educational reformer, Jan Ámos Komenský
(28 March 1592–15 November 1670), known in English as (John Amos) Comenius, having arrived in England in 1641 at the invitation of Parliament in order to help reform the English education system, was also invited to become President of the then recently founded Harvard University, the first in the USA. (Nothing came of it, however.)

Test yourself

Answer the questions using the guidelines.

a Kdy tam budete? (On Wednesday, on Sunday evening, in June, at five o'clock, next summer, on Friday, at exactly half past seven, in February, on Tuesday, this evening, in November, on the twelfth)

b Jak dlouho jste byli v Praze? (all week, a whole week, five days, three months, the whole of June, all winter, a fortnight (say 'fourteen days'), only twelve hours)

12 Děti do školy vodí manželka
It's my wife who takes the children to school

In this unit you will learn

▶ *How to talk about the most crucial types of movement: coming and going, carrying and chasing, flying and running, to and from, in and out*

▶ *How to say what things look like*

▶ *How to express the means of doing something*

Dialogue 1

Mr Navrátil is asking about the Smiths' routine at home.

 TR 37

Navrátil	Řekněte mi, jak u vás vypadá normální týden.
Smith	My oba pracujeme a děti jsou ve škole. Ráno je vodí do školy manželka, protože já odjíždím dřív. Zato večer pro ně jezdím já.
Navrátil	Nemůžou děti chodit do školy samy?
Smith	Ještě ne, jsou moc malé.
Navrátil	A jinak?
Smith	No, a večer vždycky debatujeme o tom, kdo bude muset zajít druhý den pro chleba a přinést ho nebo zajet třeba za babičkou a dědečkem. Tchyně je totiž v důchodu, nemůže chodit a někdo jí musí vynést smetí nebo ji odvézt k doktorovi a podobně. Tchán je také starý a slabý. Však to znáte.
Navrátil	Ano, u nás to vypadá podobně. Jenže my si tyto věci nepřipravujeme předem jako vy. Když přecházím naši ulici, nikdy nevím, co bude třeba: například rozvážet děti po kamarádech, zavézt ženu ke kadeřníkovi, dojít pro rohlíky nebo maso, nebo jestli si budu moct v klidu číst noviny.
Smith	Tak je to v podstatě všude stejné.

Quick vocab

jak u vás vypadá normální týden? *what's a normal week like in your house?*

týden (gen. **týdne**) *week*

vypadat (+ adverb) *to look, appear, be like*

odjíždět (3rd pl. **-ějí**)/**odjet** *to leave (by vehicle)*

pro ně jezdím *I fetch them (by car) (= 'I go for them')*

je *them* (**ně** *after a preposition*)

a jinak *and apart from that*

jinak *otherwise*

debatovat o něčem *discuss, debate something*

zacházet (3rd pl. **-ejí**)/**zajít** *to pop (on foot)*

druhý den *next day*

chleba (colloquial for **chléb**) (gen. **chleba**) *bread*

přinášet (3rd pl. **-ejí**)/**přinést** *to bring*

zajíždět (3rd pl. **-ějí**)/**zajet** *to pop (by car)*

třeba *say, for instance*

za babičkou *to see Grandma*

za (preposition + instrumental) *behind, beyond* (also used with verbs denoting *to go/come to see someone*)

babička *grandmother*

dědeček *grandfather*

tchyně je v důchodu *mother-in-law is retired*

tchyně *mother-in-law*

důchod *pension*

jí *dative of* **ona** *for her*

vynášet (3rd pl. **-ejí**)/**vynést** *to bring/take/carry out*

smetí *rubbish*

ji (acc.) *her*

odvážet (3rd pl. **-ejí**)/**odvézt** *to drive, take (away) (by vehicle)*

tchán *father-in-law*

však to znáte! *You know how it is! (idiom)*

jenže *except that*

připravovat/připravit (si) *to prepare*

předem *in advance*

jako vy *like you*

přecházet (3rd pl. **-ejí**)/**přejít** *to cross (on foot)*

třeba *necessary*

například *for example*

rozvážet (3rd pl. **-ejí**) **+ po** (+ loc.) *to take to various places (by vehicle)*

kamarád *friend*

zavézt *to take/drop (someone/something somewhere) (impfv. rare; use* **vézt**)

kadeřník *(ladies') hairdresser*

docházet (3rd pl. **-ejí**)/**dojít** *to go (so far) to get*

rohlík *bread roll*

maso *meat*

v klidu si číst *to read in peace*

klid *peace (and quiet)*

v podstatě *basically*

podstata *essence*

je to všude stejné *it's the same everywhere*

1 VERBS OF MOTION

These include fetching and carrying, coming and going, popping and dropping.

a In Unit 9 you were introduced to the 'verbs of motion'. Their main feature was their ability to distinguish between single and repeated, or targeted or random motion. They also discriminated between movement on foot or by vehicle: **jít+chodit** (*to go/walk*), but **jet+jezdit** (*to go/ride/travel/drive*), **nést+nosit** (*to carry – on foot*), but **vézt+vozit** (*to carry/take/convey – by vehicle*). If you are in any doubt about any of this, go back and look again.

The single-event (determinate) members of these pairs have one set of present-tense forms, e.g. **jdu** (*I am going*), one set of future-tense forms, e.g. **půjdu** (*I will go*), and one set of past tense forms, e.g. **šel jsem** (*I went* or *I was going*). Nothing has changed now that you have learnt about aspect: the primary verbs of motion stand outside the aspect system.

The indeterminate members of the pairs, e.g. **chodit** *to go (regularly)*, are by their very meaning imperfective, though rare perfectives may be formed from them for certain highly specialized meanings.

b Jít, nést and other determinate, durative verbs of motion attract a very wide range of prefixes. This process produces new perfective verbs in the sense in which you met them in Unit 11. The corresponding new secondary imperfectives are based on, but are not the same as, the basic indeterminate verbs of motion. Thus from **jít+chodit** there are:

 Quick vocab

procházet/projít *to go through*
přecházet/přejít *to go across, to cross*
vycházet/vyjít *to go out, to come out*
odcházet/odejít *to go away, to leave*
přicházet/přijít *to come, to arrive*
vcházet/vejít *to come or go in, to enter*
zacházet/zajít *to pop in; to go too far*
předcházet/předejít *to go before, to precede*

docházet/dojít *to go so far; to run out*
scházet/sejít *to go down, to be in decline*
scházet se/sejít se *to meet*
rozcházet se/rozejít se *to split up, to part*
ucházet/ujít *to get away, to escape, to leak*
nacházet/najít *to come upon, to find*
procházet se/projít se *to go for a walk*
obcházet/obejít *to go round, circumvent*

And some other rarer items. There are others of one aspect only:

pocházet	*to come/hail from*
ucházet se (+ **o** + acc.)	*to apply, be a candidate – for something*
scházet	*to be lacking*
zacházet (+ **s** + instrumental)	*to treat, to handle*
pojít (pfv.)	*to die – of animals*
obejít se (+ **bez** + gen.) (pfv.)	*to do without*
vejít se (pfv.)	*to fit*

These lists, which you are not expected to learn immediately, illustrate compounds of **jít** and introduce you to almost all Czech prefixes. The meanings of the prefixes in the first part of the list are practically constant, that is, you will soon come to recognize their contribution to the meaning of other prefixed verbs you may meet in future.

c Now that you can recognize the relationship between **chodit** and secondary imperfectives ending in **-cházet**, study these mutations of the other verbs of motion. The second column shows the form of their secondary imperfectives attached to the relevant prefixes.

from			
	jet + jezdit	**-jíždět**	*go by vehicle*
	nést + nosit	**-nášet**	*carry in the hand*
	vést + vodit	**-vádět**	*lead by the hand*
	vézt + vozit	**-vážet**	*carry, convey by vehicle*
	hnát + honit	**-hánět**	*chase, drive*
	táhnout + tahat	**-tahovat**	*pull*

The verbs **běžet+běhat** (*run*) and **letět+létat** (*fly*) are slightly more special. **Běžet** never takes prefixes itself; prefixed perfectives are based on **-běhnout** with secondary imperfectives ending in **-bíhat**, while **letět** can take some prefixes, though with others it is replaced by **-létnout**, with secondary imperfectives ending in **-létat**, **-létávat** or **-lítat**.

	vybíhat/vyběhnout	to run out
	vylét(áv)at/vyletět	to fly out
but	vzlétnout (pfv.)	to fly up, to take off

Exercises 1 and 2 on the next page will help you to learn these. (A limited selection of (mostly perfective) compounds appears in Dialogue 1; go back and take another look at them without referring to the **Quick vocab**.)

2 'THAT LOOKS GOOD'

Clearly in this sentence, *look* has nothing to do with *see*, but is closer to *appear*. In Czech, the verb **vypadat** (*to appear*) must usually be followed by an adverb:

To vypadá dobře/ošklivě/ modře.	*It looks good/ugly/blue.*

These adverbs are from the adjectives **dobrý** (*good*), **ošklivý** (*ugly, awful*), **modrý** (*blue*). **Vypadat** can be used very generally, as in:

Vypadá to špatně.	*Things are looking bad.*

and you can use it of people:

Miloš vypadá mladě.	*Miloš looks young.*

Accordingly, to ask what something is like or looks like, or how it appears, use the adverb **jak** (*how*):

Jak to vypadalo?	*What did it look like?/How was it?*

To say '*x looks like y*', again use **vypadat**, but with **jako** (*like, as*), but only for actual resemblance.

Petr vypadá jako fotbalista.	*Peter looks like a footballer.*

For the impersonal 'it looks like' in the sense 'it looks as if it was x (who did it)', or 'it looks as if y will happen', use **vypadat** with **to** as dummy subject (+ **na** + accusative).

Vypadá to na déšť.	*It looks like rain (rain seems probable).*
Vypadá to na Petra.	*It looks like Peter (Peter seems to be the likely culprit or victim).*
Vypadalo to na porážku.	*It was looking like defeat.*

Finally, to say 'it looks as if ...', use **vypadat** followed by a clause with **že**:

Vypadá (to), že nepřijde.	*It looks as if he isn't coming.*
Vypadalo (to), že nejsou doma.	*It looked as if they weren't in.*

With this type the dummy subject **to** is often omitted.

3 THE ODD THING ABOUT 'BREAD'

The word for *bread* is **chléb**, but you will hardly ever hear it. Its genitive case is **chleba**, and this form is widely used in the accusative and even in the nominative. This does not mean any change of gender:

Tenhle chleba nevypadá moc čerstvě.   *This bread doesn't look very fresh.*

In other respects it is an ordinary 'hard' inanimate masculine noun. The only other word that sometimes shows a similar oddity is **sýr/sýra** (*cheese*).

Exercises

1 **Guess the meaning of the following verbs. State their aspect and provide the other aspect form:**

a	přinášet	**e**	protahovat	**h**	přejet
b	proletět	**f**	přiběhnout	**i**	vyvádět
c	přenést	**g**	odvážet	**j**	odehnat
d	vyjíždět				

2 **Using appropriate primary or secondary verbs of motion, offer the following excuses or explanations:**

a We flew too far so we arrived at the airport late.

b Somebody took my suitcase away.

c Jana isn't at home because she is delivering newspapers.

d They dragged the box into the other room.

e They were just (**právě**) leaving when the phone rang.

f A van (**dodávka**) has just delivered the bread.

g We shall drive round the town. We don't like driving in foreign cities.

h She usually (**obvykle**) comes at six, but today she didn't arrive until seven.

i He ran across the street.

j Mr Navrátil came out of the house, looked at the sky (**nebe**, n; or **obloha**), thought it looked like rain, and went back inside (**dovnitř**) to fetch his coat.

3 **Translate the following into Czech:**

a He is looking well.

b She looks well.

c He looks like Napoleon.

d Cotton wool (**vata**) looks like snow.

e It (e.g. referring to cotton wool) looks like snow.

f It (the weather prospect) looks like snow.

g He is looking out of the window.

h She didn't look like coming. (Careful!)

i She looks English.

j You looked awful.

Dialogue 2

Paní Navrátilová is at the hairdresser's, complaining about the ways of the world, in particular **zločinnost** (*the crime rate*).

 TR 38

Navrátilová	Před týdnem jsem řekla naší Janě, že nemá nechávat kolo před domem. Někdo ho může ukrást.
Irena	Náš Petr měl kolo vzadu za kůlnou, a stejně mu ho někdo vzal.
Olga	A naše sousedka nedávno nechala kočárek s nákupem pod stříškou před řeznictvím a přišla o dva chleby a brambory – já nákup nosím vždycky s sebou.
Navrátilová	Já taky. Mezi námi, vaše sousedka se nesmí divit. Mezi dnešní mládeží je taková zločinnost, že musíte všechno pořád hlídat.
Irena	Mládež nemůže za všechno – mezi dospělými je určitě víc drobných zločinců, i horších. Vaše sousedka může být ráda, že jí nevzali mimino. Někdo asi nad ním držel ochrannou ruku.
Olga	Můj manžel byl jednou svědkem takového pokusu o únos. Odehnal únosce holí a jedna paní se do něho pustila kabelkou. A dítě spalo v kočárku dál.

A dítě spalo v kočárku dál

 Quick vocab

před týdnem *a week ago*
před *before, in front of, ago*
nechávat/nechat *to leave; to let*
kolo *wheel; bicycle*
vzadu *at the back*
za kůlnou *behind the shed*
za *behind, beyond, on the far side of*
kůlna *shed*
stejně mu ho někdo vzal *someone took it (from him) anyway*
stejně *anyway, as it is/was*
mu dative of on *here, from him*
kočárek s nákupem *(her) pram with the shopping*
s *with*

nákup *shopping*
pod stříškou *under the awning*
pod *under, beneath, below*
stříška *awning, shelter*, diminutive of
    střecha *roof*
před řeznictvím *outside the butcher's*
řeznictví *butcher's shop*
s sebou *here, with me*
sebou instrumental of **se**
mezi námi *between you and me, between/ among us*
mezi *between, among*
divit se (+ dat.) *to be surprised (at something)*
dnešní mládež *the youth of today*
dnešní adjective from **dnes**

mládež (f singular) *youth, young people*

taková zločinnost *so much crime*

hlídat *to guard, to watch over*

pořád *all the time*

mládež nemůže za všechno *young people can't answer for everything*

dospělý *adult* (noun and adjective)

víc drobných zločinců *more petty criminals*

drobný *small, tiny, petty*

horší *worse*

mimino *baby*

někdo asi nad ním držel ochrannou ruku *someone must have been holding a protective hand over it*

nad ním *over it*

nad *over, above*

držet *to hold*

ochranný *protective* (from **ochrana** *protection*)

být svědkem (+ gen.) *be witness (to)*

svědek *witness*

takový pokus o únos *an attempted kidnapping like that*

takový *such, like that, of that kind*

pokus (+ **o** + acc.) *attempt (at); experiment*

únos *kidnapping*

únosce (m) *kidnapper*

odhánět/odehnat *drive away*

holí (from **hůl** f) *with his stick*

pouštět se/pustit se (+ **do** + gen.) *to set about, have a go at*

kabelkou (from **kabelka**) *with her handbag*

dítě spalo dál *the child (just) kept on sleeping*

nemá nechávat kolo před domem *she shouldn't leave her bike outside the house*

přicházet/přijít + **o** + acc. *to lose (through no fault of one's own)*

4 'BY (MEANS OF)': THE INSTRUMENTAL CASE

In Dialogue 2, Olga's husband used his stick and another woman her handbag to lay about the kidnapper. The two items were the instruments used in the protection of the baby. Similarly you write *in, with* or *by means of* a biro, **pen** or **pencil**. And if a plate (**talíř**) breaks by falling (**pád** = *a fall*) on the floor, the fall is what is instrumental in the breakage. These ideas are conveyed in Czech by the last case for you to learn, the instrumental case.

Píšu perem. *I write with a pen.*

Talíř se rozbil pádem na zem. *The plate broke by falling on the floor.*

The forms of the instrumental case are almost all represented in the dialogue, and the following table summarizes them:

		Singular		Plural
'Hard' masculine and neuters	**-em**	domem, kolem	**-y**	domy, koly
'Soft' masculine and neuters	**-em**	klíčem, mořem	**-i**	klíči, moři
Masculine nouns in **-a**	**-ou**	fotbalistou	**-y**	fotbalisty
Feminine nouns in **-a**	**-ou**	kabelkou	**-ami**	kabelkami
Neuter nouns in -í	**-ím**	zelím	**-ími**	zelími
paní	**-í**	paní	**-ími**	paními
'Soft' feminines	**-í**	lekcí	**-emi**	lekcemi
i-declension nouns	**-í**	věcí	**-mi**	věcmi; lidmi

Adjectives and pronouns	Singular masc. and neut.	Singular fem.	Plural
'Hard' adjective	malým	malou	malými
'Soft' adjective	cizím	cizí	cizími
ten	tím	tou	těmi
3rd person pronouns	jím	jí	jimi
náš/váš	naším	naší	našimi
všechen	vším	vší	všemi

Study the tables and note the different endings.

Other pronouns

kdo	**kým**
co	**čím**
já/my	**mnou/námi**
ty/vy	**tebou/vámi**
se	**sebou**

5 NON-INSTRUMENTAL USES

The instrumental case and its forms exist for all nouns and related classes of words because the case has several non-instrumental uses.

a It is used after five prepositions denoting place:

před *in front of, outside, in someone's presence; ago*

Stojí před Petrem.	*He is standing in front of Peter.*
Mléko je přede dveřmi.	*The milk's outside the door.*
Před dětmi jsme opatrní.	*We're careful in the presence of the children.*
Zemřel před rokem.	*He died a year ago.*

Note the addition of **-e** before an awkward group of consonants.

za *behind, beyond, on the far side of*

Stojí za Petrem.	*He's standing behind Peter.*
Francie je za mořem.	*France is beyond the sea.*
Hotel je za řekou.	*The hotel is on the far side of the river.*

pod *under, beneath, below*

Stáli pod stromem.	*They stood under/beneath a tree.*
Metro je pod zemí.	*The underground is under the ground.*

nad *over, above*

Nad postelí je obraz.	*There's a picture over the bed.*
Výledek je nad průměrem.	*The result is above average.*

mezi *between, among*

Byl sám mezi ženami.	*He was alone among the women.*
Mezi nebem a zemí.	*Between heaven and earth.*

Place versus motion

Remember how in Unit 4, Section 10, you met some oppositions between expressions of place or position and motion towards the same place. Here, note that all five of the above prepositions combine also with the accusative case after verbs expressing motion in the direction of the positions they denote:

Postavil pivo před Petra.	*He put the beer down in front of Peter.*
Slunce zašlo za mrak.	*The sun went behind a cloud.*
Kopl bačkory pod postel.	*He kicked his slippers under the bed.*
Dal obraz nad postel.	*He put the picture over the bed.*
Kniha spadla mezi radiátor a zeď.	*The book fell between the radiator and the wall.*

Another preposition, **s** (*with*), also takes the instrumental case. It is used to mean *accompanying, together with*, not to be confused with the true instrumental *with*.

Praštila zloděje kabelkou.	*She bashed the thief with her handbag.*
Seděla tam s kabelkou.	*She was sitting there with her handbag.*
Seděl tam s manželkou.	*He was sitting there with his wife.*

In this instance, motion is usually expressed by **k** + dative.

Dala klíče ke kabelce.	*She put her keys with her handbag.*
Sedl si k manželce.	*He sat down with (next to) his wife.*

    b The instrumental case is used after a number of verbs, especially those denoting abrupt or conspicuous movement.

Když zvedal židli, hnul stolem.	*As he lifted the chair he moved the table.*
Pes mává ocasem.	*A dog wags his tail.*
Kývla hlavou.	*She nodded (her head).*
Rána zatřásla celým domem.	*The bang shook the whole house.*

but also:

Pohrdla nabídkou.	*She scorned the offer.*
Opovrhuje jimi.	*He despises them.*

It regularly expresses means or modes of travelling.

Jeli tam vlakem/tramvají/ autobusem.	*They went by train/tram/bus.*
Poletíme vrtulníkem.	*We shall fly by helicopter.*
Dostaneme se tam jenom lodí.	*We can only get there by boat.*
jet krokem	*to move at a walking pace*
jet hledmýždím tempem	*to move at a snail's pace*
jezdit (auto)stopem	*to hitchhike*

And it may convey the route or direction along which an action (viewed very broadly) takes place:

Prošli jsme branou.	*We went through the gate.*
Dívá se oknem.	*She is looking through the window.*
Šli jsme lesem.	*We went through the forest.*
Temže teče Londýnem.	*The Thames flows through London.*

This type of instrumental answers questions beginning **kudy** (which way?): **Kudy jste šli** *(Which way did you come/go)?* **Lesem** *(Via/through the woods).*

    c A special use of the instrumental is after the verb **stávat se/stát se** *(to become).* What you become goes into the instrumental:

Stává se docela dobrým básníkem.	*He's becoming quite a good poet.*
Stal se presidentem.	*He became president.*

A subtler matter is the related use after **být**. If you describe someone as, say, a teacher, or another calling, good style puts it in the instrumental.

Je učitelkou.	*She is a teacher.*
Byl instalatérem.	*He was a plumber.*

However, in spoken Czech, you can keep to the nominative. The normal way of asking after a person's profession is to use the instrumental of **co**: **Čím je?** *(What is he?)*

Nobody is born a teacher or plumber. These phrases describe an acquired, non-permanent or relative state and as such require the instrumental case. This is why it is often used in adjective + noun phrases: Petr may be a Czech, if that is what he was born, but there is no certainty that he is a *good* Czech. The permanent quality of being a Czech will always use the nominative whereas the relative quality of being a good Czech will use the instrumental.

Petr je Čech.   **Petr je dobrým Čechem.**

In some instances the instrumental use, even in speech, has become almost a formula, as in **byl svědkem** in the dialogue, or in the idiomatic **Být vámi/jim ...** *(If I were you/he ...)* (which I could never be in reality).

    d Many instrumental forms of what are or have been ordinary nouns have become adverbs or prepositions. The list below gives some of the more common ones:

 Quick vocab

Adverbs

kolem *by, past*	**většinou** *mostly*
honem *in a hurry, at once*	**právem** *rightly*
předem *in advance; by the front way*	**neprávem** *wrongly*
zadem *by the back way*	**omylem** *by mistake*
cestou *on the way*	**dnem a nocí** *by day and night*
stranou *aside, to one side*	**zuby nehty** *by tooth and nail*

Prepositions (all taking the genitive)

kolem *past, round*	**pomocí** *by means of*
během *during*	**prostřednictvím** *through (someone)*
následkem *in consequence of*	**vlivem** *due to*
vinou *owing to*	**jménem** *in the name of*

Yet others enter into whole idioms, such as **zemřít hlady** *(to die of hunger)*, **pukat smíchy** *(to split one's sides laughing)*, **krčit rameny** *(to shrug one's shoulders).*

pád *fall; (grammatical)* case
fotbalista *footballer*
instalatér *plumber*
básník *poet*
zloděj *thief*
pero *pen*
vrtulník *helicopter*
nehet (gen. **nehtu**) *(finger, toe) nail*
hlemýžď (m) *snail*
metro *underground railway*
mrak *(dark) cloud*
les (gen. **lesa**) *forest, wood(s)*
brána *gate(way)*
řeka *river*
země (f) *ground, earth, soil*
na zem *to the ground*
postel (f 'soft') *bed*
krok *(foot)step, pace, stride*
autostop *hitchhiking*
hon *hunt(ing), chase*
běh *run(ning)*
hlad *hunger*
smích *laughter*

rameno *shoulder*
strana *side, page; party*
výsledek *result, outcome*
následek *consequence*
vliv *influence, effect*
průměr *average*
omyl *error*
právo *right*
prostřednictví *mediation*
vina *guilt, blame*
ocas *tail*
opatrný *careful, cautious*
pohrdat/pohrdnout *to scorn, disdain*
opovrhovat *to despise*
praštit (pfv. only) *to bash, thump, hit*
krčit/po- *to shrug*
třást/za- *to shake*
mávat/za- *to wave, wag*
zvedat/zvednout *to lift*
hýbat (hýbe)/hnout (past **hnul**) *to move*
kopat (kope)/kopnout *to kick*
kývat/kývnout *to nod; to swing from side to side*
pukat/puknout *to burst*

Notice the last group of verbs, which are fairly representative of a type of aspect pairing not met in the last unit. The perfectives ending in **-nout** tend to denote a single, near-instantaneous action. Sometimes they stand in opposition to other perfectives denoting a composite action:

zamávat	*to wave* – giving several part-waves, as in waving good-bye
mávnout	*to wave/wag once*, as with a dismissive hand gesture

From **ťukat** (*to tap* – at a door, on a keyboard)

zaťukat	*to knock* at the door, involving several raps
ťuknout	*to tap once*, perhaps on a single key on a keyboard

Many verbs in this class describe noises:

bouchat/bouchnout	*to bang, slam; to explode*
pípat/za- or pípnout	*to tweet*

● INSIGHT

To help you remember the details of the instrumental case – some worthwhile facts:

▶ all masculines and neuters, except the masculines in -**a**, end in **-em** in the singular; even the long **-í** neuters end finally in **-m**;

▶ all masculines and feminines that end in -**a** take the ending **-ou**;

▶ most plurals across the genders and word classes end in **-mi**; the vowels (where applicable) that precede it should be fairly predictable; take care with the basic masculine and neuter instrumental plurals which alone do not end in **-mi**.

And to help you spot other instrumental plural endings overheard in the street:

In the sub-standard variants of Czech, notably Common Czech (see Unit 5, Section 9, Insight), what has evolved is a universal instrumental plural ending **-ma**, with sundry vowels (or none) before it, so the matching forms to the words given as examples in Section 4 above are: **domama, kolama, klíčema, mořema, fotbalistama, kabelkama, zelíma, paníma, lekcema, věcma, lidma, malejma, cizejma, těma, jima, našima, všema, náma, váma**. Do not yourself try to imitate this, as it represents part of the distinctive grammar of Common Czech (you can see from **malejma** that the ending alone isn't the whole story), and without knowing the rest of the grammar to match you could sound like a foreigner trying to speak Cockney but knowing only about dropped aitches..

Exercises

🔊 **TR 39**

4 Explain how you have arrived somewhere (answer using complete sentences):

a	by train;	**g**	through the town;
b	by plane;	**h**	using Čedok (the Czech
c	by car;		national travel agency);
d	by bus;	**i**	by hitchhiking;
e	on the underground;	**j**	by cab;
f	through the woods;	**k**	by the main gateway

5 Fill in the gaps using the words suggested in the right form:

a Poznámky píšu (pero), ale dopisy píšu na (počítač).

b Nerad jezdí na dovolenou s (rodiče).

c Debatuje s (partner) o (nový podnik).

d Před (my) je krásný výhled na (hrad).

e Máme před (se) velmi dobré perspektivy.

f Řeka pod (most) je velmi špinavá.

g Nemůžu přijet (auto), protože je v (opravna).

h Kdo stojí za (ty)?

i Rozdíl (*difference*) mezi (pes) a (vlk) není velký.

j Před (válka) bydleli ve městě, dnes mají (dům) na (venkov).

6 Now translate all the above sentences.

DID YOU KNOW ...?

That the ancient mining town of Jáchymov in North Bohemia gave us the word *dollar*? The town, Joachimsthal in German, produced a famous silver coin, the **Joachimsthaler groš** (or **Groschen**). The name became shortened to **Joachimsthaler**, then to **Thaler**, which gave rise to the Czech form **tolar**; which then passed into various languages in various forms including **dollar**. Other words which English owes to the Czech language or environment include *camellia*, *pistol*, *polka*, *robot* and *Semtex*; also numerous terms in the sciences, most of all mineralogy.

Test yourself

Using the verb dávat/dát (*to put***) make up sentences along the lines: (Mary) (present) (keys) in (handbag) = Marie dává klíče do kabelky.**

- **a** (Footballer) (past pfv.) (shirt) on (bed)
- **b** (I) (future pfv.) (money) with (passport)
- **c** (She) (past pfv.) (shopping) in (pram)
- **d** (Teacher) (past pfv.) (dictionary) among (the others)
- **e** (We) (past impfv.) (dustbins) outside (the house)
- **f** (Plumber) (present) (new pipe) behind (bath)
- **g** (He) (past pfv.) (books) from (table) onto (chair)
- **h** (They) must (infinitive) (china) into (boxes) (carefully)
- **i** Why (you) (past pfv.) (those letters) on (the floor)?

Quick vocab
popelnice *dustbin*
porcelán *china*
trubka *pipe*

13 *Prší!*
It's raining!

In this unit you will learn
- ▶ *How to read consecutive prose*
- ▶ *How to talk about the weather*
- ▶ *How to use personal pronouns*
- ▶ *How to say 'before' and 'after'*
- ▶ *How to form more expressions for telling the time*
- ▶ *How to express alternatives*

Text

🔊 **TR 40**

Podzimní deště táhly přes Prahu. Věže svatého Víta páraly nízká oblaka, vítr se jich chápal, rozháněl a obnažoval tu a tam hlubokou modř oblohy, vždycky jen cíp. Čeřil hladinu Vltavy mezi mosty a loďky trpělivých rybářů se houpaly na kalné vodě.

Jan Trázník se vracel po Palackého mostě z kanceláře, která hlučela od rána nervózním přebíháním úředníků. Někudy do ní vběhla zpráva o ministerské radě, jež se usnesla na nové restrikci úřednictva instituce, jejíž zbytek se měl přičlenit k ministerstvu, běžela od ucha k uchu, lidé odkládali pera, pletli si písmena na psacích strojích a nechávali vystydnout párky, které jim přinášel sluha.

Otcové rodin těšili svobodné kolegy a radovali se skrytě z myšlenky, že rodina, základ státu, nesmí být restrikcí otřesena. Prohlašoval to už před léty při velké restrikci v interviewu ministr. Šéfové oddělení krčili rameny a nevycházeli raději ze svých pokojů.

Mlhavý déšť kropil ulice ...

(from J. Hora: *Dech na skle*, Prague, 1939, p. 54.)

Quick vocab

podzimní *autumn(al)*
déšť (m, gen. **deště**) *rain*
táhnout here *draw, march*
věž (f) *tower, spire*
svatý Vít *St Vitus* (to whom Prague's cathedral is dedicated)
párat here, *rip open*
nízký *low*
oblak (m) (pl. **oblaka n!**) *cloud*
rozhánět/rozehnat *to disperse, drive everywhere*
vítr (gen. **větru**) *wind*
chápat se/uchopit se (+ gen.) *to seize hold of*
jich gen. of oni/ony/ona *them*
obnažovat/obnažit *to reveal, lay bare*
tu a tam *here and there*
hluboký *deep*
modř (f) *blue* (as noun)
cíp *a tiny corner*
čeřit/roz- *to ruffle, to cause to ripple*
hladina *surface*
loďka (rowing) *boat*
trpělivý *patient*
rybář (m) *fisherman*
houpat se/roz- (houpe), or **houpnout se** *to swing, bob*
kalný *murky*
Palackého most *Palacký Bridge*
hlučet *to be noisy*
nervózní *nervous*
přebíhání *running hither and thither*
někudy *some way* (denoting route; remember **kudy?** *which way?*)

ministerská rada *council of ministers*
rada *council, counsel;* (m) *councillor, counsellor*
jež = která *which*
usnášet se/usnést se + na (+ loc.) *to resolve*
restrikce *cutback*
úřednictvo *office staff*
jejíž *whose* (where possessor is feminine)
zbytek *remnant*
přičleňovat/přičlenit *to incorporate* (here reflexive passive)
ministerstvo *ministry*
odkládat/odložit *to put down, set aside*
psací stroj (m) *typewriter*
plést si/s- (plete) *to confuse, get wrong*
nechávat/nechat *to let*
stydnout/vy- *to get cold*
párek (pair of) *frankfurter(s)*
sluha (m) *servant,* (here) *office messenger*
radovat se/za- + z (+ gen.) *to rejoice (at)*
skrytě *secretly*
myšlenka *thought, idea*
základ *basis, foundation*
stát *the state*
nesmí být otřesena *must not be disturbed, shaken*
prohlašovat/prohlásit *to pronounce, declare*
šéf *head, boss*
oddělení *section, department, compartment*
nevycházeli raději ze svých pokojů *thought it wiser to stay in their rooms*
raději *rather, preferably*
mlhavý *misty, foggy*
kropit/po- *to sprinkle, to water*

● **INSIGHT**

You should be able to work out other words on the basis of what you have learnt in previous units. Indeed, besides revising the grammar sections, it is not a bad idea to give yourself some periodic vocabulary tests, based on everything and anything that has gone before. Not all words can – or ever would in real life – be repeated with the same frequency, so you need a little self-discipline, and possibly more outside reading, in order to embed words firmly. Using Google-type searches for any word that takes your fancy will produce masses of uses of it in different contexts; remember to do this ideally through a Czech search engine.

If you have the recording, listen to this passage. It will give you some sense for Czech as read, as opposed to spoken dialogue.

1 THE WEATHER

Contrary to their own assertions, the Czechs don't talk about the weather much less than the English! At the very least you need the following words and expressions in addition to those in the text:

 Quick vocab

sníh (sněhu) *snow*
sněhová bouře *snowstorm*
kroupy (f pl) *hail*
vánice *blizzard*
padá sníh *it is snowing*
břečka *slush*
mlha *fog, mist*
padá mlha *mist/fog is coming down*
prší (pršet) *it's raining*
leje (lít) *it's pouring*
přeháňka *shower*
mrholení (mrholit) *drizzle*
přeháňky *scattered showers*
fouká (foukat *to blow***) vítr** *it's windy*
bouřka, bouře *storm*
vichřice *gale*
od severu/jihu/západu/východu *from the north/south/west/east*
sever *north*
jih *south*
západ *west*
východ *east*
hřmí (hřmít/za-, past hřmělo) *it's thundering*
hrom *thunder*
blýská se *it's lightning*
blesk *flash*
slunce svítí (svítit) *the sun's shining*

je horko/teplo/chladno/zima *it's hot/warm(mild)/cool/cold*
je zataženo/zamračeno *it's overcast/cloudy*
polojasno/jasno *rather cloudy/bright*
tlak *pressure*
tlaková výše *ridge of high pressure*
výše (f) *height*
tlaková níže *trough of low pressure*
níže (f) *low point*
teplota stoupá/klesá *the temperature is rising/falling*
teploměr *thermometer*
stupeň (m, gen. **stupně**) *degree*
Jaká je předpověd? *What's the forecast?*
Jaké je dnes počasí? *What's the weather like today?*
Kolik je stupňů? *What's the temperature?*
pět stupňů (Celsia) *5°C*
zapadat *to set*
vycházet *to rise*
nejnižší *lowest*
nejvyšší *highest*
jako z konve (konev (f, gen **konve)** *watering-can*) *cats and dogs*
místy (instrumental plural of **místo** *place*) *in places*

2 STATING A PREFERENCE

There are two ways of doing this:

    a with **raději** or **radši** linked to the verb in the same way as **rád**.

Rádi vycházejí ven.	*They like going out.*

but

Raději nevycházejí ven.	*They prefer not to go out.*

or

Má rád město.	*He likes the town.*

while

Ona má raději venkov.   *She prefers the country.*

In direct comparison use **než** (*than*).

Mám raději salát než zelí.   *I prefer lettuce to cabbage.*

(i.e. 'I have lettuce more gladly than cabbage')

b with the phrase **dávat/dát přednost něčemu před něčím** (*to give precedence/ preference/priority to something over something*):

Dávám přednost češtině před němčinou.   *I prefer Czech to German.*

3 THE -*NÍ* ENDING: *PODZIMNÍ* – 'AUTUMNAL'

Adjectives based on nouns denoting times and locations (but not place names) often have the ending **-ní**, hence also **letní**, **zimní** and **jarní**, but also **místní** (*local*) (**místo**), **východní**, **západní**, **severní** and **jižní** and many others.

> ● **INSIGHT**
>
> A popular food: **párky** – as brought in for the clerks' lunch in the text, above.
>
> **Párek** nowadays often means a frankfurter, but originally they were sold in attached pairs, hence **párek** (**pár** = *pair*) used to mean two frankfurters. However, you definitely only get one when you buy **párek v rohlíku** (*hot dog*) at a **stánek** (a street-side *stall*). You may also find stalls selling **buřty** (**buřt** or **vuřt** a chunky *smoked sausage*, served piping hot, but not for the figure-conscious) with a slice of rye bread and a big dollop of **hořčice** (*mustard*), or **smažený sýr** (*fried cheese*), a large slice of Edam-style cheese, breadcrumbed and fried on a lightly oiled griddle. Among the many generations of students I have taught, this has tended to be the most abiding memory of Prague of the majority!

4 PERSONAL PRONOUNS

You have met many personal pronouns. Here they are systematized:

Nominative	já (*I*)	ty (*you*)	-*self*	my (*we*)	vy (*you*)
Accusative/Genitive	mě	tebe-tě	sebe-se	nás	vás
Dative	mně-mi	tobě-ti	sobě-si	nám	vám
Instrumental	mnou	tebou	sebou	námi	vámi
Locative	o mně	o tobě	o sobě	o nás	o vás

Nominative	on (m) ono/to (n)	ona (f)	oni/ony/ona (*they*)
Accusative	jeho/jej/něho/něj-ho	ji/ni	je/ně
Genitive	jeho/jej/něho/něj-ho	jí/ní	jich/nich
Dative	jemu/němu-mu	jí/ni	jim/nim
Instrumental	jím/ním	jí/ní	jimi/nimi
Locative	o něm	o ní	o nich

At first sight there seem to be a lot of variants, but they are all subject to a few simple rules:

a the third-person forms (he/she/it/they) beginning with **n-** are only used after prepositions, and must be used after them: **pro něho** (*for him*), **bez nich** (*without them*), **před ní** (*before her*). This explains why there are only forms beginning with **n-** in the locative, which can never occur without a preposition.

b the forms to the right of the dash are unstressed and are those you have been meeting tucked away in the second slot in the sentence.

Viděl jsem ho včera.	*I saw him/it* (some masculine object) *yesterday.*
Zítra mi dají párky.	*They'll give me frankfurters tomorrow.*

Where there is no choice of 'short' or 'long' forms, the sole form listed may also be unstressed.

Viděl jsem je včera.	*I saw them yesterday.*
Zítra nám dají párky.	*They'll give us frankfurters tomorrow.*

c The forms to the left of the dashes, and the forms where there is no choice, must be used where emphasis is needed; they will not then be in the second slot.

Viděl jsem včera jeho/je, ne Marii.	*I saw him/them yesterday, not Mary.*
Nám dají párky, tobě dají palačinky.	*It's us they'll give the frankfurters to, you'll get pancakes.*

The same forms must be used after prepositions.

Šli proti mně/nám.	*They were walking towards me/us.*

d **jeho/jej** and **něho/něj** are largely interchangeable, but in the accusative **jeho** and **něho** are best reserved for animates.

e **je**, neuter accusative singular *it* (not given in the table), is hardly ever to be encountered in modern Czech, though it was the standard form until fairly recent times and so will be met in older printed texts.

f *They*: **ony** (f pl) and **ona** (n pl) are invariably replaced by **oni** in the spoken language.

g With inanimates of any gender, the demonstrative pronoun **ten/ta/to** is used under emphasis:

Znáš sídliště Ládví? – Ne, to neznám, jenom Prosek.	*Do you know the Ládví estate? – No, that one I don't, only Prosek.*
Koupíš si tu novou detektivku? – Tu od Borové? Tu ne.	*Will you buy the new detective novel? – The one by Borová? Not that one.*

h You will frequently hear third-person pronouns used redundantly to emphasize the subject; this is a purely colloquial feature – recognize it if you hear it, but don't attempt to use it.

Ona paní Ježková je zase v jiném stavu.	*Mrs Ježek is pregnant again.*
v jiném stavu	*'in another state'* = the everyday euphemism for *pregnant*
Ono to bylo loni v červnu.	*It was in last June.*

i   In older textbooks you will find **mne-mě** as the accusative/genitive forms of **já** *I*. The only form given here – **mě** – has generally taken on all functions appropriate to both 'long' and 'short' pronouns, leaving its 'long' counterpart **mne** likely to be found only in older, or highly conservative, texts.

5 *JE MI ZIMA* – 'I'M COLD'

The dative of pronouns is commonly combined with those expressions from the 'weather' list that refer to temperature.

Je mi/mu/nám teplo/horko/ zima.	*I am/he is/we are* (feeling) *warm/hot/cold* (Lit. *it is warm, etc. to me*, etc.).

The type ending in **-o** are originally short neuter adjectives, now functioning as a special type of adverb. Many other expressions to do with how one feels operate in the same way.

Je jí smutno.	*She feels sad.*
Je mu úzko.	*He feels anxious.*

Just occasionally a 'true' adverb works like this too.

Je nám dobře/zle.	*We're feeling good/awful.*

Zima is a very special case, having progressed from 'winter' as a noun to 'cold' as an adverbial: **Je zima** (*It's cold*), to the 'sensation of cold' type of adverb: **Je mi zima** (*I am cold*).

The noun **tma** (*dark*) has also become an adverbial: **Je tam tma** (*It's dark in there*). The test is that in the past tense all of these sentences use the neuter form of the verb: **Bylo jí smutno, Bylo nám dobře, Bylo (nám) zima, Bylo (or Byla) tam tma**.

Several other forms in **-o** produce adverbs of place:

vysoko *high*	**hluboko** *deep*
blízko *near*	**nízko** *low*
daleko *far away*	**široko** *wide*

and time, or 'prevailing conditions'.

dlouho *(for a) long time*	**veselo** *merry, lively*
draho *marked by high prices*	

Chalupa stojí vysoko na stráni.	*The cottage stands high up on the hillside.*
Mluvil dlouho.	*He spoke for a long time.*
Bylo tam draho.	*Things there were expensive.*

Formation of 'regular' adverbs

To express the meanings *highly* (praised), *deeply* (touched), *at great length, merrily, dearly* (bought), i.e. meanings conveyed (usually) by regularly formed English adverbs, use regularly formed Czech adverbs.

To form an adverb from an adjective, remove the adjective ending **-ý** or **-í** and add **-e** or **-ě**, depending on the final consonant. Final **-k-**, **-h-**, **-ch-** and **-r-** change to **-c-**, **-z-,** **-š-** and **-ř-**.

vysoký	vysoce	drahý	draze
hluboký	hluboce	měkký (*soft*)	měkce (*softly*)
dlouhý	dlouze (*at*	strohý (*strict, severe*)	stroze (*strictly*)
	great length)	plachý (*timid*)	plaše (*timidly*)
veselý	vesele	dobrý	dobře

Adjectives ending in **-ský** and **-cký** have adverbs in **-sky** and **-cky**. You have met **český-česky** and others denoting *'how'* (in what language) someone speaks, but it applied equally to, say, **logický-logicky** (*logical/ly*). **Hezký** (*nice, good-looking*) similarly has **hezky** (*nicely*).

6 WORD ORDER: STRESSLESS WORDS

There are so many items to be located in the second slot in a sentence or clause that they have to be ordered. The order is fixed:

If present, past-tense auxiliaries take absolute precedence, followed by **se** or **si**.

Umyl ¹**jsem** ²**se** ve studené vodě.   *I washed in cold water.*

Koupili ¹**jsme** ²**si** deštník.   *We bought (ourselves) an umbrella.*

After the reflexive, if present, comes any dative pronoun.

Dívala ²**se** ³**mu** přes rameno.   *She was looking over his shoulder.*

Mu, and other datives occurring with the names of body parts or intimate belongings, denote possession. If there is no reflexive the dative follows the auxiliary.

Koupili ¹**jsme** ³**jim** auto.   *We bought them a car.*

Then come any other unstressed pronouns, usually accusative, rarely genitive, and, only in the case of **to**, the nominative.

Nechtěli ¹**jsme** ³**vám** ⁴**ho** dát.   *We didn't want to give you it.*

Strašně ²**se** ⁴**nás** báli.   *They were terribly afraid of us.*

bát se (*to be afraid*) is followed by the genitive.

Moc ²**se** ³**jim** ⁴**to** nelíbilo.   *They didn't like it much.*

Líbit se (+ dat.) (*to be pleasing to*) is used to express intellectual or esthetic pleasure, as opposed to emotional, which uses **mít rád**. Here **to** is the subject, therefore it is in the nominative.

After all the unstressed pronouns you might hear one or other adverbs such as **prý**, **teda/ tedy** (*so*), or **ale/však** (*though*). Finally one example to show the whole lot at work:

Bál ¹**jsem** ²**se** ³**jí** ⁴**ho** ⁵**ale** dát.   *I was afraid to give her it though.*

Notice that it does not matter that the **jsem se** go with **bál** to form the past tense of *to be afraid*, while the **jí ho** are the indirect and direct objects of **dát**.

Exercises

1 Jaké je počasí?

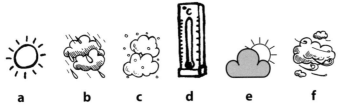

| a | b | c | d | e | f |

2 As an aid to conversation try to convert the following clichés and other weather comments into Czech:

a It looks like rain.

b I hope it doesn't rain tomorrow.

c My daughter's afraid of thunder.

d I don't like driving in fog.

e It was snowing all day yesterday.

f First it was raining cats and dogs, then the sun shone.

g The forecast says it will be cold and overcast.

h When the pressure rises I get a headache.

i What's the temperature outside? Four degrees.

j No it isn't, it's five degrees.

k The wind is blowing from the south, it's going to be warm.

3 Assume that each of the sentences follows on from something said before. First translate them into Czech, then change all the nouns (or whole noun phrases) into pronouns. (Remember to be sure of the gender of the noun to be replaced and watch out for word-order affected by the insertion of pronouns.)

🔊 **TR 41**

a But Marie told Peter that she had already washed the car.

b I didn't like the concert.

c We shall visit the Smiths tomorrow.

d I cannot do without the dictionary.

e Tell us about your journey.

f First we'll try to put the books in the box.

g The Smiths confused the pubs.

h He won't buy tickets for Anna, but he will for Štěpán.

i It wasn't the neighbours my daughter gave the umbrella to.

j When did you see the exhibition (**výstava**)?

Dialogue

The Navrátils are discussing a death in the neighbourhood.

 TR 42

On	Kdy zemřel starý pan Ježek? Před víkendem nebo po něm?
Ona	Přece v pátek. Cestou na nákup jsme viděli stát před jeho domem sanitku.
On	A pohřeb měl už před dvěma dny, v pondělí?
Ona	Ne, to byl někdo jiný. Pan Ježek má pohřeb až za tři dny.
On	A půjdeš tam?
Ona	Ano, a ty?
On	Já nemůžu, před týdnem mi v práci řekli, že od čtvrtka za týden, čili zítra, mám jet do Bratislavy.
	He looks at the clock.
On	Už je tolik? Za deset minut přijde pan Smith. Mám ho zavést do práce. Bude mě tam zastupovat za mé nepřítomnosti.
Ona	A nemám ho snad taky vzít na ten pohřeb?!

V **Quick vocab**

viděli jsme stát před jeho domem sanitku *we saw the ambulance outside his house*

sanitka = ambulance *ambulance*

někdo jiný *someone else*

má pohřeb až za tři dny *his funeral is in three days' time*

pohřeb (pohřbu) *funeral*

od čtvrtka za týden *on Thursday week*

za týden *in a week's time*

POHŘEBNÍ ÚSTAV

čili *or, that is*

Už je tolik? (hodin is understood) *Is it that late already?*

za deset minut *in ten minutes*

zastupovat *replace, stand in for, represent*

za mé nepřítomnosti *in my absence*

za (+ gen.) *during*

nepřítomnost (f, **-i**) *absence* (**přítomnost** = *presence*)

Nemám ho snad taky vzít na ten pohřeb?! *Am I supposed to take him to the funeral as well?!*

pohřební ústav *funeral directors*

ústav *institution, institute*

7 'BEFORE' AND 'AFTER'

It is important not to confuse two uses of **před** + instrumental. In one use it means *before*, as the opposite of **po** + locative *after*: **před válkou** (*before the war*), **po válce** (*after the war*), and, more crucially: **před druhou hodinou** (*before two o'clock*), **po druhé hodině** (*after two o' clock*).

In the other use, **před** will also translate as *before*, but only in past tense contexts, matching *ago* in present tense contexts. This means that **zemřel před rokem** may mean *he had died a year before* or *he died a year ago*. In this use the opposite is **za** + accusative.

Pohřeb měl/má za dva dny.   *His funeral was two days later/is in two days' time.*

Similarly, and in contrast to the first use: **před dvěma hodinami** (*two hours ago*), **za dvě hodiny** (*in two hours' time*).

8 *ZA* AND TELLING THE TIME

This **za** is what you need for telling the time between the quarters. The Czech for *ten past two* is **za pět minut čtvrt na tři** – Lit. 'in five minutes' time quarter on the way to three'. However, **půl třetí a pět minut** is just as likely as **za deset minut tři čvrtě na tři** for *twenty-five to three*.

Look at the clock now and work out the time in two different ways (do the same each time you revise this section).

9 ALTERNATIVES

You have previously met **nebo** (*or*). You use **nebo** when you are talking about distinct alternatives:

Čaj nebo kávu?	*Tea or coffee?*
Pojedete na pohřeb, nebo do Bratislavy?	*Will you go to the funeral or to Bratislava?*

However, when *or* just means saying the same or a similar thing but in different words, use **čili** (it often translates best as *in other words* or *that is*).

Nás šéf, čili Petr, jak mu říkám ...	*Our boss, or Peter, as I call him ...*
Prší, čili nemůžeme si hrát venku.	*It's raining, that's to say we can't play outside.*

To express strict alternatives use **buď ... nebo** (*either ... or*).

Dám si buď čaj nebo bezkofeinovou kávu, ale nic jiného.	*I'll have either tea or decaffeinated coffee, but nothing else.*

To deny or reject two or more alternatives use **ani ... ani** (*neither ... nor*).

Nechutná mi ani čaj, ani káva.	*I don't like either tea or coffee.*
Nepřišel ani Petr, ani Jan.	*Neither Peter nor John came.*

Note the repetition of the negative in the verb, and the use of the comma.

10 ALTERNATIVES WITH 'ELSE'

Czech uses the part-word **jin-** to express *else*. The only full form of the word goes with **kdo** and **co** and their compounds: **někdo jiný** (*someone else*), **co jiného?** (*what else?*)

Notice that after **co** in the nominative or accusative **jiné** goes in the genitive. Other cases, and all cases of **jiný** with **kdo**, agree.

s něčím jiným   *with something else*
u někoho jiného   *at someone else's place*

Other *else* expressions are based on the matching question words:

kde *where*	**(někde) jinde** *elsewhere*
kam *where to*	**jinam** *to another place*
odkud *where from*	**odjinud** *from somewhere else*
kudy *which way*	**jinudy** *another way, by another route*
jak *how*	**jinak** *in another way, otherwise*
kdy *when*	**jindy** *at another time, at other times*

11 ?!

This combined punctuation mark denotes sarcasm or irony in the question. The tone is reinforced by the inclusion of **snad** (*perhaps, maybe*) and by the fact that the question is made in the negative. Perhaps the single most frequent Czech utterance that requires it – and one that Mrs Navrátil might have used if Mr N. had replied '**Ano'** to her last sarcastic question – is **To snad nemyslíš vážně?!**, used, then, whenever an English person might say: 'You must be joking!', 'What do you take me for?' or even 'Pull the other one!'

12 *DVA/DVĚ* – 'TWO'

Nominative/Accusative	dva (m) dvě (f, n)
Genitive/Locative	dvou
Dative/Instrumental	dvěma

The same forms are shared by **oba/obě** (*both, the two*).

Dal to dvěma cizincům.	*He gave it to two foreigners.*
Mezi oběma dcerami je velký věkový rozdíl.	*There's a big age difference between the two daughters.*
Má chybu ve dvou větách.	*He has a mistake in two sentences.*
Má chybu v obou větách.	*He has a mistake in both sentences.*

13 *TŘI* AND *ČTYŘI* – 'THREE' AND 'FOUR'

These two numerals present little new to learn, since they change like the plural of the **i**-declension nouns, with one exception each:

Nominative/Accusative	tři	čtyři
Genitive	tří	čtyř
Dative	třem	čtyřem
Instrumental	třemi	čtyřmi
Locative	o třech	o čtyřech

14 BEFORE SINGULAR AND PLURAL …

… there used to be special forms every time just two things were referred to. All that is left are a few irregular plural forms, which survive in words denoting parts of the body. The main ones are arms/hands, legs/feet, eyes and ears.

Irregular plurals				
	ruka	**noha**	**oko**	**ucho**
	(*hand/arm*)	(*leg/foot*)	(*eye*)	(*ear*)
Nominative/Accusative	ruce	nohy	oči	uši
Genitive	rukou	nohou	očí	uší
Dative	rukám	nohám	očím	uším
Instrumental	rukama	nohama	očima	ušima
Locative	rukou	nohou	očích	uších

Notice where these forms are like those of **dva**. When any of these four words is accompanied by an adjective in the instrumental plural, the adjective also ends in -**ma**, not -**mi**. These 'dual' forms are the only ones where -**ma**, universal in Common Czech (see Unit 5, Section 9, Insight), is correct for the standard language.

holýma rukama	*with bare hands* (**holý** = *bare*)
mezi jejíma krásnýma očima	*between her beautiful eyes*

This even applies with 'four' in the expression

mezi čtyřma očima	*in private, tête-à-tête* (Lit. 'between four eyes')

Colloquially, and especially in contexts where arms and legs are not meant as body parts, the genitive **nohou** and locatives **rukou** and **nohou** may be replaced by the regular forms **noh**, **rukách** and **nohách**, respectively.

Rameno (*shoulder*) and **koleno** (*knee*) have regular plural forms, but also **ramenou** and **kolenou** in the genitive and locative.

Nesl ji na ramenou.	*He carried her on his shoulders.*

Exercises

4 Answer the following questions according to the dialogue:
  a Jak poznali Navrátilovi, že pan Ježek zemřel?
  b Kdo měl pohřeb v pondělí?
  c Kdo určitě bude na pohřbu pana Ježka?
  d Kde bude v tu dobu pan Navrátil?
  e Co bude dělat pan Smith za nepřítomnosti pana Navrátila?
  f Půjde pan Smith na pohřeb?

5 **Look at the newspaper weather forecast below and then answer the questions that follow:**

> **Dnes je neděle 11. dubna 2010** • Slunce vychází v 6.09 hodin a zapadá v 19.52 hodin, Měsíc vychází v 02.51 a zapadá v 12.19 letního času. • Bude oblačno až zataženo, občas déšť, na severu území déšť jen místy. Nejnižší teploty 4 st. C až nula, nejvyšší denní teploty 9 až 13 st. C. Teplota v 1000 m 5 st. C, východní až jihovýchodní vítr kolem 5m/s. •
>
> **Rekordní teploty dne 13. dubna** (**od r. 1775 v pražském Klementinu**): nejvyšší teplota 23,6 st. C v roce 1952, nejnižší teplota minus 3,2 st. C v roce 1986. Dlouhodobý teplotní normál je 8,7 st. Celsia. • **Vyhlídka na zítřek**: V pondělí bude převládat oblačné až zatažené počasí, místy s občasným deštěm, na jihu a jihovýchodě i trvalejší srážky.

a What is the date?
b What happens at 12.19?
c What is the forecast as regards rain?
d Deduce what **až** means in this context.
e What is the significance of: 1775, 1952, 1986?
f Where would you prefer not to be on Monday (unless you love rain)?
g What is the forecast wind speed?

6 **Tell the time in two different ways:**

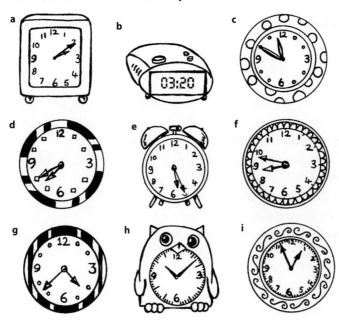

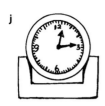

7 Draw in the hands on these watch faces to show:

a deset hodin a pět minut

b tři čtvrtě na sedm

c za sedm minut půl jedné

d za deset minutpět **e** půl třetí

f čtvrt na dvě

8 Now try to work out the meaning of these idioms:

a Stát na vlastních nohou.

b Plést se někomu pod nohama.

c Mít obě ruce levé.

d Podat si ruce.

e Nevěřit svým uším.

f Být až po uši zamilovaný.

g Nechoď mi na oči!

h Sejde z očí, sejde z mysli.

Quick vocab

plést se *to get in the way*
levý *left*

zamilovaný *in love*
scházet/sejít *to go down*

CZECHS AND THEIR ANIMALS

The country's main heraldic symbol is the Bohemian lion with two tails (**dvouocasý lev**). Moravia has a red-and-white chequered eagle (**orel**) and Silesia a black eagle. Lions and eagles, but also bears (**medvěd**) and dragons (**drak**), abound on town and city coats of arms (Beroun, Jeseník, Trutnov, Kolín), but perhaps the oddest heraldic animals are the hedgehogs (**ježek**) on the arms of Jihlava (the town is called 'Iglau' in German and *Igel* is German for 'hedgehog'), and the greyhound (**chrt**) and camel (**velbloud**) on the complex arms of the city of Pilsen. The camel recalls when the Catholic citizens of Pilsen captured a camel from the besieging Hussites (revolutionary protestants) in the 1430s. Litovel has a simple design consisting of a carp (**kapr**) and a pike (**štika**) recalling the wealth of fish in Czech rivers, while Budyně nad Ohří has hares (**zajíc**) and wild boar (**kanec**) – nothing to do with hunting, but borrowed from different old family crests. Since the 14th century, the city of Pardubice has had the front half of a charging horse, recalling the Lord of Pardubice's loss of his charger during the siege of Milan in the 12th century, but coincidentally it is a reminder that this is where the Czech Grand National (**Velká pardubická**) is held. (The English Grand National is known analogously as **Velká liverpoolská**.) The city of Brno, the capital of Moravia, is famous for (among other things) its 'dragon', which is to be seen in the form of a stuffed alligator hanging at the entrance to the Old City Hall. Several legends account for this curio, which has become famous enough to give its name – **Brněnský drak** – to one of the express trains running between Brno and Prague and to a grand prix motor race.

 Test yourself

Delete from the items in brackets the ones which will not fit the sentence (the correct version is in the Key to the exercises):

1 Dáte si kafe, nebo něco (jiné/jiného)?

2 Kdo (jiný/jiná) tu je kromě úředníků?

3 Rád jezdím do Prahy, ale jednou chci jet (někde jinde/někam jinam).

4 Tamtudy (*that way*) zloděj nešel, musel utéct (jinde/jinam/jinudy).

5 Koho (jiného/jinému) se můžu na to zeptat?

6 Teď nemám čas, budou muset přijít (jinde/jindy).

7 Líbo, s nikým (jiným/jinými) tam nejdu!

8 Nikde (jinde/jiné) jsem neslyšel tak krásnou hudbu.

9 Dáte mi ten kufr, (jinak/jinam) vás praštím!

14 Nehádejte se!
Stop arguing!

In this unit you will learn
▶ *How to give orders*
▶ *How to use some politeness formulae*
▶ *How to express wishes*

Dialogue 1

Mrs Navrátilová is organizing her family – her son Jan, her daughter Líba and her husband Zdeněk – between breakfast and going out for the day.

 TR 43

Navrátilová	Honzo, ukliď ze stolu a ty, Líbo, umyj nádobí.
Líba	Ale mami, já jsem ho myla včera, ať to udělá Honzík.
Jan	Nebuď protivná, vidíš, že uklízím stůl. Jen to umyj, ať můžeme jet.
Navrátil	Nehádejte se. Já ti, Líbo, pomůžu, ty myj a já budu utírat.
Jan	To není fér, kdo bude pomáhat mně?
Navrátil	Uklidni se, Honzo! Vždyť všichni pomáháme mamince. Nezapomeň, že většinou to všechno dělá sama.
Navrátilová	Ještěže to někdo ví! Dělejme, nebo to neskončíme nikdy.
Líba	Kam vlastně jedeme? Já mám schůzku s Pepíkem – ve tři před radnicí. Budeme zpátky včas?
Jan	Nemůže Pepík jet s námi? Já ho mám rád, minule mi koupil zmrzlinu.
Navrátil	Ovšemže může, když se mu bude chtít. Zastavíme se pro něj cestou. Dobře, Líbo?
Líba	Dobře, budu docela ráda. Doufám, že bude chtít.
Navrátilová	Tak vidíte, už je všechno hotové, vezměte si kabáty a boty a pojedeme.

ukliď ze stolu *clear the table*

uklízet/uklidit *to tidy up*

umyj nádobí *wash the dishes*

mami (domestic way children address their mother)

ať to udělá Honzík *let Johnny do it*

nebuď protivná *don't be horrible*

protivný *contrary, detestable, mean, peevish*

ať můžeme jet *let's get going*

nehádejte se *stop arguing*

hádat se *to argue, quarrel*

ty myj a já budu utírat *you wash and I'll wipe*

fér (colloquial) *fair*

uklidni se *calm down*

uklidňovat se/uklidnit se *to calm down, become calm*

uklidňovat/uklidnit *to (make) calm*

vždyť *after all*

zapomínat/zapomenout (past **zapomněl**) *to forget*

maminka (used in the family context; opposite **tatínek** = *Dad*) *Mum*

nezapomeň *don't forget*

dělejme *let's get on*

to neskončíme nikdy *we'll never be finished*

končit/s- *to finish*

schůzka *date, appointment*

radnice (f) *town hall*

včas *in time, on time*

minule *last time*

zmrzlina *ice cream*

zastavovat se/zastavit se *to stop*

vezměte si kabáty *get your coats*

kabát *coat*

1 GIVING ORDERS

In the main, commands are expressed by forms called *imperative*. There are three main forms: corresponding to **ty**, any sense of **vy**, and **my**, depending on who the command is addressed to. The **my** forms are equivalent to English forms beginning *let's* ...

How to form the imperative

Start with the third person plural. Using the verbs appearing as commands in Dialogue 1 take:

uklidí, (u)myjí, budou, hádají se,

uklidní, zapomenou, dělají, vezmou

Two main patterns emerge, depending on whether there is one consonant or two before the final vowel. You can see two consonants in **uklidn-í** and **vezm-ou**. This type produces imperatives of the form:

ty	uklidn**i**	vezm**i**
vy	uklidn**ěte**	vezm**ěte**
my	uklidn**ěme**	vezm**ěme**

Notice the change of vowel from **i** to **ě** between the singular and plural forms. And remember that **ě** will only appear in this form if the stem ends in **d**, **t** or **n**, or **b**, **p**, **m** or **v**. Otherwise there will be no 'hook', as in the case of

myslet mysl-í mysl**i**/mysl**ete**/mysl**eme**

Where there is only one consonant before the final vowel, the imperatives take the form:

ty	umyj	dělej	ukliď	zastav
vy	umyj**te**	dělej**te**	uklid**te**	zastav**te**
my	umyj**me**	dělej**me**	uklid**me**	zastav**me**

The singular form has no ending at all, while the *you* and *we* forms end typically, as in the first type and in all the conjugations, in **-te** and **-me**.

Note: Three subsidiary rules:

a if the third person plural stem ends in **-aj-,** the **a** changes to **e.**
   dělají dělaj- dělej/dělejte/dělejme (*do, make*)

b if the third person plural stem ends in **-n-, -d-, or -t-,** these consonants must be 'softened'.

zapomenou	**zapomen-**	zapomeň/zapomeňte/
		zapomeňme (*forget*)
budou	**bud-**	buď/buďte/buďme (*be*)
letí	**let-**	leť/leťte/leťme (*fly*)

c if the syllable before the final consonant is long, the vowel shortens in the imperative. (This type is not represented in the dialogue.) As is often the case, shortening may change the vowel altogether.

vrátí	**vrát-**	vrať/vraťte/vraťme (*return*)
rozpůlí	**rozpůl-**	rozpul/rozpulte/rozpulme (*halve*)
koupí	**koup-**	kup/kupte/kupme (*buy*)

What about aspect in commands?

Positive commands are based on perfective verbs – they seek to get something done. In the dialogue this is represented by **uklid', umyj** and **uklidni se**.

However, if a positive command seeks to get someone to continue with an act begun, or about to be begun, then the imperfective is used, as in **myj** and **dělejme**.

Then, though it is not shown in the dialogue, if a positive command relates to an act that is to be performed regularly or in principle, the imperfective verb is used.

Učme se česky aspoň dvě hodiny denně.   *Let's study Czech at least two hours daily.*

In other words, much of what you learnt about the uses of the aspects applies in the imperative too.

Negative commands

If you give a negative command you may be seeking to prevent something happening that is not yet happening; or to stop something happening that is already going on; or to issue a warning against an untoward event. So, if you wish to advise someone against buying something, you would say: **Nekupuj(te) to!** And if, like Mr Navrátil, you wish to stop an

ongoing argument, you will again use the imperfective imperative and say: **Nehádejte se!**
But if your command is more of a warning, e.g. *don't forget* …, you would, like Mr Navrátil,
say **Nezapomeň …!**, based on the perfective. This type is necessary for the urgent type of
warning contained in the *Mind you don't* … formula:

Nespal si prsty.	*Mind you don't burn your fingers.*
(pálit/spálit *to burn*)	
Nespadni pod autobus!	*Mind you don't fall under a bus!*

Commands based on 'be' and 'have'

As you already know, **být** and **mít** can only ever be imperfective. **Být** forms its imperatives
from its future tense: **budou; bud-: buď/buďte/buďme.**

Buďte tak hodný a kupte mi	*Be so kind as to* (Lit. and) *buy me*
jeden lístek.	*one ticket.*

Mít, however, is slightly irregular, having the forms **měj/mějte/mějme** (but remember the
past tense **měl** to see a similarity). In fact, you will really only need **měj**, etc. in the farewell
formula **Měj(te) se dobře** (*Cheerio!*), and in various set phrases:

Měj(te) rozum.	*Be reasonable/sensible.*
Mějte trpělivost.	*Be patient.*

Obviously their literal meaning is 'have reason' and 'have patience'.

English uses far more imperatives based on *have*, as in *Have a sandwich*, or *Have the schnitzel*.
If it is you making the offer, use **Vezmi si/vezměte si**, as in **Vezměte si sendvič**, but if it is a
suggestion, for example as to what someone might buy or order, it would be more usual to
use **Dej(te) si**, as in **Dejte si řízek** – the imperative form of sentences met earlier (remember
dám si kávu = *I'll have coffee*).

When you need an imperative, do not worry if it sounds too peremptory. You can always
soften a command with **prosím** (or **prosím vás**) (*please*), but this is rarely necessary.
Indeed to many Czechs the English seem over-deferential, with p's and q's all over the place.
Requests that could be expressed as commands ('Pass me the salt') can always be toned
down if you put them as questions, in both languages, so instead of saying **Podejte mi sůl**
you could use **Podáte mi sůl?**

2 OVŠEMŽE – 'OF COURSE …'

This expression combines **ovšem** (*of course*) and the conjunction **že**,
amounting to 'of course it is the case that'. Compare the two versions of *of course*:

Ovšem nevím, jak to udělal.	*Of course, I don't know how he did it.*
Ovšemže nevím, jak to udělal.	*Of course I don't know how he did it.*

The first one is more apologetic, the second insistent.

3 IDIOMS WITH *CHTÍT SE*

Chtít se is an impersonal verb denoting a wish that is (semi-) involuntary: if **chtít** most often translates as *to wish/want*, **chtít se** is closer to *to feel like*. The person upon whom the feeling acts is expressed in the dative. Compare:

Pepík chce jet s námi.	*Pepík wants to go with us.*
Pepíkovi se chce jet s námi.	*Pepík feels like going with us.*

As an impersonal verb, **chtít se** is always in the singular, neuter in the past tense (**Pepíkovi se chtělo …** as opposed to **Pepík chtěl**), and is usually followed by an infinitive.

4 BEGINNING/ENDING, STARTING/STOPPING

You saw earlier that the negative imperative may mean *stop doing something* (**nehádejte se**). However, there is a verb which itself means *to stop* (and is of course not limited to the imperative). This is **přestávat/přestat** (**přestane**). Mr Navrátil could have said: **Přestaňte se hádat.** Note:

Přestává pršet.	*The rain's stopping. (Lit. it's stopping raining)*
Loni přestal kouřit.	*He gave up smoking last year.*

The verb is always followed by an imperfective infinitive. The same thing applies to **začínat/začít** (**začne**, past **začal**) *to begin*, as in:

Začalo pršet.	*It began to rain.*
Začal kouřit v patnácti letech.	*He began to smoke at 15.*

Where, however, *begin* and *end* are followed by nouns, the verbs are **začínat/začít** and **končit/s-** respectively. You can see the opposition in:

Začal/přestal pracovat.	*He started/stopped working.*
Začal/skončil práci.	*He started/finished the/his work.*

To express *continue* with verbs, use the adverb **dál** (*further*). The verb **pokračovat** (*to continue*) may be used either absolutely, as a verb of speaking ('and then there's the cost,' he continued), or using **v** + locative:

Pracoval dál.	*He continued working.*
Pokračoval v práci.	*He continued (with) his work.*

Exercises

 TR 44

1 Practise giving orders with the following imperative sentences:

   a Do your shopping at the shop round the corner.
   b Buy me an ice cream, please.
   c Let's take our books back to the library.
   d Always help old people across the street.

e Don't wash the best china in the dishwasher.

f Look! It's raining again.

g Tell me, please, where are the toilets?

h Be patient. Peter will be here soon.

i Read me that article, please.

j Don't sleep during the film!

k Do understand, I can't get there by Thursday.

l Think about us when we're gone.

 Quick vocab

nakupovat *to shop*
knihovna *library*
myčka *dishwasher*

nejlepší *the best*
myslet na (+ acc.) *think of/about*
porcelán *china, porcelain*

2 **Interpret the following imperative forms, which you will hear or see frequently (you may use the vocabulary list or a dictionary; make sure to note both aspects of any new verbs):**

a podejte mi …

b obraťte se na …

c uschovejte v suchu

d neváhejte

e přejděte na druhý chodník

f sedněte si

g neparkujte před výjezdem

h přestaňte

i nemluvme už o tom

j vyplněný formulář vraťte do …

Dialogue 2

Mr Smith is phoning the Navrátils about his weekend visit.

Navrátil	*(picking up the phone)* Haló, Navrátil.
Smith	Dobrý den, tady Smith.
Navrátil	Jej, dobrý den. Tak kdy přijedete?
Smith	Dojedu na vaši stanici asi v půl sedmé.
Navrátil	Dobře, přijdu vám naproti.
Smith	To není třeba. Nechoďte, já trefím. Vždyť jsem u vás už jednou byl.
Navrátil	Ale ano, stejně si potřebuju koupit Večerník a cigarety – právě mi došly.
Smith	Ale já vám je můžu koupit cestou. To přece nic není.
Navrátil	To ne, neobtěžujte se, já se rád dostanu na chvilku ven. Jen přijďte. Žena se na vás těší.
Smith	Dobře. Tak na shledanou.

> *On their arrival back at the flat.*
>
> **Smith**   Dobrý den, paní Navrátilová. *(Hands her some flowers)* To je pro vás.
>
> **Navrátilová** Ty jsou krásné! Děkuju! Jak se máte? *(To her husband.)* Pomoz panu Smithovi s kabátem.
>
> **Smith**   Nemusíte, děkuju. Už to je.
>
> **Navrátilová** Tak už pojďte dál. Večeře bude asi za hodinu.

 Quick vocab

jej interjection denoting pleasant surprise

stanice (f) *(bus, tram) stop, (underground) station*

přijdu vám naproti *I'll come to meet you*

to není třeba *that isn't necessary*

třeba (see Section 5)

já trefím *I know the way*

trefit *to find the way, to hit a target*

vždyť jsem u vás už jednou byl *after all I've been at your place before*

ale ano *here, of course I will (come out to meet you)*

Večerník *the Prague evening paper*

právě mi došly *I've just run out (of them)*

to přece nic není *it's nothing, I can do that easily (etc.)*

to ne *oh no (don't even think of it)*

obtěžovat se *to go to the trouble, trouble, bother oneself*

obtěžovat *to bother, annoy (someone)*

jen přijďte *just come*

pomoz singular imperative of **pomoct** *help*

už to je *it's done, I've managed (etc.)*

tak už pojďte dál *do come along in*

5 SEMI-EMPTY 'POLITENESS'

If you read Dialogue 2 closely, you will pick up a variety of phrases which are easier to acquire by example than by any reference to dictionaries and so on. These are, in particular, such polite rejections as **To není třeba**, **To ne** and **Neobtěžujte se**; the assurances **To přece nic není** and **Už to je**; and the phrase **ale ano** to contradict a negative. Notice too the occurrences of **jen** and **už**, which are not exactly the same as **jenom** (*only*) and **už** (*already*).

6 MORE IMPERATIVES

a The imperative forms of **jít** do not fully fit the rules given in Section 1. The first one you will meet is **pojď/pojďte** (*come*) and **pojďme** (*come on, let's go*). This, and **přijď/přijďte** (*come*), have the short type of ending despite the two consonants. Other compounds of **jít** behave 'normally': **zajdi/zajděme** (*pop (round) to*), **přejdi/přejděte** (*cross*).

b *Come* versus *go*:

Come! to or with the speaker, here and now, is expressed by **pojď/pojďte**. *Come!* at a later time is expressed by **Přijď/přijďte** (notice how they appear in Dialogue 2). *Go!* (i.e. away from the speaker) is based on the present tense form of **jít: jdou – jd-,** giving **jdi/jděte**, as in **Jděte k doktorovi** (*Go to the doctor*).

184

Both *don't come* and *don't go* are expressed by the negative imperative of **chodit** (also seen in the dialogue). Generally use the indeterminate verbs of motion (**nosit**, **vozit**, **běhat**, etc.) to form negative commands.

Pojďte dál! (see **dál** above) is the normal way of saying *Come in*, but is often shortened, when the person at the door is not visible, to **Dál!**

Note the expression of mild disbelief **Ale jdi!**, **Ale jděte!** (*Get away!, You don't say!*). It can also be used in reproof as *Don't be silly!*

c Some other verbs have irregular imperatives.

stát (**stojí**) *to stand*	**stůj/stůjte!** *Stop!*
povědět (conjugates like **vědět**) *to tell*	**pověz/povězte** (similarly for **odpovědět** *reply*)
pomoct *to help*	**pomoz/pomozte** (should you ever need to shout for help, however, use the noun **pomoc**!)

vidět *to see* technically has **viz/vizte**, but this is only used in such (written) contexts as **viz strana 634** (*see page 634*).
Normal English commands using *see* will probably in fact mean *look*, and so be based on **dívat se/po-.**

Quick vocab

povídat/povědět *to say, tell*   **odpovídat/odpovědět** *to reply*
povídat si s někým *to chat to someone*

7 IMPERATIVES/WISHES: THIRD PERSON

This type of sentence is illustrated in Dialogue 1.

Ať to udělá Honzík.   *Let Honzík do it.*

This construction with **ať** can actually be used in all persons, chiefly to express wishes:

Ať vás tady už nikdy neuvidím.   *May I never see you here again.* (i.e. *Don't let me ever see you here again.*)

It also occurs in various formulae: **ať žije X** (*long live X*). Notice that **ať** combines with ordinary present or future tense forms.

8 OTHER USES OF *AŤ*

Systematically **ať** occurs with words ending in **-koli**, equivalents to English words beginning **any-** or ending in **-ever**:

Ať vám to řekl kdokoli, je to nesmysl.   *Whoever told you that, it's nonsense.*
Ať přijde kdykoli, bude už pozdě.   *Whenever he comes, it will be (too) late.*
Ať budeš mluvit s kýmkoli, stejně ti to nikdo neřekne.   *Whoever you talk to, nobody will tell you anyway.*

Similar words in the series are:

cokoli	*anything/whatever*
kdekoli	*anywhere/wherever*
kamkoli	*(to) anywhere/wherever*
kudykoli	*any way/whichever way*
odkudkoli	*from anywhere/wherever from*
kdykoli	*at any time, wherever*
jakýkoli	*any/whatever*
kterýkoli	*any/whichever*
jakkoli	*anyhow/however*

A related set of formulae dispense with **ať**, placing the **-koli** at the beginning.

Kudykoli půjdete, najdete poštu.   *Whichever way you go you'll find a post office.*

Note also the following formulae with **ať**:

Ať si myslí co si myslí, ...   *Whatever he thinks, ...*

Ať se stane co se stane, ...   *Whatever happens, ... (i.e. come what may)*

Finally, get used to seeing the **-koli** series as equivalents to *any-*:

Kdokoli vám to řekne.   *Anyone will tell you.*

Kup to kdekoli.   *Buy it anywhere.*

Of course, you must not confuse these with the *any-* words that come in English negative sentences: (*I haven't eaten anything today*) **Dnes jsem nic nejedl**, which, in Czech, will always begin with **ni-**:

Neříkej to nikomu.   *Don't tell anybody.*

And the *any-* words in English questions are likely to begin **ně-** in Czech:

Máte něco na bolení hlavy?   *Have you anything for a headache?*

Compare:

Víno koupíte **kdekoli.**	*You can buy wine anywhere.*
Víno nekoupíte **nikde.**	*You won't buy wine anywhere.*
Koupím tady **někde** víno?	*Can I buy wine anywhere here?*

Notice how the future perfective may imply possibility, as well as just future time.

9 THE VOCATIVE CASE

At the end of Unit 3 ('A few Czech conventions on titling') and in Unit 5 (Quick vocab after Dialogue 2) you met references to the vocative, the case of direct address. Dialogue 1 in this lesson contains a number of instances of the vocative in use. The time has come to systematize these forms.

Hard masculine nouns take the ending **-e**, as in **pane**, **doktore**, **profesore**, **inženýre**, **Alane**.

Hard feminine nouns and masculine nouns that end in **-a** take the ending **-o**, as in **starosto**, **Líbo**, **Honzo**.

All these have occurred previously. Two other types need to be learnt:

▶ the ending **-u** goes with hard masculine nouns ending in **k**, **h**, **g**, and **ch**, and the noun **syn**:

chirurg : chirurgu *surgeon*
Pepík : Pepíku *Joe*   **hoch : hochu** *boy*
vrah : vrahu *murderer*   **syn : synu** *(my) son*

▶ the ending **-i** goes with all soft masculine nouns except those ending in **-ec** and **-ce**, which follow their own patterns:

král : králi *(oh) king*
muž : muži *man, husband*   **správce : správce** *caretaker; administrator*
otec : otče *father*

There are three exceptions to the above:

▶ in hard masculines that end in **-r** preceded by a consonant the ending is **-e**, but **r** becomes **ř**: **Petr**: **Petře** (contrast this with **doktor** etc. above);
▶ **Bůh** (*God*) has **Bože!** and is common in such exclamations as **Bože můj!** (*Goodness me!*);
▶ **člověk** (*man, person*) has **člověče**, which is used chiefly as an 'empty' vocative, similar to 'mate' or Caribbean English 'man' and similar.

No other classes of words have a distinctive vocative form, that is, no soft feminine, no neuter, no plural, no adjectival and no pronoun declension. In all these instances the vocative shares the same form as the nominative, as in **paní Navrátilová** in Dialogue 2.

Exercises

3 Find suitable ways of requiring someone to …
  a buy you a stamp at the post office,
  b bring the book back in time,
  c come in; he needn't take his shoes off,
  d translate this letter for you,
  e stop talking aloud (**nahlas**),
  f put the light on for you, please (**rozsvěcovat** or **rozsvěcet/rozsvítit**),
  g be so kind as to help you fill in (**vyplňovat/vyplnit**) the form,
  h go away,
  i not to leave the keys on the table,
  j not to come towards you when he's got a cold like that.

Proverbs based on imperatives

▶ **Kuj železo, dokud je žhavé.** (**kovat** *to forge*; **železo** *iron*; **žhavý** *red-hot*) (Not only *Strike while the iron's hot*, but also *Make hay while the sun shines*.)

▶ **Neříkej hop, dokud nepřeskočíš.** (**hop** interjection accompanying a hop, here implying an expression of satisfaction; **přeskakovat/přeskočit** *to jump across*) (Equivalent to *There's many a slip twixt cup and lip* or *Don't count your chickens ...*)

▶ **Nechval dne před večerem.** (**chválit/po-** *to praise*; **dne** genitive of **den** *day*, in an old construction which used the genitive case after a negative) (Equivalent to *If you sing before breakfast, you'll cry before night*, or equally good for not counting chickens.)

▶ **Napřed měř, potom řež.** (**měřit/z-** *to measure*; **řezat** [**řeže**] *to saw, cut*) (Roughly equivalent to *Look before you leap*.)

▶ **Nebuď zvědavý, budeš brzy starý.** (**brzy** *soon, early*) (Equivalent in force to *Curiosity killed the cat*.)

● **INSIGHT**

There are many more proverbs in common use in Czech, at least among the older generation, than there are these days in English. This is in large measure due to the fact that one particular novel, *The Grandmother* (**Babička**) by Božena Němcová (1820–62), is compulsory reading for all Czechs at school and in it the Grandmother's language is richly larded with proverbs. This fund of folk wisdom thus filters into most Czech minds generation after generation and so passes into everyday use. *Babička* is *the* classic Czech novel, indeed the first modern novel in the language, and is one of the many products of the nineteenth-century National Revival. If this book enjoys the status of 'national novel', then Karel Hynek Mácha (1810–36) is the national poet (and his long poem *May* (**Máj**) the national poem), and František Palacký (he of the bridge in an earlier unit, 1798–1876) is the national historian. Bedřich Smetana (1824–84) is the national composer, and his *Bartered Bride* (**Prodaná nevěsta**) the national opera.

?? Test yourself

Be dogmatic and assertive. Translate the following into Czech.

    a Whatever the weather, we're going out.

    b Whoever told you that is a fool.

    c Wherever you go, send me a postcard (pohlednice).

    d Wherever you got that from, they cheated you (šidit/o-).

    e I'll study from (use podle) any book in any language.

    f Don't speak about this to anyone.

    g Who asked if I needed anything?

    h Whenever the sun shines we will play (hrát si, see Unit 5, Exercise 5) outside.

    i Have you any postcards with pictures of the river?

    j Don't come to me with your problems!

15 Kdybych věděla, že přijdete …

If I knew you were coming …

In this unit you will learn

▶ *How to express vain wishes using the conditional*
▶ *How to state actual and theoretical preferences*
▶ *How to form indirect commands*
▶ *How to express 'purpose'*

Dialogue 1

Mr and Mrs Smith have arrived at the Navrátils' flat unannounced. Mr Navrátil has just opened the door.

 TR 48

Navrátil	Jej, dobrý den. To jsou k nám hosté!
Mr Smith	Nezlobte se, že jsme přišli jen tak bez ohlášení. Rozhodli jsme se tady zastavit teprve před hodinou.
Navrátil	Z toho si nic nedělejte, jen pojďte dál!
Mrs Smith	Ano, kdybychom se rozhodli dřív, určitě bychom vám dali vědět.
Navrátilová	(*coming to the door*) Ach, dobrý den. To je milé překvapení. Pojďte dál.
Mrs Smith	Děkuju.
Navrátilová	Škoda, že jsem nevěděla, že vás dnes uvidíme. Kdybych věděla, že přijdete, upekla bych dort.
Mr Smith	My jsme s tou možností dokonce počítali: dort jsme koupili cestou – pro každý případ. Neradi bychom vás přivedli do rozpaků!
Navrátil	Ale to jste nemuseli! Já bych skočil tady do cukrárny a bylo by to.
Mrs Smith	Nevadí, už jsme tady, dort taky. Hlavně jestli na nás máte čas. Jindy bychom už nemohli přijít, aspoň ne spolu.
Navrátilová	Jak to? Stalo se něco?
Mr Smith	Žena čeká delší dobu na operaci a najednou jsme dostali zprávu, že musí ve čtvrtek do nemocnice ...
Mrs Smith	A kdybych nešla teď, kdo ví, dokdy bych musela ještě čekat. Nejde o nic vážného, ale to čekání je protivné.
Navrátil	Měli bychom váš odjezd oslavit – aspoň trochu. Můžete pít alkohol?

Quick vocab

to jsou k nám hosté! *a greeting formula registering pleasant surprise at the arrival of visitors*

nezlobte se, že jsme přišli jen tak *do forgive us for turning up just like that*

zlobit se/roz- *to be/get angry*

jen tak *just like that*

bez ohlášení *unannounced*

rozhodovat se/rozhodnout se *to make up one's mind, to decide*

zastavovat se/zastavit se *to stop; to call in*

teprve *(in time expressions) only*

z toho si nic nedělejte *don't worry about it, think nothing of it*

dělat si něco z *(+ gen.) to make an issue of*

kdybychom se rozhodli *if we had decided*

dali bychom vám vědět *we would have let you know*

dát někomu vědět *to let someone know*

překvapení *surprise*

kdybych věděla *if I knew*

upekla bych *I would (have) bake(d)*

dort *cake (strictly gâteau, torte)*

počítali jsme s tou možností *we allowed for that possibility*

počítat s *to reckon with, allow for*

možnost (-i) *possibility*

pro každý případ *just in case, for any eventuality*

případ *case, event(uality)*

rozpaky *(pl) embarrassment, awkwardness, uncertainty*

neradi bychom vás přivedli do rozpaků *we wouldn't like to embarrass you*

přivádět/přivést někoho do rozpaků *to cause someone embarrassment*

ale to jste nemuseli *but you needn't have*

já bych skočil *I would pop*

skákat (skáče)/skočit *to jump (!)*

cukrárna *confectioner's, cake shop*

a bylo by to *and that would be that*

a je to *and/so that's that*

nevadí *never mind, it doesn't matter*

vadit *to matter*

hlavně jestli máte na nás čas *the main thing is if you've got time for us*

jindy bychom už nemohli přijít *we couldn't come at any other time*

už *here, at this stage*

jak to? *how come?*

delší dobu *for some time*

delší *comparative of* **dlouhý** *long (i.e. longer, longish)*

operace *(f) operation*

nemocnice *(f) hospital*

kdybych nešla *if I didn't go*

dokdy bych musela čekat *until when I would have to wait*

dokdy *until/by when*

nejde o nic vážného *it isn't anything serious*

jít o *(+ acc.) to be a matter/question of*

vážný *grave, serious*

čekání *waiting*

měli bychom váš odjezd oslavit *we ought to celebrate your going*

mít *(in conditional) ought, should*

odjezd *departure (by transport)*

slavit/o- *to celebrate (imperfective also* **oslavovat***)*

1 UNREAL STATES OF AFFAIRS/THE CONDITIONAL

The conditional is equivalent to English forms containing *would* as in 'I would pop to the cake shop'. (The *woulds* in the 'future in the past' – *he said he would come* – or expressing regular repetition in the past – *they would do the washing on Mondays* – are different.)

In Czech, it is formed from the past tense (those forms ending in **-l**, etc.), accompanied by the conditional auxiliary, in the place of the past-tense auxiliary – like, say, *would have* *(spoken)* in place of *had (spoken)*. The conditional auxiliary conjugates according to person and follows the same word-order rules as the past-tense auxiliary. The forms, here illustrated with **dělat**, are:

dělal/-a bych	*I would make*	**dělal/-a byste**	*you would make* (singular)
dělal/-a bys	*you would make* (familiar)		
dělal/-a/-o by	*he/she/it would make*	**dělali/-y byste**	*you would make* (plural)
dělali/-y bychom	*we would make*	**dělali/-y/-a by**	*they would make*

Thus you have seen, in Dialogue 1:

Já bych skočil (*or*** Skočil bych) do cukrárny.** — *I would pop into the cake shop.*

My bychom nemohli (*or*** Nemohli bychom) přijít.** — *We couldn't come.*

Bylo by to. — *That would be that.*

One common formula using the conditional is:

To by bylo dobré. — *That would be good.*

To by bylo lepší. — *That would be better.*

Individual verbs may call for individual translation, such as **měli bychom** (**váš odjezd oslavit**) *we should/ought to (celebrate your leaving)*. This is the conditional of **mít** as a modal verb. Note also:

Neradi bychom vás přivedli do rozpaků. — *We wouldn't like/want to embarrass you.*

2 THEORETICAL PREFERENCES: 'I WOULD RATHER ...'

To state an actual preference, combine **raději** (*rather*) with the verb in the same way that you have used **rád** previously:

Píšu raději na počítači. — *I prefer writing on the computer.*

If the preference is only theoretical use **raději** and the conditional:

Raději bych psal na počítači. — *I would rather write on the computer.*

Petr by to raději zaplatil sám. — *Peter would rather pay for it himself.*

When both options are mentioned use **raději** with the conditional and the conjunction **než** (*than*). **Mít raději** is another way of saying *to prefer*. Compare the following:

(Non-conditional)

Mám raději kočky než psy. — *I prefer cats to dogs.*

(Conditional)

Měl bych raději kočku než psa. — *I would prefer a cat to a dog.*

Just as with **mít rád** (*to like*) this construction can extend to other verbs:

Šel bych raději do divadla než do kina.   *I'd rather go to the theatre than the cinema.*

3 'IF'-CLAUSES/CONDITIONAL

This is the kind of sentence that begins in English '*If I were ..., ... would ...*', '*If I had ..., ... would ...*' or other *ifs* apparently in combination with the past tense: '*If I knew you were coming, ... would ...*'.

In Czech, the *if*-clause begins with the word **kdyby**, which is actually the third-person form and has to be changed, like the conditional auxiliary, according to person. The endings of this conjugating conjunction (an odd phenomenon!) are the same as for the auxiliary. Again, in the dialogue, you have seen:

Kdybychom se rozhodli dřív, **dali bychom vám vědět.**	*If we had decided earlier, we would have let you know.*
Kdybych věděla, že přijdete, upekla **bych dort.**	*If I knew you were coming I would have baked a cake.*
Kdybych nešla teď, kdo ví, **dokdy bych musela čekat.**	*If I didn't go now, who knows how long I'd have to wait.*

To these we could add:

Koupil by si nové auto, kdyby měl **na to peníze.**	*He would buy a new car if he had the money.*
Kdybyste tak nekouřil, nekašlal **byste tolik.**	*If you didn't smoke like that, you wouldn't cough so much.*

4 *TEPRVE* – 'AS LATE AS'

This is a time adverb which can often be replaced by **až**. It is used where the sense is '*as late as*':

Ameriku objevili Evropané teprve **(až)** v šestnáctém století.	*The Europeans **only** discovered America in the 16th century.*

It also denotes a critical first occurrence in other linear sequences:

Ptali se všech; teprve Petr znal **správnou odpověď.**	*They were asking everybody; Peter was the first to know the right answer.*

It does not mean Peter alone and no others.

5 *JÍT* + O AND THE ACCUSATIVE: 'TO BE ABOUT ...'

This very common idiomatic construction is best translated by *to be*, although sometimes other expressions are needed to convey it.

Nejde o nic vážného.	*It's nothing serious.*
Jde o jeho zdraví.	*It's (a question of) his health.*
Šlo o lidské životy.	*Human lives were at stake.*
O mě nejde.	*It's not me I'm worried about.*

| **O to nešlo.** | *That wasn't the point.* |
| **Jde o to, jestli ...** | *The question is whether ...* |

In many such instances you may meet **běží** (**běželo**) replacing **jde** (**šlo**).

Notice that when the party affected by the concern needs to be expressed, the dative case has to be used:

| Jde **mi** o jeho zdraví. | *It's his health I'm concerned about.* |
| **Vládě** jde o to, jak ... | *The government is concerned about how ...* |

Quick vocab

kouřit *to smoke*	**správný** *right, correct*
kašlat *to cough*	**odpověď** *reply, response*
Evropan *European*	**lidský** *human*
objevovat/objevit *to discover*	**život** (gen. **-a**) *life*
století *century*	**vláda** *government*

Exercises

1 Make up questions and answers stating your preferences in the way suggested: Co máte raději, brambory nebo knedlíky? or: Máte raději brambory nebo knedlíky? Mám raději knedlíky než brambory.

   a Kam chodíte raději, do kina nebo do divadla?

   b Komu kupujete dárky raději, dětem nebo rodičům?

   c Kde byste seděli raději, vpředu (*at the front*) nebo vzadu (*at the back*)?

   d Máš raději Petra nebo Janu?

   e Šel byste raději do parku nebo k řece?

   f Budete platit raději v korunách nebo v dolarech?

   g Jak byste platil raději, v librách nebo v korunách?

   h Kde byste parkoval raději, na ulici nebo na parkovišti (*car park*)?

   i Šla bys tam raději sama nebo s Milošem?

   j Měli by to koupit raději za týden nebo teď?

2 Read the information about each person and their job. Make up sentences to explain what they would rather be. The first one is done for you.

	Kdo?	Jaký je?	Čím je?	Čím by byl raději?
a	Jan	velmi seriózní	taxikář	knihovník
b	Marie	ochotný každému pomáhat	v domácnosti	učitelka
c	Štěpán	vtipný	televizní hlasatel	komik
d	Radek	energický	programátor	horolezec
e	Josef	hudebně nadaný	fotbalista	dirigent
f	Sofie	krásný	písařka	modelka
g	'já'	líný	šofér	ředitel

a Jan je velmi seriózní. Zatím (*for the time being*) je taxikářem, ale raději by byl knihovníkem.

 Quick vocab

seriózní *serious, earnest*
taxikář *cab driver*
knihovník *librarian*
vtipný *witty*
hlasatel *announcer*
komik *comedian*
energický *energetic*
programátor *(computer) programmer*

horolezec *climber*
hudebně nadaný *musical*
nadaný *talented*
dirigent *conductor*
písařka *typist*
modelka *model*
líný *lazy*
šofér *driver*
ředitel *manager*

3 Supply answers to the questions using the suggestions in brackets.

a O co jde? (počasí, přednáška, Marie, my, všechno)
b O co jim jde? (peníze, dovolená, příští schůze, nový pas)
c O co vám jde? (kariéra, ta zpráva v novinách, zdraví, naše návštěva)
d O co jde panu Smithovi? (jeho zavazadla, večeře, dárek pro sousedku, práce v laboratoři)
e Komu jde o nový návrh? (Mr Smith, Miss Šetek, the director, the whole company [use **podnik**], us).

●INSIGHT

A lot of the new words you will meet in Czech will be derived from other simpler or more familiar words or elements of words – much more so than in English, where often only a knowledge of Norman French or Latin can offer this transparency; in other words Czech builds very heavily on its own resources. A case in point is the word **parkoviště**, first met in Exercise 1h. The ending **-iště** is highly productive (lots of words end in it); it always has a general meaning of 'place' where something is done or found; **park** is *park*, **parkovat** *to park* or *to be parked* (of a car), so **parkoviště** is 'a place to park'. Many units ago you met **koupelna** *bathroom*. This comes from **koupat se** *to bath* or *bathe*; **koupaliště** is an *open-air swimming-pool*. In Unit 7 you met **letiště** *airport* (also *aerodrome, flying field*), from **letět** *to fly*. In Unit 12 you met the verb **scházet** *to go down*; you should have remembered that **-cház-** is a mutation of the **chod-** of **chodit** *to go, walk*. The prefix **s-** means *down*, so **s + chod + iště**, that is, **schodiště**, is a 'place for walking down', which may seem an arbitrary creation for *(flight of) stairs, staircase*, since we walk up them as well. **Nastupovat/nastoupit** is *to board (a bus, train etc.)*, hence **nástupiště** means *platform*. **Rodit/po-** may be *to give birth*, but **rodiště** is not 'maternity hospital' (which is **porodnice**), but *place of birth*, so is associated with **rodit se/na-** *to be born*.

Evidently, many such nouns come from verbs, though others come from nouns, thus from:

semeno *seed* there is **semeniště** *seedbed*

> **brambor** *potato* gives **bramboříště** *potato field*
>
> **tábor** *camp* gives **tábořiště** *campsite*
>
> **boj** *fight(ing)* gives **bojiště** *battlefield* ... and countless others; one reversing dictionary* lists 122 items of both kinds, from **hrabiště** *rake handle*, from **hrabě** (f.pl.) *rake*, to **vržiště** the *sector* or *target area* into or towards which you throw a javelin, hammer, discus or shot, from **vrhat/vrhnout** *to throw, toss, hurl*. (*A reversing dictionary is one that lists words alphabetically from their ends, not their beginnings, hence all the words ending in **-iště** are neatly brought together.)

Dialogue 2

Continuation of the previous dialogue.

 TR 46

Mrs Smith	Snad ano. Doktor mi nikdy neřekl, abych nepila. Ale já stejně moc nepiju, jen bych nechtěla, abyste se všichni kvůli mně omezovali.
Navrátil	Nebojte se. My se nedáme. A ani o to nejde.
Navrátilová	Ale Zdeňku, radila bych ti, abys mnoho nepil, zvlášť kdybys je měl odvézt zpátky do hotelu.
Mr Smith	To v žádném případě nemusí. V nejhorším případě bychom jeli taxíkem, ale myslím, že stačí metro.
Navrátil	Tak vy vlastně letíte zítra, abyste mohla být v nemocnici ve čtvrtek.
Mrs Smith	Ano, nemám na vybranou. Doporučili mi, abych přišla.
Navrátilová	Tak Zdeňku, ty bys ji mohl odvézt ráno na letiště, ne?
Navrátil	To bych mohl, a pana Smithe taky, aby ji mohl vyprovodit.
Mr Smith	To opravdu není třeba, já ji tam dovezu letištním autobusem, aby určitě přijela na letiště včas.
Navrátil	Ne, ne, já vás tam hodím, stejně jsem měl být zítra doma. Jen buďte klidní, znám šikovnou cestu od vašeho hotelu na letiště. Pojeďte raději se mnou.
Mrs Smith	Tak děkujeme mnohokrát, jste velmi laskavi.
Navrátilová	Abys to tedy, Zdeňku, s dnešním pitím nepřeháněl. Budeš muset zítra vstávat s jasnou hlavou!
Mrs Smith	Vidíte, přece vás omezujeme. To mě mrzí.
Navrátil	Nemějte strach, paní Smithová. Nic nebudeme přehánět. Hlavně abyste si nemysleli, že já jsem alkoholik! Mně stačí teď nějaký aperitiv, sklenička vína při večeři a třeba kapka koňaku potom.

Quick vocab

snad ano *possibly, probably, I should think so*

doktor mi neřekl, abych nepila *the doctor hasn't told me not to drink*

nechtěla bych, abyste se omezovali *I wouldn't like you to limit yourselves*

omezovat (se)/omezit (se) *to limit, restrict (oneself)*

kvůli mně *on my account, because of me*

nebojte se *don't worry*

bát se (bojí se) (+ gen.) *to be afraid (of)*

my se nedáme *we won't let ourselves be (limited)*

dávat se/dát se + infinitive *to let oneself be -ed*

ani o to nejde *that's not the issue*

radila bych ti, abys mnoho nepil *I'd advise you not to drink much*

radit/po- (+ dat.) **aby ...** *to advise (someone) to ...*

to v žádném případě nemusí *he needn't (do that) at all*

v nejhorším případě *if the worst comes to the worst*

nejhorší *worst*

případ *case, event*

letíte zítra, abyste mohla ... *you're flying tomorrow so that you can ...*

nemít na vybranou *to have no option, alternative*

doporučili mi, abych přišla *they recommended me to come*

aby ji mohl vyprovodit *so that he can see her off*

vyprovázet/vyprovodit *to see off*

to opravdu není třeba *there's really no need*

dovezu ji tam, aby přijela včas *I'll take her so that she arrives on time*

já vás tam hodím *I'll drop you there*

házet/hodit *to throw, (also) to drop someone off somewhere by car (colloquial)*

buďte klidní *don't worry*

klidný *calm*

šikovný *clever, useful, handy*

abys to s pitím nepřeháněl! *You'd better not overdo the drinking*

přehánět/přehnat *to exaggerate, overdo*

to mě mrzí *I am sorry, I do regret that*

nemějte strach! *never fear!*

strach *fear*

hlavně aby(ste) ... *the main thing is that (you) should ...*

mně stačí (+ nom.) *I'll make do with*

při večeři *over dinner*

sklenička (diminutive of **sklenice** f.) *glass*

kapka *drop, also drip*

koňak *cognac, brandy*

6 ABY – 'THAT I/YOU/WE ...'

This little word, which changes according to person in exactly the same way as **kdyby**, does several related jobs, all illustrated in Dialogue 2.

a Advising, telling, recommending or requesting someone to do something.

If you say: *'Come on time'*, this can, depending on the circumstances, be interpreted as advice, an order, a request or merely a recommendation. The same would apply to a Czech command if expressed in the imperative. However, you can specify what is really meant by using the verbs that exist for the purpose:

radit/po- (*advise*)

říkat/říct (and others having the same basic meaning) (*tell*)

prosit/po- (*to request*)

doporučovat/doporučit (*recommend*)

These are then followed by a clause beginning with **aby** in the appropriate person-form and containing the past-tense form of the verb – the part that ends in **-l**. In Dialogue 2 you have the example:

Radil bych ti, abys mnoho nepil.   *I'd advise you not to drink too much.*

which, to use an old-fashioned style of English, amounts to: *I advise you that you not drink too much.*

b Reporting on the advice of others.

The same construction is especially common in the third persons, where it is equivalent to an 'indirect command', a reported version of what someone else has bidden or recommended or advised and so forth. There are a couple of these in the dialogue:

Doktor mi neřekl, abych nepila.   *The doctor didn't tell me not to drink ('that I not drink').*

Doporučili mi, abych přišla.   *They recommended me to come ('that I come').*

c Wanting and wishing.

If someone simply wants to do something, the verb **chtít** is enough, followed by an infinitive:

Chce si koupit chleba.   *He wants to buy some bread.*

But if someone wants someone else to do something, you need, again, an **aby**-clause:

Chce, abych koupil chleba.   *He wants me to buy some bread ('that I buy bread').*

The more formal verb **přát si** (**přeje si**) to wish works similarly:

Nepřejeme si, aby tady kouřili.   *We do not wish them to smoke here.*

The same construction applies when **chtít** is used in the conditional, when it often translates as 'would like':

Nechtěla bych, abyste se omezovali.   *I wouldn't like you to limit yourselves.*

This is the basis of some politely formulated sentence types such as:

Chtěl bych (*or* **Já bych chtěl**) **...**   *I would like ...*

followed by a noun, an infinitive or an **aby**-clause. Note also the way of politely offering to do something:

Nechtěl byste, abych ...?   *Would you like me to ..?*

Some wishes, like the warnings overleaf, may be expressed by an **aby** clause on its own (often with the addition of **už** to denote urgency):

Už aby tu byli!   *I wish they'd hurry up!*

Folk idiom is full of such wishes; you may hear:

Aby ho vzal čert.	*May the devil take him!*
Aby ji husa kopla!	*May a goose kick her!*

(the latter meaning: 'What a nuisance she can be sometimes', 'Why did she have to go and do that?' or some other expression of annoyance).

d Warning.

The **aby** construction may follow the verbs **varovat** (*to warn*) and the bureaucratic **upozorňovat/upozornit** (*to advise*, *draw someone's attention*), notably when they have the force of a near-command, as opposed to a warning for information:

Varuji vás, abyste nezlobili.	*I warn you not to be naughty.*
Žadatele upozorňujeme, aby formuláře odevzdali trojmo a v češtině.	*Applicants are advised to submit their forms in triplicate and in Czech.*

However, many gentle admonitions may be expressed by the **aby** construction on its own, as (from Dialogue 2):

Abys to s pitím nepřeháněl.	*You'd better not overdo the drinking.*
Hlavně abyste si nemysleli, že jsem alkoholik.	*The main thing is not to think I'm an alcoholic.*

e Purpose or reason.

Probably the most widespread function of **aby** clauses is to express purposes, where in English you would meet such phrases as '*in order to*', '*in order that*', '*so as to*', or just an infinitive. The only example in Dialogue 2 is:

Letíte zítra, abyste mohla být v nemocnici ve čtvrtek.	*You're flying tomorrow so as to be at the hospital on Thursday.*

There are endless possibilities.

Česky se učím, abych se domluvil s Čechy.	*I'm studying Czech in order to make myself understood to Czechs.*
Abychom určitě dojeli včas, objednali jsme si taxík.	*To be sure of getting there on time we've ordered a taxi.*

The **aby** clause may stand first or second in the sequence; it depends on context and emphasis.

Whatever the order, **aby** clauses must, in writing, be separated by a comma.

f Various important modalities – about possible, necessary, etc. states of affairs – not present in the dialogue types.

Je/není možné, aby …	*It is(n't) possible that …*
Je/není třeba, aby …	*It is(n't) necessary …*
Je/není žádoucí, aby …	*It is(n't) desirable …*
Je/není vyloučeno, aby …	*It is(n't) out of the question that …*
Není žádoucí, aby nás viděli spolu.	*It isn't desirable that they see us together.*

Exercises

4 Supply the appropriate form of aby and the verbs suggested to give meaningful utterances (beware of word order):

a Doporučujeme vám, (aby) (vzít si) kabát, prší.
b Je vyloučeno, (aby) (přijet) v úterý, už budeme doma.
c Chceme, (aby) Petr a Marie (vzít se).
d Upozorňujeme cestující, (aby) všechna zavazadla (vzít s sebou).
e Řekl mi, (aby) (poslat mu to) za týden.
f Poprosili nás, (aby) (půjčit jim) deset liber.
g Spěcháme, (aby) (nezmeškat) začátek představení.
h Nechtějí, Honzo, (aby) v ložnici (kouřit).
i (Aby), milí přatelé, (nemyslet si), že budu kandidovat!
j Už (aby) ty dopisy (přijít).

Quick vocab

zmeškat	*to be late for*	**představení**	*performance*
začátek	*beginning*	**kandidovat**	*to stand for election*

 TR 47

5 Compile a set of planned activities from the following, using the first one as a model. (Be careful about which clause conveys the purpose.) Example: (já) (jít do města) (koupit dceři dárek) – Jdu do města, abych koupil dceři dárek.

a (my) (hledat ve slovníku) (najít významy slov)
b (ona) (vařit zeleninu) (manžel) (stát se vegetariánem)
c (oni) (učit se česky) (moct pracovat v Praze)
d (my) (večeřet spolu) (vy) (muset přijít domů včas)
e (já) (zavolat sousedy) (pomoct nám s přípravami)
f (člověk *one*) (studovat cizí jazyky) (muset mít jisté nadání)
g (vy) (smět v Anglii řídit auto) (muset vám být aspoň 17 let)

 **Quick vocab**

nadání *talent*   **řídit** *to drive*

6 **Now convert b, d and f of Exercise 5 into the past tense.**

   (Example: Šel jsem do města, abych koupil dceři dárek.)

7 **Supply the correct form of kdyby and by in the following sentences:**
   a (kdyby) mi to Petr neřekl, nevěděl (by 'I') o tom nic.
   b (kdyby), Jano a Ivane, chtěli jet s námi, bylo (by) ještě místo.
   c My (by) v Edinburghu nekupovali nový dům, (kdyby) já tam nedostal dobré místo.
   d (kdyby) její synové tak nepili, nemusela (by) si dělat tolik starostí.
   e (kdyby 'I') byl na vašem místě, řekl (by) to také sousedům.

8 **Now translate the sentences to be sure you understand them.**

MORE PROVERBS

Look at these two versions of a common proverb; the second one should provide the 'logic' of the first, but as with proverbs in many languages, the logic is hidden. Check the **Key to the exercises** if it is unclear.
   i   **Kdyby jsou chyby.**
   ii **Kdyby nebylo kdyby, nebyly by chyby.**

Another common lament is:

Pozdě **bycha** honit!   *It's too late ['to chase "I would have" ']*

It is equivalent to *locking the stable door after the horse has bolted*, or *crying over spilt milk*. Appreciate the sheer inventiveness of converting an auxiliary verb – **bych** – into an animate noun!

Test yourself

Make aby-type warnings or recommendations to express the following (note the variety of English formulations that can be covered by this device):
   a Mind you don't burn your fingers! (use the **ty** form)
   b Mind you don't forget the keys! (use the singular **vy** form)
   c Let's park for preference in the car-park, don't you think?
   d I really had better buy a new laptop!
   e Mind you don't get the salt and sugar mixed up! (use the plural **vy** form)

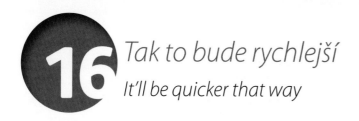

16
Tak to bude rychlejší
It'll be quicker that way

In this unit you will learn
▶ *How to make comparisons*
▶ *How to say something is the best*
▶ *How to talk about your children and pets*

Dialogue 1

The Smith children (Sharon and Graham), who both speak amazingly good Czech, are out and about with two of the Navrátil children, Líba and Štěpán (Jan was not available).

🔊 **CD2, TR 18**

Sharon	Nemohli bychom si jít někam sednout? Bolí mě nohy a mám žízeň.
Štěpán	Vždyť jsme ještě nikde nebyli, nejdřív jsme vám chtěli ukázat Hrad a pak teprve se někde zastavit na občerstvení. Nemůžeš počkat?
Graham	Jak je to daleko?
Štěpán	Pěšky asi dva kilometry, nebo kousek pěšky a potom tři stanice metra.
Sharon	Kousek?! Znám tvoje 'kousky' – jsou trochu delší než moje!
Líba	Neboj se, to není tak zlé. V Londýně byly vzdálenosti větší, a my jsme si nestěžovali.
Štěpán	Nechte toho, pojedeme metrem. Tak to bude rychlejší.
Graham	Souhlasím. Pěšky by to bylo možná hezčí …
Líba	Ano, bylo, cestou je několik skutečně pěkných pohledů na město, ale asi je musíme nechat na jindy.
They've been round the Castle and are having the promised drink. Sharon is still complaining.	
Sharon	To kafe mohlo být teplejší.
Graham	Ty jsi čím dál protivnější. Máš být ráda, že jsi vůbec tady!
Líba	(*trying to change the subject*) Ukažte mi pohlednice, které jste si koupili.
Graham	Já mám lepší. Sharon si koupila první, které jsme našli, ale mně se moc nelíbily.
Štěpán	To je její věc. (*Being diplomatic*) No, jsou taky hezké, jenom jiné. Aspoň má co lidem posílat.
Sharon	Tahle je nejkrásnější. Tu si nechám, ale koupím si další, abych jich měla dost na posílání.

Quick vocab

jít si někam sednout *to go and sit somewhere* (here, in order to have something to eat or drink)

sedat si/sednout si *to sit down*

mít žízeň *to be thirsty*

žízeň (f, gen. **žízně**) *thirst*

vždyť (protesting) *but*

ukazovat/ukázat (ukáže) *to show*

hrad *castle* (with capital H = Prague Castle)

občerstvení *refreshment(s), a snack*

kousek *a bit* (here, *a short way*)

stanice (f) *(bus or underground) stop*

to není tak zlé *it's not that bad*

zlý *wicked, evil, bad*

vzdálenost (-i) *distance*

větší *bigger*

nechte toho! *leave off!, stop it!*

rychlejší *quicker, faster*

souhlasit *to agree, concur*

bylo by to možná hezčí *it might be nicer*

možná *perhaps*

hezčí *prettier, nicer*

skutečně *really*

pohled na (+ acc.) *view of something*

musíme je nechat na jindy *we'll have to leave them for another time*

to kafe mohlo být teplejší *the coffee could have been warmer*

teplý *warm*

ty jsi čím dál protivnější *you're getting more and more obnoxious*

protivný *obnoxious*

máš být ráda, že *you should be thankful that*

lepší *better*

to je její věc *that's her affair/business*

no *hmm*

aspoň má co lidem posílat *at least she's got something to send to people*

nejkrásnější *(the) most beautiful (one)*

tu si nechám *I'll keep that one*

nechávat si/nechat si *to keep*

abych jich měla dost na posílání *so I have enough (of them) for sending*

1 GOOD, BETTER, BEST

This section deals with the second degree of adjectives (*better*), the comparative. In English, this either ends in -*er*, or is expressed by the extra word *more*, as in *more beautiful*.

In Czech, the regular equivalent of -*er* is the ending **-ější** or **-ejší** (depending once again on the spelling rules). Look at the following examples:

krásný *beautiful*	**krásnější** *more beautiful*
rychlý *quick*	**rychlejší** *quicker*
svěží *fresh*	**svěžejší** *fresher*
severní *northern*	**severnější** *more northerly*

As in other circumstances, certain consonants are affected by the **-ě-** of this ending (most of the consonants in the groups of words given further on). The main ones to study are **-r-**, **-sk-** and **-ck-**, and just a few cases of **-k-**, which become **-ř-, -šť-** and **-čť-** (but beware the spelling!), and **-č-** as in:

pestrý *colourful*	**pestřejší** *more colourful*
český *Czech*	**češtější** *more Czech*
logický *logical*	**logičtější** *more logical*
horký *hot*	**horčejší** *hotter*

So much for the rule. The exceptions are unavoidable! However, most are words of everyday meanings, so you will meet them frequently and get used to them. These can be grouped together. Use the following section for reference, as an addition to the reference section at the back of the book.

The first of the minor comparative endings is **-ší**. This occurs with the following five groups of adjectives.

Group 1

Adjectives that end in **-chý** and **-hý** (notice what happens to **ch** and **h**):

hluchý	*(deaf)*	**hlušší**
tichý	*(quiet)*	**tišší**
suchý	*(dry)*	**sušší**
jednoduchý	*(simple)*	**jednodušší**
tuhý	*(stiff, tough)*	**tužší**
drahý	*(dear; costly)*	**dražší**

Group 2

Some that end in **-ký** and lose the **k**:

těžký	*(heavy, difficult)*	**těžší**
hladký	*(smooth)*	**hladší**
sladký	*(sweet)*	**sladší**
prudký	*(abrupt, steep; quick-tempered)*	**prudší**
řídký	*(rare, sparse, thin* [of liquids]*)*	**řidší**
krátký	*(short)*	**kratší**
krotký	*(meek, tame)*	**krotší** (or **krotčejší**)

Group 3

A few others, in which **-ší** is just tacked on to the stem:

starý	*(old)*	**starší**
mladý	*(young)*	**mladší**
tvrdý	*(hard)*	**tvrdší**
hustý	*(thick, dense)*	**hustší**
čistý	*(clean)*	**čistší**
tlustý	*(fat)*	**tlustší**
sprostý	*(rude, vulgar, uncouth)*	**sprostší**
bohatý	*(rich, wealthy)*	**bohatší**
hrubý	*(rough, coarse)*	**hrubší**
slabý	*(weak, thin)*	**slabší**
tmavý	*(dark)*	**tmavší**

Group 4

It also occurs with a family of words to do with space:

vysoký	*(tall, high)*	**vyšší**
nízký	*(low, base)*	**nižší**
hluboký	*(deep, profound)*	**hlubší**
široký	*(wide, broad)*	**širší**
úzký	*(narrow, tight)*	**užší**
blízký	*(near, close)*	**bližší**
daleký	*(far, remote)*	**další** (NB *another, a further*)
dlouhý	*(long)*	**delší** (of time or space)

Group 5

Irregular items:

malý	*(small)*	**menší**
velký	*(big, great)*	**větší**
dobrý	*(good)*	**lepší**
špatný	*(bad)*	**horší**
snadný	*(easy)*	**snazší**

The second exceptional ending, **-čí**, is associated with words ending in **-ký**:

Group 6

hezký	*(pretty, nice)*	**hezčí**
lehký	*(light, easy)*	**lehčí**
křehký	*(frail, fragile)*	**křehčí**
měkký	*(soft)*	**měkčí**
tenký	*(thin – not of people)*	**tenčí**
mělký	*(shallow)*	**mělčí**
trpký	*(tart, acid)*	**trpčí**
vlhký	*(damp, moist)*	**vlhčí**

You need to know two other common words that are comparatives in form:
   a dřívější (*former, previous*) for which there is no basic form.
   b pozdější (*later, subsequent*) for which the adjective **pozdní** (*late*) is not widely used.
      (To say 'I am late' use **Jdu pozdě** or **Mám zpoždění**. The adjective cannot be used.)

Finally, the most minor type of comparatives. Just as English sometimes has to resort to *more*, so too Czech has comparatives based on **víc(e)**. Not many are involved and they all end in **-cí**:

žádoucí	*desirable, preferable*
víc žádoucí	*more desirable*

You may nonetheless occasionally hear such substitutes as **žádoucnější**, but do not imitate them.

2 MORE/EVEN MORE/MUCH MORE

Comparative adjectives form part of other expressions beyond merely those followed by **než** (*than*).

a *Even more* is expressed by **ještě** + comparative:

Jana je hezčí než Milena a Helenka je ještě hezčí.	*Jana is prettier than Milena and Helena is even prettier.*

b *Much more* is expressed by **mnohem** or **o mnoho** + comparative:

Jan je mnohem (or **o mnoho**) **starší než Milena.**	*Jan is much older than Milena.*

c **O mnoho** (*by much*) shows how Czech expresses the measure of the difference. **O mnoho krásnější** means, in effect, *more beautiful by much*. This 'by' construction appears in many contexts:

Petr je o dva roky starší než Jan.	*Peter is (by) two years older than John.*
Sklo je o centimetr užší než okno.	*The glass is (by) a centimetre narrower than the window.*

d Where two sets of circumstances change in parallel, *the more ... the more ...*, Czech uses **čím ... tím ...** (instrumental case of **co** and **to**, just as **mnohem** above was the instrumental of **mnoho**).

Čím jsem starší, tím jsem zapomnětlivější.	*The older I am, the more forgetful I am.*

A simpler version of this uses **čím dál** + comparative:

Jsem čím dál zapomnětlivější.	*I am ever more forgetful (more and more forgetful).*

3 BEST/FASTEST

The English forms in *-est* are called the *superlative*. Nothing could be simpler than forming the superlative in Czech – provided you get the comparative right. Without exception, all you need is to add **nej-** at the front:

dobrý	lepší	**nej**lepší
rychlý	rychlejší	**nej**rychlejší
hezký	hezčí	**nej**hezčí

There are again one or two useful constructions based on the superlative:

a *the best (fastest, ...) (out) of* is simply expressed by the superlative + **z** + genitive:

Petr je nejlepší ze všech.	*Peter is the best of all.*
Jan je z nás nejrychlejší.	*John is the fastest of us.*

b the English *as ... as possible* and *most ... possible* constructions also use the superlative in Czech, preceded simply by **co**:

Kupte si co nejlevnější boty.	*Buy the cheapest shoes possible.*
Vařila co nejzdravější večeři.	*She cooked as healthy a dinner as possible.*

You may meet the word **možná** between the two parts of the idiom: **co možná nejlevnější boty**. It makes no difference to the meaning.

4 COMPARISONS BASED ON (NON-)SAMENESS

To say that x is or isn't as (old) as y, use **je stejně (starý) jako** or **není tak (starý) jako** if what follows is a noun:

Petr je stejně starý jako Marie.	*Peter is as old as Mary.*
Čeština není tak těžká jako čínština.	*Czech isn't as hard as Chinese.*

If what follows is a clause, replace **jako** by **jak**:

Čeština není tak těžká, jak jste si myslel.	*Czech isn't as hard as you thought.*

5 *NECHÁVAT/NECHAT* – WAYS OF SAYING 'TO LEAVE'

Nechávat/nechat něco někde is *to leave something somewhere* (by accident or design).

Nechal jsem klíče doma.	*I've left the keys at home.*
Nechá nám vzkaz v hotelu.	*He'll leave us a message at the hotel.*
Nechte to!	*Leave it alone!*

Nechat + genitive means *to leave off doing something*, but is largely confined to commands with **toho**.

Nechte toho!	*Stop it!*

Nechávat/nechat si něco means *to keep*, in the sense of 'take possession' or 'fail to return'.

Půjčili jsme jim židle a oni si je nechali!	*We lent them some chairs and they kept them!*
Nechte si to.	*Keep it* (often used about change, as a tip).

Nechávat/nechat si něco pro sebe means *to keep something* (a secret) *to oneself*.

Nechte si to pro sebe.	*Don't tell anyone.*

a **Nechat** forms its imperative: **nech/nechte**. There is also a regularly formed regional variant **nechej/nechejte**.

b *Leave* **nechat** must not be confused with *leave* meaning *to go away, to depart* (**odjet, odejít**):

Odjeli/Odešli jsme v deset.	*We left at ten.*

nor with the meaning *to abandon* (**opustit**).

Loď jsme opustili, než se potopila.	*We left the ship before it sank.*

6 *SEDĚT* AND *SEDNOUT* – 'TO BE SEATED' AND 'TO SIT DOWN' – AND OTHER VERBS

Czech, as you know, firmly distinguishes between positions and movements (e.g. at a place/ to a place). Verbs denoting various postures need some care, since one and the same English verb may have two functions, kept apart in Czech:

The verbs denoting position, posture, can only be imperfective.

sedět (sit)	**Sedím v křesle.**	*I'm sitting in an armchair.*
ležet (lie)	**Leží na pláži.**	*They're (lying) on the beach.*
stát (stand)	**Stála ve frontě.**	*She was standing in a queue.*
klečet (kneel)	**Klečel před oltářem.**	*He was kneeling before the altar.*
viset (hang)	**Visel na provaze.**	*He was hanging on the rope.*

Verbs meaning to adopt a posture denote an act, and therefore have both aspects:

sedat si/sednout si (do křesla)	*to sit (down) (in an armchair)*
lehat si/lehnout si (na pláž)	*to lie (down) (on the beach)*
vstávat/vstát	*to get up, rise*
klekat si/kleknout si (před oltář)	*to kneel (down) (before the altar)*
věšet se/pověsit se (na provaz)	*to suspend oneself (on a rope)**

*This is not suicide: suicidal hanging is almost exclusively perfective and uses **oběsit se**.

Of these only **věšet/pověsit** also occurs with an object:

Věšela prádlo na šňůru.   *She was hanging the washing on the line.*

There is also a verb **posazovat/posadit** (*to seat*):

Posadila ho vedle sebe.   *She sat him down next to her.*

This has a reflexive form, usually only perfective **posadit se** (*to sit down*), as a common alternative to **sednout si**. So listen out for both **sedněte si** and **posaďte se** (*do*) *sit down* – they are equally common.

7 WHAT DOES 'MEAN' MEAN?

When you are asking after the significance or meaning, of a word, sentence, abbreviation or even an event, you must use **znamenat**.

Co znamená zkratka OSN?   *What does the abbreviation UNO mean?*
Co to znamená, když kočka přede?   *What does it mean when a cat purrs?*

When, however, you are talking more about a person's intended meaning, use **myslet**.

Jak to myslíš?   *What do you mean? (Lit. How do you mean it?)*
On to nemyslí vážně.   *He doesn't mean it./He can't be serious.*
Kdo ví, co tím myslel?   *Goodness knows what he meant by that!*

Quick vocab

levný *cheap*
zapomnětlivý *forgetful*
loď (lodi or **lodě** f *) ship*
opouštět/opustit *to leave, abandon*
topit se/po- *to sink*
pláž (f) *beach*
fronta *queue*
oltář (m) *altar*
prádlo *linen, the washing*

šňůra *(washing) line*
provaz *rope, string*
zkratka *abbreviation*
kočka *cat*
příst (přede) *to purr; to spin* (thread)
OSN = Organizace spojených národů *UNO*
spojený *united*
národ (gen. **-a**) *nation*
čínština *Chinese* (the language)

● **INSIGHT**

Czech is no less rich than English in onomatopoeia, words that paint sounds. A few onomatopoeic verbs are borrowed from pre-existing ideas, like **příst** above. The noise made by the spinning wheel as it carries out the ordinary act of spinning is transferred to the cat (in English it's probably the other way round); both peoples clearly sense a 'p' sound and an 'r' sound in the quiet noise a cat makes. Most sound verbs exist primarily to express the noise, and only a few get re-used for other meanings as well. For now, let's stick to some more animal noises and see how Czechs perceive them, whether similarly to English ears, or not. So, the other noise a cat makes is expressed by the Czech verb **mňaukat**. A dog **štěká** or **hafá** (and *bow-wow* is **haf-haf**). A hen **kdáká**, while a cockerel **kokrhá** (but *cock-a-doodle-doo* is **kikiriki**). A crow **kráká**, a cuckoo **kuká**, small birds variously **čirikají**, **cvrlikají** or **štěbotají**, and an owl, like a car, **houká**. A pig **chrochtá**, a horse **ržá**, a goose **kejhá** (covers *cackle* and *honk*) and a turkey **hudrá** (and *gobble-gobble* is **hudry-hudry**). All these (and many more) are **a**-conjugation verbs. Another range are **i**-conjugation verbs, all of which have the infinitive in **-et/-ět**. They include **bučet** (bulls and cows), **pištět** (mice and chicks), **mečet** or **bečet** (sheep and goats), and **syčet** (snakes and geese; it also means other kinds of hissing, fizzing and sizzling).

Non-animal words of the same types include **kýchat** *sneeze* (but *atishoo!* is **hepčí(k)!**), **svištět** *whiz, whirr* or *swish*, **dunět** *thunder* (e.g. of distant traffic), **šuštět** *rustle*, **klinkat** *tinkle*, **crčet** *trickle, gurgle* (of water in a drainpipe), **bublat** *bubble*, **klokotat** *babble* (of a brook), also *trill* (nightingale), but **kloktat** *gargle*. And so we could go on ...

Exercises

 TR 49

1 Make up sentences on the basis of the following preferences (the first has been done for you). Use the present tense.

c Lenka (mít) radši (Praha) krásná Londýn
  Lenka má radši Prahu, protože je krásnější než Londýn.

d Studenti (číst) radši (překlad) jednoduchý originál

e (My) radši (letět) letadlo rychlý vlak

f Petr (sedět) radši vedle (Sára) protivná Marie

g Zuzana (mluvit) radši slovensky slovenština pro ni lehká čeština

h Skotové (pít) radši whisky silná pivo

i Štěpán (nosit) radši džínsy nový jeho kalhoty

Ⅴ Quick vocab

překlad	*translation*	**džínsy** (f pl)	*jeans*
whisky (f)	*whisky*	**kalhoty** (f pl)	*trousers*

2 Now convert your sentences a to g in question 1 above to the past tense (think carefully about whether to do so in the second clause would always make sense).

3 Using the pairs, make the different types of comparisons as indicated:

a Londýn – New York (*older*)

b Pražský hrad – Hluboká (*much older*)

c Můj soused – otec (*even older*)

d Jeho manželka – on (*six months older*)

e Jejich dům – náš (*not as old as*)

f Tento hotel – hotel na náměstí (*two hundred years older*)

g Moje auto – jeho (*as old as*)

h Tenhle kufr – ten druhý (*not much older*)

● **INSIGHT**

The Hluboká mentioned in Exercise 3b above is a large, 19th-century country house with a fine park south of Prague, inspired pre-eminently by what the Czechs call 'Tudor' or 'English Gothic'. The reconstruction (1840–71) came at the instigation of Johann Adolf II von Schwarzenberg and his wife the Princess Eleonora (née Lichtenstein) following their visits to England, especially Windsor. Perhaps the second most famous house of the kind is at Lednice in South Moravia, whose present appearance dates from 1846–58, after Prince Alois II von Lichtenstein decided that Vienna was no good for summer parties and had his Lednice seat completely redone in the favoured neo-Gothic style imitative of Windsor Castle. Both houses have impressive, easily found websites, usefully in Czech and English (so a good source of parallel texts).

Dialogue 2

This time it is the Navrátil children arguing, about their homework.

Líba	Já jsem ti přece řekla, že budu hotová dřív než ty.
Štěpán	No a! Ale já jsem to udělal líp!
Líba	To si myslíš ty! Vypadá to hůř, než kdyby to psalo naše kotě.
Štěpán	A ten tvůj úkol snad vypadá líp?
Líba	Vypadá. Nenakreslila jsem sice ten obrázek právě nejkrásněji, ale naše učitelka říká, že každý nemůže být Rembrandt.

Štěpán	Tak já píšu škaredějí než kotě, a ty kreslíš jen o něco méně hezky, než maloval Rembrandt!

Their father enters in time to hear the last remark.

Navrátil	Podívejte se, má tohle smysl? Kdybyste radši uvažovali rozumněji a hlavně se hádali tišeji.
Děti	Promiň, tati.
Navrátil	Jak by to vypadalo, kdyby mi maminka pořád vytýkala, že neumím natírat, nebo já jí zase říkal, že se zřejmě neučila vařit v Hiltonu? K čemu by to vedlo?
Líba	(*giggling*) Tak tys ji neslyšel minulý týden?
Navrátil	Co? Kdy? Co řekla?
Líba	Jak jsi natřel venku okna ... Já jsem potom slyšela, jak maminka povídá: Tohle snad natřelo prase zadní levou.
Navrátil	Počkej, děvče. To jsem slyšel. Jednak řekla prasata, a navíc jí šlo o práci natěračů z komunálu, kteří právě přetřeli lavičky na hřišti.
Líba	To jsem nevěděla, promiň.
Navrátil	O mé práci se vždycky vyjadřuje mnohem šetrněji. Nebo ji spíš přejde mlčením.
Štěpán	Dejte pokoj s tím, jak kdo natírá. Mě spíš zajímá, jak vaří v tom Hiltonu a jestli pestřeji než u nás!

Quick vocab

budu hotová dřív než ty *I'll be finished before you (are)*

dřív(e) než *before (conjunction)*

no a *so what*

líp (adverb) *better*

To si myslíš ty! *That's what you think!*

hůř comparative of **špatně**

kotě (n. **kotěte**) *kitten*

úkol *exercise, task, homework*

kreslit/na- *to draw*

obrázek *picture*

právě (here goes with **ne-**) *not exactly*

nejkrásněji *most beautifully*

každý nemůže být Rembrandt *not everyone can be a Rembrandt*

škaredějí comparative adverb from **škaredý** *ugly, awful, bad, gross*

jen o něco *just slightly*

méně hezky *less nicely*

malovat *to paint*

podívejte se (here) *look here!*

má tohle smysl? *What's the point of this?*

uvažovat *to think, consider, use one's head*

rozumněji comparative of **rozumně** adverb from **rozumný** *sensible*

hlavně (here) *above all*

tišeji comparative of **tiše/ticho** *more quietly*

tati domestic usage for *Dad(dy)*

natírat/natřít (**natře,** past **natřel**) *to paint*

vytýkat/vytknout (**někomu něco**) *to reproach*

zřejmě *apparently, evidently*

k čemu by to vedlo *where would that lead/get us*

tys = ty jsi

jak jsi natřel venku okna *when you had painted the windows outside*

tohle snad natřelo prase zadní levou *this must have been painted by a pig with its left hind leg*

prase (n, **prasete**) *pig*
zadní *rear, back* (adj.)
levý *left*
počkej, děvče! *wait a moment, my girl!*
děvče (n, **děvčete**) *girl, lass*
jednak ... a navíc *for one thing ...*
  and what's more
natěrač *(house) painter*
komunál *council services department*
přetírat/přetřít *to repaint*
lavička *bench*
hřiště (n) *(children's) playground*

vyjadřovat (se)/vyjádřit (se)
  to express (oneself)
šetrněji comparative adverb from **šetrný**
  sparing; considerate
spíš(e) *more likely, rather*
přecházet/přejít mlčením *to pass*
  over in silence
mlčení *silence, non-talking*
dát pokoj s + instrumental (idiom)
  to stop going on about something
pestřeji comparative adverb from
  pestrý *colourful, varied*

8 LOOKING BETTER/THINKING MORE SENSIBLY

Forming comparative adverbs (*more quickly*) is relatively straightforward. For the majority, the 'regular' words, just replace the normal adverb ending **-ě (-e)** with **-ěji (-eji)**:

krásně → krásněji   *beautifully → more beautifully*

rychle → rychleji   *quickly → more quickly*

also:

pomalu → pomaleji   *slowly → more slowly*

However, one or two variants are associated with adjectives in the groups listed in Section 1, so you do need to know how the comparative adjective is formed.

For the regular types, replace **-ější (-ejší)** with **-ěji (-eji)**:

krásnější → krásněji   rychlejší → rychleji

logičtější → logičtěji   pozdější → později

(**Dřívější** is an exception and uses **dřív(e)** *earlier, sooner,* which is the comparative of **brzo, brzy** *early, soon.*)

For most of Group 1 and Group 3, replace **-ší** by **-eji** and **-ěji** respectively; in Group 3 words this will have consequences for pronunciation and/or spelling.

tišší → tišeji   mladší → mlaději

jednodušší → jednodušeji   slabší → slaběji

(The exception **dražší** has **dráž(e)** *more dearly.* **Starši** has **stáře** and, less commonly, **stařeji** *older.*)

For most of Group 2 and Group 6, replace **-ší** or **-čí** with **-čeji** (the **č** is because of the **k** in the base adjective):

prudší → prudčeji   hezčí → hezčeji

kratší → kratčeji   měkčí → měkčeji

(The exception **těžší** has **tíž(e)** *with more difficulty.*)

Groups 4 and 5, which were exceptional in how their adjectival comparatives behaved, need to be learned separately:

vyšší → výš(e)	bližší → blíž(e)	větší → víc(e)
nižší → níž(e)	další → dál(e)	lepší → lépe/líp
hlubší → hloub(ěji)	delší → déle/dýl	horší → hůř(e)
širší → šíř(e)	menší → méně/míň	snazší → snáz(e)
užší → úže		

  a The adjectives have a short vowel, the adverbs a long vowel.

  b Almost all the exceptions given have optional longer forms. These are used in higher or more formal styles, or sometimes for rhythm or ease of pronunciation; the shorter forms are more informal. The short forms with a vowel change (**dýl**, **líp**, **míň**) are the most informal, though not unacceptably 'low'.

  c There is a special adverb, comparative in form, **spíš(e)**, which means *probably*, *more likely*, *rather (more)* and sometimes just *more*, where it expresses a conjecture more than a fact, or qualifies other word-classes than adjectives:

  Řekl bych, že to je spíš modré   *I'd say it was more blue than green.*
    než zelené.

  Udělá to spíš Petr než Marie.   *Peter's more likely to do it than Mary.*

  d Like superlative adjectives, all superlative adverbs are formed by mere addition of **nej-** to the comparative:

  Petr vaří ze všech nejlíp.   *Peter cooks best of all.*

9 WHEN TO USE COMPARATIVE ADVERBS

  a Whenever an adverb is, in Czech, unavoidable, such as (often) after **vypadat**.

  Vypadá líp než včera.   *He's looking better than yesterday.*

  Here, however, the comparative adjective is often used instead: **Vypadá starší** is more probable than **stáře** or **stařeji**.

  b As in English to accompany other verbs:

  Zpívala krásněji než Marie.   *She sang more prettily than Mary.*
  Zůstali jsme déle, než jsme chtěli.   *We stayed longer than we intended.*

  c In the case of **víc(e)** (*more*) and **méně/míň** (*less/fewer*) to express quantity. This means that they are also the comparatives of **mnoho** (*much/many*) and **málo** (*little/few*) and, like them, are followed by the genitive:

  Má víc knih než já.   *He has more books than I.*
  Měla míň času, než potřebovala.   *She had less time than she needed.*

  d **Méně/míň** has an extra use in being the only way of expressing negative comparison in both adjectives and adverbs:

  Kanály jsou méně důležité než železnice. *Canals are less important than railways.*
  Štěpán píše méně hezky než Líba.   *Štěpán writes less nicely than Líba.*

10 CHILDREN AND YOUNG ANIMALS

Czech has a special class of neuter nouns, always ending in **-ě** or **-e**, reserved mostly for the names of young animals. In Dialogue 2 you met **kotě** (*kitten*), but in the same group there is **štěně** (*puppy*), **jehně** (*lamb*), **tele** (*calf*), **sele** (*piglet*), **hříbě** (*foal*), **kuře** (*chick*), **ptáče** (*baby bird*) and many others, often derived from the name of the adult: **slon** (*elephant*), **slůně** (*baby elephant*).

The peculiarity of the declension is the addition of an ending before the case endings, moreover that ending differs between singular and plural:

	Singular	Plural
Nominative	kotě	koťata
Accusative	kotě	koťata
Genitive	kotěte	koťat
Dative	kotěti	koťatům
Locative	(o) kotěti	koťatech
Instrumental	kotětem	koťaty

Note that the singular case endings, after the inserted ending, are like the 'soft' declensions, and the plural endings like those of 'hard' neuter nouns.

The young human, **dítě** (*baby, child*) also belongs in this family, but beware: its plural **děti** (*children*) is feminine (not neuter) and declines like the **i**-declension nouns.

Other human young in the group are **nemluvně** (*baby*), **batole** (*toddler*), **děvče** (*little girl*), **dvojčata** (*twins*).

Some common words happen also to share this declension: **prase** (*adult pig*), **koště** (*broom*), **poupě** (*flower bud*) and about half a dozen others, some of them colloquial, like **štamprle** (*tot, dram* or the glass you would have one in).

11 NOT EVERYONE CAN BE REMBRANDT!

This expression was used in Dialogue 2 – and you can imagine plenty more similar. Note that the negation comes on the verb: **Každý *ne*může být Rembrandt**. Similarly you might say: **Každý tohle neví.**   *Not everyone knows that.*

12 *NE- PRÁVĚ NEJLEPŠÍ* – 'NOT EXACTLY THE BEST'

In Dialogue 2, Líba uses a version of this construction, which consists of **právě** (or more colloquially **zrovna**) and a superlative after a negative verb. It is used in irony and is equivalent to *not exactly (not what you'd call) the best* and similar.

13 ON THE SUBJECT OF PAINTING

Malovat is to paint pictures, or for interior decorating using water or emulsion paints. **Natírat** is for gloss paints. **Malíř** (m) = *a painter*, as artist, **natěrač** = *a house painter* or *painting contractor*, while a painter and decorator doing interiors is a **malíř pokojů.**

Exercises

4 Complete the sentences in an appropriate manner, using up all the adverbs in the box below without repeating them.

a Vypadá ___ než včera.

b Anna se dostala na poštu ___, protože běžela ___.

c Je to ___ kotě než kočka.

d Píše ___ perem než propisovačkou.

e Spali jsme ___ na gauči, než loni na zemi.

f Tady je ___ místa než v kuchyni.

g Pojďte ___!

h Koupil to ___, než počítal.

i Chovala se ___ v patnácti letech, než když byla starší.

j ___ tam nechoď, maminka se zlobí.

čitelněji   pohodlněji   raději
rychleji   víc   zdravěji   spíš
dráž   dál   dřív   rozumněji

 Quick vocab

propisovačka	*biro*	**v patnácti letech**	*at fifteen*
čitelný	*legible*	**pohodlný**	*comfortable*
chovat se	*to act, behave*		

4 Read the following and answer the questions below.

Martin cestuje nejraději na kole. Ale když se potřebuje někam dostat rychleji, jede radši vlakem. Loni byl v Čechách, ale letos chce jet na Moravu, protože si myslí, že se mu tam bude líbit víc. V Čechách se mu nejvíc líbila Praha. Pro něho je jedním z nejzajímavějších měst, která zná, a on už poznal mnoho ještě větších hlavních měst. V Praze si dokonce půjčil kolo. Nejhorší však bylo, že na něm nemohl jezdit všude – kvůli kočičím hlavám.

a Jak jezdí Martin nejraději? **d** Líbí se mu Praha? Proč?

b Kdy používá vlak? **e** Měl možnost po Praze jezdit na kole?

c Zná Martin Moravu? **f** Proč se mu to nevyplatilo?

 Quick vocab

kolo *bicycle*

letos *this year*

poznávat/poznat *to get to know*

půjčovat si/půjčit si *to borrow, hire*

hlavní město *capital*

kočičí hlavy *cobblestones* (Lit. cats' heads)

používat/použít *to use*

vyplácet se/vyplatit se (někomu)
to be worth it (to someone)

ANIMALS ...

As Dialogue 2 suggests, animals are just as common in comparisons as in English. So add an idiomatic flavour to your Czech and look for opportunities to use some of the following:

škrábat jako kocour/kočka	*to scratch/scrawl like a cat*
být utahaný jako pes	*to be dog-tired*
dřít se (dře) jako kůn/mezek/vůl	*to slave/slog away*
	('like a horse/mule/ox')
potit se jako prase	*to sweat like a pig*
mít hlad jako vlk	*could eat a horse ('be as hungry as a wolf')*
být mlsný jako kocour	*to be choosy about food (**mlsný** liking good food, choosy)*
mlčet jako ryba	*to say nothing, stay (stubbornly) silent ('like a fish')*
být zdravý jako ryba	*to be as fit as a fiddle ('as a fish')*
být tichý jako myška/myš	*to be as quiet as a mouse*
být chudý jako (kostelní) myš	*to be as poor as a church mouse*
být slepý jako krtek	*to be as blind as a bat ('as a mole')*
být (and some other verbs)	*to be like a bull ('elephant') in a china shop*
jako slon v porcelánu	

... AND ARISTOCRATS

In the changing conditions since 1989, Czech society has seen some of the old aristocratic families return, or simply resurface. Thus not only has the word **soudruh** (*comrade*) gone into decline, but such words as **kníže** (*prince*) and **hrabě** (*count*) have come back into service. They need mentioning if only because they share the forms of the 'young animal' words! However, in the singular they are masculine (and animate), therefore the accusative and genitive are the same (**knížete**, **hraběte**), but in the plural they are, oddly, neuter.

 Test yourself

In various situations you are a bit put out. Seek to have matters improved.

    a People are talking loudly in the library: say, 'Talk more quietly.'

    b Your friends are dawdling: say, 'Hurry up (Come more quickly).'

    c You are desperate for some help: say, 'Come as quickly as possible.'

    d You cannot understand some directions: say, 'Please speak more slowly.'

    e You think a friend is being foolish: say, 'Think more sensibly.'

    f Some children are misbehaving: say, 'Be (act) more politely.'

(Do not worry if the English sounds a little odd; your Czech sentences should sound entirely natural, then you will appreciate how the common, simple Czech structures fit things that, in English situations, you might have expressed differently.)

17 Kvůli politice se nerozčiluj!
Don't get worked up over politics!

In this unit you will learn

▶ *How to describe what people/things are doing, e.g. singing policemen/rising unemployment*

▶ *How to deal with some features of written Czech*

▶ *How to say 'whose'*

Dialogue 1

Pan Navrátil is mulling over the evening paper and grumbling about the state of the country to his wife.

 TR 50

On	Tak se mi zdá, že naši mladí politici to ještě moc neumějí.
Ona	Jak to myslíš?
On	Tady čtu, že se jistý 'vedoucí činitel' – nepíšou, které strany – 'divil, že zhoršující se hospodářská situace a stoupající zahraniční dluh jsou nezastavitelné'.
Ona	A co tě na tom tak překvapuje?
On	Já nejsem ekonom, ale i mně, rychle stárnoucímu inženýrovi je jasné, že to nějaký rok potrvá, než se postavíme na nohy.
Ona	Samozřejmě. Ale ty se kvůli politice nerozčiluj!
On	Já se nerozčiluju, jenom se divím, že se diví ten činitel. Kdyby šlo o rostoucí nezaměstnanost – určitě by se divil zas.
Ona	Dej pokoj už s tou politikou – ty bys to taky neuměl.
On	Já vím. Co je dnes v televizi?
Ona	Program snad máš v ruce, ne? Ve Večerníku.
On	Ach ano. (*He looks for the TV page*) Hele, zrovna dávají údajně šokující anglický film o zpívajícím policistovi. Chceš ho vidět?
Ona	Viděla jsem první díl a moc se mi nelíbil, ale můžeš se dívat, když nic jiného není.
On	Zdá se, že není.
Ona	Hlavně se zas nerozčiluj, i kdyby to náhodou bylo pro tebe víc šokující než naši politikové.

Program
TELEVIZE
na celý víkend

LIDOVÉ NOVINY

3 přílohy
na víkend
NEDĚLE
ORIENTACE
VĚDA

Sobota 1. února 2003   NEZÁVISLÝ DENÍK ZALOŽENÝ 1893   Cena 10 Kč

 Quick vocab

tak se mi zdá *well it seems to me*

moc to neumět *to be not much good at it*

vedoucí činitel *leading official*

které strany *of which party*

strana *side, page; party* (political, contractual, in litigation)

zhoršující se *deteriorating*

hospodářský *economic*

situace *situation*

divit se (+ dat.) *to be surprised* (at)

stoupající *rising*

zahraniční *foreign*

dluh *debt*

nezastavitelný *unstoppable*

co tě na tom překvapuje *what surprises you about that*

překvapovat/překvapit *to surprise*

stárnoucí *ageing*

nějaký rok *a year or so*

trvat/po- *to last, endure*

postavit se (pfv) **na nohy** *to get (back) on one's feet*

rozčilovat se/rozčilit se *to get excited*

rostoucí nezaměstnanost *rising unemployment*

v televizi *on television*

dávat film *to put on, show a film*

údajný *alleged*

šokující *shocking*

zpívající *singing*

policista (m) *policeman*

1 ADJECTIVES ENDING IN '-ING' AND THE CZECH IMPERFECTIVE ACTIVE PARTICIPLE

Dialogue 1 includes words ending in **-ící** and **-oucí**, translated by English forms ending in *-ing*. Clearly, they are all used as adjectives, but originate in verbs. The verbs in question are:

vést (a familiar primary verb of motion, here in an abstract sense)

zhoršovat se (*to get worse*) from **zhoršovat/zhoršit** (*to make worse*)

stoupat (*to rise, climb, go up*)

stárnout (*to grow old*)

růst (roste) (*to grow*)

šokovat (*to shock*)

zpívat (*to sing*)

They are from various different conjugations, yet there is little variety in the formation of these *-ing* words. This is because they are based on the *they* forms of verbs with the addition of **-cí** – and all verbs end in either **-í** or **-ou** in the 3rd person plural.

The version of Czech that you are learning includes some forms that have become 'tolerated' only in fairly recent times. They include any *I* and *they* forms ending in **-u** and **-ou** that you meet in the **-e** and **-uje** conjugations after 'soft' consonants. The higher-style equivalents of endings are **-i** and **-í**, and it is the **-í** ending of the *they* form that has to be used to form the 'active participle', as these **-ící/-oucí** forms are called. In other words, *writing* and *buying* have to be **píšící** and **kupující**.

2 MORE ABOUT VERBAL ADJECTIVES

Aspect

These participles can only be formed from imperfective verbs. This makes sense, since it is the imperfective that is used to denote ongoing actions or states.

Word order

Objects or adverbs precede the participle when the participle is to the left of the noun:

cigaretu kouřící žena	*the cigarette-smoking woman*
rychle stárnoucí inženýr	*a rapidly ageing engineer*

Many compound words have their origins in this rule:

dlouhohrající	*long-playing*
protijedoucí	*oncoming*
rychlerostoucí	*quick-growing*

But if a participle is from a reflexive verb, the **se** will be treated as part of the noun phrase, not the overall clause: **zhoršující se situace** follows **že** in Dialogue 1. Combining these two facts, you have:

Rychle se zhoršující situace.	*A rapidly deteriorating situation.*

Style

Participles proper, which follow the noun, for example:

žena sedící vpředu je ministryně kultury. *The woman sitting in front is the minister of culture.*

are largely a feature of written styles, but as adjectives to the left of the noun they often have to be used as the only possibility. Some such adjectives may actually be commoner than the verb they come from: **překvapující** (*surprising*), **vynikající** (*excellent, outstanding* – **vynikat** *to stand out, excel*). Others occur in set phrases:

létající talíř	*flying saucer (plate)*
vařící/tekoucí voda	*boiling/running water* (**vařit** and **téct** (**teče, tekl**) *to flow*)

Other English equivalents

English has many words ending in *-ent* or *-ant*, versions of the Latin active participle. Some of these will then also have Czech participles as their equivalent:

blížící se	*imminent* (**blížit se** *to approach*)
převládající	*predominant* (**převládat** *to predominate*)
odpovídající	*equivalent, corresponding* (**odpovídat** *reply, correspond, match*)

Notice also the special case of **budoucí** (*future*).

Changing status

A number of participle-adjectives, including some compound words, have taken on the function of nouns:

cestující	*passenger*
vedoucí	*manager/-ess*
kolemjdoucí	*passer-by*
dílovedoucí	*foreman*

Since the participles are 'soft' adjectives, gender can only follow from context: **stará vedoucí** (*the old manageress*).

Exercises

1 Fill the gaps with active participles from the verb suggested.

   a Někdo nechal (**hořet**) cigaretu tady na stole.

   b (**Tonout [tone]**) se i stébla chytá. (In this proverb the participle has become a noun: *a drowning man*.)

   c Nech (**spát**) psa ležet.

   d Mluvili jsme s několika (**vést**) činiteli.

   e Nechtěli zvýšit (**stávkovat**) horníkům mzdy.

   f Vyhodila už (**vadnout**) květiny.

   g Proti (**rozhodovat**) gólu nemohli protestovat.

   h (**Štěkat**) pes nekouše.

   i Otec spravoval (**padat**) omítku.

 Quick vocab

hořet *to burn*	**vadnout/u-** *to wilt*
tonout/u- *to drown*	**rozhodovat/rozhodnout** *to decide, settle*
chytat se/chytit se (+ gen.) *to catch at*	(*something*)
stéblo *stalk*	**rozhodující** *decisive*
zvyšovat/zvýšit *to increase, raise*	**štěkat/za-** *to bark*
stávkovat *to strike*	**kousat (kouše)/po-** or **kousnout** *to bite*
horník *miner*	**spravovat/spravit** *to repair*
mzda (gen. pl **mezd**) *wage*	**omítka** *stucco, plaster*

3 MORE VERBAL ADJECTIVES ENDING IN '-ING'

It is vital to appreciate that *-ing* in English has several functions. There is another set of adjectives which must not be confused with the participles. This is a set that in some sense denotes a function – *what something is for*, or *what it does*. In Czech, these also, like the participles, end in **-cí**, but this time they are made from the infinitive: **šít** (*to sew*) gives **šicí** as in **šicí stroj** (*sewing machine*, a machine 'for sewing'). You have already met **psací** from **psát** in **psací stroj** (*typewriter*). From **plnit** (*to fill*) there is **plnicí** as in **plnicí pero** (*fountain pen*) (notice how minimally different this type is from the participle – **plnící**). Many such words occur in conjunction with only a few nouns, often to produce technical terms:

plánovací výbor	*planning committee*
rýsovací prkno	*drawing board*
bicí nástroje	*percussion instruments*
holicí strojek	*shaver*
startovací pistole	*starting pistol*
nulovací tlačítko	*reset button*
tankovací karta	*fuel card, petrol card*
šroubovací uzávěr	*screw top, cap*
vítací výbor	*welcoming committee*

Verbal adjectives of this type have a short vowel when the infinitive is a monosyllable.

 Quick vocab

výbor *committee*
rýsovat *to draw* (technical drawing)
prkno *plank, board*
bít (bije) *to hit, strike*
nástroj (m) *tool, instrument*
pistole (f) *pistol*

nulovat/vy- *to return to zero*
tlačítko *(push-)button*
tankovat *to fill up* (car with petrol)
karta *card*
šroubovat *to screw* (from **šroub** *screw*)
uzávěr *closure, top, cap* (of bottles etc.)

4 '-IBLE/-ABLE'

Many English words ending in *-ible* or *-able* have direct Czech equivalents in **-telný**:

nezastavitelný	*unstoppable*
nepopíratelný	*undeniable*
srovnatelný	*comparable*
(ne-)stravitelný	*(in)digestible*
nepolepšitelný	*incorrigible*
(ne-)představitelný	*(un)believable, (un)imaginable*

There are scores of others (notice how many are negative). If all you have is a small dictionary, you should be able to work out the meaning of such adjectives on the basis of verbs, which are more likely to be in it. One or two important words of the same class – in terms of meaning – cannot be readily deduced from the motivating verb, especially where it doesn't belong to one of the main types. They include:

(ne-)jedlý	*(in)edible*
(ne-)pitný	*(un)drinkable, (un)fit to drink*
(ne-)čitelný	*(il)legible*
(ne-)proveditelný	*(not) feasible*

 **Quick vocab**

zastavovat/zastavit *to stop* (someone or something)
popírat/popřít (popře, popřel) *to deny*
srovnávat/srovnat *to compare*
trávit/strávit *to digest*

představovat si/představit si *to imagine*
provádět/provést (-ved/-vedl) *to carry out, perform, implement, execute*
polepšovat/polepšit *to improve, correct* (as in criminology)

Exercises

2 Using the verbs and nouns suggested create the terms in brackets below.

a krýt + jméno (*false name, alias,* 'covering name')
b balit + papír (*wrapping paper*)
c rozkazovat + věta (*imperative sentence*)
d školit + zařízení (*training centre, facility*)
e obývat + pokoj (*living room*)
f skladovat + prostor (*storage space*)
g oddat + list (*marriage certificate*)
h poznávat + značka (*licence plate,* 'recognition mark')
i mýt + houba (*bath sponge,* 'washing fungus')
j hrát + karty (*playing cards*)
k In what respect is **g** the 'odd man out'?

Dialogue 2

Paní Navrátilová is in the kitchen cooking. Mr Smith is sitting out of the way, killing time with a Czech crossword. (Czech crosswords rely heavily on general knowledge and synonyms and are not cryptic.)

 TR 51

Mr Smith	Něco jsem přece jenom uměl, ale budete mi muset trochu pomoct, pokud vás to nebude zdržovat.
Navrátilová	Samozřejmě, jen se ptejte.
Mr Smith	Jaká je zkratka 'kódu umožňujícího včasné doručení dopisů'?
Navrátilová	To myslí 'poštovní směrovací číslo', čili PSČ.
Mr Smith	A meziválečný český spisovatel pocházející ze židovské rodiny?
Navrátilová	Na kolik písmen?
Mr Smith	Sedm, a třetí je L.
Navrátilová	To bude asi Poláček. Zkuste to.
Mr Smith	Dobře. O je třetí písmeno města ležícího západně od Londýna. Předposlední je G a celé slovo má šest písmen.

Navrátilová	To byste měl znát spíše vy než já!
Mr Smith	Já vím, ale nic mě nenapadá. Budu mít první písmeno, když uděláme ještě tohle: značka křemíku. Co je to křemík?
Navrátilová	Anglicky nevím, ale je to prvek a značka je Si.
Mr Smith	Už vím, jaké je to město: Slough.
Navrátilová	Slau? A jak se to píše?
Mr Smith	s-l-o-u-g-h. Nic si z toho nedělejte! Vždyť víte, jaký máme pravopis. A vychází taky Poláček.
Navrátilová	To jsem ráda.
Mr Smith	Ještě mi řekněte jedno a potom už dám pokoj: já bohužel neznám české dějiny: jméno dvou českých knížat panujících v desátém století: mezera, o, dvě mezery, s, mezera, a, mezera.
Navrátilová	To zřejmě bude Boleslav, první a druhý. Skončil jste přesně včas, budeme obědvat.
Mr Smith	Ještě jsem neskončil. Čí jsou ty noviny? Mohl bych si je ponechat?
Navrátilová	Samozřejmě. Jsou včerejší!

Here is a miniature crossword like the one Mr Smith is trying to do. Have a go! The answers are in the **Key to the exercises**. If a word contains **ch**, both 'letters' (which are one in Czech) go in the same space.

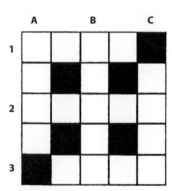

A Kousek něčeho.
B Katedrály.
C Mužské jméno.

1 Kde žijí Češi.
2 Bez přestávky.
3 Velká kočka.

 Quick vocab

něco jsem přece jenom uměl
   I did know some things
zdržovat/zdržet *to delay, hold up*
umožňovat/umožnit *to make possible, facilitate,* (with dat.) *enable*
včasný *timely, punctual*

doručení *delivery*
to myslí *what they mean is*
meziválečný *inter-war* (**válka** *war*)
spisovatel *writer*
židovský *Jewish* (**žid** *Jew*)
na kolik písmen *(in/with) how many letters*

224

písmeno *letter*
západně od *to the west of*
předposlední *next to last, last but one*
dohromady *together, all told*
napadat/napadnout *to occur/come to, dawn on*
značka *sign, brand, mark, marque, symbol*
křemík *silicon*
co je to křemík? *what's silicon?*
prvek (-vku) *element*

pravopis *spelling, orthography*
vycházet/vyjít *here, come out, work out*
to jsem ráda *I'm glad*
dějiny (f. pl) *history*
panovat *to reign*
mezera *gap*
to zřejmě bude ... *I expect that's ...*
budeme obědvat *we're about to have lunch*
čí *whose*
včerejší *yesterday's*

5 *PŘECE JENOM:* SHOWING A POSITIVE ATTITUDE

This expression is hard to translate, and conveys more an attitude than a definable meaning. Basically it affirms that something *has* happened after there had been some doubt. Possible translations (in addition to letting intonation or forms of *do* suffice) include *so* at the beginning of the sentence, or *after all* at the end.

6 MORE ABOUT *TO*

The **to** at the beginning of Mrs Navrátilová's second response (**to myslí ...**) is a kind of particle referring back to the previous question, but built into the sentence only loosely. A similar instance is her **to jsem ráda**, where the **to** picks up the preceding fact that has made her pleased.

The **to** in **co je to křemík** is part of the common formula for asking what something is when that something already has a name:

Co je to? *What is this/that/it?*

Co je to ptakopysk? *What is a platypus?*

All other occurrences of **to** in Dialogue 2 are various types of pronouns, equivalent to *it* or *that*, but often used indefinitely, ignoring the gender of the thing referred to.

7 'YESTERDAY'S, TODAY'S, TOMORROW'S'

Learn the following adjectives from *time* adverbs.

včera	→ **včerejší**	*yesterday's*
dnes	→ **dnešní**	*today's*
zítra	→ **zítřejší**	*tomorrow's*
loni	→ **loňský**	*last year's*
letos	→ **letošní**	*this year's*

8 'WHICH', 'THAT' AND 'WHO': AND THEIR SUBSTITUTES

The lady who ..., The man with whom ..., The town outside which ..., etc. all contain forms of the English relative pronoun, the device which introduces relative clauses, and all could be translated by forms of **který**. The Czech word has also to be used where English uses *that* or indeed nothing:

Návštěva, která tu byla ...	*The visitor that was here ...*
Boty, které jsem koupil včera ...	*The shoes (which) I bought yesterday ...*

English commonly drops both the pronoun (when it is the subject of the relative clause) and any forms of the auxiliary verb 'to be', leaving just the participle:
The woman (who is) sitting at the front is ...

Czech may also use a participial construction:

žena, která sedí vpředu, je ...,   **žena sedící vpředu je ...**

The relative pronoun **který** must share the gender and number of the noun to which it refers (**která** in the last example is feminine and singular), its case is that required by its function in its own clause (here nominative, as the subject of **sedí**). As soon as it is replaced by the participle, which is a special kind of adjective, it must agree with the noun it is qualifying by case as well:

Vidím muže, který sedí vzadu.	*I can see the man who is sitting at the back.*

but

Vidím muže sedícího vzadu.	*I can see the man sitting at the back.*

Muže and **sedícího** are both masculine singular accusative whereas **který** is masculine singular nominative.

If you return to Dialogue 2 you can now see that:

    a **umožňujícího** agrees (masculine singular genitive) with **kódu**, but replaces (only in the economical language of crossword clues and some scholarly or official styles) **který umožňuje**;

b **pocházející** agrees (masculine singular nominative) with **spisovatel**, but replaces **který pocházel**;

c **ležícího** agrees (neuter singular genitive) with **města**, and replaces **které leží**;

d **panujících** agrees (plural genitive) with **knížat**, and replaces **která panovala**. (For neuter plural agreement, see the end of Unit 16.)

Examples **b** and **d** show that the imperfective active participle can replace relative clauses in any tense, even if equivalent English sentences with full relative clauses do not have part of *be* as auxiliary: a writer *who came* ... (replacement by *[who was] coming* would be odd).

You need above all to be able to recognize this type of sentence in the various written styles where it may occur. You will have no active spoken need of it. You do, however, need to understand where the active participle comes from because of the numerous instances where it has evolved into an adjective.

9 HOW TO SAY 'WHOSE'

a When *whose* is a question word, use **čí**, a soft adjective. As the questioning word it has to stand at the front of the sentence. Since what is asked about is the other important element in the sentence, it stands at the end, as in English:

Čí jsou ty noviny?   *Whose is that newspaper?*

But notice where **to**, the indefinite word for *it/this/that thing*, stands when needed:

Čí jsou to noviny?

or

Čí to jsou noviny?   *Whose paper is it/this?*

b The same **čí** applies in indirect questions:

Nevěděl, čí to jsou noviny.   *He didn't know whose paper it was.*

c When *whose* is used as a relative possessive pronoun, as in *The man whose dog bit me* ..., *The girl whose friends I danced with* ..., you need different forms, but in essence you already know them: just take the possessive pronouns **jeho**, **její** and **jejich**, and add **-ž**:

Muž, jehož pes mě kousl ...   *The man whose dog bit me ...*
Dívka, jejíž pes mě kousl ...   *The girl whose dog bit me ...*
Lidé, jejichž pes mě kousl ...   *The people whose dog bit me ...*

Remember that **jehož** and **jejichž** will never change in form, but **jejíž**, like **její**, behaves like a 'soft' adjective:

Dívka, s jejímiž přáteli jsem tančil ...   *The girl with whose friends I danced ...*

In writing, they are, like **který**, always preceded by a comma.

Exercises

3a Insert appropriate forms of čí, jehož, jejíž or jejichž (it might be worth considering 3b first):

a Dáma, ... psi se ztratili, je hraběnka.

b To je ta kniha, ... autor zemřel v koncentračním táboře.

c Cestující, v ... kufrech jsou drobné elektrické spotřebiče (rádio, holicí strojek, kulma atd.), musí tuto skutečnost hlásit (*announce, report*).

d Zeptali se, ... je kufr, ... obsah vzbudil pozornost.

e Tady je ta židle, ... noha potřebuje opravu.

f Řidiči, ... světla nesvítila, dali pokutu 1,500 korun.

g V ... je to zájmu?

h Dáma, o ... psech nikdo nic nezjistil, žaluje hotel, kde je viděla naposled.

Quick vocab

hraběnka *countess*	**obsah** *content(s)*
hlásit/na- *to report*	**atd. = a tak dále** *etc.*
drobný *small*	**žalovat/za-** *to sue*
skutečnost *reality, fact*	**řidič** *driver*
vzbuzovat/vzbudit *to arouse*	**pokuta** *fine*
pozornost *attention*	**zájem (-jmu)** *interest*
spotřebič *appliance*	**tábor** *camp*
kulma *curling tongs*	

3b Translate all the sentences in 3a into English. If you get any wrong, re-do them all in 3 hours' time.

THE CZECH ANTHEM

When the Czechoslovak Republic broke up, there was much arguing about whose was what, or how much of it, between the two daughter states. One matter, however, was very simple: the national anthem. Czechoslovakia had always had an anthem consisting of two distinct parts, one Czech and one Slovak. Each part then simply became the anthem of the respective new country.

The journalist and playwright Josef Kajetán Tyl's (1808–56) words, from his play **Fidlovačka**, run to several verses, but only the first verse is the official Czech anthem. The stage music, including the tune to which the anthem is still sung, is by František Škroup (1801–62), who also wrote the first original Czech opera.

Kde domov můj?

Kde domov můj, kde domov můj?

Voda hučí po lučinách,
bory šumí po skalinách,
v sadě skví se jara květ,
zemský ráj to na pohled.
A to je(st) ta krásná země,
země česká, domov můj,
země česká, domov můj.

Where is my home, where is my home?

Water murmurs among the meadows,
Pine-woods sigh among the cliffs,
Orchards are radiant with spring blossom,
An earthly paradise to the gaze.
And that is that beautiful land,
Land of Bohemia, my home,
Land of Bohemia, my home.

Test yourself

Identify the imperfective active participles in the following passage and replace them by full relative clauses. (**Který** must always be preceded by a comma.)

Cizí státní příslušníci, disponující dostatkem kapitálu a přející si založit joint-venture s českým podnikem majícím k tomu oprávnění, musí svůj záměr ohlásit příslušnému ministerstvu. Adresy a telefonní čísla kanceláří zabývajících se těmito otázkami, lze obdržet na českých velvyslanectvích. Dokumentaci charakterizující celkový podnikový plán můžete zaslat poštou.

V minulosti zahraniční žadatelé, mající v úmyslu podnikat v ČR, často neznali, nebo plně nepochopili platné právní předpisy, proto se nejdříve přesvědčte, že máte k dispozici znění všech předpisů upravujících tuto činnost.

Quick vocab

cizí státní příslušník *alien, foreign citizen*
disponovat + inst. *to have available*
dostatek *sufficiency*
přát si *to wish*
zakládat/založit *to found, set up*
podnik *enterprise, company, firm*
mít oprávnění k *be authorized to*
záměr *intention*
ohlašovat/ohlásit *to announce*
příslušný *the relevant*
zabývat se + inst. *to deal with*
lze *one can, it is possible*
obdržet (pfv. only) *to obtain*
velvyslanectví *embassy*
charakterizovat *to describe*
celkový *overall*

podnikový *corporate*
zasílat/zaslat (zašle) *to send*
minulost *the past*
žadatel *applicant*
mít v úmyslu *to intend*
ČR = Česká republika
platný *valid, in force*
právní *legal*
předpis *prescription, regulation*
přesvědčovat/přesvědčit
    to persuade, convince
přesvědčit se *to make sure*
mít k dispozici *to have at one's disposal*
znění *wording, text*
upravovat/upravit *to adjust, amend, regulate*
činnost *activity*

Note the irregular imperative of **přesvědčit**.

18 Nejdřív uděláme pořádek v Líbině skříni
First we'll tidy Líba's wardrobe

In this unit you will learn

▶ *How to say more about possession*
▶ *How to make suggestions*
▶ *How to use the Czech equivalent of '-ed'*

Dialogue 1

It is a spring Saturday and Mrs Navrátilová would dearly like to do the spring-cleaning (**jarní úklid**).

 TR 53

Navrátil	Dnes je patnáctého března a je docela hezky. Co budeme dělat? Nechcete někam jet?
Navrátilová	Řekla jsem ti přece včera, že chci začít jarní úklid. Nemusíš u toho být, jestli nechceš.
Navrátil	Tak já půjdu do laboratoře. Aspoň se ti tu nebudu plést. Jenom mi nic nevyhazuj!
Navrátilová	Dobře. Nejdříve uděláme pořádek v Líbině skříni, potom se pustím do Štěpánova pokoje.
Navrátil	Tak ahoj. Vrátím se kolem půl šesté.
Navrátilová	(*volá děti*) Líbo, Štěpo, uklízíme! Budete mi pomáhat?
Líba	Ale mami, já mám pořádek a nechci věci přehazovat.
Navrátilová	Musíme odtáhnout nábytek a všechno důkladně vyčistit. A zeď za postelí potřebuje přemalovat.
Líba	Tak dobře, ale já to udělám sama.
Štěpán	Když budete malovat v Líbině pokoji, pak já chci, abyste vymalovali taky můj – na zelenou. Ta růžová, kterou tam mám, je pro holky.
Líba	(*matce*) Mně růžová nevadí. Co kdybychom si pokoje vyměnili? Já se pohodlně vejdu do Štěpovy ložnice.
Navrátilová	No nevím. Co ty na to, Štěpo? Máme to udělat?
Štěpán	To víte, že ne. Já přece nepůjdu do menšího! Ledaže do tátovy pracovny. Tam jsou krásné poličky na moje věci.
Navrátilová	A kam s tátou? Nesmíme vyhazovat jeho věci, natož jeho samotného!

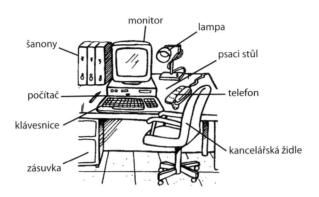

Quick vocab

nemusíš u toho být *you needn't be around*
u toho *at it, there (at the time)*
vyhazovat/vyhodit *to throw away/out*
v Líbině skříni *in Líba's wardrobe*
skříň (f. **-ně**) *cupboard, wardrobe*
Štěpánův (pokoj) *Stephen's (room)*
Štěpa affectionate form of **Štěpán** *Steve*
uklízet/uklidit *to tidy (up)*
já mám pořádek *my room's tidy*
přehazovat/přehodit *to throw (something)*
   over, to jumble, cause disarray
odtahovat/odtáhnout *to pull out*
čistit/vy- *to clean*
důkladný *thorough*
přemalovávat/přemalovat
   to repaint, paint over
když .., pak ... *if ..., then ...*
(malovat něco) na zelenou
   (to paint something) green

růžový *pink*
holka (informal) *girl*
mně růžová nevadí *I don't mind pink*
co kdyby ..? *what if ..?*
vyměňovat (si)/vyměnit (si) *to exchange,*
   swap (with one another)
do Štěpovy ložnice *into Steve's bedroom*
no nevím *I don't know about that*
co ty na to? *what do you think?*
máme to udělat? *should we do it?*
to víte, že ne *certainly not*
ledaže (conjunction) *unless*
tátova pracovna *Dad's study*
polička (diminutive of **police**) *shelf*
kam s tátou? *where do we put your dad?*
natož *let alone*
opouštět/opustit *leave, abandon*
samotný (emphatic pronoun) *(him-, etc.) -self*

1 MAKING SUGGESTIONS

You have already seen polite enquiries expressed as negative questions. Pan Navrátil's
Nechcete někam jet? is an example of the type. Paní Navrátilová's positive question
Budete mi pomáhat? is slightly more abrupt.

Two other questioning phrases are also used:

a **co kdyby**, which will have to change according to the subject (we – **kdybychom**, in
   Dialogue 1). It is very close to English *What if* **with** *were* and similar.
b **co X na to?** asks what X thinks about it and seeks either agreement or a counter-
   proposal. The **na** 'accompanies' the verb **říkat/říct**, which is simply understood. The full
   version of paní Navrátilová's question would be: **Co na to říkáš ty?**

Outside the present tense, the same question merely asks for facts or predictions:

Co on (řekl) na to? *What did he say to that?*

2 COLOURS

You have met several colour terms in passing, usually describing something other than the colours themselves, as in **černý mrak** (*black cloud*) or **hnědý kufr** (*brown suitcase*). To talk about colours themselves, use the adjective form, but in the feminine: **růžová** is really short for **růžová barva** (*pink colour*) (**barva** also means *paint* and *dye*).

Painting a thing a certain colour means achieving a change of state, the new colour is a goal, hence the need for the preposition **na**:

přemalovat zdi na fialovou *to repaint the walls purple*

The noun forms of colour names are not much used outside the realm of art, poetry, fashion or paintmaking, though these are worth knowing:

berlínská modř *Prussian blue*

tiskařská čerň *printers' ink/'black'*

Here is a summary of basic colour terms (some already met, some new):

černý *black*	**bílý** *white*
červený *red*	**hnědý** *brown*
modrý *blue*	**fialový** *purple*
zelený *green*	**růžový** *pink*
žlutý *yellow*	**šedý, šedivý** *grey*
oranžový *orange*	**stříbrný** *silver*
zlatý *gold(en)*	**odstín** *shade, tint*
tmavomodrý *dark blue*	**bleděmodrý** or **bledě modrý** *pale blue*
světle modrý *light blue*	

3 ŠTĚPÁNOVA LOŽNICE AND LÍBIN POKOJ – EXPRESSING POSSESSION WHERE THE POSSESSOR IS NAMED

The English expression of possession by **'s** is matched in Czech by special endings to form possessive adjectives.

The ending **-ův (-ov-**; see table in Section 5) is added to the stem of masculine words:

Štěpánův, tátův, sousedův *Stephen's, Dad's, the neighbour's*

and **-in** to feminines:

Líbin, mámin, sousedčin *Líba's, Mum's, the (female) neighbour's*

These are the basic nominative singular masculine forms.

As you can see, the **-i-** of the feminine ending causes some final consonants to change. The full range of changes is:

d → ď	Milada/Miladin	*Milada's*
t → ť	teta/tetin	*(my) aunt's*
n → ň	žena/ženin	*the woman's, my wife's*

These three show only in pronunciation, not spelling.

r → ř	dcera/dceřin	*(my) daughter's*
k → č	matka/matčin	*mother's*
ch → š	snacha/snašin	*daughter-in-law's*
g → ž	Olga/Olžin	*Olga's*

4 WHEN CAN'T YOU USE POSSESSIVE ADJECTIVES?

Possessive adjectives may be formed from given names, pet names, surnames and common nouns of most types.

You cannot form them if:

▶ the possessor is expressed by more than one word;
▶ the possessor is plural;
▶ the word denoting the possessor is adjectival in form;
▶ the word denoting the possessor is grammatically neuter;
▶ the 'possessor' is not human.

In the first three instances you must use the genitive:

romány Karla Poláčka	*K. P. 's novels*
tradice Angličanů	*the traditions of the English*
politika Thatcherové	*Thatcher's policy*
knihy Škvoreckého	*Škvorecký's books*

In this type, where the adjectival noun is masculine, inversion is common: **Škvoreckého knihy**, similar to which you have already seen in **Palackého most** (*Palacký Bridge*).

In the case of neuter nouns, the genitive is also more likely: **hlava prasete** (*the pig's head –* as opposed to **prasečí hlava** *a pig's head*, i.e. 'what sort of head', not 'whose'), but sometimes a 'normal' adjective is used: **dětský pokoj** (*the child's room*, as well as *a/the children's room, nursery*).

For non-human 'possessors', generally use the genitive: **listy dubu** (*the oak tree's leaves*) (but **dubové listy** *oak leaves*).

Bear in mind that 'more than one word in the possessor phrase' refers to Czech, not English. In English, you would have to say 'my brother's', 'our mother's', but Czech kinship terms usually dispense with **můj/náš**, so: **bratrovo auto** will, usually, itself mean *my brother's car*.

5 POSSESSIVE ADJECTIVES: *JANŮV* – 'JOHN'S'

	Singular Masculine	Feminine	Neuter	Plural Masculine	Feminine	Neuter
Nominative	Janův	Janova	Janovo	{ Janovi* / Janovy	Janovy	Janova
Accusative	{ Janův / Janova*	Janovu	Janovo	Janovy		Janova
Genitive	Janova	Janovy	Janova		Janových	
Dative	Janovu	Janově	Janovu		Janovým	
Locative	(o) Janově				Janových	
Instrumental	Janovým	Janovou	Janovým		Janovými	

Points to notice:

a forms marked with an asterisk are for masculine animate agreement (**Janovi rodiče** *Jan's parents*);

b the case-endings are short, very like familiar hard noun endings, except in the instrumental singular and plural, and genitive, dative and locative plural.

c the male-possessor ending changes from **-ův** to **-ov-** when any further ending is added.

d the case endings after the female-possessor ending **-in** are exactly the same as above (**Janini rodiče** = *Jana's parents*).

Exercises

1 Revise the sections in earlier units on dates (see Unit 11, Section 8) and times (see Unit 9, Sections 2 and 9), then give the dates (Dnes je ...) and times (Je ...) in Czech as shown on the various calendar pages and clock faces:

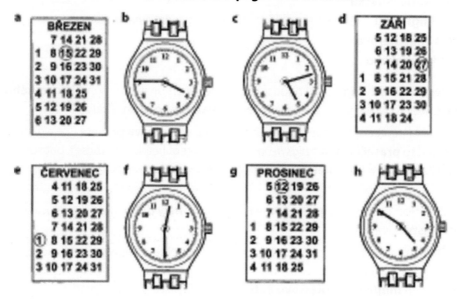

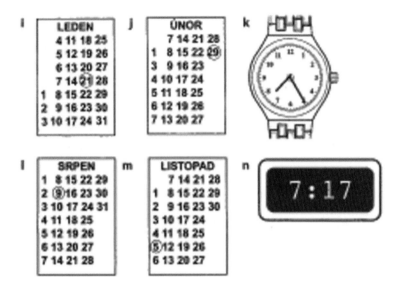

The answers are in the **Key to the exercises** at the back of the book, and they offer just one possibility. Some other solutions are possible, so double-check with the earlier sections or ask a Czech friend for confirmation.

2 Complete the following sentences:

a (*My brother's wife*) ztratila klíče od auta.

b Byla na procházce s (*the neighbour's dog*).

c Nikdy nečetla (*Shakespeare's plays*).

d Koupili jsme parcelu (*behind Peter's cottage*).

e Během jarního úklidu našla (*under Vera's bed*) starého medvídka.

f Bál se, že ho (*Stephen's friends*) nepoznají.

g Na (*Mrs Smith's fridge*) stála láhev mléka.

h Šli mu naproti na (*Wilson Station*).

i Udělali to (*without Mary's agreement*).

j Nevyhazujte (*Zdeňka's old books*)!

k (*St Vitus' Cathedral*) vidíte odevšad.

l Studenti hráli na kytaru (*on Charles Bridge*).

m (*My sister's cat*) má pět koťat.

n (*The guide's last words*) jsme kvůli letadlu neslyšeli.

 **Quick vocab**

parcela *plot (of land)*   **medvídek** *teddy bear*

lednička *fridge*   **chrám** *cathedral*

3 **Compose questions and suggestions along the following lines (there will be two acceptable possibilities):**

  a What if we were to ask Peter?

  b Suppose Líba didn't know?

  c How about going to a restaurant for dinner?

  d Shall we have a beer?

  e What do you say to that?

  f What did she say to that?

4 **Are you good with flag colours? Six flags are reproduced below, but unfortunately they are in black and white. Say what their colours are in Czech!**

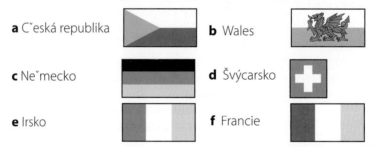

a Cˇeská republika   **b** Wales

c Neˇmecko   **d** Švýcarsko

e Irsko   **f** Francie

Dialogue 2

Continuation of the previous dialogue.

 TR 54

Štěpa	Myslíš, že by mu to hodně vadilo? Většinu věcí má stejně v laboratoři.
Navrátilová	No nevím. Musíme se ho večer zeptat. Kdoví, možná bude souhlasit.
Líba	To asi ne. Náš otec nemá rád změny.
Navrátilová	Nebudu ho přemlouvat, jenom se o tom u večeře zmíníme jako o možnosti a uvidíme, jak zareaguje.

Štěpa	Můj pokoj je asi o dva metry delší a o metr širší, vejde se mu tam třeba i křeslo a bude si tam moct vodit návštěvy. Vsadím se, že to ocení!
Líba	Kdypak tu měl někoho naposled?
Navrátilová	Náhodou před týdnem. Zastavil se nějaký kolega pana Smithe z Anglie – ty jsi nebyla doma, zřejmě proto o tom nevíš.
Štěpa	A kde ho tatínek přijal?
Navrátilová	V obýváku – a zrovna když jsem chtěla luxovat. Proto byla pozdě večeře, všechno se tím posunulo.
Štěpa	Vidíte, o co by bylo lepší, kdybychom si s tatínkem vyměnili pokoje. Já dostanu poličky, on bude mít místo pro návštěvy a ty si budeš moct luxovat, kdykoli se ti bude chtít.

Evening, and the suggestion has just been made.

Navrátil	To je sice velmi hezké, ale: za prvé ve Štěpánově pokoji není přípoj na telefon, za druhé je málo zásuvek, abych tam mohl mít počítač, tiskárnu, kopírku, stolní lampu, konvici a rozhlas, za třetí Štěpovo okno je rozbité a já nemám čas ho spravit, za čtvrté nějaké poličky navíc bych zřejmě potřeboval i tam a za páté dnes ráno jsem odvezl do práce ty dvě bedny knih, které už nepotřebuju, a z práce přivezl na jejich místo vyřazené křeslo, aby si moje návštěvy měly kam sednout!
Navrátilová	Tušila jsem, že bude někde háček.

 Quick vocab

vadilo by mu to *he would mind*
možná bude souhlasit *he may agree*
to asi ne *I shouldn't think so*
změna *change*
přemlouvat/přemluvit *to talk someone round, persuade*
zmiňovat se/zmínit se + o (+ loc.) *to mention, increasingly expressed as* **zmiňovat/zmínit** (+ acc.)
o tom ... jako o možnosti *about it as (about) a possibility*
reagovat/za- *to react*
i křeslo *even an armchair*
vsadím se, že ... *I bet (that ...)*
sázet/vsadit *to bet*
oceňovat/ocenit *to appreciate; to price*
kdypak *when (see Section 6b)*

náhodou před týdnem *a week ago, as it happens*
zřejmě proto *that's perhaps why*
přijímat/přijmout (přijme, přijal) *to see, receive*
obývák *informal for* **obývací pokoj**
zrovna když jsem chtěla luxovat *just as I was about to hoover*
luxovat/vy- *to 'hoover', in fact to '(electro)lux'*
posunovat/posunout *to shift, delay*
o co by bylo lepší *how much better it would be*
za prvé (etc.) *firstly, for one thing*
přípoj (m) *connection*
tiskárna *printing works; printer*
kopírka *photocopier*
stolní lampa *table lamp*
konvice *kettle*

i tam *there too*
bedna (large) *box, crate*
vyřazený *discarded, scrapped, thrown out*
aby si návštěvy měly kam sednout *so visitors have somewhere to sit*

tušit *to guess, have a presentiment*
háček *here, snag*

6 ATTITUDES

a Czech has many words to convey various types of conjecture. Some have direct equivalents in English, such as **kdoví**, the rhetorical *who knows*, **pravděpodobně** (*probably*) or the informal **vsadím se** (*I bet*). Others may have direct equivalents in English, but the tendency is to use something different. This applies above all to the modal particles that express possibility and probability. It would be more natural to translate **možná bude souhlasit** as *he may* (or *might*) *agree*, rather than 'perhaps he will agree'. Líba's **To asi ne**, short for **asi nebude souhlasit,** is perhaps best expressed by *I don't think he will* or *I shouldn't think so* than by 'perhaps not'. The conjecture in **zřejmě proto o tom nevíš** is far closer in tone to *I expect that's why you don't know* than to 'apparently for that reason you don't know'; and **zřejmě bych potřeboval** has more the force of *I might well need* than 'evidently I would need'.

This is a subtle area in which the dictionary can only help in part. In English the verb forms (*may, might, should, expect, guess* and others) are heavily used in contrast to the Czech particles (**asi, možná, zřejmě, třeba, patrně**). Much conversational practice is needed for the learner to appreciate fully the subtleties of the equivalences.

b Adding **-pak** to the question words adds a degree of informality, which can come across as sarcasm, irony, sympathy, condescension or irritation. In Líba's **kdypak** utterance in Dialogue 2 a reasonable equivalent might be with *Now when ..?* A brusque **Kdepak jsi byl?** could well be *Where on earth have you been?*, while a solicitous **Copak se ti stalo?** could be *Dear me, what have you done?*

Thanks to the extra shade of meaning one or two words have special uses:

  ▸ **kdepak!** in reply to a suggestion is abruptly dismissive – *not a bit of it!*, *not likely!* (or the modern *no way!*);

  ▸ **copak**, in addition to being a pronoun, is also a particle that usually conveys surprise:

  Copak si už kupuje další nové auto?   *Do you mean to say he's buying another new car already?*

c Adding a fundamentally redundant **si** (*for oneself*) to the verb gives the sense that the activity is a source of enjoyment, pleasure, comfort or other positive feeling. For this reason many verbs occur almost automatically with **si: sednout si** (*to sit down*), **lehnout si** (*to lie down*) or **hrát si** (*to play*) are common examples. Even a simple sentence like **Čte** (*He is reading*) can be converted to **Čte si** (*He's having a read* – presumably purely for leisure).

Si may be added even in the case of activities that are perhaps not inherently enjoyable, though that may mean adding a hint of irony. Paní Navrátilová had merely wanted to vacuum (**luxovat**) the living room. But when Štěpán uses **luxovat si**, he is conveying an attitude, saying, in effect, that she will no longer be deprived of the pleasure, she will be able to hoover to her heart's content. These English attempts to convey this use of **si** are too wordy; the actual English equivalent is an appropriate tone of voice.

Any other function of **si** in a sentence predominates and the 'pleasure dimension' doesn't enter into it.

Kupuje si novou kravatu.   *He is buying a new tie.*

This does not suggest that this is a pleasurable exercise, but that the intended wearer is *he*.

vyměnit si s někým pokoje   *to change rooms with someone*

Si here guarantees the meaning that *A* has *B*'s old room and vice versa, not that *A* and *B* swapped their present rooms for different ones.

7 *ZA PRVÉ, ZA DRUHÉ*: ORDERING FACTS AND EVENTS

Use **za** and the neuter singular form of ordinal numerals to express *firstly*, *secondly*, etc. Do not confuse these with **poprvé**, **podruhé**, **potřetí**, etc. (*for the first/second/third time*) or **pokaždé** (*every time*).

Next (time) is either **příště**, implying that the next event is just one of many:

Příště budeme opakovat číslovky.   *Next time we shall revise numerals.*

or **podruhé**, suggesting only that 'this time' is, or 'last time' was, the first time:

Až člověk přistane na měsíc podruhé ...   *Next time man lands on the moon ...*

Some contexts allow for both:

Až tu budeme příště/podruhé, ...   *Next time we're here, …*

8 'LAST'

There are two Czech adverbs meaning *(for the) last (time)*.

a To refer to the most recent occurrence of an event like the present event use **minule** or **naposled(y)**:

Když jsme tu byli minule/naposled,   *Last time we were here it was raining.*
pršelo.

b To refer to the last occurrence of a particular event use **naposled(y)**:

Kdy tu byl naposled?   *When was he here last?*
Byl tu naposledy v červnu.   *He was last here in June.*
Tos udělal naposled!   *That's the last time you do that! (Lit. 'you have done that for the last time!')*

9 *ROZBITÝ* AND *VYŘAZENÝ* – 'BROKEN' AND 'CAST OUT' (PASSIVE PARTICIPLES)

Like the active participles learned in Unit 17, the 'passive participles' (forms denoting something *done*, not *doing*) are also common as adjectives. In English, the vast majority of forms end in *-ed*, frequently pronounced as *t*, as in, say, *cropped* (neatly cropped lawn). Sometimes a form with *t* may coincide with other forms of the same verb, as in *cut* (the freshly cut grass). So *t/d* is the main type. Rather fewer use *n* instead: *done, given, hidden*.

In Czech, the proportions are reversed: the vast majority use **n**, in the ending **-aný** or **-ený** (**-ěný**), while just a few use **t**, in **-tý**. You have already met **unavený** (*tired*), **zklamaný** (*disappointed*) and **rozbitý** (*broken*), and in Dialogue 2 **vyřazený** (*cast off, thrown out*).

How to form the passive participle

▶ Most monosyllabic verbs use forms with **-tý**, with a short vowel in front of it:

bít → bitý	*beaten*	**hnout → hnutý**	*moved*
vzít → vzatý	*taken*		

and so will their, often commoner, compounds:

zabitý	*killed*	**ohnutý**	*bent*
převzatý	*taken over*	**přejetý**	*run over*

including some compounds of 'dead' words:

přijmout → přijatý	*received, accepted*
najmout → najatý	*hired*

Monosyllables ending in **-át**, and their compounds, generally use **-n-**:

dát → daný	*given*
vybrat → vybraný	*chosen, selected*
pozvat → pozvaný	*invited*
napsat → napsaný	*written*

▶ Verbs whose infinitives end in **-at** use **-aný**:

udělat → udělaný	*made*	**slibovat → slibovaný**	*promised*
poslat → poslaný	*sent*		

irrespective of conjugation.

▶ Most others use **-ěný/ený:**

otevřít → otevřený	*open(ed)*
pochopit → pochopený	*grasped, understood*
vyplnit → vyplněný	*filled in* (of a form)
objevit → objevený	*discovered*
zkoušet → zkoušený	*examined* (of a student)
vyrábět → vyráběný	*manufactured*

but because of the **-ě-** there will be some consonant changes, and
spellings with **-ený**:

t → **c** as in **ztracený**	*lost* (**ztratit**)
d → **z** as in **vyřazený**	*thrown out* (**vyřadit**)
s → **š** as in **ohlášený**	*reported* (**ohlásit**)
z → **ž** as in **vožený**	*transported* (**vozit**)
sl → **šl** as in **vymyšlený**	*fictitious* (**vymyslet** = *think up*)
st → **šť** as in **pojištěný**	*insured* (**pojistit**)

though not all verbs show such changes, e.g.:

cítěný	*felt*	(**cítit**)
zazděný	*bricked-up*	(**zazdít**)
odsouhlasený	*carried* (in a vote)	(**odsouhlasit**)
omezený	*limited*	(**omezit**)
kreslený	*drawn*	(**kreslit**)

Which verbs do or do not change can usually be verified in the dictionary. The form
of any secondary imperfectives is often a guide (**ztrácet**, **nahrazovat** and **ohlašovat**
would help in the first three examples, **vymýšlet**, **pojišťovat**, **zazdívat** and **omezovat**
in some of the others).

▶ Verbs whose infinitives end in **-st** or **-ct** usually use the present tense to form the passive
participle:

přinést-přinese → **přinesený**	*brought* (on foot)
opéct-opeče → **opečený**	*roasted*
vyvést-vyvede → **vyvedený**	*led out*
krást-krade → **kradený**	*stolen* (impfv.), but
ukrást-ukradne → **ukradený**	*stolen* (pfv.)
říct-řekne → **řečený**	*said*

▶ Verbs ending in **-nout** behave variously, according to whether **-nout** is dropped or not,
and should be learned individually as you meet them:

zapomenout → **zapomenutý**	*forgotten*
vytisknout → **vytištěný**	*printed*
dosáhnout → **dosažený**	*achieved*
nadchnout se (to enthuse) → **nadšený**	*enthusiastic*
zahrnout → **zahrnutý**	*included*
stisknout → **stisknutý**	*squeezed*

10 ASPECT AND THE PASSIVE PARTICIPLES

Passive participles are formed from verbs of either aspect, and the usual differences apply:

Kradené věci are simply *stolen things* in general, as opposed to **ukradené**
věci, some particular items that have been stolen and the effects of their particular loss

are felt. **Kupovaný chleba** is of the type normally bought, 'shop bread', as opposed to **koupený chleba**, the bread that has (just) been bought as intended. **Uznávaná autorita** (*a recognized authority*) is expressed by the imperfective, because the recognition has gone on, been renewed and still applies.

Exercises

5 Make your own phrases with participles formed in this way:

(rozlít *to spill*) + (mléko)	**a** *spilt milk*
(nezvat) + (host)	**b** *uninvited guest*
(přibít *to nail up/on*) + (plakáty *posters*)	**c** *nailed-up posters*
(připsat) + (písmena *letters*)	**d** *letters added*
(zahnout *to bend*) + (nos)	**e** *crooked nose*

6 Form more phrases of your own:

(zadat *to reserve*) + (stůl)	**a** *reserved table*
(uznávat *to recognize, acknowledge*) + (autorita)	**b** *recognized authority*
(zakázat *to ban, forbid*) + (ovoce)	**c** *forbidden fruit*
(informovat) + (zdroj [m] *source*)	**d** *informed sources*

7 Make some more phrases of your own:

(vyžehlit *to iron*) + (košile)	**a** *an ironed shirt*
(zlepšit *to improve*) + (výkon *performance*)	**b** *improved performance*
(ztratit) + (Ráj *Paradise*)	**c** *Paradise Lost*
(přihlásit *to register*) + (cizinec)	**d** *unregistered alien*
(omezit) + (prostředky)	**e** *unlimited resources*
(vypůjčit si *to borrow*) + (kolo)	**f** *a borrowed bicycle*
(promyslet *to think through*) + (návrh)	**g** *a well thought-out proposal*
(spojit *to join*) + (národ)	**h** *United Nations*

8 Make some phrases of your own:

(dovézt) + (stroj)	**a** imported machines
(nalézt *to find*) + (štěstí)	**b** new-found happiness
(unést *to hijack*) + (letadlo)	**c** the hijacked plane
(okrást *to rob*) + (turista)	**d** the robbed tourist

9 Describe your needs to a Czech friend, beginning Potřebuju ..:

 TR 55

a a freshly washed (**prát/vyprat**) shirt.
b those two recently published (**vydávat/vydat**) translations.
c to find your lost watch.

d to see the newly opened bridge before (**než**) you go home.

e to rest, because your feet are tired.

f to repeat the forgotten words from Unit 8.

g to open the locked (**zamykat/zamknout**) wardrobe.

h three talented young people for the film you want to make (**natáčet/natočit** *to make [a film]*).

i a cautiously formulated (**formulovat**) letter which you want to send the hotel manager.

j to mend your broken briefcase (**aktovka**).

POSSESSIVES AND PLACE NAMES

On any Czech street map you will see countless instances of possessive adjectives. In effect the Czechs say *Wilson's Station, Smetana's Embankment, Jirásek's Square, Charles' Bridge* – **Wilsonovo nádraží, Smetanovo nábřeží, Jiráskovo náměstí, Karlův most** – not to mention *Palacký's Bridge* **Palackého most**, that you met long ago – where English uses just the name (*Victoria Street, Russell Square*). Similar forms are found in the names of many towns and villages: **Králův Dvůr** (*King's Court*) (but **Dvůr Králové** *Queen's Court*, with the post-positioned genitive of **králová** *queen-consort*, which declines like an adjective), **Kardašova Řečice, Golčův Jeníkov**. The final **-ov** of the last, occurring in many Czech and other Slav place names, is itself an historic version of **-ův**.

Some very ancient Prague and other street names based on the names of people use the adjective ending **-ský** that now cannot be used this way, for example **Václavské náměstí** (*Wenceslas Square*), the very heart of Prague. Others of the same sort refer not to a person, but to an adjoining church: **Voršilská ulice** refers not to an *Ursula* (**Voršila**), but to the nearby Ursuline convent, while **Havelská ulice** refers not to some medieval Havel, but to the church of St Havel. Were the first president of the Czech Republic to have, say, a bridge named after him, today it would have to be either **Havlův most** (so not 'Havelský') or **most Václava Havla**, with the order given by the use of both parts of his name.

⍰ Test yourself

Express the following ideas without using modal verbs:

a He may come.

b I expect you're right.

c He must have left the keys at home.

d There may have been 20 people there.

e He's unlikely to come.

19 Dejte si něco na ochutnání
Have something to taste

In this unit you will learn

▶ *How to use '-ing' (as a noun) to state your likes and dislikes*
▶ *How to say what things are good for*
▶ *How to recognize and form 'passive' sentences*

Dialogue 1

 TR 56

Paní Navrátilová telefonuje Smithovým, aby je pozvala.

Navrátilová	Dobrý večer, paní Smithová. Poslyšte, dělám zítra malé pohoštění pro Zdeňkova kolegu. Mohli byste přijít?
Mrs Smith	Myslím, že ano. Zeptám se manžela, až přijde – šel s dětmi do galerie moderního umění.
Navrátilová	Dobře. Zavoláte mi pak?
Mrs Smith	Samozřejmě. Nebudete potřebovat pomoc s vařením? Nechci se chlubit, ale kdysi jsem vyhrála cenu za pečení dortu!
Navrátilová	Jste velmi hodná. Sladkosti jsem už objednala, ale jestli chcete pomoct s napichováním jednohubek ...
Mrs Smith	Velmi ráda. V kolik mám přijít?
Navrátilová	Řekněme v půl páté. Dobře?
Mrs Smith	Dobře. A děkuju za pozvání.
Navrátilová	Nemáte vůbec zač. Potěšení je na naší straně.

Druhý den večer. Paní Smithová je už u Navrátilů, kde pomáhala, jak se s paní Navrátilovou dohodly. Pan Smith přichází pozdě – zapomněl na včerejší pozvání.

Mr Smith	(*paní Navrátilové*) Nezlobte se, že jdu pozdě. Úplně jsem na to zapomněl – měl jsem spoustu vyřizování, a navíc autobus měl zpoždění. Nejhorší je, že jsem se i najedl. Nebylo to už k vydržení.
Navrátilová	To nevadí. Dáte si aspoň něco na ochutnání.
Navrátil	Ano, pojďte mezi nás a povězte tady Ježkovým něco o sobě.
Ježek	Vaše paní nám právě říkala, jak má ráda vaření, ale o vás víme jen to, že si libujete v luštění křížovek. Máte ještě jiné koníčky?
Mr Smith	Hlavně plavání a pěší turistiku, ale na pěstování jakýchkoli koníčků nemám mnoho času.
Ježek	To já znám – já jsem musel nechat domácího kutění, které mě dost bavívalo.
Mr Smith	Děti jsou na tom líp – syn tráví celé hodiny vymýšlením nových počítačových her a dcera se věnuje hře na housle a jednou týdně chodí do kursu aranžování květin.
Navrátil	Ano, Smithovy děti jsou opravdu šikovné a mají pěkné chování.
Mrs Smith	Ale zlobit umějí taky.

 Quick vocab

poslyšte *listen, I say*
dělat pohoštění *to give/have a (small formal) party*
zavoláte mi pak? *Will you ring me later?*
vaření *cooking*
chlubit se *to boast*
vyhrávat/vyhrát *to win*
pečení *baking; roasting*
sladkost *sweetness; something sweet*
objednávat/objednat *to order*
napichování *spiking, putting on cocktail sticks*
jednohubka *canapé or other titbit that goes into the mouth* (**huba** vulg.) *at one go* (**jednou**)
nemáte vůbec zač *not at all*
potěšení *the pleasure*
dohodnout se *to agree, come to an agreement*
vyřizování *things to sort out*
nejhorší je, že jsem se i najedl *is the worst thing that I've even eaten*
nebylo to k vydržení *it was beyond endurance*
vydržet *to (with)stand, bear*

dáte si něco na ochutnání *you can have a bite to taste*
ochutnávat/ochutnat *to try, taste* (food, drink)
pojďte mezi nás *come and join us*
libovat si v něčem *to take satisfaction in, enjoy*
luštění křížovek *doing crosswords*
luštit/vy- or **roz-** *to solve*
koníček *hobby*
plavání *swimming*
pěší turistika *hiking*
pěstování *cultivation*
nechávat/nechat (+ gen.) *to give up*
domácí kutění *DIY*
kutit (si) *to tinker about*
bavívat (from **bavit** *to amuse, give pleasure*)
na tom jsou líp děti *the children are better off*
být na tom dobře *to be well off*
trávit/s- *to spend* (time)
vymýšlení *thinking up*
počítačová hra *computer game*
věnovat se (+ dat.) *to devote oneself to*

hra na housle *violin-playing*
housle (f. pl.) *violin*
jednou týdně *once a week*
kurs *course*

aranžování květin *flower-arranging*
Smithovy děti *the Smith(s') children*
chování *behaviour*

1 SAYING YOU LIKE (DOING) SOMETHING

Not only can you **mít rád** something or combine **rád** with any other verb to say you like doing such and such, you can **trávit** (*spend time*) (+ inst.) on it – which need not always mean that it is for pleasure. You might also **věnovat** (*devote*) time to it, using the dative, or **věnovat se** (*devote oneself, one's energies*) to it. Then, from the same origin as **líbit se** (*to please, to appeal to*) (**Líbí se mi to** = *I like it*) there is the verb **libovat si + v** (+ locative case), meaning *to enjoy, relish*. The verb **pěstovat** means *to cultivate, grow* of plants, but is widely used for the cultivation of all kinds of activities. Most of these are illustrated in the dialogue. Yet another possibility is the verb **bavit** (*to amuse*):

Baví mě chodit na houby.   *I like going mushrooming.*
Nebaví mě sedět doma.   *I don't like sitting at home.*

The reflexive **bavit se** means either *to amuse oneself* (+ inst. for the result of the activity, or **s** + inst. for the means) or *to chat*:

Bavili se tapetováním ložnice.   *They were amusing themselves by wallpapering the bedroom.*

Bavíme se s počítačem.   *We're having fun with the computer.*
Baví se venku se sousedkou.   *She's outside chatting to her neighbour.*

2 -ÁNÍ/-ENÍ: '-ING' WORDS

These are the verbal nouns from the various verbs concerned – usually translated, once again, by the English *-ing* form. You have met several in the course of the book, simply as extra neuter nouns ending in **-í**. Some, like **umění** (*art*), **pohoštění** (*party, refreshments*) or **potěšení** (*pleasure*), have become separated from their verbs (**umět** *to know how*; **hostit/po-** *to host, treat*; **těšit/po-** *to console, give pleasure*), some are the only available way of expressing an activity as a noun, as opposed to the verb (**plavání** *swimming*); yet others could be used, but might be avoided because some other, preferable noun may exist in competition with it (**hraní** *playing* could be used to refer to the manner of someone's playing, as opposed to **hra**, denoting the fact of playing).

You form the verbal noun in the same way as the passive participle (Unit 18), except for the noun ending **-í** and the lengthening of **a** in words from **-at** verbs – but not from most verbs of one syllable: **hrát: hraní** (*play-ing*), **prát: praní** (*wash-ing*), but note, for example, **přát: přání** (*wish, a wish*).

A small number end in **-tí**: **bytí** (*being*), **šití** (*sewing*), **použití** (*use*), **hnutí** (*movement* in various senses). Moreover, while the passive participle can only be formed from verbs that can have a direct object, the verbal noun can be formed from almost all verbs and from both aspects: **čtení** (*reading* – in general), **přečtení** (*the* – completed – *reading* of a particular thing). Sometimes there may be a conspicuous meaning change (viewed from the English perspective):

vydávání knih   *book publishing*

but

první vydání knihy   *the first edition of the book*

▶ As in English, what was the direct object of the verb goes into the genitive (*of*) after the verbal noun:

    prát košile   *to wash shirts*
    praní košil   *the washing of shirts*

▶ If the noun following a verb (what would be the English direct object) is in any other case, or needs a preposition, then that other case or prepositional phrase is also used after the verbal noun:

    mávat kapesníkem   *to wave one's handkerchief*
    mávání kapesníkem   *handkerchief-waving*
    prát v pračce   *to wash by (in a) machine*
    praní v pračce   *washing by machine*

▶ The verbal noun from reflexive verbs loses **se**, except to avoid ambiguity:

    chovat se   *to act, behave*
     chování   *behaviour*
    učit jazyky   *to teach languages*
     učení jazyků   *language-teaching*
    učit se jazyky   *to study languages*
     učení se jazyků   *language-learning*

(An older construction uses the dative of subjects taught or learnt, hence **učení (se) jazykům**.)

▶ English has some variety in the way it uses its verbal nouns: '*the washing of shirts*', '*washing shirts*' or '*shirt-washing*'. Watch out for them, beware when an *-ing* form is to be understood as a noun (and not one of its other uses), and always rethink it so that it is like the first structure: the only one that matches Czech.

3 IDIOMS BASED ON THE VERBAL NOUN

Two common ones are:

a být k + verbal noun *to be -able*, or *to be for -ing*: this is very common in the negative:

Není to k vydržení.	*It is not endurable.*
Pokoj je k pronajmutí.	*The room is for rent(ing).*
Slovník není k dostání.	*The dictionary cannot be got, isn't gettable, to be had.*

Or the even more idiomatic:

Je to k zbláznění.   *It's enough to drive you mad.*

This can often be met in a reduced form, without the verb:

pokoj k pronajmutí	*room to let*
něco ke čtení	*something to read*

Interpret the following signs, versions of which you will see in buses, trams and underground trains:

72 míst k sezení		140 míst k stání

b být na + verbal noun *to be (good, used) for -ing*. This is used to denote either the permanent use to which something may be put: **tyto brýle jsou na čtení** (*these glasses are for reading*), and from this: **brýle na čtení** (*reading-glasses*), or the temporary:

To je jen na ochutnání. *This is just* (**for you**) *to taste.*

The difference between the two types may sometimes be minimal. In instructions you will often find the version with **k**: **k čištění používejte vlhký hadřík** (*to clean, use a damp cloth*), but a *cloth for cleaning* is likely to be **hadřík na čištění**. This is one of those features of Czech best learned by observation.

4 *BAVÍVALO*: FREQUENTATIVE VERBS

One of the meanings of imperfective verbs is to express a regular repeated activity. Czech has a set of forms which, in the present or past tense, suggests fairly regular or merely sporadic repetition:

Chodili jsme do divadla ve čtvrtek.	*We used to go to the theatre (regularly) on Thursdays.*
Chodívali jsme do divadla ve čtvrtek.	*We used to go to the theatre (if at all) on Thursdays.*

The frequentative form of some verbs is fairly common (**bývat** from **být**, **mívat** from **mít** are obvious ones, but others will be heard). Most are formed by insertion of an extra **-va-** before the **-t** of the infinitive, with the vowel in the syllable before lengthened, as in **bavívat**. One or two verbs have special forms, such as **slýchat** for **slyšet**, **vídat** for **vidět** and **čítat** for **číst**. Sometimes you may even meet a type of double frequentative, especially from **být**, namely **bývávat**, as in the idiom **Bývávalo!** (*Those were the days!*). You need not try to use frequentatives at all, but be prepared to spot them.

5 *BÝT NA TOM DOBŘE* – 'TO BE GOING WELL'

This idiom uses a form of **to** which is 'empty' when it comes to meaning. The phrase means *to be well off, to be getting along OK*, but need not be to do with material wealth. It is commonly followed by **s** + instrumental:

Jak jste na tom s prací?	*How's your work coming along?*
Jak jste na tom s češtinou?	*What's your Czech like?*

6 *NEMÁTE ZAČ* – 'DON'T MENTION IT'

This formula is reduced from:

Nemáte za co mi poděkovat.	*You don't have anything for which to thank me.*

Co is reduced to **č** in one or two other words, of which **proč** (**pro co**) you know. Another is **nač** (*for what purpose*):

Nač tam jít teď?	*What's the point of going there now?*

7 *CHODIT* OR *JÍT NA HOUBY* – 'TO GO MUSHROOMING'

The Czechs are great gatherers of wild mushrooms (**houby**). To say *to go -ing*, use a suitable verb *to go* with **na** 'for' and the collected item in the accusative plural.

chodit na ostružiny/maliny/ borůvky/ryby	*to go blackberrying/raspberrying/ bilberrying/fishing*

> ● **INSIGHT**
>
> One conspicuous side effect of the liberation of travel after the 'Velvet Revolution' in 1989 was the number of Czech (and Slovak) au pairs, their boyfriends and/ or their visiting parents and friends, scouring the English countryside, especially woodland, for edible fungi – old habits die hard. And they know and collect far more species than the occasional Englishman and his field mushroom. One journalist, Benjamin Kuras, even wrote a book on the subject: Anglie je na houby (*England is good for mushrooms*). This is a cheeky title, possibly misleading at first sight, since **houby** is a longstanding euphemism for **hovno** (*shit*), and the phrase **x je na houby** is widely used to mean *x is rubbish, useless, no earthly good,* so euphemistically total crap.

8 *SMITHOVI*: FORMING PLURALS OF SURNAMES

The plural form of surnames, denoting the whole family, may be treated like the possessive adjectives or as nouns:

Jdeme k Smithovým/Smithům. *We're going to the Smiths'.*

The nominative is the odd man out: for the whole family use **-ovi**; the noun ending **-ové** is reserved for two or more males or two or more females of the same surname:

bratři Čapkové *the Čapek brothers*
slečny Smithové *the misses Smith*

Exercises

 TR 57

1 Convert the rád (+ verb) construction to mít rád (+ verbal noun).
   a Petr rád vaří.
   b Rádi létáme na kluzácích (**kluzák** *glider*).
   c Nerad utírá nádobí (**utírat/utřít [utře, utřel]** *to wipe*).
   d Radši si hrál s počítačem, než dělal úkoly.
   e Nejraději ze všeho četl dlouhé romány.
   f Ráda pěstovala malé druhy azalek (**druh** *kind, type, species;* **azalka** *azalea*).

2 Create sentences using the suggestions in brackets.
   a (vyřizovat žádost) trvalo tři měsíce.
   b Nelíbilo se nám její (provést poslední část).
   c (Učit se matematiku) většinu dětí nebavilo.
   d Někteří byrokraté (*some bureaucrats*) si libují v (klást překážky). (**překážka** *obstacle*)
   e Nestojí to za (utrácet tolik peněz).
   f (psát kondolenční dopis) nebylo pro něho lehké. (**kondolenční dopis** *letter of condolence*)
   g Podnik musí provádět (hodnotit výsledky) aspoň jenou za rok. (**hodnotit/o-** *assess, evaluate;* **výsledek** *result*)

Be sure you can translate the sentences in **1** and **2** into English.

3 Find (at least) two ways of putting the following into Czech.
   a I don't like washing shirts.
   b We aren't much into mushrooming.
   c She didn't devote much time to writing the letter.
   d They like tinkering about with cars.

Text

 TR 58

What follows is a series of little extracts, typical of encyclopedia entries, history textbooks and newspaper reporting:

a Pražský orloj byl sestaven koncem 15. století. Je opředen legendami, například o tom, jak byl jeho tvůrce oslepen, aby nemohl své znamenité dílo opakovat jinde.

b Jako oběti demonstrací byli hlášeni jeden mrtvý a patnáct zraněných. Převážně jsou postiženi Češi, avšak také četní Němci byli zraněni. (*from a report in October 1939*)

c Jan Hus byl odsouzen roku 1415 k smrti, protože trval na tom, čemu věřil. Když mu byla nabídnuta milost, odvolá-li své bludy, odmítl.

d Všechny počáteční potíže pobytu československých letců v Anglii byly brzy odstraněny. Když počátkem srpna 1940 navštívil první čs. stihací peruť president Beneš, zastihl desítky letců, mechaniků a jiných v nejhorlivějších přípravách k boji na strojích Hurricane, které jim byly přiděleny.

 Quick vocab

orloj (m) *astronomical clock*
sestavovat/sestavit *to construct*
koncem *at the end of*
být opředen (+ inst.) *to be wreathed (in)*
legenda *legend*
o tom, jak *about how*
tvůrce (m) *maker, creator*
oslepovat/oslepit *to blind*
znamenitý *magnificent*
oběť (f) *victim; sacrifice*
ranit/z- *to wound*
převážně *predominantly*
postihovat/postihnout *to affect, afflict*
četní *numerous*
odsuzovat/odsoudit k *to condemn to*
trvat na (+ loc.) *to insist on*
milost (-i) *mercy*
odvolávat/odvolat *to withdraw, repeal, cancel*
-li *if (added to verb at start of clause)*
blud *heresy*

odmítat/odmítnout *to refuse*
počáteční *initial*
potíž (f) *problem, difficulty*
pobyt *stay*
letec *airman*
odstraňovat/odstranit *to remove*
počátkem *at the beginning of*
čs. = československý
stihací peruť *fighter squadron*
stihat *to pursue*
stihat/stihnout *to have time for*
peruť (poetic and military) *wing*
zastihnout (usually limited to pfv.) *to catch, find*
desítka *a tensome, (loosely) dozen*
mechanik *mechanic*
horlivý *eager, keen, diligent, urgent*
připravy k *preparations for*
boj (m) *battle*
přidělovat/přidělit *to assign*

9 PASSIVE FORMS: *JE OPŘEDEN* – 'IS WREATHED'

The Text items were selected as the type of Czech where you will find most occurrences of the passive voice. (If you are not familiar with the term, 'Peter killed Paul' is in the active voice:

Peter, the subject, is the active party; 'Paul was killed by Peter' is in the passive voice, in which the subject Paul is the passive 'target' of the action.)

The English passive is usually expressed by *be* + the *-ed* form of the verb. So too in Czech, but a shorter version of it than what you learned in Unit 18. To form the short passive participle as needed for this purpose, imagine the verbal noun without the final -**í**:

vydání (*edition*) → vydán (*published*)

This gives the masculine singular form. Then simply add the usual gender and number endings as required:

Slovník byl vydán.	*The dictionary was published.*
Zpráva byla vydána.	*The report was issued.*
Město bylo vydáno nepříteli.	*The city was surrendered to the enemy.*
Rukojmí byli vydáni.	*The hostages were handed over.*
Slovníky/Zprávy byly vydány.	*The dictionaries/reports were published.*

If the verb is one of those that requires an 'object' in a case other than the accusative, a passive participle can still be formed, but it will always be neuter singular in form, and the 'object' stays in the same case:

Hnuli stolem.	*They moved the table.*
Bylo hnuto stolem.	*The table was moved.*

10 WHEN TO USE THE PASSIVE

The examples which you were given at the outset were not put into a dialogue because, while passives can be heard, they are not the most common feature of spoken Czech. Indeed, there is relatively little need for them. To go back to the initial example of 'Peter killed Paul': this is simply expressed by **Petr zabil Pavla**. The English passive version, 'Paul was killed by Peter', which has its uses in the right context, is equally simply expressed in Czech by inversion: **Pavla zabil Petr**.

There is in neither case any doubt as to who was dead and who was responsible, and both the English and the Czech version are conveying a fact chiefly about Paul, namely his being killed by Peter. It is the flexibility of Czech word order – here the fact of being able to open a sentence with the object, the accusative – which not only guarantees that it can adapt to context, but also accounts for the low incidence, outside certain special styles, of 'true passive' constructions. That is to say, in a different type of Czech, the sentence might be expressed: **Pavel byl zabit Petrem**, or **Král byl zabit davem**. *The king was killed by the crowd.* But not for everyday purposes.

11 THE MAN (WHO WAS) KILLED BY PETER ...

Just as the active participle could be used to replace a relative clause, so too can the passive participle. And it too will have to agree with the noun it follows:

Compare:

Muž, který byl zabit Petrem, byl jeho tchán.
The man who was killed by Peter was his father-in-law.

and

Muž zabitý Petrem byl jeho tchán.
The man killed by Peter …

and

Pochovali muže, který byl zabit Petrem.
Pochovali muže zabitého Petrem.
They buried the man (who was) killed by Peter.

This type of 'participial' clause is more frequent than the relative clause with the passive verb.

12 OTHER FACTS ABOUT THE PASSIVE

a As early as Unit 4 you met the 'reflexive passive'. This is an alternative to the passive construction you have just been reading about, but only if the 'passive subject' is not human, sometimes not even animate, and provided there is no need to state who the agent was, that is, by whom the act was performed.

Talíř se rozbil. *The plate was (or got) broken.*

A plate is not animate, and no culprit is named. If the culprit is known and to be named, the obvious solution is inversion:

Talíř rozbil Petr. *The plate [obj.] broke Peter [subj.].*

But if circumstances dictated that a passive of some kind had to be used, then it would have to be the 'true' passive:

Talíř byl rozbit Petrem. *The plate was broken by Peter.*

b If you try to make a human the subject of a reflexive passive construction, remembering you cannot add the agent, you will either produce nonsense, or, more probably, a different sentence, since reflexivization produces so many different results with different types of verbs. To stay with poor Paul: **Pavel se zabil**. This can only mean that Paul was in some sense the cause of his own death. In fact more often, though not exclusively, it implies involuntary death rather than suicide:

Pavel se zabil na lyžích. *Lit. Paul killed himself on skis.*

This means he died, perished, was killed while skiing. Just one more example: with the 'true passive':

Turisté byli vráceni od hranic. *The tourists were turned back from the frontier.*

And with a reflexive verb form:

Turisté se vrátili od hranic. *The tourists returned (came back) from the frontier.*

Here **vracet se/vrátit se** is an intransitive reflexive verb (intransitive means 'not requiring a direct object'). The way to avoid using the true passive construction is, of course, to invert the sentence again: **Turisty vrátili od hranic**. In this **turisty** is accusative (like **Pavla** earlier) and **vrátili** contains the impersonal, unnamed 'they'.

c Now look back to the Texts. Most talk about past events: the clockmaker *was* blinded, Germans *were* injured, the planes *had been* assigned, and so on. But there are two phrases where the passive participle is combined with the present tense of *be*: **je opředen** and **jsou postiženi**.

These examples serve to illustrate the two English counterparts of the combination, namely *is/are -ed* and *has/have been -ed* respectively. To interpret them you have to think of the past 'moment' when the clock became wreathed in legends, or the Czechs were affected by the outcome of the demonstrations, coupled with the present relevance of the facts. (The choice of the different English tense forms is irrelevant to Czech, so it can be left aside here.) In speech you will often hear the long passive participles used for this function, but strictly there is a difference – between the present state resulting from a past act:

Tento pokoj je (už) vytapetován.　　*This room has (now) been papered.*

but

Tento pokoj je (už) vytapetovaný.　　*This room has already got wallpaper (is already papered).*

The long form, therefore, is much like any other adjective after *be*.

13 *DESÍTKY* – 'TENS'

Numerals ending in **-ka**: Round numerals are often expressed by this type of noun, which will also be met in the plural: **stovky** (*hundreds*), **desítky** (*'tens'*, as a low number best treated as *dozens*: the real Czech word for 'dozen' is **tucet**). *Tens of thousands* is **desítky tisíců**. Smaller clusters use the words: **dvojice/trojice/čtveřice/pětice** *a twosome (couple)/ threesome/foursome/fivesome*.

The other use of **-ka**, which works with all numerals, denotes anything that carries the particular number (hotel rooms, trams, school grades up to five, dress sizes, strengths of beer – see Unit 7), as well as naming the number itself:

So **desítka** is a *No. 10* tram, room *No. 10*, the lightest common beer strength, or, in **Nakreslila velkou desítku**, 10 itself: *She drew a big 10.*

In the plural these numerals are used for any numbered items associated with plurals: **potřebuju desítky** (*I need size 10*) probably refers to shoes.

To form these numerals, add **-ka** to the end of the ordinary numbers, but if these end in **-et** change **e** to **í**: třicet → **třicítka**. Two-digit numerals use the inverted form: **dvacet čtyři** →

čtyřiadvacítka. Three-digit numerals usually use just the last: **sto trojka** *103*, **sto dvacet trojka** *123*. The odd ones out are:

jednička	**dvojka**
trojka	**čtyřka**
sedmička	**osmička**
devítka	**stovka**
tisícovka	

14 COUNTING DOORS AND TROUSERS

You have met several nouns which were plural in form but referred to single items: **dveře** (f pl) is *one door*, **housle** (f pl) is *one violin*, **kalhoty** are *one pair of trousers*, as **brýle** are *one pair of spectacles*. To count them a special set of numerals has to be used:

jedny dvoje troje čtvery patery šestery

and so on.

Jedny is merely the plural of **jeden** and changes like **ten**:

Šel jedněmi dveřmi tam a druhými ven.	*He went in through one door and out through the other.*

The others decline as follows:

Nominative/Accusative	dvoje	čtvery (čtvera for n pl)
Genitive/Locative	dvojích	čtverých
Dative	dvojím	čtverým
Instrumental	dvojími	čtverými

Note the similarity to adjectives.

(There are some other rather more specialized types of numerals, but you can ignore them.)

15 FRACTIONS

These are formed by adding **-ina** to the basic numbers: **pětina** (*one-fifth*), **sedmnáctina** (*a seventeenth*), **tisícina** (*thousandth*). Again there are some odd ones out:

polovina	*half*	**třetina**	*third*
čtvrtina	*quarter*	**setina**	*hundredth*

Exercises

4 The following pairs of similar sentences hint at different styles, requiring different ways of handling the verb. Put them into Czech forms appropriate to the style.

a i My suitcase was removed by a tall man with long hair.

  ii My suitcase was stolen by the tall man with long hair.

b i In 1884 the village was abandoned so that the valley could be flooded.

  ii The village was deserted so a dam was built.

c i The king was unceremoniously executed by his enemies.

  ii The king's been killed by his doctor!

d i The accused was observed by three witnesses at 4.30 p.m.

  ii They say the man was seen by three witnesses at half past four.

e i The bedroom was painted to schedule.

  ii This room is nicely painted already.

f i The suitcase removed by the man with long hair was found near the river.

  ii Her passport was in the suitcase stolen by the man with long hair.

 Quick vocab

odcizovat/odcizit *to remove*
vesnice (f) *village*
údolí *valley*
topit/za- *to flood*
přehrada *dam*
bez ceremonie *unceremoniously*
nepřítel *enemy*

popravovat/popravit *to execute*
obžalovaný *accused*
pozorovat/z- *to observe*
v termínu (termín *deadline)* *to schedule*
**nalézat/nalézt (nalezne, nalezl,
  nalezený)** *to find*

WATER RESOURCES

The Czechs have no sea (they are fond, however, of blaming Shakespeare for alleging in *The Tempest* that Bohemia had a coast), but they are not short of water.

The longest river in the Czech Republic, at 271 miles, is the **Vltava** (often known by its German name, the *Moldau*). It flows from the southern hills northwards and through Prague to join the **Labe** (*Elbe*) at Mělník in Bohemia's most northerly wine-producing area. Many impressive rivers descend from all the country's encircling mountains, including the **Morava** (historically known in English as the *March*), which cuts across Moravia eventually to form the southern end of the Czech–Slovak frontier before joining the Danube. The *mor-, mar-* element in these names is historically to do with the idea of frontier, border, as in the Welsh *Marches*, or the *Mark* element in some German place-names. The ending **-ava** of **Morava** and countless other Czech rivers is a leftover from pre-history when the area was inhabited by Celts; it shares its origin with **Avon** (of which England also has more than one) and thus with the Welsh word **afon** *river*, which is feminine, hence so too is the Czech name **Avona** for the river at Stratford – **Stratford nad Avonou**.

The biggest natural lake is **Černé jezero**, which is 18.4 hectares in area and nearly 40 metres deep. It lies in the part of the hills that make up the frontier with Germany in the South-West known to the Czechs as **Šumava** (the north-western end of this range of forest-covered hills is called **Český les**; the English name *Bohemian Forest* covers both parts of the range).

The largest man-made lake is the **Rožmberk** fishpond (**rybník**) in South Bohemia (489 hectares), one of many in the region. It is here that the carp which Czechs eat at Christmas is farmed and from where fish was exported as far away as England in Henry VIII's time. There are of course many larger, more recent artificial lakes – reservoirs (**vodní nádrž**), especially where valleys have been dammed (**údolní nádrž**, or **přehrada** *dam* for short).

Then there are the famous mineral springs (**pramen** or, if hot, **vřídlo**) all over Bohemia and parts of Moravia, hence the number of spa towns (you can often spot them on the map from the word **lázně** (*baths*) in their name); the hottest is one of the 12 that made Carlsbad (**Karlovy Vary**) famous – it leaves the ground at 72 degrees Celsius and at the record rate of about 1,800 litres a minute. The popular liqueur or aperitif known as **Becherovka**, produced at Karlovy Vary, is jocularly known as the town's **třináctý pramen** (*thirteenth spring*).

Test yourself

The extra numeral types cannot be avoided, as these specimen sentences show. Put them into Czech.

   a I'm in (**na**) number 17.

   b I would like you to wash these four pairs of trousers.

   c He prefers 12-degree beer to 10-degree beer.

   d Can you change (**rozměnit**) a 500-crown note for me?

   e They gave us a sixth and kept five sixths, but I think we should have got three quarters.

   f We had to replace (**vyměnit**) the locks on (**v**) two doors.

Supplement

Remember that throughout the book you have been taught a neutral version – not too bookish and not over-colloquial – of Standard Czech. It is as well, however, to be aware of some of the key features of higher-style (chiefly written) and lower-style (chiefly spoken) versions of the language.

Selected features of high-style Czech

Key features of high-style Czech are likely to occur in more pretentious or archaic texts.

1 GERUNDS

Unfortunately this is yet another *-ing* form of English, which we may call the verbal adverb. It is the kind of thing you have in *Running after the bus she slipped and fell* – meaning *as*, *when* or *because she was running* …, or *Having admired the cake, they proceeded to eat it*, that is *when or after they had admired it* …

In Czech, the equivalent forms of the first type are a short version of the active participle, which means that, although they are 'adverbial', they show some agreement according to gender, the gender of the subject of the sentence ('*she*' or '*they*' in the English examples).

As there were two types of present active participle (ending in **-oucí** or **-ící**), so there are two ways of forming the gerund. If the stem of the third person plural (the '*they*' form) ends in a 'soft' consonant, or if the verb is of the **í**-conjugation, the endings are **-e/-ě**, **-íc**, **-íce**, otherwise **-a**, **-ouc**, **-ouce**.

		Masculine	Feminine/neuter	Plural
dělat	dělaj-	dělaje	dělajíc	dělajíce
psát	píš-	píše	píšíc	píšíce
myslet	mysl-	mysle	myslíc	myslíce
hledět	hled-	hledě	hledíc	hledíce
chodit	chod-	chodě	chodíc	chodíce
vést	ved-	veda	vedouc	vedouce
být	js-	jsa	jsouc	jsouce

An accessible, if rather theoretical, example:

Zpívajíc nahlas, vzbudila   *Singing loudly, she woke the*
  sousedy.   *neighbours.*

This shows all you need to know: this type is used for economy to express a simultaneous action, whatever the tense. It can only be formed from imperfective verbs.

There is a perfective gerund to express an action that precedes the action in the main clause. This is formed in the same way as the past tense, except that instead of **-l**, a **-v** is added; this gives you the masculine form. The feminine/neuter and plural forms are then based on it and end in **-vši** and **-vše**.

		Masculine	Feminine/neuter	Plural
udělat	udĕla-	udĕlav	udĕlavši	udĕlavše
napsat	napsa-	napsav	napsavši	napsavše
vymyslet	vymysle-	vymyslev	vymyslevši	vymyslevše
vzít	vza-	vzav	vzavši	vzavše
přežít	přeži-	přeživ	přeživši	přeživše

If, however, the past tense uses a consonantal stem, this alone is the masculine form, to which the feminine/neuter and plural endings are then added:

přivést	přived-	přived	přivedši	přivedše
vytisknout	vytisk-	vytisk	vytiskši	vytiskše

Again, let one example suffice:

Král, propustiv komorníka,   *The king, having dismissed his*
   brzy toho litoval.   *chamberlain, soon regretted it.*

Only two verbs need to be thought of as anomalous. One is **být**, which has the forms **byv**, **byvši**, **byvše** (the oddity is that here a past gerund is formed from an *im*perfective verb). The other is **jít**, or more importantly its forms with prefixes, which have **-šed, -šedši, -šedše**:

Přišedši pozdě, ani se   *Having arrived late, she didn't even*
   neomluvila.   *apologize.*

One or two words that are gerunds in origin have become divorced from their respective verbs and taken on new functions. They include: **nehledě na** (*disregarding*); **chtě nechtě** (*willy-nilly*) and **počínaje** and **konče**, which may work as prepositions or post-positions (and they are accompanied by the instrumental) meaning *beginning with* and *ending with*:

Umí všechno, počínaje   *He knows everything from biology*
   biologií a hudbou konče.   *to music.*

and a few others.

Even rarer than the perfective, past, gerund is the perfective active participle based on it. This is formed by replacing the **-i** of the feminine form of the gerund by **-í** and treating it as a 'soft' adjective. Some are also to be seen in adjectival functions proper: **vrátivší se emigranti** (*returning émigrés – 'the having returned émigrés'*). Far commoner in a related function are adjectives formed from the past tense: from **zbohatnout** (*to get rich*) there is **zbohatlý** (*nouveau riche*), from **zmrznout** (*to freeze*) there is **zmrzlý** (*frozen*), while **zkamenět** (*to turn to stone*) gives **zkamenělý** (*fossilized*). Some are highly restricted, **došlá (korespondence)** *incoming* (*mail*), from **dojít** (*to have arrived*), while others have become far removed from their verbs: **umělý** (*artificial*: **umět** *to know how*). This type of adjectivalization of the part tense is a highly productive source of 'changed state' adjectives that are by no means confined to high-style usage – the examples just given are the 'ordinary' words for the given meanings.

2 *JENŽ:* ANOTHER WAY OF SAYING 'WHO', ETC.

This is a higher-style alternative to **který**, the relative pronoun. It declines like the long forms of **on**, **ona**, **ono**, **oni**, etc., but has distinct nominative and accusative forms.

	Singular			Plural		
	Masculine	**Feminine**	**Neuter**	**Masculine**	**Feminine**	**Neuter**
Nominative	jenž	jež	jež	již*	jež	jež
				jež		
Accusative	jenž	již	jež	jež	jež	jež
	jehož*					
(*denote animate forms.)						

Konference, na niž nás	*The conference to which they had*
pozvali, byla zrušena.	*invited us was cancelled.*
Konference, jichž jsme se	*The conferences which we*
zúčastnili, byly nudné.	*attended were boring.*

(**účastnit se/z-** + gen. = *to participate in, attend*)

Notice that, like the third-person pronouns, this word must start with **n-** after prepositions.

If you are alert, you will gradually observe that there is considerable interference between (confusion about) these forms in 21st-century usage.

● INSIGHT

Czechs have been traditionally concerned about correct usage. Similar in function to the language side of the Académie Française, there is **Ústav pro jazyk český** (*Institute for the Czech Language*), part of the Academy of Sciences of the Czech Republic. Besides publishing learned language journals, it also has an office that answers language questions from the general public and offers guidance on matters where current rules have plainly become out of date, that is, where normal usage is now at variance with an older standard. Areas where it has given advice include the gerunds (above), the forms of **jenž**, and those of **tentýž** (below). What unites both these is that they are unequivocally confined to high-style written versions of Czech; they are not part of the spoken language, therefore Czechs cannot acquire them with their mothers' milk, so they have to be learned at school, and like anything learned at school, they may not be learned fully – hence the 'mistakes' people may make and the need for guidance from an authoritative source.

---

3 *TENTÝŽ/TÝŽ*– 'THE VERY SAME'

This means *the same, the very same*. In everyday speech it is replaced by **stejný**, which strictly means *'same'* as to type, appearance and so on. If I and another write **týmž perem**, we are sharing the pen, if we write **stejným perem**, strictly we each have our own, but they look the same.

The declension of **(ten)týž** is rather unstable, but the approved current pattern is as follows:

	Singular Masculine		Neuter	Feminine
Nominative	týž/tentýž		totéž	táž/tatáž
Accusative	týž/tentýž		totéž	touž/tutéž
	téhož (anim.)			
Genitive		téhož		téže
Dative		témuž		téže
Instrumental		týmž/tímtéž		touž/toutéž
Locative		(o) témž(e)/tomtéž		téže

	Plural Masculine	Neuter	Feminine
Nominative	tíž/titíž (anim.)	táž/tatáž	tytéž
	tytéž		
Accusative	tytéž	táž/tatáž	tytéž
Genitive		týchž	
Dative		týmž	
Instrumental		týmiž	
Locative		(o) týchž	

Various 'non-approved' forms such as **těchže** also occur as a natural consequence of the mixture of pronoun and adjectival endings already present in this approved set of forms. Just one form, the neuter singular, enjoys an everyday use, as the absolute pronoun *'the same (thing)'*:

Dnes ráno umyla okna a   *This morning she washed the windows*
  zase dělá totéž.   *and she's doing the same again.*

4 DĚLATI, VÉSTI, ZAPOMENOUTI: ARCHAIC INFINITIVES

You learnt early on that such verbs as **moct** and **říct** are still used also in their more conservative forms **moci**, **říci**. Until fairly recently all infinitives ended, or could end, in **-i**, but this is now a 'dead' feature, occasionally surviving in legalese, or in fossilized bits of Czech, such as proverbs:

Nouze naučila Dalibora   *Necessity taught Dalibor to play*
  housti.   *the fiddle.*

equivalent to *Necessity is the mother of invention*.

Selected features of low-style Czech

Now for a glimpse of overlapping types of Czech called 'Common Czech', 'Spoken Colloquial Czech' or 'Spoken Urban Czech'. It would need a whole new book to describe them all properly, but the most readily observed points are listed here.

5 SOUND CHANGES

ý is almost regularly replaced by **ej**: **být → bejt, dobrý → dobrej**.

é is almost regularly replaced by **í/ý**: **péct → píct, dobré → dobrý**.

initial **o-** is largely replaced by **vo**: **on → von, okno → vokno**

6 FORM CHANGES

Many of these are a consequence of the above, but there are others.

a the instrumental plural ends in all circumstances in **-ma**, with various vowels preceding it:

pánama	**oknama**
ženama	**klíčema**
židlema	**dětma**
krásnýma	**cizíma**
mýma	**našima**
třema	

b the 1st person plural of **e-**conjugation verbs often shortens from **-eme** to **-em**: **vedem** from **vedeme**. Other conjugations cannot do this because the resulting form would be the same as the 1st person singular.

c the third person plural of all **i-**conjugation verbs (not just those limited sets which you have learnt) ends in **-ějí/-ejí**, though usually shortened first to **-ěji/-eji**, or more often even to **-ěj/-ej**: **choděj(i)**, **myslej(i)** and so on. Similarly, the **-ají** of the **a-**conjugation verbs shortens to **-aj(i)**: **dělaj(i)**. This has no effect on how the imperative is formed; that remains based on standard conjugation.

d In **e-**conjugation verbs where the third person plural and the first person singular may have either **-ou** or **-í** and **-u** or **-i**, only **-ou** and **-u** will be heard.

e the past tense of verbs whose stems end in a consonant drops the **-l** in the masculine form: **ved** from **vedl**, **moh** from **mohl**. Those from verbs ending in **-nout** may behave similarly, or retain a version of the ending: **spad** or **spadnul** from **spadnout**, for the standard form **spadl**. The other forms are generally as you have learnt (**spadla**), but alternatives with **-nu-** may also occur (**spadnula**).

f the conditional auxiliary has its own, more 'regular' conjugation: **bysem, bys(i), by, bysme, byste, by**.

g the second-person singular of **být** as *to be*, but not as auxiliary, is **seš** instead of **jsi**.

h forms of **který**, when used (see next page), will often be heard without the **-t-**, and many other words will turn up in simplified pronunciation: **dy** from **kdy**, **dyť** or even **dyk** from **vždyť**; **pudu**, etc. from **půjdu** (and imperative **poď(te)**); the verb **vzít** conjugates **vemu, vemeš**, etc. (imperative **vem(te)**).

7 GRAMMATICAL CHANGES

The most conspicuous is replacement of **který** by **co**, and the various case-forms of **který** by **co** with the corresponding forms of the third-person pronouns: **muž, se kterým jsem mluvil** becomes **muž, co jsem s ním mluvil**. Another is the use of the conjunction **jak** for **když** (*when, if*), **jakmile** (*as soon as*), **pokud** (*if, insofar as*) and some others. For the rest it follows that there will be a total absence of the features described for high-style Czech.

8 VOCABULARY CHANGES

These are far too numerous to mention and no systematic rules can be given. One or two are well known and widely acknowledged, such as **táta** for **otec**, or **brácha** for **bratr, Pražák** for **Pražan, anglina** for **angličtina, ten samej, ta samá, to samý** for both **stejný** (etc.) and **tentýž** (etc.) (a borderline hybrid style may use **ten samý, ta samá, to samé** here). However, the stylistic diversity of many words remains a huge and open problem. Only practice will teach you what words may be used when – what is admissible as standard colloquial, and what is by any measure substandard – so for safety and propriety's sake, stay with standard forms for a long time yet!

Taking it further

Some suggested other works you might use, now that you have the basics of Czech firmly in your mind:

F. Čermák, M. Šára, J. Holub, J. Hronek & D. Short *Czech: a Multi-Level Course for Advanced Students*, Prague: Charles University; Brno: Masaryk University; London: School of Slavonic and East European Studies, University of London, 1993 (ISBN: 8021007699 and 8021007702). A substantial, two-volume, somewhat technical course usable at two levels of intensity or speeds of progression; includes a reader, tables and a generous vocabulary.

Tom Dickins *Spoken Czech: Situational Dialogues for Intermediate Level Students*, Wolverhampton: Univ. of Wolverhampton, 1993. A set of 13 video recordings of situations with an accompanying book of transcripts and exercises.

Josef Fronek, Světlana Obenausová, David Bickerton *Mluvte s námi česky! Audiovizuální kurs*, Glasgow: Department of Slavonic Languages and the Language Centre of the University of Glasgow, 1995 (ISBN: 0852615361). Book, video-cassette and audio-cassette. The ten lessons, for intermediate learners, rely on simultaneous use of the book and both cassettes. The scenes, set in the university environment, theatre, shops, stations, the countryside etc., were filmed in Olomouc and the whole course arose from close co-operation between the universities of Glasgow and Olomouc.

Michael Heim *Contemporary Czech*, Columbus, Ohio: Slavica Publishers, 1991 and later reprints (ISBN: 0-89357-098-2). A course for more advanced students assumed to have a knowledge of a related language; your knowledge of Czech after completing *Complete Czech* puts you in a similar position, making *Contemporary Czech* an excellent revision tool.

James Naughton *Czech: An Essential Grammar*, London, New York: Routledge, 2005 (ISBN: 0415287847 [hbk], 0415287855 [pbk]). A readily available 'practical reference guide to the core structures and features of modern Czech'.

Laura A. Janda & Charles E. Townsend *Czech*, Munich: Lincom Europa, 2000 (ISBN: 389561421). An excellent survey grammar and reference work by two of the leading US scholars in the field of Czech language studies.

David Short 'Czech', in Bernard Comrie (ed.): *The Slavonic Languages*, London: Routledge, 1993, pp. 455–532; reprinted with amendments 2001 (hbk, ISBN: 0415047552) and 2002 (pbk, ISBN: 0415280788). Another linguistic survey of the language.

Charles E. Townsend *A Description of Spoken Prague Czech*, Columbus, Ohio: Slavica Publishers, 1990 (ISBN: 089357211X). A valuable attempt to distil the core features of modern urban speech in Prague; least reliable is the section on vocabulary.

DICTIONARIES

Josef Fronek *Anglicko–český - Česko–anglický slovník*, Prague: LEDA, 1998; published since in several revised editions and frequent reprints (ISBN: 8085927489). Also available on CD-ROM. The best by far of the available two-way dictionaries, excellent for contemporary vocabulary; the separate English–Czech and Czech–English dictionaries from the same author and publisher provide a much wider vocabulary overall.

Karel Hais & Břetislav Hodek *Velký anglicko-český slovník*, Prague: Academia, 1992–94. A comprehensive, four-volume work, considerably updated in the intervening years, but most readily available on CD-ROM (Prague: LEDA, 2006), which is not cheap (EAN: 8594037280501).

Oxford photo dictionary anglicko–český. Praktická cvičení pro potřebu škol a samouků, Oxford University Press, 1992 (ISBN: 019431376X; EAN: 9780194313766). The Czech mutation of a work intended for learners of English that can be used profitably by English-speaking learners of Czech; includes exercises. Hard to get hold of, but well worth the effort.

Ivan Poldauf, with Robert Pynsent *Czech–English Dictionary*, Prague: SPN, 1986; 10th ed. Prague: WD Publications, 2002 (EAN: 9788090218031), distributed in the USA by Hippocrene Books. A fairly comprehensive dictionary, enabling the user to cope with literature, as well as the press and everyday spoken Czech; the 3rd and subsequent editions contain some 'modernizations and other modifications' by **Sinclair Nicholas**, who has also compiled a Czech–American dictionary.

Bruce Davies & Jana Hejduková *401 Czech Verbs*, Prague: Bruce Davies, 3rd expanded edition, 2006 (EAN: 9788023972603). An excellent resource that offers far more than its main focus of the language's most troublesome verbs.

Lukáš Vodička *Anglicko–český slovník frázových sloves*, Prague: Fragment, Práh, 2nd edn, 2002 (ISBN: 807200588X, EAN: 9788072005888). A good resource for coping with English phrasal verbs – interpreted here very broadly. It contains 12,000 entries.

ON-LINE DICTIONARIES (A SMALL SELECTION)

http://users.ox.ac.uk/~tayl0010/links.html. Created by James Naughton of Oxford. Not in itself a dictionary, but a large database of Czech language-learning materials, including links to some dictionaries. The other associated page, http://users.ox.ac.uk/~tayl0010/czech.html, provides a mixed range of links, chiefly on literature, but providing plenty of useful reading matter, in and about Czech. Another set of very useful links can be found on http://www.blinkpro.com/members/neilber, compiled by Neil Bermel.

Ectaco Online Dictionaries

www.ectaco.com/online/diction. php3?lang=4. A site designed to sell more powerful dictionaries in software form. The free online version at http://www.ectaco.com/English–Czech-Dictionary/ nonetheless gives access to a reasonable range of Czech–English–Czech equivalents.

Moravia Translations:

http://www.moravia-it.com/dictionary/. A reasonable dictionary that tends to show less frequent equivalents first. It also exists in a WAP version at http://wap.moravia-it.com

The Langsoft Multilingual Dictionary

http://www.slovnik.cz/. Offers translation from and into a variety of languages, including English and Czech, and contains within its alphabetized lists entire phrases – the siting of some of which might not have occurred to the user, e.g. 'a babe in the woods' early in the A section, with a translation meaning 'a helpless person'.

Wordbook multi-dictionary

http://www.wordbook.cz. An English-language online dictionary which permits searches with or without diacritics ('accents'). Contains a system for typing in letters with accents for those without a Czech keyboard.

PHRASE BOOKS

Many well-known publishers produce books under the generic title **Czech Phrase-book and Dictionary**, for example Berlitz and Chambers, or **Czech Phrase-book**, for example Hugo's or Dorling Kindersley. The market in them is fairly fluid, and the content of each one may not be exactly what each individual needs. Try to inspect as many as you can (under whatever title) in the travel or dictionary section of a good bookseller in your nearest large town. Many more are produced inside the Czech Republic, only a few of which will reach bookshops abroad. Here are details of just two from the recent and less recent harvest:

Richard Nebeský *Lonely Planet Czech Phrasebook and Dictionary, London: Lonely Planet, 2013.*

Zuzana Zrůstová *Czech Phrase Book Travel Pack*, London: BBC Books, 1996. One of the best general phrase books in its day – so still worth looking for; includes a 3000-word dictionary and is accompanied by a 60-minute cassette.

USEFUL WEBSITES – A SELECTION

www.bohemica.com – one of the most varied sites, which includes masses of background information and links to a wide range of other sites, on all aspects of learning Czech, including exercises, textbooks, dictionaries, glossaries, information about the Czech Republic day to day, its literature, culture etc., and much else. It is created and constantly updated by Dominik Lukeš.

www.czech-language.cz/ – a rich site associated with Charles University, Prague, offering in summary or inventory form, and often more discursively, all aspects of the language from pronunciation to sentence structure. Includes a 500-word vocabulary and a variety of quirky bits, such as the language's longest words, games and quizzes. There is a small selection of translations and parallel texts, some areas which sidestep to the Czech National Corpus, and a valuable links button.

http://www.seelrc.org/webliography/czech.ptml?PHPSESSID=0217d0a0402c22c6e7204c 540603c435 – one of several excellent US sites, this one from the Slavic and East European Resource Center of the University of North Carolina, includes among much else a Czech reference grammar and games for language practice, masses of cultural background material and links to the other main US sites.

http://ucnk.ff.cuni.cz/verejny.php – the 'public access' (**veřejný přístup**) site of the Czech National Corpus, enabling searches for examples of words in use (up to 50 examples for each word or form keyed in), drawn from the corpus, which grows by the day. It is also possible to get full access to all the facilities offered by the corpus site on payment of a subscription.

http://www.locallingo.com/countries – 'A site that helps you learn Czech', particularly good for beginners, including exercises and a phrase-book. It also has a number of eminently useful links. Its sister site, http://www.myczechrepublic.com/, has a wealth of information of all kinds pertaining to the country and its language; it also provides a forum for like-minded learners.

www.seznam.cz – one of the major Czech general search engines, with a comprehensive range of links to everything Czech, including a multilingual online dictionary, though it needs using with caution. In Czech.

http://pages.cs.wisc.edu/~bolo/travel/czech_lang.html – a teaching and learning site with a comprehensive set of internal and external links. It is another of the good US university-based sites.

USEFUL BOOKSELLERS

Bay Foreign Language Books, Unit 4, Kingsmead Park Farm, Folkestone, Kent, CT19 5EU, England, is the main UK importer and worldwide distributor of foreign language books, including an impressive range of Czech grammars, dictionaries and other language-learning aids. For contact details etc. see http://www.baylanguagebooks.co.uk. This company supplies most UK (and many foreign) bookshops with dictionaries etc.

The Talking Bookshop offers audio language resources in addition to those accompanying some of the above book titles. See http://www.talkingbooks.co.uk/ttbs/results.asp?TAG= &CID=&sf1=kword_index&st1=Czech&x=8&y=5.

Bohemia Books USA – 'Czech Book Store Since 1978', prop. John Sramek, 53321 Villa Circle, Shelby Township, Michigan, 48316. They have over 6000 titles in stock, including the main contemporary language-learning materials. Contact and other details at http://bohemiabooksusa.com/About_Us.html.

ORGANIZATIONS AND INSTITUTIONS

The British Czech and Slovak Association has a membership of largely UK-based Czechs, Slovaks and Britons interested in what is going on in the Czech and Slovak Republics. It publishes the bi-monthly BCSA Review, which contains topical news items, general-interest articles, reports on Czech events in the UK, book reviews, a letters page and a calendar of future events. See www.bcsa.co.uk. It also organizes an annual essay competition (on Czech/Slovak/Czechoslovak subjects).

The International Association of Teachers of Czech publishes a half-yearly journal, *Czech Language News*, which contains articles on the language, book reviews and news of conferences, language summer schools etc. Membership (by modest subscription payable in US$, UK£ or Czech crowns) is open to learners as well as teachers. See http://www.language.brown.edu/NAATC/.

The Czech Centre London, 116 Long Acre, London, WC2E 9PA, organizes regular events on site, and coordinates closely with the Czech Embassy and various cultural bodies (theatres, local authorities, the British Film Institute etc.) in the promotion of Czech events, including regular film festivals, anywhere in the UK. The Centre also runs language evening courses. The excellent website is at www.czechcentre.org.uk.

The Czech Center New York, 321 East 73rd Street, New York, NY 10021 operates in a very similar manner. For contact and activities, and some more useful links see http://www.czechcenter.com/. The same address is home to the Czech Tourist Authority.

EMBASSIES OF THE CZECH REPUBLIC

3900 Spring of Freedom Street, N.W.
Washington, DC 20008, USA
Tel. (202) 274-9123, Fax (202) 363-6308
E-mail: washington@embassy.mzv.cz
Website: http://www.mzv.cz/washington

26-30 Kensington Palace Gardens
London, W8 4QY, UK
Tel. (020) 7243 1115, Fax (020) 7727 9654
E-mail: london@embassy.mzv.cz
Website: http://www.mzv.cz/london/

251 Cooper Street
Ottawa, Ontario, K2P 0G2, Canada
Tel. (613) 562-3875, Fax (613) 562-3878
E-mail: ottawa@embassy.mzv.cz
Website: http://www.mzv.cz/ottawa

Main consulates
Consulate General of the Czech Republic, New York
1109-1111 Madison Avenue
New York, NY 10028, USA
Tel. (212) 717-5643, ext. 1, Fax (212) 717-5064
E-mail: consulate.newyork@embassy.mzv.cz
Website: http://www.mzv.cz/newyork

Consulate General of the Czech Republic, Chicago
205 N Michigan Av., Suite 1680
Chicago, IL 60601, USA
Tel.: (312) 861-1037, Fax: (312) 861-1944
E-mail: chicago@embassy.mzv.cz
Website: http://www.mzv.cz/chicago

Consulate General of the Czech Republic, Los Angeles
10990 Wilshire Blvd., Suite 1100
Los Angeles, CA 90024-4879, USA
Tel. (310) 473-0889, Fax (310) 473-9813
E-mail: losangeles@embassy.mzv.cz
Website: http://www.mzv.cz/losangeles

Consulate General of the Czech Republic, Toronto
Richard Krpač, consul general
2 Bloor Street West, Suite 1500
Toronto, Ontario, M4W 3E2, Canada
Tel. (416) 972 1476, fax. (416) 972 6991
E-mail: montreal@embassy.mzv.cz
Website: http://www.mzv.cz/toronto

Key to the exercises

UNIT 1

1 (a) Dobré ráno (b) Dobrý den (c) Dobrý večer **2** (a) Dobrý den. Jak se máte? (b) Velmi dobře, děkuju. (c) A jak se máte vy? (d) Dobrou noc a na shledanou. **3** (a) Dobrý večer. Vítám vás v Praze. (b) Jak se máte? **4** (a) Velmi dobře, děkuju. (b) Jde to. (c) Špatně. **5** (a) Na shledanou večer. (b) Na shledanou ráno. (c) Na shledanou zítra. (d) Na shledanou zítra večer. **6** Jsem rád, že jsem tady/v Praze. **English imports:** (a) sandwich, (b) shaker (for mixing drinks), (c) (pork) lunch(eon) meat, (d) jam, (e) weekend, (f) team, (g) showman, (h) sweater, jumper, (i) training, (j) goal, (k) combine (harvester), (l) hooligan (the last two entered Czech via Russian!)

UNIT 2

1 (a) Smím se vám představit. Jmenuju (jmenuji) se XY. (b) Smím vás představit? To je Jane Williamsová. (c) Těší mě. **2** (a) Jsem vlastně Angličan/-ka, ne Čech/Češka. (b) John je vlastně Skot, ne Angličan. (c) Sabine je vlastně Francouzka, ne Němka. **3** (a) Slečno Schmidtová, odkud jste? (b) Ale odkud pocházíte původně? **4** (a) Patrick je Ir. Je student. (b) Paní Evansová je Velšanka. Je průvodkyně. (c) Mária Slobodová je Slovenka. Je doktorka. (d) Heinz Bayer je Němec. Je tlumočník. **5** (a) Patrick je student. Je z Irska. (b) Paní Evansová je průvodkyně. Je z Walesu. (c) Mária Slobodová je doktorka. Je ze Slovenska. (d) Heinz Bayer je tlumočník. Je z Německa. **6** (a) Jsem z Prahy/Londýna/Anglie/Walesu. (b) Smím/Můžu se vám představit? (c) Známe se z letadla. (d) Naproti, to je pan Smith/paní Smithová/to jsou Smithovi. (e) (i) Kdo je to tady? (ii) Kdo je to tam? (f) Je to student/-ka z Edinburghu. (g) Co je to? (h) Promiňte (Omlouvám se), ale musím spěchat na konferenci. **7** (a) Jak se máte? (b) Profesor pochází z Brna. (c) Jsem rád, že jsem tady v Praze. (d) Vítám vás v Londýně. (e) Můžu vás představit, slečno Navrátilová? (f) Smím se vám představit? **Test yourself:** (a) Hledá hotel. (b) Musím spěchat. (c) Neznáme vás. (d) Pocházejí z Londýna. (e) Bydlí v hotelu Jalta. (f) (Vy) jste pan Smith. (g) Nemáme kufr. (h) Ona je Irka a on je Američan. (i) Mluvíte česky? (j) Smím rušit? (k) Musíme se představit.

UNIT 3

1 (a) Kde pracujete? A co dělá vaše žena? (b) (i) Jsem novinář/-ka, (ii) doktor/-ka, (iii) učitel/-ka, (iv) úředník/úřednice. **2** (a) Pracuju v Londýně/New Yorku/Praze/Edinburghu. (b) Pracuju v továrně/v kanceláři/v divadle/ve škole. (c) Pracuju ve školství/v návrhářství/v bankovnictví/v dopravě. **3** (a) Kde pracuje vaše žena? (b) A co dělá váš syn? (c) Můj syn pracuje v divadle, je herec. (d) Promiňte (Omlouvám se, Pardon), mám telefon. **5** (a) Ne, není to pravda. (b) Ano, je to pravda, (c) Ne, není to pravda. (d) Ano, je to pravda. (e) Ne, není to pravda. (f) Ne, není to pravda. **6** (to **5** (a)) Neznají se. (to **5** (c)) Nemluví česky. (to **5** (e)) Je herečka. (to **5** (f)) Je úřednice. **7** (a) Co děláte, pane Navrátil? (b) Kde pracujete? (c) Máte dobré místo? **8** Jsem doktor/-ka, inženýr/-ka, novinář/-ka, učitel/-ka. **9** (a) Co dělá váš syn? A co dělá vaše dcera? (b) Vaše žena má také dobré místo, že? **10** Vy nemáte děti, že? **11** Bohužel nemám děti. **12** Bylo to na poště, ve škole, v Brně, doma, na univerzitě, v práci, v bance, v letadle.

UNIT 4

1 (a) Kde bydlíte, Jano? Jak bydlíte? (b) Doma bydlíme v domě; Doma bydlíme v bytě, v činžáku; Doma bydlíme v bytě ve věžáku. (c) Bydlím v hotelu. **2** (a) Ivane, kolik máte místností? *Or:* Kolik máte pokojů? (b) Náš (*or* Můj) byt je malý, ale dcera má velký dům. (c) Má čtyři velké pokoje, kuchyň a koupelnu. (*Or:* Má čtyři plus jedna.) **3** (a) Kdy jste doma? (b) Někdy bydlím v Londýně. (c) Jaký je váš byt? *or* Jaký máte byt? (d) Telefon je někde v kanceláři. (e) Který pokoj je můj/náš? (f) Který je můj/náš pokoj? (g)

Bohužel musím někam jít. (h) Slečno Brabcová, co děláte? **4** (a) Chci/Chceme vás pozvat k nám na návštěvu. (b) Přijďte až v sedm. (c) Pojďte dál! Nemusíte se zouvat. (d) Já se zouvám doma také (taky). My se zouváme doma také (taky). **5** (a) Máte krásný byt. (b) Kde je u vás záchod, prosím? (c) (i) Mám (Máme) dvě ložnice; (ii) Mám (Máme) čtyři plus jedna. (d) Omlouvám se, ale musím spěchat domů. **Test yourself**: Individual answers.

UNIT 5

1 (a) Ano, je to pravda. (b) Ne, není to pravda. (c) Ne … (d) Ano … (e) Ne … (f) Ne … (g) Ano … **2** to (b) Pan Smith neví, kde je; to (c) Na rohu je hotel; to (e) Pan Smith není slepý, jenom špatně vidí. *Or* Pan Smith je jenom unavený; to (f) Pan Smith mluví česky. **3** (a) pravdu, (b) ta taška, (c) benzínovou pumpu, (d) pana Čermáka a paní Čermákovou, (e) tu poštu, (f) toho starého cizince, (g) moje židle, (h) vaši matku a vašeho otce **4** Promiňte prosím, potřebuju pomoc. … Nevíte náhodou, kde je hotel Forum? … Jak daleko přesně? … To není daleko – (já) nemám kufr. **5** (a) Ano, hraju fotbal/Ne, nehraju fotbal. (b) Pana Navrátila chválí paní Navrátilová. (c) Ano, můj muž/moje žena mluví hodně/Ne, můj muž/ moje žena nemluví hodně. **6** (a) Prosím vás, máte sirky? (b) Nevíte náhodou, kde je paní Navrátilová? (c) Rád(a) slyšíte kritiku? (d) Těšíte se na oběd? (e) Je unavená? (f) (Ne)chce si nejdříve odpočinout? (g) Není to paní Smithová? **7** (a) bank official, (b) annually, (c) one month, (d) for a rest and to be alone, (e) a flat in a tenement block and a luxury hotel room. **Test yourself:** (1) Jmenuju se XY. (2) Ano, bydlím v Londýně/Ne, nebydlím v Londýně. (3) Ano, rád čekám/Ne, nerad čekám. (4) Ano, paní Smithová poslouchá historky ráda. (5) Těšíte se na Prahu? (6) Těší se do Prahy? (7) Hraje venku fotbal?

UNIT 6

1 (a) Jsme cizinci. (b) Dívky jsou Velšanky. (c) Chceme knihy. (d) Mají tašky a kufry. (e) Kanaďané si myslí, že vidí celníky. (f) Manželé Smithovi jsou v Praze dva týdny. (g) Fotografy neznáme, jsou to Irové. (h) Synové nemají zavazadla. (i) Hosté nevědí, kde jsou záchody. **2** (a) pneumatika na škodovku, (b) papír na dopisy ('paper for letters' – *letter paper*), (c) hadr na podlahu (*floorcloth*), (d) kartáček na zuby (*toothbrush*), (e) asfalt na silnici (*asphalt for the road*) *or:* asfalt na silnice (*asphalt for roads*), (f) pila na dřevo (*a wood saw*), (g) váza na růže (*a vase for [the] roses*), (h) nůžky na papír (*paper-scissors*), (i) nový zámek na dveře (*a new lock for the door*). **3** (a) Ano. Tento kufr a taška. (b) Ne. Má jenom osobní věci – oblečení, fotoaparát a podobně. (c) V tašce má věci na cestu – mycí potřeby, nějaké jídlo, knihu. (d) Má tam kameny (*or:* Jsou tam kameny). (e) Bude je v Praze potřebovat na konferenci. **4** Promiňte, prosím./ Je to hotel Jalta?/Ano, mám objednávku./(your name, ending in **-ová** if female)/Děkuju (-ji)./Bydlím v Manchestru./Bohužel ne. Manchester je velké město./To je v pořádku. Musím spěchat a ještě nemám klíč./Děkuju (-ji). Na shledanou. **5** (a) Kde máte tašku? (b) Proč chcete kupovat mapu? (c) Co znamená m a ž? (d) Jaký máte byt? (e) Co máte v kufru? (f) Na co je tento papír? (g) Kdo to je? **Test yourself:** (1) Nominative plural: **nouns** – zavazadla (n), kameny (m), vědci (m. anim.), geologové (m. anim.), kolegové (m. anim.); **pronouns** – vaše (n), mí (m. anim.). Accusative plural: **nouns** – věci (f), potřeby (f), kameny (m), důvody (m); **adjectives** – osobní, mycí, jaké, různé, těžká (n); **pronouns** – je (them), ty, své, vaše (n). (2) Novák is, like Smith, a very common name.

UNIT 7

1 (a) Pan Smith studoval v Edinburghu. (b) Protože se na doktorát připravoval v Praze. (c) Doktor Stuart teď pracuje v New Yorku a dřív pracoval v Edinburghu. (d) Profesor Williams pracoval v Londýně, ale minulý týden zemřel. (e) Setkali se na geologické konferenci. **2** (a) Neměli mapu. (b) Byli jsme na návštěvě u pana Navrátila. (c) Mluvil/Mluvila/Mluvili/Mluvily celý den česky. (d) Chtěl(i)/Chtěla/ Chtěly jste si večer odpočinout? (e) Doma jsme se zouvali. (f) Konference nás velmi unavovala. (g) Co to znamenalo? (h) They didn't have a/the map. – We were visiting Mr Navrátil. – He/she/they spoke Czech all day. – Did you want to rest in the evening? – At home we used to change our shoes. – The conference tired us greatly. – What did it/that mean? **3** (a) Kde jste studoval *or* Na které univerzitě jste studoval? (b) Proč nepijete kávu? (c) Slyšel jste, že profesor Williams zemřel? (d) Kdy se to stalo? (e) Máte rádi Prahu? (f) Co mají v tašce? **4** (a) Ve městě je osm divadel. (b) Do hospody u Fleků je to jenom pět minut pěšky. (c) Mají (unikátní) černé pivo. (d) Protože chce přepsat několik pasáží ve svém referátu. (e) Ve své laboratoři má (doktor Navrátil) pár kuriozit, které pan Smith určitě nikdy neviděl. **5** (a) Mám dvě dcery a pět synů; je to jenom deset minut pěšky do práce; doma mám několik druhů piva. (b) Máte ve městě hodně cizinců? Máte dost času? Máte šest kufrů? (c) Včera byly dvě smutné zprávy; Na stole bylo pět různých klíčů; Kromě toho německého kolegy bylo v letadle sedm anglických geologů. **Test yourself:** (a) Pojďte na pivo/na kávu/kafe. (b) Přijďte k nám (dnes) večer. (c) Kde se cítíte víc jako doma, v kanceláři nebo v hospodě? (d) Můžeme jít do divadla nebo do kina spolu? (e) Chcete si nejdřív odpočinout? (f) Pojďte do kuchyně na čaj.

UNIT 8

1 (a) Ano, je smolař; Ne, není smolář. (b) Klíče má na televizi; jsou to klíče od kanceláře. (c) Protože tramvaje dělaly hluk. (d) Protože (ví, že) staré zlobí (*or* nejdou). (e) Rozhlas má v pracovně. (f) Ne, bolí ho hlava. (g) U Navrátilů si stěžuje pan Navrátil. **2** (a) Bolí ji (*or* ho) hlava. (b) Bolí ho krk (*or* v krku). (c) Bolí ho záda/kříž (*or* v kříži). (d) Bolí ji oči. (e) Bolí ho zub(y). (f) Bolí ji ruka (*or* zápěstí). **3** Bolí mě hlava. To nepomáhá. Moc ne. Budily mě pořád tramvaje. Tak to jsme dva **4** (a) Jak se dostanu do kina? (b) Neviděl jste moje klíče? (c) Máte hodinky? Moje nejdou (*or* nefungujou). (d) Kolik máte aspirínů? Potřebuju dva, protože mě bolí hlava a jeden nestačí. (e) Může mě recepční vzbudit? (f) Nevíte náhodou, kde je pošta (nádraží)? **5** (a) Kolik stojí/stál ten nový kufr? (b) Kolik stojí/stály hodinky? (c) Kolik stojí/stála hodina práce? (d) Kolik stojí/stála (you may say **stály**) dvě piva? (e) Kolik stojí/stálo pět čajů? (f) Kolik stojí/stál koncert? (g) Kolik stojí/stála ta krásná kytice? (h) Kolik stojí/stál ten otvírák na konzervy? (i) Kolik stojí/stála nová střecha? (j) Kolik stojí/stál ten anglický holicí strojek? **6** (a) Máte lístky? (b) Kolik stojí? (c) To je moc! (d) Potřebuju tři, prosím. (e) Bohužel mám jenom pětistovku. (f) Řekněte mi, prosím, kde jsou (*or* máte) tady záchody? (g) Jste velmi laskava. Děkuji. (h) You were probably entering the ladies', having turned right instead of left! **Test yourself:** Individual answers.

UNIT 9

1 (a) Kdy tady budete? (b) Kolik je (teď) hodin? (c) (Ne)Víte náhodou, kolik je hodin? (d) Kdy začíná koncert? (e) Co znamená poledne? (f) Kolik máš/máte peněz? (g) Kdy tam pojedeme/pojedete? (h) Kolik mám/máš/máme/máte času? **2** (a) Je pět (hodin) pryč. (b) Čekali jsme tě/vás v osm. (c) Večeříme až v devět. (d) Jen (ten) nový, starý nefunguje. (e) (Do práce) Půjdu v sedm. (f) (Budu/Budeme čekat) na nádraží ve tři hodiny/v patnáct hodin. **3** (a) Protože pan Navrátil (*or* její muž) jde pozdě domů (*or* domů pozdě). (b) Protože (jeho přítel) Ivan měl narozeniny. (c) Měl tři piva. (d) Platil Ivan, protože dostal zvláštní odměnu. (e) Protože Maruška chtěla koupit za zvláštní odměnu nový gauč. (f) (Večer) Půjdou do vzorkovny nábytku. (g) Myje každý den nádobí. (h) *Answer appropriately:* Já/Můj muž/Moje žena/syn/dcera, etc. **4** (a) Zítra bude mít moje žena narozeniny. (b) Kolik peněz ponesete do banky? (c) Ve tři hodiny budou dávat krásný film. (d) Otec zítra povede naši dceru do školy. (e) (won't work in the future) (f) Promiňte, paní, budete číst tyto noviny? (g) Co si o tom bude/budou myslet? (h) V Praze nebudeme nikoho znát. (i) Vy se budete mít! **5** (a) Včera měla moje žena narozeniny. (b) Kolik peněz jste nesl/nesla/nesli/nesly do banky? (c) Ve tři hodiny dávali krásný film. (d) Otec včera vedl naši dceru do školy. (e) Zuzano, kde jsi viděla moje klíče? (f) Promiňte, paní, četla jste tyto noviny? (g) Co si o tom myslel/myslela/mysleli/myslely? (h) V Praze jsme nikoho neznali. (i) Vy jste se měl/měla/měli/měly! **6** (a) Můžete na mě čekat v práci (na pracovišti) ve čtvrt na jednu. (b) Můžete číst, dokud nebudu zpátky v půl čtvrté. (c) Můžete jít do banky, kde budu čekat v devět (hodin). (d) Můžete mě čekat (očekávat) ve tři čtvrtě na pět přesně (*or* přesně ve tři čtvrtě na pět). (e) Můžete spolupracovat a mýt auto v poledne. (f) Můžete tento týden vodit mého syna a (mou/moji) dceru do školy ve čtvrt na devět? (g) Můžete jít za mě do obchodu? Je pozdě – půl páté pryč – a já sám/sama nemám čas. (h) Můžete mi podat knihy ze stolu? (i) Můžete najít čtvrtou lekci a číst mi pomalu první rozhovor? (j) Víte, kolik je hodin? **Test**

yourself: (a) Je půl jedné; (b) je tři čtvrtě na čtyři; (c) je čtvrt na dvanáct; (d) je půl deváté; (e) je čtvrt na deset; (f) je tři čtvrtě na deset; (g) je půl sedmé; (h) je čtvrt na pět; (i) je půl třetí; (j) je půl jedenácté.

UNIT 10

1 vám after pomáhat; rodině indirect object after koupit; manželce, synovi, dceři indirect objects after koupit understood from previous sentence; někomu indirect object after shánět; otci a matce, sousedům a sekretářce indirect objects after shánět understood from previous question; tolika lidem ditto; sousedům a sekretářce 'beneficiaries' after chci; vám beneficiary of the act of typing; nám beneficiaries of the neighbours' care. **2** (a) cizincům, (b) Věře, (c) vám, (d) sousedům, (e) svým studentům, (f) sekretářce, (g) Našim lidem, (h) hotelu, nádraží, (i) krásnému počasí, (j) studentkám, (k) Petr and Jarmila don't understand (the) foreigners. We are going (will go) to Věra's for dinner. Because of you we haven't had dinner yet. We looked after our neighbour's flowers (plants). We recommend our students a month's stay in Prague. He is buying his secretary a souvenir of ('from') his trip. Our people will be issued passports tomorrow ('To our people they will issue …'). Opposite the hotel and opposite the station there are (some) new shops. Thanks to the beautiful weather we are playing outside today. We give the students (fem.) few exercises. **3** (a) Musím jít k řezníkovi/doktorovi/tetě/profesorovi. (b) Co máte proti novému návrhu/anglickému počasí/českému jídlu/těm lidem/jeho manželce (or ženě)/ nám? (c) Je to kvůli vlaku/autům/celníkům/počasí/mým hodinkám. (d) Bylo to díky našim přátelům/ Slovákům/jejich sousedům/vašemu starému psovi. (e) Nerozuměli jsme Petrovi/Marii/starému profesorovi/prvnímu slovu/jeho dlouhému dopisu. **4** (a) Posílám tento (tenhle) dopis příteli v Anglii (or do Anglie). Kolik bude stát? (b) Musím jít k druhé přepážce? (c) Prosím, můžete půjčit této (téhle) paní propisovačku? (d) Snažím se sehnat (or just Sháním) české známky své dceři. (e) Nerozumím těmto (těmhle) předpisům. (f) Zavíráte v pět nebo (v) šest? (g) Máte pražsky telefonní seznam? **5** (a) O Vánocích. (b) V těchto (těchhle) kufrech. (c) Mluvíme o svých sousedech. (d) Protože v těchhle malých bytech je málo místa. (e) Na všech nádražích. **6** Petrovi, konferenci, Praze, chyb, většinu příležitostí, hospodách, pivo, bance, peníze, ulici, cestu, anglická, německá slova, cestách, zítřka. **Test yourself**: (1) Loni o prázdninách. (2) V Čechách. (3) O pražských hospodách. (4) Po Velikonocích. (5) O Češích a Slovácích a jejich problémech.

UNIT 11

1 Individual answers **2** (a) Nabídli nám výlet do hor. (b) Kde jste vyměnil (vyměnila, vyměnili) peníze? (c) Vadilo vám to? (d) Nejdřív jsme se podívali do galerie, potom jsme se najedli. (e) Celý den jsem nedělal nic. (f) Pršelo. (g) Marie udělala strašnou chybu, když si ho vzala. (h) Kupovali celý den suvenýry. (i) V neděli jsme jeli domů. (j) Nekoupil (-la, -li) jste dceři něco k narozeninám? **3** (a) jsem vydělal; (b) nekoupili; (c) udělal; (d) uslyšíme; (e) pomoct; (f) se najíte (navečeříte, *etc.*); (g) si … odpočinout; (h) řeknete; (i) pochopil; (j) Najíme se. **4 Monday** – V pondělí půjdu do banky, kde vyměním (nějaké) libry, na poštu, kde si koupím známky, na nádraží pro zavazadla a odpoledne budu odpočívat. **Tuesday** – V úterý navštívím přátele v Benešově; přivezou mě zpátky v půl osmé. **Wednesday** – Ve středu změním hotel, zkusím hotel na konci ulice; nelíbí se mi pokoj (nemám rád [svůj] pokoj) a v druhém hotelu budu mít pěkný výhled na hrad. Nesmím zapomenout vrátit klíč. Odpoledne budu kupovat knihy, ale nevím, jestli seženu/dostanu to, co chci. Večer nebudu mít co dělat. **Thursday** – Ve čtvrtek ráno budu zase na poště, budu tam čekat, dokud nezavolá manželka – je na dovolené na Kypru, takže já telefonovat nemůžu. Odpoledne chci zkusit aspoň tři dobré pražské hospody, a večer si budu muset zase odpočinout. **Friday** – V pátek, pokud (když) nebudu mít kocovinu, přijmu pozvání pana Nováka na víkend a zkusím život na českém venkově. Má chatu. Nebudu ale odpočívat – (pan Novák a já) budeme čistit zahradu po zimě. **Sunday night** – V neděli večer se vrátím do Prahy; chci se dobře vyspat, protože v pondělí ráno (po)letím domů. **5** (a) seděli jsme v hospodě/četli jsme noviny/šli jsme do divadla; (b) all answers possible; (c) v půl dvanácté/hned po představení/až zavoláš/pátého ledna/ zítra večer …; (d) nevím/na televizoru/byly v téhle kapse/zůstaly v kanceláři/klíče si vzal Petr/které?/leží u dveří; (e) čtyři dny/dokud budou stačit peníze/dvě hodiny/celý příští měsíc/dokud nám nenapíšeš …/do čtvrtka/do března. **Test yourself**: (a) Ve středu, v neděli večer, v červnu, v pět hodin, příští léto (napřesrok v létě), v pátek, přesně v půl osmé, v únoru, v úterý, dnes večer, v listopadu, dvanáctého. (b) celý týden, jeden celý týden, pět dní/dnů, tři měsíce, celý červen, celou zimu, čtrnáct dní/dnů, jenom dvanáct hodin.

UNIT 12

1 (a) Impfv. *to bring (on foot)* přinést; (b) Pfv, *to fly through* prolét(áv)at; (c) Pfv. *to transfer, carry across* přenášet; (d) Impv. *to drive/go out (by vehicle)* vyjet; (e) Impv. *to pull/drag through* protáhnout; (f) Pfv. *to come/arrive running* přibíhat; (g) Impv. *to carry/take away (by vehicle)* odvézt; (h) Pfv. *to cross/drive over* přejíždět; (i) Impv. *to lead out* vyvést; (j) Pfv. *to drive/shoo away/repel* odhánět. **2** (a) Zaletěli jsme daleko, takže jsme přiletěli na letiště pozdě. (b) Někdo mi odnesl kufr. (c) Jana není doma, protože roznáší noviny. (d) Přetáhli/Přetahovali krabici do druhého pokoje/do druhé místnosti. (e) Právě odcházeli, když zazvonil telefon. (f) Dodávka právě přivezla chleba. (g) Město objedeme. Neradi jezdíme v cizích městech. (h) Obvykle chodí (přichází) v šest, ale dnes přišla až v sedm. (i) Přeběhl ulici. (j) Pan Navrátil vyšel z domu, podíval se na nebe, pomyslel si, že to vypadá na déšť a vrátil se dovnitř pro kabát. **3** (a) Vypadá dobře. (b) Vypadá dobře. (c) Vypadá jako Napoleon. (d) Vata vypadá jako sníh. (e) Vypadá jako sníh. (f) Vypadá to na sníh. (g) Dívá se (ven) z okna. (h) Vypadalo to, že nepřijde. (i) Vypadá anglicky. (j) Vypadal jste strašně. **4** (a) Přijel jsem vlakem. (b) Přiletěl jsem letadlem. (c) Přijel jsem autem. (d) Přijel jsem autobusem. (e) Přijel jsem metrem. (f) (Při)šel jsem lesem. (g) (Při)šel jsem městem. (h) Přijel jsem prostřednictvím Čedoku. (i) Přijel jsem stopem. (j) Přijel jsem taxíkem. (k) Přišel jsem hlavní branou. **5** (a) perem, počítači. (b) rodiči. (c) partnerem, novém podniku. (d) námi, hrad. (e) sebou. (f) mostem. (g) autem, opravně. (h) tebou. (i) psem, vlkem. (j) válkou, dům, venkově. **6** (a) I write notes with a pen, but I write letters on the computer. (b) He/She/They don't like going on holiday with his/her/their parents. (c) He's discussing the new company with his partner. (d) Ahead of us there's a beautiful view of the castle. (e) We have some very good prospects ahead of us. (f) The river beneath the bridge is very dirty. (g) I can't come by car because it's in the repair shop. (h) Who's standing behind you? (i) The difference between a dog and a wolf isn't great. (j) Before the war they lived in the city, today they have a house in the country. **Test yourself:** (a) Fotbalista dal košili na postel. (b) Dám peníze k pasu. (c) Dala nákup do kočárku. (d) Učitel dal slovník mezi ostatní. (e) Dávali jsme popelnice před dům. (f) Instalatér dává novou trubku za vanu. (g) Dal knihy ze stolu na židli. (h) Musí dávat porcelán do krabic opatrně. (i) Proč jste dal ty dopisy na zem?

UNIT 13

1 (a) Slunce svítí. (b) Prší. (c) Sněží. (d) Je zima. (e) Je zataženo/zamračeno. (f) Fouká vítr. **2** (a) Vypadá to na déšť. (b) Doufám, že zítra nebude pršet. (c) Moje dcera se bojí hromu. (d) Nerad jezdím v mlze. (e) Včera padal sníh celý den. (f) Nejdřív lilo jako z konve, potom svítilo slunce. (g) Předpověď říká, že bude zima a zataženo. (h) Když stoupá tlak, bolí mě hlava. (i) Kolik stupňů je venku? Jsou čtyři stupně. (j) Ne, nejsou, je pět stupňů. (k) Vítr fouká od jihu, bude teplo. **3** (a) Ale Marie řekla Petrovi, že auto už umyla. > Ale řekla mu, že ho už umyla. (b) Koncert se mi nelíbil > Nelíbil se mi. (c) Navštívíme Smithovy zítra > Navštívíme je zítra. (d) Neobejdu se bez slovníku > Neobejdu se bez něho. (e) Řekněte nám o své cestě > Řekněte nám o ní. (f) Nejdřív zkusíme dát knihy do krabice > Nejdřív je zkusíme dát do ní. (g) Smithovi si spletli hospody > Spletli si je. (h) Nekoupí lístky Anně, ale Štěpánovi koupí > Nekoupí je jí, ale jemu koupí. (i) Dcera nedala deštník sousedům > Nedala ho jim (or: Sousedům dcera deštník nedala > Jim ho nedala). (j) Kdy jste viděl (-la, -li) výstavu? > Kdy jste ji viděl (-la, -li)? **4** (a) Viděli před jeho domem sanitku. (b) Někdo jiný. (c) Paní Navrátilová. (d) V Bratislavě. (e) Bude ho zastupovat v práci/v laboratoři. (f) Nevíme. **5** (a) Sunday, 13 April 2003. (b) The moon sets. (c) Rain will be occasional, and only localized in the north. (d) **až** means 'to', between points on a scale. (e) 1775 is the year when records began at the Klementinum in Prague; 1952 saw the highest temperature for 13 April since records began; 1986 saw the lowest temperature since records began. (f) In the south and south-east, where more persistent rain is forecast. (g) 5 metres per second. **6** (a) Jsou dvě hodiny a deset minut *or* Je za pět minut čtvrt na tři. (b) Je čtvrt na čtyři a pět minut *or* Je za deset minut půl čtvrté. (c) Je tři čtvrtě na dvanáct a pět minut *or* Je za deset minut dvanáct. (d) Je půl osmé a deset minut *or* Je za pět minut tři čtvrtě na osm. (e) Je za pět minut půl šesté (the other possibility is unlikely here). (f) Je tři čtvrtě na devět a tři minuty *or* Je za dvanáct minut devět. (g) Je půl páté a sedm minut *or* Je za osm minut tři čtvrtě na pět. (h) Je deset hodin a sedm minut *or* Je za osm minut čtvrt na jedenáct. (i) Je tři čtvrtě na jednu a jedenáct minut *or* Je za čtyři minuty jedna. (j) Je dvanáct (hodin) čtrnáct (minut) *or* Je za minutu čtvrt na jednu. (k) Je dvanáct (hodin) dvacet devět (minut) *or* Je za minutu půl jedné. **7** Watches to show: (a) 10.05, (b) 6.45, (c) 12.23, (d) 4.50, (e) 2.30, (f) 1.15. **8** (a) to stand on one's own two feet; (b) to get under someone's feet; (c) to be all fingers and thumbs ('to have two left hands'); (d) to shake hands; (e) not to be able to believe one's ears; (f) to be head over heels (up to the ears) in love; (g) stay/keep out of my sight; (h) out of sight, out of mind. **Test yourself:** (a) jiného. (b) jiný. (c) někam jinam. (d) jinam/jinudy. (e) jiného. (f) jindy. (g) jiným. (h) jinde. (i) jinak.

UNIT 14

1 (a) Nakupujte v obchodě za rohem. (b) Kupte mi, prosím, zmrzlinu. (c) Donesme (*or* Odnesme) (svoje) knihy zpátky do knihovny. (d) Vždycky pomáhejte starým lidem přes ulici. (e) Nemyjte nejlepší porcelán v myčce. (f) Podívejte se! Zase prší. (g) Řekněte mi, prosím, kde jsou záchody. (h) Mějte trpělivost. Petr tu brzy bude. (i) Přečtěte mi, prosím, ten článek. (j) Nespěte během filmu. (k) Pochopte, já se tam do čtvrtka nedostanu (nemohu/nemůžu dostat). (l) Myslete na nás, až budeme pryč. **2** (a) Pass me the … (b) Apply/Refer to … (c) Store in a dry place. (d) Don't hesitate. (e) Cross to the opposite pavement. (f) Sit down. (g) Don't park in front of the exit. (h) Stop (it). (i) Let's say no more about it. (j) Return your form, duly filled in, by/to. **3** (a) Kupte mi, prosím, známku na poště. (b) Přineste/Doneste mi knihu zpátky včas. (c) Pojďte dál. Nemusíte se zouvat. (d) Přeložte mi, prosím, tento dopis. (e) Nemluvte nahlas! (f) Rozsviťte mi, prosím. (g) Buďte tak hodný a pomozte mi vyplnit formulář. (h) Jděte pryč. (i) Nenechávejte klíče na stole. (j) Nechoďte ke mně, když máte takovou rýmu. **Test yourself:** (a) Ať je počasí jakékoli, jdeme ven. (b) Ať vám to(hle) řekl kdokoli, je hlupák. (c) Ať pojedete kamkoli, pošlete mi pohlednici. (d) Ať jste to koupil kdekoli, ošidili vás. (e) Budu se učit podle kterékoli knihy v kterémkoli jazyce. (f) Nemluvte o tom s nikým. (g) Kdo se (ze)ptal, jestli něco potřebuji (-ju)? (h) Kdykoli bude svítit slunce, budeme si hrát venku. (i) Máte (nějaké) pohlednice s obrázky řeky? (j) Na mě se svými problémy nechoďte.

UNIT 15

1 (a) Chodím raději do divadla než do kina. (b) Kupuji dárky raději (*or* Raději kupuji dárky) rodičům než dětem. (c) Seděli bychom raději vzadu než vpředu. (d) Mám raději Janu než Petra. (e) Šel bych raději k řece než do parku. (f) Budu platit raději v dolarech než v korunách. (g) Platil bych raději v korunách než v librách. (h) Parkoval bych raději na parkovišti než na ulici. (i) Šla bych tam raději s Milošem než sama. (j) Měli by to koupit raději teď než za týden. **2** (b) Marie je ochotná každému pomáhat. Zatím je v domácnosti, ale raději by byla učitelkou. (c) Štěpán je vtipný. Zatím je televizním hlasatelem, ale raději by byl komikem. (d) Radek je energický. Zatím je programátorem, ale raději by byl horolezcem. (e) Josef je hudebně nadaný. Zatím je fotbalistou, ale raději by byl dirigentem. (f) Sofie je krásná. Zatím je písařkou, ale raději by byla modelkou. (g) Jsem líný. Zatím jsem šoférem, ale raději bych byl ředitelem. **3** (a) Jde o počasí/přednášku/Marii/nás/všechno. (b) Jde jim o peníze/dovolenou/příští schůzi/nový pas. (c) Jde nám o kariéru/tu zprávu v novinách/zdraví/naši návštěvu. (d) Panu Smithovi jde o jeho zavazadla/večeři/dárek pro sousedku/práci v laboratoři. (e) O nový návrh jde panu Smithovi/slečně Šetkové/řediteli/celému podniku/nám. **4** (a) .., abyste si vzali … (b) .., abychom přijeli … (c) .., aby se Petr a Marie vzali. (d) .., aby všechna zavazadla vzali s sebou. (e) .., abych mu to poslal … (f) .., abychom jim půjčili … (g) .., abychom nezmeškali … (h) .., abys v ložnici kouřil. (i) Abyste si, milí přátelé, nemysleli … (j) Už aby ty dopisy přišly! **5** (a) Hledáme ve slovníku, abychom našli významy slov. (b) Vaří manželovi zeleninu, aby se stal vegetariánem. (c) Učí se česky, aby mohli pracovat v Praze. (d) Abychom večeřeli spolu, musíte přijít domů včas. (e) Zavolám sousedy, aby nám pomohli s přípravami. (f) Aby člověk studoval cizí jazyky, musí mít jisté nadání. (g) Abyste směl v Anglii řídit auto, musí vám být aspoň 17 let. **6** (b) Vařila … (d) Musel jste přijít … (f) .., musel mít … **7** (a) Kdyby mi to Petr neřekl, nevěděl bych o tom nic. (b) Kdybyste, Jano a Ivane, chtěli jet s námi, bylo by ještě místo. (c) My bychom v Edinburghu nekupovali nový dům, kdybych já tam nedostal dobré místo. (d) Kdyby její synové tak nepili, nemusela by si dělat tolik starostí. (e) Kdybych byl na vašem místě, řekl bych to také sousedům. **8** (a) If Peter hadn't told me, I wouldn't know anything about it. (b) If, Jana and Ivan, you would like to go with us, there would still be room. (c) We wouldn't be buying a new house in Edinburgh if I hadn't got a good job there. (d) If her sons didn't drink so, she wouldn't have to worry so much. (e) If I were in your place, I would tell the neighbours as well. **Test yourself:** (a) Aby sis nespálil prsty! (b) Abyste nezapomněl klíče! (c) Abychom radši/raději (za-)parkovali na parkovišti, nemyslíte? (d) Abych si opravdu raději koupil nový notebook! (e) Abyste si nespletli sůl a cukr (sůl s cukrem)! **Proverbs:** (i) *Ifs are errors (something wrong)*; (ii) *If there were no ifs, there'd be no errors* (nothing wrong). They mean that if nothing is wrong, we would not have been led to wish for alternatives. The English equivalents are the rather more colourful: *If wishes were horses, beggars would ride*, or *If ifs and ans were pots and pans there'd be no need for tinkers* and perhaps others.

UNIT 16

1 (a) Lenka má radši Prahu, protože je krásnější než Londýn. (b) Studenti čtou radši překlad, protože je jednodušší než originál. (c) Radši (po-)letíme, protože letadlo je rychlejší než vlak. (d) Petr sedí radši vedle Sáry, protože není tak protivná jako Marie. (e) Zuzana mluví radši slovensky, protože slovenština je pro ni lehčí než čeština. (f) Skotové pijí radši whisky, protože je silnější než pivo. (g) Štěpán nosí radši džínsy, protože jsou novější než jeho kalhoty. **2** (a) Lenka měla radši Prahu, protože je krásnější než Londýn. (b) Studenti četli radši překlad, protože byl jednodušší než originál. (c) Radši jsme letěli, protože letadlo je rychlejší než vlak. (d) Petr seděl radši vedle Sáry, protože nebyla/není tak protivná jako Marie. (e) Zuzana mluvila radši slovensky, protože slovenština je/byla pro ni lehčí než čeština. (f) Skotové pili radši whisky, protože je silnější než pivo. (g) Štěpán nosil radši džínsy, protože byly novější než jeho kalhoty. **3** (a) Londýn je starší než New York. (b) Pražský hrad je mnohem starší než Hluboká. (c) Můj soused je ještě starší než otec. (d) Jeho manželka je o šest měsíců starší než on. (e) Jejich dům není tak starý jako náš. (f) Tento hotel je o dvě stě let starší než hotel na náměstí. (g) Moje auto je stejně staré jako jeho. (h) Tenhle kufr není o mnoho starší (je jen o málo starší) než ten druhý. **4** (a) zdravěji. (b) dřív, rychleji. (c) spíš. (d) čitelněji. (e) pohodlněji. (f) víc. (g) dál. (h) dráž. (i) rozuměji. (j) raději. **5** (a) Nejraději jezdí na kole. (b) Vlak používá, když se potřebuje někam dostat rychleji. (c) Ne, Moravu nezná. (d) Ano, Praha se mu líbí, protože je velmi zajímavá. (e) Ano, měl. Někdo mu ho půjčil. (f) Protože tam jsou kočičí hlavy. **Test yourself:** (a) Mluvte tišeji! (b) Pojďte rychleji! (c) Pojďte co nejrychleji. (d) Mluvte, prosím, pomaleji. (e) Uvažujte rozumněji. (f) Chovejte se slušněji.

UNIT 17

1 (a) hořící. (b) tonoucí. (c) spícího. (d) vedoucími. (e) stávkujícím. (f) vadnoucí. (g) rozhodujícímu. (h) štěkající. (i) padající. **2** (a) krycí jméno. (b) balicí papír. (c) rozkazovací věta. (d) školicí zařízení. (e) obývací pokoj. (f) skladovací prostor. (g) oddací list. (h) poznávací značka. (i) mycí houba. (j) hrací karty. (g) is the odd-man-out because the adjective is formed from the perfective – and logically so. **Crossword:** A = ČÁST, B = CHRÁMY, C = PETR; 1 = ČECHY, 2 = STÁLE, 3 = TYGR. Did you remember that CH counts as one letter? **3a** (a) jejíž. (b) jejíž. (c) jehož or jejichž. (d) čí, jehož. (e) jejíž. (f) jehož. (g) čím. (h) jejíchž. **3b** (a) The lady whose dogs went missing (got lost) is a countess. (b) This is that book whose author died in a concentration camp. (c) Passengers in whose luggage there are small electrical appliances (radio, shaver, curling tongs etc.) must declare this fact. (d) They asked whose was the suitcase that had aroused attention. (e) Here is the chair the leg of which needs mending. (f) They gave the driver whose lights were out a fine of 1,500 crowns. (g) In whose interest is it? (h) The lady about whose dogs nobody had found anything out is suing the hotel where she last saw them. **Test yourself:** disponující = kteří disponují; přející = kteří si přejí (*or:* a přejí si); majícím = který má; zabývajících se = které se zabývají; charakterizující = která charakterizuje; mající = kteří měli; upravujících = které upravují.

UNIT 18

1 (a) patnáctého března; (b) tři čtvrtě na čtyři; (c) za dvě minuty čtvrt na šest; (d) sedmadvacátého září; (e) prvního července; (f) půl jedné; (g) dvanáctého prosince; (h) za deset minut pět; (i) jednadvacátého ledna; (j) devětadvacátého února; (k) za pět minut půl osmé; (l) devátého srpna; (m) pátého listopadu; (n) čtvrt na osm a dvě minuty. **2** (a) Bratrova manželka…, (b) se sousedovým psem. (c) Shakespearovy hry. (d) za Petrovou chalupou. (e) pod Věřinou postelí. (f) Štěpánovi přátelé. (g) ledničce paní Smithové. (h) Wilsonovo nádraží. (i) bez Mariina souhlasu. (j) Zdeňčiny staré knihy. (k) Chrám svatého Víta. (l) na Karlově mostě. (m) Sestřina kočka. (n) Průvodcova poslední slova. **3** (a) Co kdybychom se zeptali Petra? *or* Nemohli bychom se zeptat Petra? (b) Co když to Líba nevěděla? *or* Co kdyby to Líba nevěděla? (c) Co kdybychom šli na večeři do restaurace? *or* Nechcete jít na večeři do restaurace? (d) Nedáme si pivo? *or* Co kdybychom si dali pivo? (e) Co na to říkate? *or* Co vy na to? (f) Co na to řekla? *or* Co ona na to? **4** (a) modrá, bílá a červená. (b) bílá, zelená a červená (s červeným drakem). (c) černá, červená a žlutá. (d) červená a bílá (s bílým křížem). (e) zelená, bílá a oranžová. (f) modrá, bílá a červená. **5** (a) rozlité mléko; (b) nezvaný host; (c) přibité plakáty; (d) připsaná písmena; (e) zahnutý nos. **6** (a) zadaný stůl; (b) uznávaná autorita; (c) zakázané ovoce; (d) informované zdroje. **7** (a) vyžehlená košile; (b) zlepšený výkon; (c) Ztracený Ráj; (d) nepřihlášený cizinec; (e) neomezené prostředky; (f) vypůjčené kolo; (g) dobře promyšlený návrh; (h) Spojené národy. **8** (a) dovezené stroje; (b) nově nalezené štěstí; (c) unesené letadlo; (d) okradený turista. **9** (a) Potřebuju čerstvě vypranou košili. (b) … ty dva nedávno vydané překlady. (c) … najít svoje ztracené hodinky. (d) … vidět nově otevřený most, než pojedu/ odjedu domů. (e) … si odpočinout, protože mám unavené nohy. (f) … si opakovat zapomenutá slova z osmé lekce. (g) … otevřít zamčenou (*or:* zamknutou) skříň. (h) … tři talentované mladé lidi pro film, který chci natočit. (i) … opatrně formulovaný dopis, který chci poslat manažerovi (*or:* vedoucímu) hotelu. (j) … spravit rozbitou aktovku. **Test yourself:** (a) Možná (*or:* Třeba) přijde. (b) Máte asi pravdu. (c) Zřejmě nechal klíče doma. (d) Bylo tam asi dvacet lidí. (e) Patrně (*or:* Asi) nepřijde.

UNIT 19

1 (a) Petr má rád vaření. (b) Máme rádi létání na kluzácích. (c) Nemá rád utírání nádobí. (d) Měl radši hraní s počítačem než dělání úkolů. (e) Nejraději ze všeho měl čtení dlouhých románů. (f) Měla ráda pěstování malých druhů azalek. **2** (a) Vyřizování žádosti … (b) … provedení poslední části. (c) Učení se matematiky (*or:* matematice) … (d) … v kladení překážek. (e) … utrácení tolika peněz. (f) Psaní kondolenčního dopisu … (g) … hodnocení výsledků … **3** (a) Nerad peru košile/Nemám rád praní košil. (b) Nechodíme příliš rádi na houby/Chození (*or:* Chodit) na houby se nám moc nelíbí. (c) Psaní dopisu nevěnovala mnoho (*or:* moc) času/Psaním dopisu nestrávila mnoho času. (d) Mají rádi kutění s auty/ Baví se kutěním s auty. **4** (a) (i) (Můj) Kufr byl odcizen vysokým mužem/člověkem s dlouhými vlasy. (ii) Kufr mi ukradl ten vysoký člověk/muž s dlouhými vlasy. (b) (i) Roku (R.) 1884 byla vesnice opuštěna, aby údolí mohlo být zaplaveno. (ii) Vesnice byla opuštěná, proto postavili přehradu. (c) (i) Král byl popraven bez ceremonie svými nepřáteli. (ii) Krále zabil jeho lékař! (d) (i) Obžalovaný byl zpozorován třemi svědky v 16 hodin a třicet minut. (ii) Toho muže prý viděli tři svědkové (svědci) v půl páté. (e) (i) Ložnice byla vymalována v termínu. (ii) Tento pokoj hezky vymalovaný už je. (f) (i) Kufr odcizený mužem s dlouhými vlasy byl nalezen blízko řeky. (ii) Její pas byl v kufru ukradeném tím mužem s dlouhými vlasy. **Test yourself:** (a) Jsem na sedmnáctce. (b) Chtěl bych, abyste mi vypral(a) tyto čtvery kalhoty. (c) Má radši dvanáctku než desítku. (Dává přednost dvanáctce před desítkou.) (d) Můžete mi rozměnit pětistovku? (e) Nám dali šestinu a sobě nechali pět šestin, ale já si myslím, že jsme měli dostat tři čtvrtiny. (f) Museli jsme vyměnit zámek (zámky) ve dvojích dveřích.

Glossary of grammatical terms

Adjectives Adjectives are used to provide more information about nouns, e.g. *That school is very good*. Ta škola je velmi *dobrá*. *The new hotel is expensive*. *Nový* hotel je *drahý*. In a language like Czech adjectives must agree in **gender** and **number** and, where relevant, **case** with the noun they qualify, e.g. *good* school *dobrá* škola, *good* hotel *dobrý* hotel, *good* people *dobří* lidé, *with* *good* people *s dobrými* lidmi.

Adverbs Adverbs mainly provide more information about verbs: *She was singing quietly*. Zpívala *tiše*. They may also provide more information about adjectives: *It was completely unnecessary*. *Bylo to úplně zbytečné*. The typical English adverb ends in **-ly** while in Czech the main type ends in **-ě** or **-e**. Simple words expressing additional information about *time*, *place*, *manner* or *degree* such as *then* **tehdy**, *here* **tady**, *somehow* **nějak**, *very* **velmi** are also adverbs.

Articles English has a *definite* article *the* and an indefinite article *a/an*. Czech has no articles, though forms of **ten** and **nějaký** may sometimes appear to act as substitutes for them. Czech frequently compensates for its lack of articles by changes of word order: *The book is on the table* **Kniha je na stole**, but: *There is a book on the table* **Na stole je kniha**.

Aspect Aspect is a category in Czech which expresses whether a verbal action is (*perfective* aspect) or is not (*imperfective* aspect) completed. With the perfective, the fact of completion is in some sense relevant (consequences may follow from it). The imperfective can express both ongoing states or acts (by definition not completed), or those that are regularly repeated (by definition not one completed event), or those which may have been completed, but where that completion has no particular relevance or consequence. Examples: *I've read the paper* **Noviny jsem přečetl** (perfective; possible consequence: you can have the paper). *At home I (used to) read the* Guardian **Doma jsem četl** Guardian (imperfective; implied regularity). *I read* War and Peace *as a child* **Četl jsem Vojnu a mír jako dítě** (imperfective; no particular relevant consequence, even if I did read the whole book).

Auxiliary verb This term applies to those bits of the verbal expression in a sentence which give it its 'grammar' as opposed to just its 'meaning'. In *I have been cooking since ten o'clock* the verb is *to cook*, while *have* and *been* are the auxiliary, 'helping', words that place the cooking in a particular time frame; similarly the 'will' in *I will cook today* or the *do* in *Do you cook?* Being grammatical, these English auxiliaries have no direct equivalent in Czech, though Czech does have auxiliary verbs of its own, in the past tense, the imperfective aspect of the future tense and the conditional.

Case Case is that feature of a noun (or adjective, pronoun or numeral) by which it is integrated into the sentence; it is revealed by 'endings'. For example, the function of 'subject of the sentence' is expressed by the nominative case. Most of the cases, which are conventionally ordered in Czech as nominative, genitive, dative, accusative, vocative, locative, instrumental, have more than one function: a noun in the genitive (with its genitive ending) will frequently have to do with possession or some other relation expressed in English by *of*, but it is also the case required by many **prepositions**. Case has long gone from English, but we see shades of it in some pronouns: *he v. him*, *we v. us* and others.

Clause This is a technical term for a sentence, but used specifically to denote each of the part-sentences that make up a whole, more complex 'space between full stops'. *She was knitting and her husband was working in the garden* **Ona pletla a manžel pracoval na zahradě** consists of two simple clauses, either of which could stand on its own. *He made some tea because he was thirsty* **Udělal si čaj, protože měl žízeň** likewise has two clauses, the first potentially free-standing, the *main* clause, the second a so-called *subordinate* clause introduced by the **conjunction** *because*. A **clause** can be recognized by having a *finite* verb-form, here *was knitting, was working, made* and *was* (as opposed to the **infinitive** or **participles**).

Comparative The comparative form of adjectives and adverbs is used in making comparisons. In English this means adding -*er* to most adjectives and some adverbs or putting *more* in front of them; Czech adds endings of the type **-ější, -ší, -čí** to adjectives and, most frequently, **-ěji** to adverbs: *This shirt is **cheaper/more expensive** than that one*. **Tahle košile je levnější/dražší než tamta**. *The baby is sleeping **more calmly** than yesterday*. **Dítě spí klidněji než včera**.

Conditional This term applies in Czech to a set of verb forms which look like a **tense**, but which apply to acts or states that are in some sense 'unreal' or merely 'possible' or 'desirable'. It is akin to the much rarer English *subjunctive*. Examples: *If he **felt** worse [but he doesn't], he **would go** to the doctor [but he probably won't]*. **Kdyby se cítil hůř, šel by k doktorovi**. *He insisted that **I go** to the doctor* [at the time I hadn't gone, wasn't going; it was merely desirable]. **Naléhal, abych šel k doktorovi**. The Czech 'conditional auxiliary' – forms of **by** – are embedded, where applicable, in the conjunctions **kdyby** *if* and **aby** *that, so that, in order to*.

Conjugation This term applies to the fact that, and the manner in which, verbs change – *conjugate* – according to their formal class. For example, an **a-**conjugation verb will be marked by having an **-a-** or **-á-** appearing in its various forms. However, **-a-** in the **infinitive** need not guarantee that the verb is itself of the **a-**conjugation, though it often will.

Conjunction Conjunctions are the words that literally *conjoin* **clauses**. They are divided between *co-ordinating* conjunctions, such as *and* **a,** *but* **ale** and *or* **nebo**, and *subordinating* conjunctions, which introduce clauses which would not normally be able to stand on their own. They include *when* **když**, *although* **ačkoli**, *because* **protože** and many others.

Declension This term applies to the fact that, and the manner in which, nouns, pronouns, adjectives and some numerals change – *decline* – according to their formal class. Patterns of declension are associated with **gender**, **case** and **number**.

Demonstratives These are words like *this* and *that* – **tenhle** and **tamten**; they indicate, 'point to', items that are relatively closer to or farther from the speaker, or, in the case of *that* – **ten**, indicate something that the speaker believes the hearer will know of, remember etc.: *He was washing **that** new car of his*. **Myl to svoje nové auto**. In Czech, demonstratives, like **adjectives** and other qualifying expressions, agree with their **noun** in **gender**, **number** and **case**.

Gender In English, gender is usually linked to the sex of persons and animals and is expressed by the use of *he* and *she* for males and females respectively; objects and beings of indeterminate sex are referred to as *it*. These are the *masculine*, *feminine* and *neuter* personal **pronouns** of English, where gender is a 'natural' category. In Czech, gender is a grammatical category and nothing to do with sex; it broadly matches natural gender with humans and some animals, so *man* **muž**, *husband* **manžel**, *judge* **soudce**, *bull* **býk** are masculine, and *woman* **žena**, *wife* **manželka**, *(lady) judge* **soudkyně**, *cow* **kráva** are feminine, while all other items, whether living, non-living or abstract, have *grammatical* gender, which may appear arbitrary: **vrabec** *sparrow* is masculine, **ryba** *fish* is feminine, **prase** *pig* is neuter; **stůl** *table* is masculine, **židle** *chair* is feminine, **křeslo** *armchair* is neuter; **zájem** *interest* is masculine, **krása** *beauty* is feminine, **zdraví** *health* is neuter. In many cases a word's gender is predictable from its form, but you must accept that the gender of each new noun you meet has to be learnt at the first encounter.

Imperative The imperative is the form of the verb used to give directions, instructions or commands: ***Insert*** *the CD in drive A.* **Vložte cédéčko do diskové jednotky A**. *Pop to the shop for me and **buy** some tea.* **Skoč mi do krámu a kup čaj**. *Halt!* **Stůjte!**

Infinitive The infinitive is the basic form of the verb as you will find it in dictionaries. In Czech the infinitive ends in **-t**, though until fairly recently the ending **-ti** was the norm, and those you meet ending in **-ct** ended in **-ci**; these earlier forms may still be encountered in older texts or dictionaries. In large measure, the letters to the left of the final **-t** give some guidance as to a verb's **conjugation**, but this is not reliable enough; therefore with each new verb be prepared to learn not only the infinitive, but also the third-person singular and, especially in the case of *monosyllabic* verbs, the past tense. Examples: **mít-má-měl** *to have*, **říct-řekne-řekl** *to tell*, **brát-bere-bral** *to take*.

Irregular verbs Not all verbs conjugate (see **conjugation**) according to the small number of main patterns, nor is their conjugation necessarily obvious from the **infinitive**. All languages have such verbs, called 'irregular verbs'; the crucial ones in Czech tend to be monosyllabic and their individual peculiarities have to be learnt (see **infinitive**).

Nouns Nouns are words like *house* **dům**, *teacher* **učitel**, *wealth* **bohatství**; they are often called 'naming words' – they name persons, objects or ideas etc.

Number This is the name for the grammatical category indicating whether something is 'one' or **singular** (house) or 'more than one' or **plural** (houses).

Object This term describes the **noun** or **pronoun** affected by the action (or other operation) of the verb. In *The cat caught the mouse* **Kočka chytila myš** or *Kamila is writing a book* **Kamila píše knihu**, the mouse and the book are the objects in their respective sentences. In Czech, the object is typically expressed by the accusative case (see **case**). In more complicated sentences such as *My mother gave the driver some money* **Matka dala šoférovi peníze**, the expression *some money* expresses what was given (just as the mouse was what was caught and the book what was being written) and so is the **object**; here, however, we refer to it as the *direct object*, to distinguish it from the driver, who as recipient or beneficiary of the giving, is said to be the *indirect object*. In Czech the indirect object is typically expressed by the dative case.

Participles In English these are the *-ing* and *-ed* forms, 'parts', of verbs. The former is the *active*, as in *killing*, the latter the *passive* participle, as in *killed*. They have various uses and various formal equivalents in Czech.

Passive See Unit 19, Section 9.

Person Person is what characterizes the different conjugated forms of verbs. **Zpívám** and **zpíváme** are the *I* and *we* or 'first person' singular and plural forms of **zpívat** *sing* respectively. Similarly **zpíváš** and **zpíváte** are the *you* or 'second person' forms. The 'third person' forms – singular **zpívá**, plural **zpívají** – are not only used for third persons *he/she/it* and *they*, but for any other singular or plural **subject** expressed as a noun. Thus on its own **Zpívá** is *S/he is singing*, but the same form is needed in **Matka zpívá**. *Mother is singing.*

Personal pronouns While the name of this class of pronouns (see **pronouns**) suggests an association with one or other person or persons – *I* **já**, *she* **ona**, *we* **my** etc., it also embraces expressions such as *it* **ono**, **to** and *they* as referring, for example, to some previously mentioned books. You should appreciate that in Czech, a language with grammatical gender (see **gender**), forms of **on** or **ona**, apparently 'he' or 'she', may refer to any masculine (that is, not merely male) or feminine (not just female) noun, hence **To je můj nový slovník. Koupil jsem si ho včera** *This is my new dictionary. I bought 'him' yesterday.* (See also **subject**.)

Plural See **Number**.

Possessives or possessive pronouns These are the words that express possession, after the manner of '*my* book' *moje* **kniha**, 'the book is *mine*' **kniha je** *moje*. Also forms of **tvůj** *your*, **jeho** *his*, **její** *her(s)*, **náš** *our(s)*, **váš** *your(s)*, **jejich** *their(s)*, and **Čí?** *Whose?* In some works (for some languages) this class of pronoun is referred to as possessive adjectives, a term better reserved in Czech for words like **Petrův** *Peter's*, **matčin** *mother's*.

Prepositions Words like *in* **v**, *for* **pro**, *without* **bez** are called prepositions; they establish all manner of spatial and other relations between different things mentioned in a sentence, whether as nouns or pronouns: *The milk's* **in** *the fridge*. **Mléko je v ledničce**. *I'll do it* **for** *you*. **Udělám to pro tebe**. *She came* **without** *her husband*. **Přišla bez manžela**. Some expressions in both Czech and English count as prepositions even if consisting of more than one word: *He took the money* **out of** *his pocket*. **Vzal peníze z kapsy**. *Irrespective of the weather…* **Bez ohledu na počasí …** Each Czech preposition is associated with (must be followed by a noun or pronoun in) one or other of the **cases**. In the above examples **v** is followed by the **locative**, **pro** and **bez ohledu na** by the **accusative**, **bez** and **z** by the **genitive**. This means that you must learn the case(s) that each preposition governs.

Pronouns There are several categories of these items, which fulfil functions similar to nouns. They often stand in the place of nouns which have already been mentioned, e.g. *My girlfriend* (noun) *is Czech* **Moje přítelkyněje Češka.** *I love her* (personal pronoun) *very much*. **Mám** *ji* **velmi rád**. *I'll show you her* (possessive pronoun) *photo*. **Ukážu ti** *její* **fotku**. In the same example, **moje** and **ti** are also pronouns, referring to the speaker and addressee in their own right rather than replacing their names as 'previously mentioned' nouns. Among the most widely used Czech pronouns is **se**, called the 'reflexive pronoun', because it refers back to, 'reflects', the **subject** of the sentence: **Kočka se líže** *The cat is licking* ***itself***. **Petr se myje** *Peter is getting washed (washing himself)*. With a plural subject **se** may express reciprocity: **Petr a Marie se mají rádi** *Peter and Mary love* ***each other***; **Petr a Marie se myjí** is theoretically ambiguous between *Peter and Mary are getting washed (washing themselves)* and *Peter and Mary are washing each other*, but the context will usually suggest which interpretation is appropriate. **Se** has many other, largely grammatical, functions, but it is nonetheless always referred to as a pronoun.

Reflexive pronouns See **Pronouns**.

Reflexive verbs Primarily, this term applies to verbs of which the subject and object are one and the same: Czech **mýt se** *to get washed* is structurally equivalent to *to wash oneself*. A secondary type is **zabít se** *to perish, get killed*, **nudit se** *to be bored*; though structurally like *to kill oneself* or *to bore oneself*, they do not actually mean 'take one's life ...' or 'bore oneself deliberately ...'. The term also applies to the numerous Czech verbs of which **se** is a necessary part although it cannot be interpreted as a reflexive pronoun-object. These include **dívat se** *to look*, **bát se** *to be afraid*, **smát se** *to laugh* (there is no free-standing *dívat*, *bát* or *smát*; English has very few verbs like this, but think of *overreach* or *perjure*).

Singular See **Number**.

Subject This term expresses the **noun** or **pronoun** denoting the person or thing that performs the verbal action or is described as being in such and such a state. So in *My mother gave the driver some money* or *They are asleep* the subjects are *my mother* and *they* respectively. Unlike English, in Czech a *pronoun subject* is often not a separate word, being expressed by the ending of the verb: **Zpívá** *S/he is singing*; whether the person who is singing is a he or a she follows from the context.

Superlative The superlative is used for the most extreme degree of a quality expressed as an adjective or adverb. In English it is expressed by *-est* or *most*. Examples: *This shirt is **the cheapest/most expensive** of all*. **Tato košile je *nejlevnější/nejdražší ze* všech**. *Peter runs **fastest***. **Petr běhá nejrychleji**. (See also **comparative**.)

Tense This term applies to sets of verb forms that apply to a particular time – in Czech *present*, *past* and *future*. *He is working/was working/will be working*. **Pracuje/pracoval/bude pracovat**. Importantly, Czech does not have the English patterns known as 'sequence of tenses', as in *He **said** he **was** just **leaving**.* (two past tense forms since the whole event happened in the past). Instead it uses patterns like **Řekl** [past], **že právě odchází** [present], i.e. *He **said** that he **is** just **leaving***, reflecting the tense that applied at the moment of speaking – he had said '*I am leaving*'. This explains in part the need for a term – **tense** – that makes a distinction between the verb *forms* and any actual present, past or future *times*.

Verb The verb is the linchpin of the sentence, expressing the action, state or sensation that is performed or experienced by the **subject**. *The children **were playing** outside*. **Děti si hrály venku**. *The dog **is sleeping** in his kennel*. **Pes spí v boudě**. *I **smell** gas*. **Cítím plyn**. Czech has many kinds of subjectless sentences: **Prší** *It is raining*. **Tady *se pracuje*** *People are working here* [literally: *Here **is worked***].

Appendices

Appendix 1 – Reference tables

This section systematizes the declensional types which you necessarily had to meet piecemeal. For verbs, refer back to the table in Unit 2.

Nouns

As you progressed through the book, you met the cases more or less in line with the frequency with which you would need them. In these reference tables, the order is that which is conventionally used in Czech reference works, which you should now be able to use.

Masculine

Inanimate	Hard		Soft	
	Singular	Plural	Singular	Plural
Nominative	hrad	hrady	klíč	klíče
Genitive	hradu[1]	hradů	klíče	klíčů
Dative	hradu	hradům	klíči	klíčům
Accusative	hrad	hrady	klíč	klíče
Vocative	hrade	hrady	klíči	klíče
Locative	(o) hradě/-u[2]	hradech	klíči	klíčích
Instrumental	hradem	hrady	klíčem	klíči

[1] Many common nouns, or groups of nouns (some names of months), have **-a** in the genitive singular. See Unit 11, Sections 4 and 7 and **Glossary of grammatical terms**.

[2] For variation in the locative singular see Unit 3, Section 11.

Animate	Hard		Soft	
	Singular	Plural	Singular	Plural
Nominative	pán	pánové/páni[1]	muž	muži
Genitive	pána	pánů	muže	mužů
Dative	pánovi[2]	pánům	muži	mužům
Accusative	pána	pány	muže	muže
Vocative	pane	pánové/páni	muži[4]	muži
Locative	(o) pánovi[2]	pánech[3]	muži	mužích
Instrumental	pánem	pány	mužem	muži

[1] For variation in the nominative/vocative plural see Unit 6, Section 3.

[2] For variation in the dative/locative singular see Unit 7, Section 2 and Unit 10, Section 2.

[3] For variation in the locative plural see Unit 10, Section 11.

[4] Nouns ending in **-ec** have the vocative ending **-če**.

Feminine

	Hard Singular	Plural	Soft Singular	Plural
Nominative	žena	ženy	růže[1]	růže
Genitive	ženy	žen	růže	růží[3]
Dative	ženě	ženám	růži	růžím
Accusative	ženu	ženy	růži	růže
Vocative	ženo	ženy	růže[2]	růže
Locative	(o) ženě	ženách	růži	růžích
Instrumental	ženou	ženami	růží	růžemi

[1] Words with stems ending in **b**, **p**, **v** or **m**, **ť**, **ď** or **ň** have **-ě** for **-e**. Some have no final vowel; **dlaň**, pl. **dlaně** *palm* shows both points.

[2] Members of this class that have a zero ending in the nominative have the vocative ending **-i**, e.g. **dlani**.

[3] Some groups of words have a zero ending; see Unit 7, Section 4.

Masculine *a*-declension

	Hard Singular	Plural	Soft Singular	Plural
Nominative	hrdina	hrdinové	průvodce	průvodcové[1]
Genitive	hrdiny	hrdinů	průvodce	průvodců
Dative	hrdinovi	hrdinům	průvodci	průvodcům
Accusative	hrdinu	hrdiny	průvodce	průvodce
Vocative	hrdino	hrdinové	průvodce	průvodcové[1]
Locative	(o) hrdinovi	hrdinech	průvodci	průvodcích
Instrumental	hrdinou	hrdiny	průvodcem	průvodci

[1] Also **průvodci**, i.e. like **muži** above.

Neuter

	Hard Singular	Plural	Soft Singular	Plural
Nominative	okno	okna	moře	moře
Genitive	okna	oken	moře	moří[1]
Dative	oknu	oknům	moři	mořím
Accusative	okno	okna	moře	moře
Vocative	okno	okna	moře	moře
Locative	(o) okně	oknech	moři	mořích
Instrumental	oknem	okny	mořem	moři

[1] Some groups have a zero ending in the genitive plural; see Unit 7, Section 4.

Neuter *í*- and *t*-declensions

	Singular	Plural	Singular	Plural
Nominative	nádraží	nádraží	kotě	koťata
Genitive	nádraží	nádraží	kotěte	koťat
Dative	nádraží	nádražím	kotěti	koťatům
Accusative	nádraží	nádraží	kotě	koťata
Vocative	nádraží	nádraží	kotě	koťata
Locative	(o) nádraží	neádražích	kotěti	koťatech
Instrumental	nádražím	nádražími	kotětem	koťaty

Feminine *i*- and *í*-declensions

	Singular	Plural	Singular	Plural
Nominative	věc	věci	paní	paní
Genitive	věci	věcí	paní	paní
Dative	věci	věcem	paní	paním
Accusative	věc	věci	paní	paní
Vocative	věci	věci	paní	paní
Locative	(o) věci	věcech	paní	paních
Instrumental	věcí	věcmi	paní	paními

Hard adjectives

	Singular			Plural		
	(m)	(f)	(n)	(m)	(f)	(n)
Nominative	dobrý	dobrá	dobré	dobří*/ dobré	dobré	dobrá
Genitive	dobrého	dobré	dobrého		dobrých	
Dative	dobrému	dobré	dobrému		dobrým	
Accusative	dobrý/ dobrého*	dobrou	dobré	dobré	dobré	dobrá
Locative	(o) dobrém	dobré	dobrém		dobrých	
Instrumental	dobrým	dobrou	dobrým		dobrými	

*animate forms

Soft adjectives

	Singular			Plural		
	(m)	(f)	(n)	(m)	(f)	(n)
Nominative	cizí	cizí	cizí	cizí	cizí	cizí
Genitive	cizího	cizí	cizího		cizích	
Dative	cizímu	cizí	cizímu		cizím	
Accusative	cizí/ cizího*	cizí	cizí		cizí	
Locative	(o) cizím	cizí	cizím		cizích	
Instrumental	cizím	cizí	cizím		cizími	

*animate form

Můj, tvůj, svůj

Like the hard adjectives (e.g. gen. **mého**, **mé**, **mých**) except for:

	Singular			Plural		
	(m)	(f)	(n)	(m)	(f)	(n)
Nominative	můj	má/moje	mé/moje	mí*/moji*	mé/moje	má/moje
Accusative	můj/mého*	mou/moji	mé/moje	mé/moje	mé/moje	má/moje

*animate forms

The two-syllable forms are more informal. Other (colloquial) forms based on **moj-, tvoj-, svoj-** followed by the same endings as in **náš**, **váš** below may be heard, but you should avoid them.

Náš, váš

	Singular			Plural		
	(m)	(f)	(n)	(m)	(f)	(n)
Nominative	náš	naše	naše	naši*/naše	naše	naše
Genitive	našeho	naší	našeho		našich	
Dative	našemu	naší	našemu		našim	
Accusative	náš/	naši	naše		naše	
	našeho*					
Locative	(o) našem	naší	našem		našich	
Instrumental	naším	naší	naším		našimi	

*animate forms

Ten, ta, to

	Singular			Plural		
	(m)	(f)	(n)	(m)	(f)	(n)
Nominative	ten	ta	to	ti*/ty	ty	ta
Genitive	toho	té	toho		těch	
Dative	tomu	té	tomu		těm	
Accusative	ten/toho*	tu	to	ty	ty	ta
Locative	(o) tom	té	tom		těch	
Instrumental	tím	tou	tím		těmi	

*animate forms

Note that all pronouns and adjectives have vocative the same as the nominative.

For the declension of possessive adjectives, see Unit 18, Section 5.

For **oči**, **uši**, **ruce**, **nohy** see Unit 13, Section 14.

For **dva**, **oba**, **tři**, **čtyři** see Unit 13, Sections 12 and 13.

For **tentýž** see Supplement, Section 3.

For personal pronouns see Unit 13, Section 4.

For **jenž** see Supplement, Section 2.

For **dvoje**, **čtvery** see Unit 19, Section 14.

For **všechen** see Unit 10, Section 13.

Appendix 2 – Voicing and devoicing

You met the main facts about spelling and pronunciation in the **Introduction.** There are some other systematic details which you ought to master in addition. Turn to this Appendix from time to time to remind yourself of the key factors.

While the value of the Czech letters is more or less consistent, there are two sets of circumstances where you will hear sounds other than what you might expect from the spelling. These apply to consonants.

The simpler pattern with which you must come to terms is what happens at the end of a word, before a pause. Any word ending in: **b, d, ď, g, h, v, z** or **ž** will be pronounced as if it ended in **p, t, ť, k, ch, f, s** or **š**.

The former set are called *voiced* (the vocal chords vibrate during their pronunciation); the latter are their *voiceless* equivalents (the vocal chords are at rest). To test the relationship between the two sets, except **h** and **ch**, try whispering any of the first set: you should produce the equivalent member of the second set.

Try pronouncing the following isolated words:

zub (pron. zup)   *tooth*   **oděv** (pron. oďef)   *clothing*
oběd (pron. objet)   *lunch*   **mráz** (pron. mrás)   *frost*
nechoď (pron. nechoť)   *don't go*   **muž** (pron. muš)   *man*
dialog (pron. dialok)   *dialogue*

The pair **h** and **ch** are not strictly the same sound with and without 'voice', but they nevertheless function as a pair: **vrah** (pron. vrach) *murderer*.

These *devoicing* patterns were said above to apply before a pause. This means both a literal break in speaking or a momentary, detectable pause, and the special circumstances where the next word begins with a vowel. For although it is not shown in writing, every word beginning with a vowel is actually preceded by a glottal stop, the tiny sound break in English that replaces the -tt- in some dialect pronunciations of, say, *butter* or *little*. This glottal stop, which is marked below as ', amounts to a minimal pause, and so devoicing will occur before it. Try:

oběd a večeře (pron. objet 'a večeře)   *lunch and dinner*
bez Anny (pron. bes 'anny)   *without Anna*
v okně (pron. f 'okňe)   *in the window*
z Edinburghu (pron. s 'edinburgu)   *from Edinburgh*
dialog o Praze (pron. dialok 'o praze)   *a dialogue about Prague*

The second set of circumstances in which letters acquire their 'opposite' value is when a mixture of two or more consonants from both the lists above meet within a word or at word boundaries. This time the change works both ways – a voiced sound may become voiceless and a voiceless voiced, depending, with a few exceptions, on the type of the last consonant in the cluster. Thus in the expression **v Praze**, **p** is voiceless and causes the preceding **v** to devoice to *f*, hence *f praze*. Similarly:

z Prahy (pron. s prahy)   *from Prague*

bez kterého (pron. bes kterého)   *without which*

budka (pron. butka)   *(telephone) booth*

nůžky (pron. nůšky)   *scissors*

In the following examples the reverse applies, voiceless sounds becoming voiced:

kdo (pron. **g**do)   *who*

sbírat (pron. **z**bírat)   *to collect*

s Davidem (pron. **z** davidem)   *with David*

náš dům (pron. ná**ž** dům)   *our house*

svatba (pron. sva**d**ba)   *wedding*

The 'exceptions': refinements to the rule about voice assimilation apply to the behaviour of **v/f** and **h/ch**, and to **c** and **č**, which were not in the original list of paired consonants.

v and f

a before a voiceless consonant **v** does become pronounced as *f*, as you saw in **v Praze**, also **vstup** (pron. fstup) *entrance* (seen on the relevant doors of buses and trams); **Kavka** (pron. kafka), a common surname (it also means *jackdaw*). Because of the famous Prague–German writer, Franz Kafka, you will already be aware that the name has an alternative spelling reflecting the pronunciation.

b **v** following a voiceless consonant has no effect on it, hence **tvar** (*shape*) is pronounced as spelled; similarly **svět** (pron. svjet) (*world*).

c as noted above, final **v** before a pause devoices to *f*, e.g. **ostrov** (pron. ostrof) *island*, **dav** (pron. daf) *crowd*, and the case of **v okně** (pron. f 'okňe) *in the window*.

d **f** itself occurs mostly in foreign borrowings, e.g. **forma** *form, shape, mould*, **fifty-fifty** (more widely used in Czech than you might suppose!), **golf**, **konference** (*conference*), and there is little scope for the voicing processes to work.

h and ch

a **h** devoices to *ch* at the end of a word before a pause: **vrah** (pron. vrach) *murderer*, **Bůh** (pron. bůch) *God*.

b However, following a voiceless consonant two patterns occur: the word **shoda** (*agreement*) may be pronounced *zhoda* (obeying the rules, as it were), or *schoda*. The latter type is preferred in Bohemia, the former in Moravia. The pronunciation of the expression *good-bye*, **na shledanou** (with *schl-*), which you met in Unit 1, is explained by this rule.

c If **ch** is followed by a voiced consonant it becomes voiced, but as a true voiced *ch*, not *h* – to get an idea of what this alien sound is like try making an er sound as you pronounce **ch**; this should force you to produce the right 'growl'! This assimilation occurs in **kdybych byl**. *If I were*.

c and č

c and **č** are fairly common voiceless consonants, without true voiced counterparts *dz* and *dž*. However, where **c** and **č** occur before a voiced consonant, they do change to *dz* and *dž* in pronunciation, as in **moc dobře** (pron. mo**dz d**obře) *very well*, **lečba** (pron. lé**džb**a) *treatment, cure*.

No other consonants than those mentioned here are involved in voice assimilation.

Czech–English vocabulary

Abbreviations used:

acc. *accusative*; adj. *adjective*; adv. *adverb*; coll. *colloquial(ly)*; comp. *comparative*; conj. *conjunction*; dat. *dative*; f. *feminine*; gen. *genitive*; impfv. *imperfective*; inf. *infinitive*; inst. *instrumental*; loc. *locative*; m. *masculine*; n. *noun*; nt. *neuter*; pl. *plural*; pfv. *perfective*; prep. *preposition*; sg. *singular*; vb./vbs *verb(s)*.

| is used to separate pairs of verbs of motion (see Unit 9) and to mark off the common section of entry-words and their subentries.

~ indicates repetition of the headword or its common section (to the left of |).

/ separates aspectual verb-pairs; it also separates alternatives, such as *How much/many*.

a *and*
ahoj *hello, hi; cheerio, 'bye*
aktovka *briefcase*
ale *but*
alespoň *at least*
adresa *address*
americký *American*
Američan/-ka *American*
Amerika *America*
Angličan/-ka *Englishman/-woman*
anglicky *(in) English*
anglický *English*
Anglie *(f.) England*
ani … ani *neither … nor*
ano *yes*
apod. *etc.*
aranžování květin *flower-arranging*
asi *about, perhaps, possibly, probably, I expect*
aspoň *at least*
atd. = a tak dále *etc.*
auto *car*
autobus *bus*
autorita *authority*
autostop *hitchhiking*
azalka *azalea*
až *when; not until; as many as*

babička *grandmother*
bačkora *slipper*
banka *(adj. **bankovní**) bank*
bankéř *banker*
bankovnictví *banking*
barva *colour; paint, dye*
básník *poet*

batole *(-ete, nt.) toddler*
bát se *(bojí se) to be afraid/scared*
bavit *to amuse, give pleasure*
bavit se/za- *+ inst. to amuse oneself*
bavit se s někým *to chat to somebody*
bedna *(large) box, crate*
běh *run(ning)*
běhat *(see Unit 12)*
během *+ gen. during*
benzín *petrol*
benzínová pumpa *petrol pump, filling station*
bez *+ gen. without*
běžet *(běží) to run; to be on (of a film)*
běžný *common, ordinary*
bílý *white*
biolog/bioložka *biologist*
bít *(bije) to hit, strike*
bitva *battle*
blatník *mudguard, wing from **bláto** mud*
blbý *stupid*
blesk *flash*
blízko *(adv.) nearby; (prep. + gen.) near*
blízký *(comp. **bližší**) near, close*
blížící se *imminent*
blížit se/při- *to approach*
blok *block (esp. of flats)*
blud *heresy*
blýskat se/zablesknout se *to flash (of lightning)*
bohatý *(comp. **bohatší**) rich*
bohudík *thank goodness, fortunately*
bohužel *unfortunately*
boj *(m.) battle*
bolet *to hurt, ache*
bonboniéra *box of chocolates*

borůvka bilberry
bos/-ý barefoot
bota shoe
botník shoe cupboard
brambor potato
brána gate(way)
brát (si) (bere)/vzít (si) (vezme, vzal) to take; marry
brát se/vzít se to get married (of two people)
bratr brother
brýle (f. pl.) glasses
brzo or brzy (adv.) early
břečka slush
břeh (river) bank; shore
březen (-zna) March
břicho belly
bříza birch
buď ... nebo either ... or
budit/vz- to wake (someone)
budit se/pro- se to wake up
budova building
Bůh (Boha) God
bydlet to live = dwell
bydliště (nt.) dwelling, place of residence
byt flat, apartment
být to be
být k + verbal noun (see Unit 19)
bytí being
byznysmen businessman

cédéčko CD
celkový overall
celník customs officer
celý all, whole
centimetr centimetre
cesta trip, journey, way, path, track
cestou on the way
cestovat to travel
cestující passenger
cigareta cigarette
cíp tip, corner (of garment, etc.)
cítit (se) to feel
cizí strange, foreign
cizí státní příslušník alien, foreign citizen
cizina foreign country (-ies)
cizinec (-ce)/cizinka foreigner
co what
cokoli anything, whatever
cukr sugar
cukrárna confectioner's, cake shop
cvičení exercise
čaj (m.) tea
čas time
část (-i, f.) part

Čech/Češka Czech
Čechy (f. pl.) Bohemia
čekat/počkat to wait, expect
čerň (f.) black; **tiskařská čerň** printer's ink
černý black
čerstvý fresh
čert devil
červen (-vna) June
červenec (-nce) July
červený red
čeřit/roz- to ruffle, to cause to ripple
česky (in) Czech
český Czech
čeština Czech (language), **spisovná ~** Standard Czech, **hovorová ~** Colloquial Czech, **obecná ~** Common Czech
četba reading (matter)
četný numerous
čí whose
čili or, that is
činitel official
činnost (-i, f.) activity
čínština Chinese
činžák tenement block
číslo number
číslovka numeral
číst/pře- (čte, četl) to read
čistit/vy- to clean
čistý (comp. čistší) clean
čitelný legible
člověk (pl. lidé) man, person, one
čokoláda chocolate
čtení reading
čtvrt quarter
čtvrtek (-tka) Thursday
čtvrtina quarter
čtyři four

ďábel (-bla) devil
dál(e) further; come in
daleko far (adv.)
daleký far, remote
další (an)other, more, further (ones); next
Dán/-ka Dane
daný given
dárek (-rku) present
datum (data, nt.) date
dav crowd
dávat/dát to give, put; **dát se** + inf. can be -ed
dávat/dát někomu vědět to let someone know
dávno long ago
dcera (dat./loc. dceři) daughter
debatovat o něčem to discuss, debate something
dědeček (-čka) grandfather

dějiny (f. pl.) history
děkovat/po- (někomu) + za + acc. to thank
dělat/u- to do, make; to work
dělat si něco z + gen. to make an issue of
děl|ník/~nice worker
delší longer; longish
demokrat (pl. **-té**) democrat
den (dne) day
denně daily
deset ten
desetník ten-heller coin
desítka a tensome, (loosely) dozen
déšť (deště, m.) rain
děti (f. pl.) children
dětský child's
děvče (-čete, nt.)girl, lass
devět nine
dialog dialogue
díky thanks; + dat. thanks to
dílna workshop
dílo (gen. pl. **děl**) work
dílovedoucí foreman
dirigent conductor
disponovat + inst. to have available
dispozice disposal; **mít k dispozici** to have at one's disposal
dítě (-ěte, n.; pl. **děti,** f.) child
divadlo theatre
dívat se/po- + na + acc. to look (at)
divit se + dat. to be surprised (at)
dívka girl
divný strange, odd
dizajn design
dlouho (for) a long time
dlouhohrající long-playing
dlouhý (comp. **delší**) long
dluh debt
dnes today
dnešek (-ška) today (as a noun)
dnešní today's
do + gen. to, into, until, by
doba time, period, do **té doby** by/until then
dobrý good
dobře well; OK
dodávka van; delivery, shipment
dodělávat/dodělat finish doing/making
dohoda agreement
dohodnout se to agree, come to agreement (pfv.)
dohromady together, all told
dokdy until/by when
dokonce even
doktor doctor
dokud while; **dokud ne-** until
dole down, downstairs (place)

doleva to the left
dolů down, downstairs (motion)
doma at home
domácí kutění DIY
domácnost (-i, f.) household
domluvit se to reach agreement, to make oneself understood
domov (-a) home
domů home(wards)
dopis letter
dopoledne (nt.) morning
doporučovat/doporučit to recommend
doprava (adv.) to the right
doprava traffic
dort cake (strictly gâteau, torte)
doručení delivery
dosahovat/dosáhnout to achieve
dosažený achieved
dospělý adult
dost (+ gen.) enough, plenty of
dostatek (-tku) sufficiency
dostávat/dostat (dostane) to get (something)
dostávat se/dostat se to get = reach (somewhere)
doufat to hope
dovážet (3rd pl. **-ejí**)/**dovézt** to import
dovést be able, capable
dovnitř inside
dovolená holiday
dráha course, track, railway
drahý (comp. **dražší**) dear; costly
drobnost (-i, f.) something small, trifle
drobný small, tiny
droga drug
druh type, sort, type, kind, species
druhý second, the other
držet to hold
dřevo wood
dřív(e) sooner, earlier, before
dřív(e) než before (conjunction)
dřívější previous, former
dub oak
duben (-bna) April
důchod pension
důkladný thorough
důležitý important
dům (domu) house
důvěřovat + dat. to trust
důvod reason
dva/dvě two
dvacetník twenty-heller coin
dvakrát twice
dveře (f. pl.) door
dvojče (-čete, n.) twin

džem *jam*
džínsy *(f. pl.) jeans*

ekonom *economist*
emigrant/-ka *émigré(-e)*
energický *energetic*
esemeska *text (message)*
Evropa *Europe*
Evropan/-ka *European*

farmacie *pharmacy*
fax *fax*
fér *(coll.) fair*
fialový *purple; violet*
film *film*
flek *spot; stain*
formulář *(m.) form*
formulovat *to formulate*
fotbal *football*
fotbalista *footballer*
fotograf *photographer*
fotoaparát *camera*
foukat/za- *to blow*
Francie *France*
Francouz/-ka *Frenchman/-woman*
fronta *queue*
fungovat *to work, function*

galerie *(f.) gallery*
garáž *(f.) garage*
gauč *(m.) couch, settee, sofa*
geolog *geologist*
geologický *geological*
geoložka *geologist (f.)*
gól *goal*

háček (-čku) *hook, snag*
had *snake*
hádat se/po- *to argue, quarrel, have a row*
hadr *cloth, rag*
haléř *(m.) heller*
házet (3rd pl. -ejí)/hodit *to throw; drop (someone)*
  off (somewhere)
herec (herce) *actor*
herečka *actress*
hezký (comp. hezčí) *nice, pretty*
historka *story; tale*
hlad *hunger; mít ~ be hungry*
hladina *surface*
hladký (comp. hladší) *smooth*
hlasatel/-ka *announcer*
hlásit/na- *to report*
hlasovat *to vote*
hlava *head*

hlavně *mainly, above all*
hlavně aby ... *the main thing is that ...*
hlavní *main, principal*
hlavní město *capital*
hledat *to look for*
hlemýžď *(m.) snail*
hlídat *to guard, to watch over*
hluboko (comp. hlouběji) *deep (adv.)*
hluboký (comp. hlubší) *deep, profound (adj.)*
hlučet *to be noisy*
hluchý (comp. hlušší) *deaf*
hluk *noise*
hnát (žene) *to chase (see Unit 12)*
hned *immediately; at once*
hnědý *brown*
hnutí *movement*
hoden *+ gen. worthy of*
hodina *hour*
hodinky *(f. pl.) watch*
hodiny *(f. pl.) clock*
hodit se *+ dat. to suit*
hodně *much; a lot of; plenty of*
hodnotit/o- *to assess, evaluate*
hodný *good, kind, nice*
holicí strojek (-jku) *shaver*
holit se/o- *to shave*
holka *(informal) girl*
hon *hunt(ing), chase*
honem *in a hurry, at once*
honit *to chase (see Unit 12)*
hora *mountain*
horko (adv.) hot
horký *hot*
horlivý *eager, keen, diligent, urgent*
horník *miner*
horolezec (-lezce) *climber*
horší *worse*
hořet *to burn*
hospoda *pub*
hospodářský *economic*
host *guest*
hostinec (-nce, m.) *inn*
hostit/po- *to host, treat*
hotov/-ý *ready, finished*
houba *mushroom, fungus; sponge*
houpat se/roz- (houpe) *to swing, bob*
housle *(f. pl.) violin*
hovězí *(nt.) beef*
hra *game; play*
hra na housle *violin-playing*
hrabě (-ěte, m.) *count*
hraběnka *countess*
hrad *castle*
hraní *playing*

hranice *(f.) border, frontier*
hrát (si) *to play*
hrát na *+ acc. to play (an instrument)*
hrom *thunder*
hrozný *terrible, awful, dreadful*
hrubý *(comp.* **hrubší***) rough, coarse*
hříbě (-běte, *nt.)* *foal*
hřiště *(nt.) playground*
hřmít/za- (hřmělo) *to thunder*
hůl (holi, *f.) stick*
husa *goose*
hustý *(comp.* **hustší***) thick, dense*
hýbat (hýbe)/hnout (hnul) *to move*
chalupa *cottage*
chápat (chápe)/pochopit *to understand,*
  appreciate
chápat se/uchopit se *+ gen. to seize hold of*
charakter *character*
charakterizovat *to describe*
chlapec (-pce) *boy*
chléb *(coll.* **chleba***) bread*
chlubit se *to boast*
chodit *to go, walk*
chodit *or* **jít na houby** *to go mushrooming*
chodník *pavement, sidewalk*
chování *behaviour*
chovat se *to act, behave*
chrám *cathedral, temple*
chróm *chromium, chrome*
chtít *to want (see Unit 4)*
chudý *poor*
chutnat *to taste (good)*
chuť *(f.) appetite; (sense of) taste*
chválit/po- *to praise*
chvíle *(f.) while, moment*
chyba *mistake*
chytat se/chytit se *+ gen. to catch at*

i *and, also, even*
informace *(f.) (piece of) information*
informovat *to inform*
instalatér *plumber*
inženýr *engineer*
Ir/-ka *Irishman/-woman*
Irsko *Ireland*

já *I*
jablko *apple*
jabloň *(f.) apple tree*
Jadran *Adriatic*
jak *how*
jakkoli *anyhow, however*
jako *as, like*
jaký *what, what kind of*

jakýkoli *any, whatever (kind of)*
jakžtakž *(coll.) more or less, also so-so*
jarní *spring (adj.)*
jaro *spring*
jasný *bright, plain, obvious*
jazyk (-a) *tongue, language*
je *is; them (acc.)*
jeden, jedna, jedno *one*
jednak … jednak *for one thing … for another*
jednička *one*
jednoduchý *(comp.* **jednodušší***) simple*
jednohubka *canapé*
jehně (-ěte, *nt.)* *lamb*
jelen *stag*
jen, jenom *only, just*
jenže *except that*
jestli(že) *if, whether*
ještě *else, still, after a negative verb (not) yet*
ještěže *it's a good thing that*
jet (jede) *to go (involving a means of transport)*
jezdit *(see Unit 12)*
jídlo *food, dish, meal*
jih *south*
jinak *otherwise*
jinam *to another place*
jinde *elsewhere*
jindy *at another time*
jiný *other; else*
jíst (jí, jedí)/najíst se *to eat, to have a meal*
jíst/sníst *to eat (something)*
jist (být si j.) *(be) sure*
jistě *surely, certainly, I expect*
jistý *certain*
jít (jde, šel, šla) *to go (on foot)*
jít o *+ acc. to be a matter/question of*
jitro *morning*
jižní *southern*
jméno *name*
jmenovat se *to be called*
jogurt *yoghurt*

k *+ dat. to, towards, up to; for (the purpose of)*
kabát *coat*
kabelka *handbag*
kadeř|ník/~nice *(ladies') hairdresser*
kafe *(nt.) (coll.) coffee*
kakao *cocoa*
kalhoty *(f. pl.) trousers*
kalný *murky*
kam *where (to)*
kamkoli *(to) wherever, anywhere*
kamarád/-ka *friend*
kámen (kamene) *stone*
Kanaďan/-ka *Canadian*

kanál *canal*
kancelář (f.) *office*
kandidovat *to stand for election*
kapesník *handkerchief*
kapka *drop; drip*
kartáček (-čku) *brush*
kastrol (sauce-) *pan*
kašel (-šle, m.) *cough*
kašlat (kašle) *to cough*
káva *coffee*
každý *everyone, everybody; each, every*
kde *where*
kdekoli *wherever, anywhere*
kdepak *not at all; of course not*
kdo *who*
kdokoli *whoever, anyone*
kdy *when*
kdykoli *whenever*
když *when, as; since; + future if*
kilometr *kilometre*
kino *cinema*
klást (klade, kladl)/položit *to lay, place, put;* **klást překážky** *to hinder*
klávesnice *keyboard*
klečet *to kneel*
klekat si/kleknout si *to kneel (down)*
klesat/klesnout *to fall, drop*
klíč (m.) *key*
klid *peace*
klidný *calm*
kluk *boy*
kluzák *glider*
knedlík *dumpling*
kniha *book*
knihkupectví *bookshop*
knihovna *library*
knihovník *librarian*
kníže (-ete, m.) *prince*
koberec (-rce) *carpet*
kocour *tomcat*
kocovina *hangover*
kočárek (-rku) *pram, pushchair*
kočka *cat*
kód *code*
kohoutek (-tku) *tap*
kolega (m.), **kolegyně** (f.) *colleague*
kolem + gen. *round, past; (adv.) by, past*
kolemjdoucí *passer-by*
koleno *knee (see Unit 13)*
kolik + gen. *how much; how many*
kolikátý *the how many-eth*
kolikrát *how many times*
kolo *wheel; bicycle*
komik *comedian*

komunál *council services department*
koňak *brandy, cognac*
konat se *to be held, to be going on, to take place*
koncem (+ gen.) *at the end of*
koncert *concert*
končit/s- *to finish, end*
kondolenční dopis *letter of condolence*
konec (-nce) *end*
konečně *at last*
konev (-nve, f.) *watering-can*
konference (f.) *conference*
koníček (-čku) *hobby*
kontrola *control, check*
konvice (f.) *kettle, teapot, jug*
konzerva *tin, jar (of food)*
kopat (kope)/kopnout *to kick; dig*
koruna *crown*
kosit/po- *to scythe*
kostel (-a) *church*
kostkovaný *chequered, check(ed)*
košile (gen. pl. košil, f.) *shirt*
koště (-ěte, nt.) *broom*
kotě (-ěte, nt.) *kitten*
koule (f.) *sphere, globe, ball*
koupě (f.) *purchase*
koupelna *bathroom*
kouřit *to smoke*
kousat (kouše)/po- or kousnout *to bite*
kousek (-sku) *a bit*
kovat/u- *to forge*
krabice (f.) *box*
kradený *stolen (impfv.)*
král (-e) *king*
krásný *beautiful, handsome*
krást (krade, kradl)/u- (ukradne) *to steal*
krát, -krát *times*
krátký (comp. kratší) *short*
kráva (gen. pl. krav) *cow*
kravata *tie*
krčit/po- (rameny) *to shrug*
kreslený *drawn*
kreslit/na- *to draw*
kritika *criticism*
krk *throat; neck*
krok *(foot)step, pace, stride*
kromě + gen. *besides, except*
kropit/po- *to sprinkle, to water*
krotký (comp. krotší) *tame, meek*
kroupy (f. pl.) *hail stones*
křehký (comp. křehčí) *frail, fragile*
křeslo *armchair*
kříž (m.) *cross; small of the back*
křižovatka *crossroads*
křížovka *crossword puzzle*

který *which*
kterýkoli *any, whichever*
kudy *which way*
kufr *suitcase, boot/trunk (of car)*
kuchyň or **kuchyně** *(f.) kitchen; cuisine*
kulma *curling tongs*
kůlna *shed*
kůň (koně) *horse*
kupovat/koupit *to buy*
kuriozita *curio, (item of) curiosity*
kurs *course*
kuře (-ete, nt.) *chick*
kutit (si) *to tinker about*
kvalita *quality*
kvést/vykvést (kvete, kvetl) *to bloom*
květen (-tna) *May*
kvůli + *dat. for the sake of, because of*
Kypr *Cyprus*
kytice *(f.) bunch of flowers*
kytka *colloquial for* **květina** *flower and for* **kytice**
  bouquet
kývat/kývnout *to nod; to swing from side to side*

laboratoř *(f.) laboratory*
lampa *lamp*
laskav/-ý *kind*
laskavost (-i, f.) *kindness*
lavice *(dim.* **lavička***) bench*
leccos *all manner of things*
led *ice*
ledaže *(conj.) unless*
leden (-dna) *January*
lednička *fridge*
lehat si/lehnout si *to lie (down)*
lehký *(comp.* **lehčí***) light, easy*
lekce *(f.) lesson*
lépe/líp *(adv.) better*
lepší *better*
les (-a) *wood, forest*
letadlo *aeroplane*
létat *(see Unit 12)*
letec (-tce) *airman*
letět *to fly*
letiště *(gen. pl.* **letišť***, nt.) airport*
léto *(adj.* **letní***) summer*
letos *this year*
letošní *this year's*
lev (lva) *lion*
levný *cheep*
levý *left*
ležák *lager*
ležet *to lie*
-li *if*
líbit se + *dat. to please, to appeal to*

libovat si v + *loc. to take satisfaction in, enjoy*
libra *pound (£ or lb.)*
lidé *people*
lidský *human*
líný *lazy*
lípa *lime, linden (tree)*
list *leaf, page*
lístek (-tku) *ticket*
listí *leaves, foliage*
listopad *November*
litovat + *gen. to regret*
loď(lodi or **lodě, f.)** *ship, boat*
loďka *rowing boat*
logický *logical*
loket (-kte, m.) *elbow*
Londýn (-a) *London*
loni *last year*
loňský *last year's*
ložnice *(f.) bedroom*
luštit/vy- or **roz-** *to solve*
luxovat/vy- *to hoover*
luxus (*adj.* **luxusní***) luxury*
lyže *(f.) ski*
lze + *infin. one can, it is possible*

majitel/-ka *owner, proprietor*
malina *raspberry*
malíř *(m.) painter*
málo + *gen. few, little*
malovat *to paint*
malý *(comp.* **menší***) small, little*
manažer *manager*
manžel *husband*
manželé *husband and wife, Mr & Mrs*
manželka *wife*
mapa *map*
marně *in vain*
marný *vain, pointless*
maso *meat*
matematika *mathematics*
matka *mother*
mávat/za- or **mávnout** *to wave, wag*
medvěd *bear*
medvídek (-dka) *teddy bear*
mechanik *mechanic*
měkký *(comp.* **měkčí***) soft*
mělký *(comp.* **mělčí***) shallow*
méně/míň *less*
měnit/z- *to change*
měsíc *(m.) month; moon*
město *town*
metro *underground railway*
mezi + *inst. or acc. between, among*
mezitím *meanwhile, while I wait (etc.)*

meziválečný *inter-war*
míle *(gen. pl.* **mil***, f.) mile*
milost (-i, *f.) mercy*
milovat *to love*
milý *kind, charming*
mimino *baby*
mimochodem *by the way*
mimořádn|ý *exceptional, extraordinary;* **~á odměna** *bonus*
ministerstvo *ministry*
ministr *minister*
minule *last (time)*
minulost (-i, *f.) the past*
minulý *past, last*
minuta *minute*
místnost (-i, *f.) room*
místo *place; space; job;* + *gen. instead of*
mít *to have; to be (supposed, due, expected) to*
mládež *(f. sg.) young people*
mladý *(comp.* **mladší***) young*
mlčet *to be silent*
mléko *milk*
mlha *mist, fog*
mlhavý *misty, foggy*
mluvit/pro- *to speak; talk*
mnich *monk*
mnohem + *comp. much*
mnoho + *gen. much, many*
mobil *mobile (phone)*
moc (-i, *f.) power;* + *gen. a lot, much, many*
moct *or* **moci (může, mohl)** *can, be able*
modelka *model*
moderní *modern*
modrý *blue*
modř *(f.) blue (as noun)*
mop *mop*
Morava *Moravia*
Moravan/-ka *Moravian*
moře *(nt.) sea*
most *bridge*
moucha *(gen. pl.* **much***) fly*
mouka *flour*
možná *perhaps*
možnost (-i, *f.) possibility*
možný *possible*
mrak *(dark) cloud*
mrholit *to drizzle*
mrtev/mrtvý *dead*
můj, má (moje), mé (moje) *etc. my*
muset *must; to have to*
muž *man; husband*
my *we*
myčka *dishwasher*
mýlit se/z- *to be mistaken*

mysl (-i, *f.) mind*
myslet/po- (si) *to think*
myslet/po- na + *acc. to think of/about*
myš (-i, *f.) mouse*
myšlenka *thought, idea*
mýt/u- (se) (myje) *to wash*
mzda *(gen. pl.* **mezd***) wage*

na + *loc. on, at;* + *acc. (on)to; for*
nabízet *(3rd pl.* **-ejí***)/***nabídnout** *to offer*
nábřeží *embankment*
nábytek (-tku) *furniture*
nač *for what purpose, why*
nad + *inst. or acc. over, above*
nadání *talent*
nadaný *talented*
nadělat + *gen. to make a lot of something*
nadchnout se *to enthuse*
nadšený *enthusiastic*
nádobí *the dishes, the washing up*
nádraží *station*
nahlas *aloud*
náhoda *chance, coincidence;* **náhodou** *by chance*
nahrazovat/nahradit *to replace, compensate*
nacházet *(3rd pl.* **-ejí***)/***najít** *to find*
najímat/najmout (najme, najal) *to hire*
najít *see* **nacházet**
nakládat/naložit *to load*
nakonec *in the end*
nákup *shopping*
nakupovat/nakoupit *to shop*
nalevo *on the left*
nalézat/nalézt (nalezne, nalezl) *to find*
náměstí *square*
nápad *idea*
napadat/napadnout *to occur/come to, dawn on*
napichovat/napíchnout *to spike, put on cocktail sticks*
nápomocen/-cný *helpful*
naposledy *(for the) last (time)*
napravo *on the right*
naproti *opposite*
napřesrok *next year*
například *(abbreviated* **např.***) for example*
národ (-a) *nation*
narodit se *to be born (pfv.)*
narození *birth*
narozeniny *(f. pl.) birthday*
následek (-dku) *consequence*
naspěch: mít naspěch *be in a hurry*
nástroj *(m.) tool, instrument*
náš, naše, naše *etc. our*
natáčet *(3rd pl.* **-ejí***)/***natočit** *to make (a film)*
natěrač *(house) painter*

natírat/natřít (natře, natřel) to paint
natož let alone
navíc moreover, on top of that; extra
návod instructions
návrat return
návrh suggestion, proposal, motion; design
návrhář/-ka designer
návrhářství design
návštěva visit(or)
název (-zvu) name
ne no
nebe (nt.) sky, heaven
nebo or (between real alternatives)
neboli or (between synonyms)
něco something
nečekaný unexpected
neděle (f.) Sunday; week
nehet (nehtu) (finger) nail
nehoda accident
nechávat/nechat (imperative **nech** etc.) to leave;
   to let
nechávat si/nechat si to keep
nějak somehow
nějaký some, a
nejdříve first
nejhorší worst
nejlepší best
nejprv(e) first of all
někam somewhere (motion)
někde somewhere (place)
někdo someone
někdy sometime(s)
několik + gen. several
několikrát several times
některý a certain
někudy some way
Němec/Němka German (m./f.)
Německo Germany
nemluvně (-ěte, nt**.)** baby
nemnoho + gen. not many
nemocen/-cný ill, sick
nemocnice (f.) hospital
neprávem wrongly
nepřítel (pl. **nepřátelé**) enemy
nepřítomnost (-i, f.) absence
nervózní nervous
nést (nese, nesl) to carry
nezaměstnanost (-i, f.) unemployment
nezastavitelný unstoppable
než than; before (conj.)
nic nothing
nikde nowhere
nikdo nobody
nikdy never

nízký (comp. **nižší**) low, base
no hmm, well
no a so what
noc (-i, f.) night
noha leg, foot (see Unit 13)
nos nose
nosit to carry, wear
novinář/-ka journalist, reporter
novinářství journalism
noviny (f. pl.) newspaper
nový new
nudný boring
nulovat/vy- to return to zero, re-set
nůžky (f. pl.) scissors

oba (f. **obě**) both
občan (pl. **-é**)/**-ka** citizen
občas sometimes, from time to time
občerstvení refreshment(s), a snack
obdržet (pfv. only) to obtain
oběd (-a) lunch
obědvat/naobědvat se to have lunch
obejít se + bez + gen. to do without
oběsit se to hang oneself
oběť (f.) victim; sacrifice
obchod trade, business; shop
obchodní commercial, business-
obchodní dům department store
obilí corn
objednávat/objednat to order
objevovat/objevit to discover
oblak (m., pl. **oblaka** nt.) cloud
oblečení clothing
oblékat se/obléknout se to get dressed
obloha sky; garnish, side vegetables
obnažovat/obnažit to reveal, lay bare
obracet se/obrátit se to turn, apply to
obraz (obrázek) picture
obsah content(s)
obtěžovat to pester, annoy, intrude
obtěžovat se to take the trouble, to bother oneself
obvyklý usual, customary
obývací pokoj living room
obžalovaný accused
oceňovat/ocenit to appreciate; to price
ocet (octa) vinegar
očekávat to expect
od + gen. (away) from
odbočovat/odbočit to turn off; to digress
odcizovat/odcizit to remove
oddělení section, department, compartment
oděv clothing
odevšad from all sides
odevzdávat/odevzdat to submit, hand in

odhánět (3rd pl. **-ějí**)/**odehnat** (**odžene**) to drive/ chase away

odcházet (3rd pl. **-ejí**)/**odejít** to leave, depart, go away

odchod departure, leaving

odjezd departure (by transport)

odjíždět (3rd pl. **-ějí**)/**odjet** to leave (by vehicle)

odkládat/odložit to put down, set aside, postpone

odkud from where

odlet departure (by air)

odměna reward, remuneration

odmítat/odmítnout to refuse

odpočívat/odpočinout si to (have a) rest

odpoledne (nt.) afternoon

odpověď (**-di**, f.) answer, response, reply

odpovídající equivalent, corresponding

odpovídat/odpovědět to reply, (cor)respond; match

odstín shade, tint

odstraňovat/odstranit to remove

odsud from here

odsuzovat/odsoudit k + dat. to condemn to

odtahovat/odtáhnout to pull away

odvážet (3rd pl. **-ejí**)/**odvézt** to drive/ take away

odvolávat/odvolat to withdraw, repeal, cancel

ohlášení announcement

ohlašovat/ohlásit to announce, report

ohnutý bent

ohýbat/ohnout to bend

ochrana protection

ochranný protective

ochutnávat/ochutnat to try, taste (food, drink)

okno window

oko (pl. **oči**) eye (see Unit 13)

okrádat/okrást (**okrade**) to rob

okurek (**-rku**) cucumber; gherkin

oltář (m.) altar

omezený limited

omezovat/omezit (**se**) to limit, restrict, confine (oneself)

omítka stucco, plaster

omlouvat se/omluvit se to apologize

omyl error

on/ona/ono he/she/it

opakovat to revise; repeat

opatrný careful, cautious

opékat/opéct (**opeče, opekl**) to roast

operace (f.) operation

opouštět (3rd pl. **-ějí**)/**opustit** to leave, abandon, desert

opovrhovat + inst. to despise

oprava repair

opravdu really

opravna repair shop

oprávnění (nt.) authorization; **mít oprávnění k** + dat. be authorized to

oranžový orange

orloj (m.) astronomical clock

ořech nut

osm eight

osoba person

osobní personal

ostatní the rest of, the other(s), remainder

ostružina blackberry

ošklivý ugly, awful

otec (**otce**) father

otvírák opener

otvírat/otevřít (**otevře, otevřel**) to open

ovoce (nt.) fruit

ovšem/že of course

pacient patient

pád fall; (grammatical) case

padat/spadnout to fall

palačinka pancake

palec (**-lce,** m.) thumb, big toe

pálit/s- to burn (something)

pamatovat si/za- to remember, memorize

pan Mr

pán (gentle)man

paní Mrs; lady

panovat to reign

papír paper

paprika paprika, green/red pepper

pár pair, couple, a few

párat/roz- to rip open, unpick

parcela plot (of land)

párek (**-rku**) (pair of) frankfurter(s)

parkoviště (nt.) car park

Paříž (f.) Paris

pas (adj. **pasový**) passport

pasáž (f.) passage

pašerák smuggler

pátek (**-tku**) Friday

patrně perhaps, probably

péct or **péci** (**peče, pekl**) to roast, bake

péče (f.) care

pečení baking; roasting

pěkný lovely, nice

peníz coin

peníze (gen. **peněz,** m. pl.) money

pero pen, feather

pes (**psa**) dog

pěstovat/vy- to cultivate, grow

pestrý colourful

pěší turistika hiking

pěšky on foot

pět *five*
pětina *one fifth*
pila *saw*
pípat/za- *to tweet*
písařka *typist*
písmeno *letter*
pistole *(f.) pistol*
pít (pije)/napít se *to have a drink*
pít/vy- *to drink*
pivnice *(f.) pub*
pivo *beer*
pivovar *brewery*
plachý *timid*
plakát *poster*
plánovat *to plan*
platit/za- + za *+ acc. to pay (for)*
platný *valid, in force*
plavat (plave) *to swim*
pláž *(f.) beach*
plést se/při- (plete, pletl) *to get in the way*
plést se (plete)/s- *to make a mistake*
plést si/s- *to confuse, get wrong*
plnicí pero *fountain pen*
plnit/na- *to fill*
pneumatika *tyre*
po *+ loc. up, down, along, all over; after*
pobyt *stay*
pocit *feeling*
počasí *weather*
počáteční *initial*
počátkem *+gen. at the beginning of*
počítač *(m.) (adj.* **počítačový***) computer*
počítat/s- or za- *to count (up, in)*
počítat s *+ inst. to reckon with, allow for*
pod *+ inst. or acc. under, beneath, below*
podávat/podat *to serve; offer, pass, hand*
podezřívat *to suspect*
podlaha *floor*
podle *+ gen. according to*
podnik *(adj.* **podnikový***) enterprise, business;
    company, firm*
podruhé *for the second time*
podstata *essence;* **v podstatě** *basically*
podzim *(adj.* **podzimní***) autumn*
pohlaví *sex*
pohled *view; look*
pohlednice *(f.) postcard*
pohodlný *comfortable*
pohoštění *entertainment, treat; refreshments, party;*
    dělat pohoštění *to give/have a (small formal) party*
pohrdat/pohrdnout *+ inst. to scorn, disdain*
pohřeb (-řbu) *funeral*
pocházet *(3rd pl.* **-ejí***) to come from*
pochovávat/pochovat *to bury*

pojišťovat/pojistit *to insure*
pojišťovna *insurance company*
pojišťovnictví *insurance (profession)*
pokaždé *every time*
pokoj *(m.) room; peace (and quiet)*
pokračovat *to continue*
pokud *insofar as, if*
pokus *+ o + acc. attempt (at); experiment*
pokuta *fine*
pole *(nt.) field*
poledne *(nt.) midday*
police *(f.) shelf*
policista *(m.) policeman*
polička *(diminutive of* **police***) shelf*
polit|ik/~ička *politician*
politika *policy, politics*
polojasno *rather cloudy*
polovina *half*
pomačkaný *bent, crumpled*
pomáhat/pomoct (pomůže, pomohl) *help*
pomalu *slowly*
pomalý *slow*
poměr *relationship; proportion, ratio; attitude; pl.
    condition(s); circumstances*
pomoc (-i, f.) *help*
pomocník/-nice *assistant*
pondělí, pondělek (-lka) *Monday*
popelnice *(f.) dustbin*
popírat/popřít (popře, popřel) *to deny*
popisovat/popsat *to describe*
poprvé *for the first time*
poradenství *consultancy, counselling*
porážka *defeat*
porodnice *maternity hospital*
porucha *something wrong, breakdown*
pořád *all the time*
pořádek (-dku) *(good) order, orderliness, tidiness*
posazovat/posadit *to seat*
posílat/poslat (pošle) *to send*
poslouchat *to listen (to); obey*
poslyšte *listen, I say*
postel *(f.) bed*
postihovat/postihnout *to affect, afflict*
postup *progression, procedure*
posunovat/posunout *to shift, delay*
pošta *(adj.* **poštovní***) post (office)*
pot *sweat*
potěšení *pleasure*
potit se *to sweat*
potíž *(f.) problem, difficulty*
potkávat/potkat *to meet*
potom *then, afterwards*
potomek (-mka) *descendant; offspring*
potřeba *to need, (item of) necessity*

potřebovat *to need, want, require*
potřetí *for the third time*
poupě (-ěte, *nt.) (flower) bud*
pouštět se/pustit se + do + *gen. to set about*
použití *use*
používat/použít *to use*
povídat/povědět *to say, tell*
povídat si s někým *to chat to someone*
povolání *profession*
pozdě *late (adv.)*
pozdější *later, subsequent*
pozítří *the day after tomorrow*
poznámka *note; remark, comment*
poznávat/poznat *to recognize, identify, get to know*
pozornost (-i, *f.) small gift, token (of gratitude etc.);*
    attention, attentiveness
pozorný *attentive*
pozorovat/z- *to observe*
pozvání *invitation*
pozvat *see* **zvát**
práce *(f.) work*
pracovat *to work*
pracoviště *(nt.) workplace*
pracovna *study, private office*
pračka *washing machine*
prádlo *the washing, laundry; (under-, bed-) linen*
Praha *Prague*
prase (-ete, *nt.) pig*
prášek (-šku) *powder; pill*
praštit *(pfv.) to thump, bash*
prát/vyprat (pere) *to wash*
právě *just, exactly, precisely*
právem *rightly*
právní *legal*
právo *right, claim, entitlement; law*
pravopis *spelling, orthography*
prázdniny *(f. pl.) holidays*
pražský *adj. from* **Praha**
prkno (gen. pl. prken) *plank, board*
prodávat/prodat *to sell*
prodej *(m.) sale*
proč *why*
programátor *(computer) programmer*
prohlašovat/prohlásit *to pronounce, declare*
promíjet (3rd pl. -ejí)/prominout + *dat. to forgive*
promýšlet (3rd pl. -ejí)/promyslet *to think through*
pronajímat/pronajmout (-najme, -najal) *to let*
propisovačka *biro, ballpoint*
prosinec (-nce, *m.) December*
prosit/po- *to ask, to beg*
prostřednictví *mediation*
proti + *dat. against, opposite*
protijedoucí *oncoming*
protivný *obnoxious*

proto *that's why, therefore*
protože *because*
provádět *to show round*
provádět (3rd pl. -ějí)/provést *to execute, carry out,*
    perform, do
provaz *string, rope*
prst *finger, toe*
pršet *to rain*
prudký (comp. prudší) *abrupt, steep; quick-tempered*
průměr *average*
pruhovaný *striped*
průvod|ce/~kyně *guide (m./f.)*
prvek (-vku) *element*
první *first*
prý *he/she/someone says, allegedly, apparently*
pryč *gone, past, away*
přát (si) (přeje) *to wish*
přebírat/přebrat *to have too much of; something*
přece *but, nevertheless, surely, still, after all*
před + *inst. or acc. before, in front of; (inst. only) ago,*
    before
předělávat/předělat *to redo*
předem *in advance; by the front way*
přednášet (3rd pl. -ejí) *to lecture*
přednáška *lecture*
předpis *regulation; prescription*
předposlední *next to last, last but one*
předpověď (-di, *f.) forecast*
předsíň *(f.) hallway*
představovat/představit (se) *to introduce (oneself)*
přehánět (3rd pl. -ějí)/přehnat (-žene) *to*
    exaggerate, overdo
přeháňka *shower*
přehazovat/přehodit *to throw (something over);*
    to jumble, to cause disarray
přehrada *dam*
přecházet (3rd pl. -ejí)/přejít *to cross (on foot);*
    přecházet/přejít mlčením *to pass over in*
    silence
přechod *pedestrian crossing; transition*
přejet *see* **přejíždět**
přejezd *level crossing*
přejímat/přejmout (přejme, přejal) *or* **převzít**
    (-vezme, -vzal) *to take over*
přejít *see* **přecházet**
přejíždět (3rd pl. -ějí)/přejet *to run over*
překážka *obstacle*
překlad *translation*
překládat/přeložit *to translate*
překvapení *surprise*
překvapovat/překvapit *to surprise*
přemalovávat/přemalovat *to repaint, paint over*
přemlouvat/přemluvit *to talk someone round,*
    persuade

přepážka *window (in e.g. post office)*
přepisovat/přepsat *to rewrite, overwrite*
přes *+ acc. over, across; despite*
přesně *precisely, exactly*
přesný *precise, accurate, precision*
přesnídávka *'second breakfast'*
přestávat/přestat (přestane) *to stop (doing something)*
přesvědčovat/přesvědčit *to persuade, convince;* ~ **se** *to make sure (that)*
přetírat/přetřít (-tře, -třel) *to repaint*
převážně *predominantly*
převládat *to predominate*
převoz *ferry*
při *+ loc. at, by, with, during*
příběh *story*
přibíjet *(3rd pl. -její)*/**přibít (-bije)** *to nail*
přičleňovat/přičlenit *to incorporate*
přidělávat/přidělat *to make more*
přidělovat/přidělit *to assign, apportion*
přihlašovat/přihlásit *to register*
přicházet *(3rd pl. -ejí)*/**přijít** *to come, arrive*
příchod *arrival (on foot)*
příjezd *arrival*
přijímat/přijmout (přijme, přijal) *to accept; to receive*
přijít *see* **přicházet**
příjmení *surname*
přílet *arrival (by air)*
příležitost (-i, f.) *occasion; opportunity*
přinášet *(3rd pl. -ejí)*/**přinést** *to bring*
přínos *contribution*
případ *case, event(uality)*
připisovat/připsat *to add (writing)*
přípoj *(m.) connection*
příprava *preparation*
připravovat/připravit (se) *to prepare (oneself), get ready; train, study*
přípravy *(k + dat.) preparations (for)*
příroda *nature*
přírodopis *natural history, biology*
příslušenství *lavatory + bathroom*
příslušný *the relevant*
příst (přede) *to purr (of a cat); to spin*
přistávat/přistát (-stane, -stál) *to land*
příště *next time*
příští *next*
přítel *(pl. **přátelé**),* **přítelkyně** *friend (m./f.)*
přítomnost (-i, f.) *presence*
přivádět *(3rd pl. -ějí)*/**přivést (-vede)** *to bring (in), lead (in)*
přívoz *ferry*
psací stroj *(m.) typewriter*
psací stůl *desk*

psát (píše)/napsat *to write*
pstruh *trout*
ptáče (-ete, nt.) *little bird*
pták *bird*
ptát se/zeptat se *+ gen. to ask*
pučet *to burst, come into bud*
půjčovat/půjčit *to lend;* ~ **si** *to borrow, hire*
pukat/puknout *to burst*
půl *half*
půlit/roz- *to halve*
pumpa *pump, petrol/gas pump, petrol/gas station*
původ *origin*
původní *original*

rabín *rabbi*
rád *glad;* **mít rád** *to like, love*
rada *(piece of) advice, counsel, council; (m.) councillor, counsellor*
raději *preferably*
rádio *radio*
radit/poradit *+ dat. to advise*
radnice *(f.) town hall*
radovat se/za- *+ z + gen. to rejoice (at)*
radši = raději
ráj *(m.) paradise*
rajče (-čete, nt.), rajské jablíčko *tomato*
rameno *shoulder (see Unit 13)*
ramínko *coathanger*
ranit/z- *to wound*
ráno *morning*
reagovat/za- *to react*
recepční *(adjectival noun, m. or f.) receptionist*
referát *(conference, seminar, etc.) paper, report*
republika *republic*
restrikce *(f.) cutback*
revidovat *to revise*
rodiče *parents*
rodina *family*
rodit/po- *to give birth*
rodit se/na- *to be born*
roh *corner; horn*
rohlík *bread roll*
rok *year*
román *novel*
rostoucí *rising, growing*
rovně *straight on*
rozbíjet *(3rd pl. -ejí)*/**rozbít (-bije)** *to break*
rozbitý *broken, damaged*
rozčilovat se/rozčilit se *to get excited*
rozhlas *radio*
rozhodně *definitely*
rozhodný *decisive, critical, crucial; definite*
rozhodovat se/rozhodnout se *to make up one's mind, decide*

rozhovor *talk, conversation, dialogue*
rozlévat/rozlít (rozlije *or* **rozleje)** *to spill*
rozpaky *(m. pl.) embarrassment, awkwardness, uncertainty*
rozsvěcet *or* **rozsvěcovat/rozsvítit** *to put the light on*
rozum *sense, intelligence*
rozumět *(3rd pl.* **-ějí)** *+ dat. to understand*
rozumný *sensible*
rozvážet *(3rd pl.* **-ejí)/rozvézt (-veze)** *to take/drop to various places*
ruka *(pl.* **ruce** *) arm, hand (see Unit 13)*
rukojmí *(declines as adj.) hostage*
růst (roste, rostl) *to grow*
různý *various*
růže *(f.) rose*
růžový *pink*
ryba *fish;* **chodit/jít na ryby** *to go fishing*
rybář *fisherman*
rychlý *quick, fast*
rýma *a cold*
rýsovat *to draw (technical drawing)*
řada *row, line, series; several, many*
ředitel/-ka *manager, director; headmaster/-mistress*
řeka *river*
řeznictví *butcher's shop*
řezník *butcher*
řidič *(m.) driver*
řídit *to drive (car); run, be in charge, manage, govern*
řídký *(comp.* **řidší)** *rare; sparse; thin (of liquids)*
říje *(f.) the rutting season*
říjen (-jna) *October*
říkat/říci (řekne, řekl) *to say, tell*
řízek (-zku) *schnitzel*

salám *salami*
salát *lettuce; salad*
sám, sama, samo, *etc. alone; by oneself*
samotný *(him-, etc.) -self*
samouk *self-taught person*
samozřejmě *of course, obviously; by all means*
samozřejmý *evident, obvious*
sanitka *ambulance*
sázet *(3rd pl.* **-ejí)/vsadit** *to bet (money)*
sedat si/sednout si *to sit down*
sedět *to sit*
sedm *seven*
sekretářka *secretary*
sem *(to) here*
semafor *traffic light(s)*
senior *senior citizen*
seriózní *serious, earnest*
sestavovat/sestavit *to construct, compile*

sestra *sister*
setina *hundredth*
sever *(adj.* **severní)** *north*
seznam *list;* **telefonní** *~ phonebook*
shánět *(3rd pl.* **-ějí)/sehnat (sežene)** *to (try to) get, 'to chase up'*
schopen *+ gen. capable of*
schopný *able*
schůzka *appointment, date*
sice *concessive conjunction while, though*
sídliště *(nt.) housing estate*
silnice *(f.) (main) road*
sirka *match*
situace *(f.) situation, predicament*
skákat (skáče)/skočit *to jump*
sklenice *(f.) glass*
sklenička *(diminutive of* **sklenice***) glass*
sklep (-a) *cellar*
sklo *glass*
skoro *almost*
Skot/-ka *Scot (m./f.)*
Skotsko *Scotland*
skříň *(f.) cupboard, wardrobe*
skutečně *really*
skutečnost (-i, f.) *reality, fact*
skutečný *real, genuine*
slabý *(comp.* **slabší)** *thin, weak*
sladkost (-i, f.) *sweetness; something sweet*
sladký *(comp.* **sladší)** *sweet*
slavit/o- *to celebrate*
slečna *Miss, young lady*
slepý *blind*
sleva *(price) reduction, concessionary price/rate*
slibovat/slíbit *to promise*
slon *elephant*
Slovák *Slovak*
Slovenka *Slovak woman*
Slovensko *Slovakia*
slovenština *Slovak (language)*
slovník *dictionary*
slovo *word*
složitý *complicated*
sluha *(m.) servant; office messenger*
slunce *(nt.) sun*
slušný *decent, respectable*
slyšet/u- *to hear*
směrovat *to direct, aim*
smět (smí, smějí) *to be allowed*
smích *laughter*
smrt (-i, f.) *death*
smutný *sad*
smysl *meaning; sense*
snad *perhaps, possibly*
snadný *(comp.* **snazší)** *easy*

snažit se *to try*
snídaně *(f.) breakfast*
snídat/na- se *to have breakfast*
sníh (sněhu) *snow*
sobota *Saturday*
sotva *hardly*
soud *court; judgement*
souhlasit *to agree, concur*
soused/-ka *(pl. **sousedé**) neighbour*
spát (spí) *to sleep*
spěchat *to hurry, to rush*
spisovatel/-ka *writer*
spíš(e) *more (likely)*
spod *+ gen. from under*
spojovat/spojit *to unite, join*
spokojen *satisfied; **-ý** contented*
spolu *together*
spolupracovat *to co-operate, collaborate*
spotřebič *(m.) appliance*
správce *(m.) administrator; caretaker*
správný *correct, right*
spravovat/spravit *to repair*
sprcha *shower*
sprostý *(comp. **sprostší**) rude, vulgar*
srdce *(nt.) heart*
srovnávat/srovnat *to compare*
srpen (-pna) *August*
stačit *to suffice; to be enough*
stále *all the time, constantly*
stánek (-nku) *stall*
stanice *(f.) (bus or underground) stop*
starat se/po- se *+ o + acc. to look after*
stárnout/ze- *to age*
starost (-i, f.) *care, worry; **dělat si starosti** to worry*
starosta *mayor*
starý *(comp. **starší**) old*
stařík *old man*
stát *state*
stát (stojí, stál) *to cost; to stand*
stávat se/stát se (stane se, stalo se) *to happen*
stávkovat *to strike*
stéblo *stalk, straw*
stejně *anyway; as it is/was*
stejný *(the) same*
stěžovat si *to complain*
stihat *to pursue, prosecute*
stihat/stihnout *to have time for*
stisknout *to squeeze*
sto *hundred*
stolek (-lku) *small table*
století *century*
stolní lampa *table lamp*
stoupat *to rise, climb, go up*

stovka *a hundred crowns, also a hundred-crown (or dollar or rouble etc.) note, also the number 100 expressed as a noun*
strach *fear*
strana *page, side; party; **stranou** to one side*
strohý *strict, severe*
stroj *(m.) machine*
středa *Wednesday*
střecha *roof*
střevo *intestine*
stříbrný *silver*
stříška *awning, shelter*
střízlivý *sober*
student/-ka *student (m./f.)*
studený *cold*
studovat *to study*
stůl (stolu) *table, desk*
stupeň (-pně, m.) *degree*
stydnout/vy- *to get cold*
styl *style*
sud *barrel*
sucho *dry(ness), drought; a dry place*
suchý *(comp. **sušší**) dry*
sůl (soli, f.) *salt*
svačina *snack, packed lunch*
svačit *to have a snack*
svědek (-dka) *witness*
světlo *light*
světlý *light, bright*
svěží *fresh*
svítit *to shine*
svobodný *single (unmarried); free*
svůj *reflexive possessive pronoun*
syn *(pl. **synové**) son*
šanon *box-file*
šaty *(m. pl.) a dress, clothes*
šedý, šedivý *grey*
šéf *head, boss*
šek *cheque*
šeptat/za- *to whisper*
šeptem *in a whisper*
šest *six*
šetrný *sparing; considerate*
šetřit/u- *to save, spare*
šicí stroj *sewing machine*
šidit/o- *to cheat (someone)*
šikovný *clever, useful, handy*
široko *(comp. **šíře**) (adv.) wide*
široký *(comp. **širší**) wide, broad*
šít (šije) *to sew*
šití *sewing*
škaredý *ugly, awful, bad, gross*
škoda! *pity!*
škodovka *Škoda (car)*

škola school
školství education
škrtat/škrtnout to strike (out)
šňůra (washing) line
šofér driver
šok shock
šokovat to shock
Španěl/-ka (pl. Španělé) Spaniard (m./f.)
špatně (comp. **hůř(e)**) badly
špatný (comp. **horší**) bad
šroub screw
šroubovací screw (adj.)
šroubovat to screw
štamprle (-lete, nt.**)** tot, dram
šťasten-/tný happy
šťáva juice
štěkat/za- to bark
štěně (-ěte, nt.**)** puppy
štěstí happiness; luck
Švéd/-ka Swede (m./f.)

ta the; that (f.)
tábor camp
tady here
tahat (see Unit 12)
táhnout to pull, to draw; march
tak so; thus; like this/that
také/taky also, too, as well
takhle like this/that; in this way
takový such, like that, of that kind
taky ne- not either
takže so (that), therefore
talentovaný talented
talíř (m.) plate
tam (to) there
tancovat, tančit to dance
tankovat/na- to fill up (with petrol)
tapetovat/vy- to paper (walls)
tapety (f. pl.) wallpaper
taška bag
tát/roztát (taje) to melt
taxík taxi
taxikář cab driver
téct (teče, tekl) to flow, run (of water)
tedy therefore; then
tekoucí (voda) running (water)
tele (-ete, nt.**)** calf
telefon telephone
televize (f.) TV
televizor television (the receiver)
téměř almost
ten/ta/to etc. the; that
tenhle/tento this, this one
tenký (comp. **tenčí**) thin (not of people)

teplo warm(th)
teploměr thermometer
teplota temperature
teplý warm
teprve (in time expressions) only
termín deadline, **v termínu** to/on schedule
těšit/po- to comfort, console
těšit se + na + acc. to look forward to
teta aunt
těžký (comp. **těžší**) heavy; difficult
tchán father-in-law
tchyně mother-in-law
tichý (comp. **tišší**) quiet
tisíc (m.) thousand
tiskárna printing works, printer
tisknout/s- to squeeze
tisknout/vy- to print
tiše (comp. **tišeji**) quietly
tlačítko (push-) button
tlak pressure
tlumoč|ník/~nice interpreter (m./f.)
tlustý (comp. **tlustší**) fat
tma dark
tmavo- dark- (in compounds)
tmavý (comp. **tmavší**) dark
to it, this, that
tolik + gen. so much/many
tonout/u- to drown
topit (se)/u- (se) to drown
topit se/po- to sink
topit/za- to flood
totiž you see; namely
továrna factory
tradice (f.) tradition
tramvaj (f.) tram, streetcar
trávit/s- to spend, pass; to digest
trefit to find the way, to hit (a target)
trochu a bit
trojmo in triplicate
trpělivost (-i, f.**)** patience
trpělivý patient
trpký (comp. **trpčí**) tart, acid
trvalý permanent, enduring
trvat/po- to last, endure
trvat na + loc. to insist on
třást/za- + inst. to shake
třeba say, for instance, perhaps; necessary
třetina one third
tři three
třikrát three times
tu here
tucet (-ctu) dozen
tuhý (comp. **tužší**) stiff, tough
turist|a/~ka tourist

tušit to guess, have a presentiment
tvrdý (comp. **tvrdší**) hard
tvůj yours
tvůrce (m.) maker, creator
ty you
týden (-dne) week
typický typical

u + gen. near, at; in the case of
účastnit se/z- (+ gen.) to attend, participate in
učení teaching; apprenticeship
účet (účtu) account; bill
učit/na- to teach
učit se/na- to learn; study
učitel/-ka teacher
údajný alleged
údolí valley
uhel (uhle or **uhlu)** (a) coal
úhel (úhlu) angle, corner
uhlí coal
ucho (pl. **uši**) ear (see Unit 13)
ukazovat/ukázat (ukáže) to show
úklid cleaning
uklidňovat/uklidnit to (make) calm
uklidňovat se/uklidnit se to calm down
uklízet (3rd pl. **-ejí)/uklidit** to tidy (up)
ukradený stolen
ulice (gen. pl. **ulic,** f.) street
umělý artificial
umění art
umět (3rd pl. **umějí)** to know (how to); to be good at
umožňovat/umožnit to make possible, facilitate; (with dat.) to enable
úmysl intention; **mít v úmyslu** to intend
unášet (3rd pl. **-ejí)/unést (-nese)** to hijack, kidnap
unavovat/unavit to tire
uniforma uniform
unikátní unique
univerzita university
únor (-a) February
únos kidnapping, hijack
únosce (m.) kidnapper, hijacker
upozorňovat/upozornit to advise, draw someone's attention
upravovat/upravit to adjust, amend; regulate
určitě certainly, definitely
určitý a certain
úřednictvo office staff
úřed|ník/~nice clerical worker, civil servant
uschovávat/uschovat to keep, store
usnášet se/usnést se + na + loc. to resolve
úspěch success
ústa (nt. pl.) mouth
ústav institute, institution

útěcha consolation
úterý, úterek (-rka) Tuesday
utírat/utřít (utře, utřel) to wipe
uvažovat to think, consider, use one's head
úvod introduction (to a book)
uzávěr closure, cap, top (of container, bottle)
úzký (comp. **užší**) narrow, tight
uznávaný recognized
uznávat/uznat to recognize, acknowledge
už already, now
užitečný useful

v(e) + loc. in; at
vadit + dat. to matter; to be a nuisance to
vadnout/u- to wilt
váhat/za- to hesitate
válka war
vana bath
vánice (f.) gale, blizzard
Vánoce (pl.) Christmas
varovat to warn
vaření cooking
vařící boiling
vařit/u- to cook, boil
váš, vaše, vaše your(s)
vata cotton wool
váza vase
vážný serious, grave
včas in/on time
včasný timely, punctual
včera yesterday
včerejšek (-ška) yesterday (as noun)
včerejší yesterday's
věc (-i, f.) thing, object
večer (-a) evening
večeře (f.) dinner; supper; tea
večeřet to dine, have dinner/supper/tea
vědec (-dce, m.) scientist
vědět (ví, 3rd pl. **vědí)** to know
vedle + gen. beside
vědom/-ý aware, conscious
vedoucí manager/-ess
vedoucí leading
vegetarián/-ka vegetarian
vejce (nt.) egg
vejít se (vejde se, vešel se) to fit
Velikonoce (pl.) Easter
vel(i)ký big, large; great
velmi very, (very) much
Velšan/-ka Welshman/-woman
velvyslanectví embassy
ven out
venkov (-a) country (opp. of town)
venku outside

věnovat (se) + *dat.* to devote (oneself) to
vepřové *pork*
věřit + *dat.* to believe, trust
veselý *merry, lively*
vesnice *(f.) village*
vést (vede, vedl) *to lead*
věšet/pověsit *to hang (something)*
věta *sentence*
větší *bigger*
většina *the majority*
většinou *mostly, usually*
vézt (veze, vezl) *to carry, convey*
věž *(f.) tower, spire*
věžák *tower block*
víc(e) *more*
vidět *to see*
víkend *weekend*
vina *guilt, blame*
víno *wine; grapes*
viset *to hang*
vítat/u- *or* **při-** *to welcome, greet*
vítr (větru) *wind*
vláda *government, rule; reign*
vlas(y) *hair*
vlastně *actually*
vlastní *(one's) own*
vlevo *on the left*
vliv *influence, effect;* **vlivem** + *gen.* due to
vlhký *(comp.* **vlhčí***) damp, moist*
vlk *wolf*
vlna *wave; wool*
voda *water*
vodit *(see Unit 12)*
volat/za- *to call, phone*
volno *time off*
vozit *(see Unit 12)*
vpravo *on the right*
vpředu *in front*
vracet *(3rd pl.* **-ejí***)/***vrátit** *to return, take/send back*
vracet se/vrátit se *to return, come back*
vrah *murderer*
vrata *(nt. pl.) gate*
vrtulník *helicopter*
vsadit se *to bet*
vstávat/vstát (vstane) *to get up, rise*
však *but, though, however*
všechen/všechna/všechno *all*
všechno *everything*
všichni *all, everybody*
všude *everywhere; all over the place*
vtipný *witty*
vůbec *at all, generally*
vůl (vola) *ox; (coll.) idiot*
vy *you*

vybírat/vybrat (-bere) *to choose, select*
výbor *committee*
vybraný *chosen, select(ed)*
vydání *edition*
vydávat/vydat *to issue, publish; to hand over; surrender*
vydělávat/vydělat *to earn*
vydržet *to with(stand), bear (pfv. only)*
vyhazovat/vyhodit *to throw away/out*
výhonek (-nku) *shoot (on a plant)*
vyhrávat/vyhrát (-hraje) *to win*
vyhýbat se/vyhnout se + *dat.* avoid
vycházet *(3rd pl.* **-ejí***)/***vyjít** *to come/go out; work out; rise (of sun)*
východ *(adj.* **východní***) east; exit*
vyjadřovat (se)/vyjádřit (se) *to express (oneself)*
výjezd *vehicular exit*
výkon *performance*
výlet *trip, day out*
vyměňovat/vyměnit *to replace*
vyměňovat (si)/vyměnit (si) *to exchange (money); to swap (with one another)*
vymýšlet *(3rd pl.* **-ejí***)/***vymyslet** *to think up*
vynášet *(3rd pl.* **-ejí***)/***vynést** *to bring/take/carry out*
vynikající *excellent, outstanding*
vynikat *to stand out, excel*
vynořovat se/vynořit se *to emerge*
výnos *decree*
vypadat + *adv.* to look, appear, be like
vypínač *(m.) switch*
vypisovat/vypsat *to write out*
vyplácet se/vyplatit se (někomu) *to be worth it (to someone)*
vyplňovat/vyplnit *to fill in (form)*
vypotřebovat *to use up*
vyprovázet *(3rd pl.* **-ejí***)/***vyprovodit** *to see off/out*
vypůjčovat si/vypůjčit si *to borrow*
vyrábět *(3rd pl.* **-ějí***)/***vyrobit** *to produce, manufacture, make*
vyřazený *discarded, scrapped, thrown out (from* **vyřadit***)*
vyřizování *things to sort out*
vyřizovat/vyřídit *to attend to, settle*
výsledek (-dku) *result, outcome*
vysoko *(comp.* **výš(e)***) (adv.) high*
vysoký *(comp.* **vyšší***) high, tall*
vyspat se *to have had a decent sleep*
výstava *exhibition*
vysvětlovat/vysvětlit *to explain*
vytýkat/vytknout (někomu něco) *to reproach*
vzadu *at the back*
vzbuzovat/vzbudit *to arouse*
vzdálenost (-i, f.) *distance*

vzít (si) *see* **brát (si)**

vzkaz *message*

vzkazovat/vzkázat (vzkáže) *to send a message*

vzorek (-rku) *sample*

vzorkovna *showroom*

vždy(cky) *always*

vždyť *(protesting) but, after all*

z(e) *+ gen. from*

za *+ acc. for, in exchange for; + inst. or acc. beyond, behind*

zabíjet *(3rd pl. -ejí)/***zabít (-bije)** *to kill*

zabývat se *+ inst. to deal with*

zač *what for, how much for*

začátek (-tku) *beginning*

začínat/začít (začne, začal) *to begin*

záda *(nt. pl.) back*

zadávat/zadat *to reserve; set a task*

zadem *by the back way*

zadní *rear, back (adj.)*

zahnutý *crooked*

zahrada *garden*

zahraniční *foreign*

zahrnovat/zahrnout *to include*

zahrnutý *included*

zahýbat/zahnout *to bend*

zacházet *(3rd pl. -ejí)/***zajít** *to pop (on foot)*

záchod *toilet*

zájem (-jmu) *interest*

zájezd *excursion, tour*

zajímat *to interest; ~ **se** + **o** + acc. to be interested in*

zajímavý *interesting*

zakazovat/zakázat (-káže) *to ban, forbid, prohibit*

základ *basis, foundation*

zakládat/založit *to found, set up*

zalévat/zalít (-lije or -leje) *to water (flowers)*

zámek (-mku) *lock; château*

záměr *intention*

zaměstnání *employment, occupation; job, post*

zaměstnaný *employed*

zaměstnavatel *employer*

zamilovaný *in love*

zamykat/zamknout *to lock*

zanechávat/zanechat *to give up, leave behind*

západ *(adj. ***západní***) west*

zapadat/zapadnout *to set (of sun); fall behind, disappear from sight*

zaplaťpánbůh *thank God!*

zapomenutý *forgotten*

zapomínat/zapomenout (zapomněl) *to forget*

zapomnětlivý *forgetful*

září *September*

zásada *principle*

zásadní *fundamental, basic;* **zásadně** *in principle; fundamentally*

zase *again*

zasílat/zaslat (-šle) *to send*

zastavovat/zastavit *to stop (someone or something); ~ **se** to stop; to call in*

zastihnout *(usually used in pfv. only) to catch, find*

zastupovat *to replace, represent, stand in for*

zásuvka *socket, drawer*

zatím *for the time being*

zato *but, on the other hand*

zavazadlo *piece of luggage*

zavézt *to take (someone somewhere)*

zavírat/zavřít (-vře, -vřel) *to close*

zboží *goods*

zbytečný *useless, superfluous*

zbytek (-tku) *remnant, rest*

zde *here*

zdejší *local*

zdráv/zdravý *well, healthy*

zdraví *health*

zdroj *(m.) source*

zdržovat/zdržet *to delay, hold up*

zeď (zdi, f.) *wall*

zelený *green*

zelí *cabbage*

zem *in (***spadnout,*** etc.) **na zem** (to fall etc.) to the ground*

země *(f.) ground, earth, soil; country*

zemřít (zemře, zemřel) *to die (pfv.)*

zhoršovat/zhoršit *to make worse; ~ **se** to get worse, deteriorate*

zima *(adj. ***zimní***) winter; cold*

zítra *tomorrow*

zítřek (-řka) *tomorrow (as noun)*

zítřejší *tomorrow's*

zklamaný *disappointed*

zkoušet *(3rd pl. -ejí)/***zkusit** *to try, test*

zkratka *abbreviation*

zkušenost (-i, f.) *experience*

zlatý *gold(en)*

zlepšovat/zlepšit *to improve*

zlobit *to annoy, be naughty, cause trouble*

zlobit se/roz- *to be/get angry*

zločin *crime*

zločinec (-nce, m.) *criminal*

zločinnost (-i, f.) *crime (rate)*

zloděj *(m.) thief*

zlý *wicked, evil, bad*

změna *change*

zmeškat *to be late for*

zmiňovat se/zmínit se *+ o + loc. to mention*

zmrzlina *ice cream*

značka *sign, brand, mark, marque*
znamenat *to mean*
znamenitý *magnificent*
známka *stamp*
známý *well known, familiar; friend*
znát *to know*
znění *wording, text*
znova/znovu *again*
zouvat/zout (zuje, zul) *to take off (footwear);* **~ se**
  to take one's shoes off
zpátky *back*
zpívat *to sing*
zpráva *report, (item of) news (pl.* **zprávy** *the news)*
zrovna *just, exactly, precisely*
zřejmě *apparently, evidently, I believe*
zřejmý *evident, apparent, obvious*
ztrácet *(3rd pl.* **-ejí**)/**ztratit** *to lose*
zub *tooth*
zůstávat/zůstat (zůstane) *to stay*
zvát (zve)/pozvat *to invite*
zvedat/zvednout *to lift*
zvědav/-ý *curious, inquisitive*
zvlášť *especially; separately*
zvláštní *special; separate; odd*

zvonek (-nku) *bell*
zvonit/za- *to ring*
zvyk *custom, habit*
zvyšovat/zvýšit *to increase, raise*
žadatel/-ka *applicant*
žádost (-i, f.) *application*
žádoucí *desirable*
žalovat/za- *to sue*
žaludek (-dku) *stomach*
že *that*
žehlit/vy- *to iron*
železnice *(f.) railway*
železo *iron*
žena *woman; wife*
žid *(pl.* **židé**)**, židovka** *Jew (m./f.)*
židle *(f.) chair*
židovský *Jewish*
žít (žije) *to live*
živ/-ý *alive, living; lively; vivid*
život (-a) *life*
žízeň (-zně, f.) *thirst*
žlutý *yellow*
žrát (žere)/sežrat *to eat (only of animals)*
žurnalist|a/~ka *journalist*

English–Czech vocabulary

about (roughly) **asi;** *(concerning)* **o** + *loc.*
above **nad** *(Unit 12)*
abroad **v cizině, v zahraničí**
accident **nehoda, úraz;** *road, traffic ~*
    autonehoda, havárie
actual **skutečný, vlastní;** *~ly* **vlastně**
adapter **adaptér**
address **adresa**
administration **správa**
adult (n., adj.) **dospělý**
advance: in ~ **předem**
advantage **výhoda**
advert **reklama;** *(small ad)* **inzerát**
advice **rada**
advise **radit/po-**
afford **dovolit si** *(pfv.)*
afraid: be ~ (concern) **obávat se,** *(fear)* **bát se**
after **po** + *loc.*
afternoon **odpoledne** *(nt.)*
afterwards **potom, později**
again **opět, znova, zase**
against **proti** + *dat.*
age **věk**
agency **agentura**
ago **před** + *inst.*
agree (be in ~ment) **souhlasit;** *(come to an ~ment)*
    dohodnout se
ahead (adv.) **napřed, předem;** *~ of* **před** + *inst.*
aid **pomoc (-i)** *(f.);* *first ~* **první pomoc**
aim **cíl, záměr;** *(vb.)* **mířit**
air **vzduch;** *(vb.)* **větrat/vy-;** *by ~ (mail)* **letecky,**
    letadlem; *~ conditioning* **aklimatizace;** *~mail*
    letecká pošta; *~port* **letiště** *(nt.)*
alcohol **alkohol;** *~ic beverages* **alkoholické**
    nápoje
alive **živý, naživu**
all **celý, všechen, všichni, všechno;** *~ right*
    dobře, správně, v pořádku; *that's ~* **to je**
    všechno
allerg|ic **alergický;** *~y* **alergie**
allow **dovolovat/dovolit, povolovat/povolit,**
    umožňovat/umožnit
almost **skoro, téměř**
alone **sám**
along **podél** + *gen.,* **po** + *loc.*
aloud **nahlas**
already **už**
also **také, taky, rovněž**

although **i když, ačkoli**
altogether **celkem**
always **vždy(cky), stále**
a.m. **dopoledne**
ambassador **velvyslanec**
America **Amerika;** *~n* **americký,** *(person m./f.)*
    Američan/-ka
among **mezi** *(Unit 12)*
amount (sum) **částka, obnos;** *(quantity)* **množství,**
    kvantita
amusement **zábava**
and **a,** *(emphatic)* **i**
angry **rozzlobený,** *be ~* **zlobit se**
animal **zvíře (-te)** *(nt.),* **živočich**
ankle **kotník**
anniversary **výročí**
announce **oznamovat/oznámit**
annoy **obtěžovat, zlobit, otravovat;** *~ing*
    nepříjemný
annual **každoroční**
another (one more) **ještě jeden, další,** *(different)* **jiný**
answer **odpověď,** *(vb.)* **odpovídat/odpovědět**
any **jakýkoli,** *(in a question)* **nějaký,** *(after negative)*
    žádný; *~body* **kdokoli, někdo, nikdo;** *~thing*
    cokoli, něco, nic; *~ where* **kdekoli, někde,**
    nikde; *~ way* **stejně;** *~ way (you like)* **jakkoli**
    (chcete)
apart **stranou, zvlášť;** *~ from* **kromě** + *gen.,* **mimo**
    + *acc.*
apartment **byt**
apparatus **zařízení, přístroj, aparát**
appear (turn up) **objevit se,** *(seem)* **vypadat**
apple **jablko**
apply (for) **podávat/podat žádost, žádat (o** +
    acc.)
area **plocha, areál**
argue **hádat se, dohadovat se**
arm **ruka, paže**
arrangement (disposition) **uspořádání;** *(agreement)*
    ujednání
arrival (on foot) **příchod,** *(by or of vehicles)* **příjezd,**
    (by air) **přílet**
arrive **přicházet/přijít, přijíždět/přijet, přilétat/**
    přiletět, dorazit
arrow **šíp, šipka**
art **umění;** *~ gallery* **galerie**
article (written, in a law, contract etc.) **článek,** *(item)*
    předmět

artist **umělec**

as **jako**, *(conj. = since)* **když**

ashtray **popelník**

ask *(question)* **ptát se/zeptat se**, *(request)* **prosit/
po-, žádat/po-**

asleep, be ~ **spát (spí)**

aspirin **aspirin**

at: ~ the hotel **v hotelu**; ~ the station **na nádraží**; ~
home **doma;** ~ five o'clock **v pět hodin** *(see Units
9 and 13)*

ATM **bankomat**

attack *(by assailant)* **útok**, *(fit)* **záchvat**

attempt **pokus**, *(vb.)* **pokusit se** *(pfv.)*

attraction **atrakce**

audience **obecenstvo, diváci**

August **srpen (-pna)**

Australia **Austrálie;** ~n **australský**, *(person m./f.)*
Australan/-ka

Austria **Rakousko;** ~n **rakouský**, *(person m./f.)*
Rakušan/-ka

autumn **podzim,** in the ~ **na podzim**

available **k dostání, k dispozici**

average **průměr**, *(adj.)* **průměrný**

awake **vzhůru**

away **pryč**

awful **hrozný**

baby **(malé) dítě** *(nt.)*

back *(of body)* **záda** *(n.pl.);* *(rear part)* **zadní část** *(f.);*
(adv.) **zpátky;** at the ~ **vzadu;** ~ pack **batoh**

bad **špatný**

bag **taška;** paper-~ **sáček;** hand~ **kabelka**

baggage **zavazadla** *(n.pl.)*

bakery **pekárna**; *(shop)* **pekařství**

balcony **balkón**

ballpoint **propisovačka**

banana **banán**

bandage **obvaz, fáč**

bank **banka;** ~ holiday **den pracovního klidu**

bar **bar**

barber's **holičství**

basket **koš;** *(in shop)* **košík**

bath **vana;** ~room **koupelna**

battery **baterie**

be **být** *(see Unit 2)*

beautiful **krásný**

because **protože;** ~ of **kvůli** + dat.

bed **postel;** ~room **ložnice;** ~ and breakfast **nocleh
se snídaní**

beef **hovězí** *(n., as nt. adj.)*

beer **pivo;** bottled ~ **láhvové p.;** draught ~ **točené
p.**

before **před** *(Unit 12)*

begin **začínat/začít (začne, začal)**

behind **za** *(Unit 12)*

below **pod** *(Unit 12)*

belt **pásek**

beside **vedle** + gen.; ~s **kromě** + gen.

best **nejlepší**

better **lepší**

between **mezi** *(Unit 12)*

beyond **za** *(Unit 12)*

bicycle **kolo**

big **velký**

bill *(account)* **účet;** The bill, please **Platit, prosím;**
(US [banknote]) **bankovka**

bin **popelnice**

bird **pták**

biro **propisovačka**

birthday **narozeniny** *(f.pl.)*

biscuit **sušenka**

bit: a little ~ **trochu, trošku;** a ~ far **trochu
daleko**

bite *(by insect)* **štípnutí**, *(by animal)* **kousnutí**

black **černý**

blame: Who's to blame? **Čí je to vina?**

blanket **deka**

blind *(adj.)* **slepý**

blind *(across window)* **roleta**

blood **krev** *(gen.* **krve***) (f.)*

blouse **blůza, halenka**

blue **modrý**

boat **loď**, *(small, rowing ~)* **člun**

body **tělo**

boiler **bojler**

bone **kost (-i)** *(f.)*

book **kniha;** ~shop **knihkupectví;** to ~
rezervovat

boot *(of car)* **kufr**

boots **(těžké) boty** *(sg.* **bota***)*

border *(frontier)* **hranice**

boring **nudný**

borrow **půjčovat si/půjčit si**

both **oba** *(m.),* **obě** *(f. and n.);* ~ ... and ... **jak ...
tak ...**

bottle **láhev (láhve)** *(f.);* ~-opener **otvírák**

bottom: at the ~ **na dně;** ~ of the street **na konci
ulice;** ~ of the stairs, hill **pod schody, kopcem**

box **krabice;** ~ of chocolates **bonboniéra**

boy **chlapec, kluk**

bra **podprsenka**

brake *(n.)* **brzda**, *(vb.)* **brzdit/za-**

brandy **koňak**

bread **chléb, chleba**

break *(a thing)* **rozbít;** *(a limb)* **zlomit**

breakdown *(on road)* **havárie;** I've broken down
Mám poruchu, Havaroval jsem

breakfast **snídaně** *(f.)*

bridge **most**

bring *(on foot)* **přinášet/přinést**, *(by car etc.)* **přivážet/přivézt**

Brit|ain **Velká Británie**; *~ish* **britský**

brochure **brožur(k)a, letá(če)k**

broken *(of thing)* **rozbitý**; *(of limb)* **zlomený**

brother **bratr**

brown **hnědý**

bruise **modřina**

brush **kartáč**; *tooth~* **kartáček (na zuby)**

building **budova**

bulb: *(light ~)* **žárovka**

bunch of flowers **kytice**

burn *(n.)* **spálenina**; *sun~* **opálení**

bus **autobus**; *by ~* **autobusem**; *~ station* **autobusové nádraží**; *~ stop* **(autobusová) zastávka**

busy *(public space)* **rušný**, *(person)* **zaneprázdněný**, *(phone, toilet = engaged)* **obsazeno**

but **ale**

butcher's **řeznictví**

butter **máslo**

button **knoflík**

buy **kupovat/koupit**

by *(near)* **u** *+ gen.*; *~ (e.g.) car* **autem** *(i.e. inst.)*; *~ (a certain time)* **do** *+ gen.*; *~ the way* **mimochodem**

cabbage *(white, red)* **zelí** *(nt.)*; *(Savoy, spring)* **kapusta** *(NB an important distinction to the Czechs)*

cable railway **lanovka**; *cable car* **kabina (visuté lanovky)**

café **kavárna**; *internet ~* **internetová k.**

cake *(sponge type)* **bábovka**, *(gâteau type)* **dort**

call *(vbs)* **volat/za~, telefonovat/za-**; *What's this ~ed* **Jak se tomu říká**; *(n.)* **hovor**; *collect ~* **hovor na účet volaného**

camera **fotoaparát**, *(coll.)* **foťák**

camp **tábor**; *~ site* **(auto)kempink**; *(vb.)* **stanovat, kempovat**

can *(tin, of food)* **konzerva**; *~ opener* **otvírák konzerv**

can *(= be able)* **moct (může)** *+ inf.*

Canada **Kanada**; *Canadian* **kanadský**, *(person m./f.)* **Kanaďan/-ka**

cancel **rušit/z-**

candle **svíčka**

car **auto**; *~ accident* **autonehoda**; *~ hire* **pronájem automobilů**; *~ park* **parkoviště**

card **kart(ičk)a**; *greetings ~* **blahopřání, gratulace**; *business ~* **navštívenka**; *phone ~* **telefonní karta**; *credit-~* **kreditní karta**

carpet **koberec**

carrot(s) **mrkev (mrkve, f.)**

carry **nést**

cash **hotovost**; *~ point, dispenser* **bankomat**

castle *(fortified)* **hrad**; *(château)* **zámek**

cat **kočka**

cathedral **katedrála, dóm, chrám**; *St Vitus' C~ (in Prague)* **Chrám svatého Víta**

cave **jeskyně** *(f.)*

CD **cédéčko**

ceiling **strop**

centimetre **centimetr**

centre **střed**: *(of town)* **centrum**; *(cultural, health, shopping ~ etc.)* **středisko**

certain **jistý, určitý**; *~ly* **jistě, určitě**

chair **židle**; *arm~* **křeslo**

chambermaid **pokojská**

champagne **šampaňské**

change *(vbs)* **měnit/z (se)**; *(money)* **proměňovat/proměnit**; *(trains, buses)* **přesedávat/přesedat, přestupovat/přestoupit**; *(get changed)* **převlékat se/převléknout se**; *(n.)* **změna**, *for a ~* **pro změnu**; *small, loose* **drobné**

cheap **levný, laciný**

check *(vb.)* **kontrolovat**; *~ in* **registrovat**; *~ out* **odhlašovat se/odhlásit se**; *(n. US = UK cheque)* **šek**; *(US = UK bill)* **účet**

Cheers! **Na zdraví!**

cheese **sýr**

chemist's **lékárna**

cheque **šek**; *~ book* **šeková knížka**; *~ card* **průkaz majitele konta**

chest **hruď** *(f.)*

chicken *(meat)* **kuře(cí maso)**

child **dítě** *(nt.)* *(pl.* **děti**, *f.)*

chips **hranolky** *(sg. -ek)*, *(US = UK crisps)* **bramborové lupínky** *(sg.* **b-á lupínka***)*

chocolate **čokoláda**

Christmas **Vánoce**; *~ Eve* **Štědrý večer**; *~ present* **vánoční dárek**; *for ~* **k Vánocům**; *at ~* **o Vánocích**

church *(institution)* **církev (církve, f.)**, *(building)* **kostel (-a)**

cigar **doutník**; *~ette* **cigareta**

cinema **kino**

city **město**

clean *(adj.)* **čistý**; *(vb.)* **čistit/vy-**

clock **hodiny** *(f.pl.)*

close *(vb.)* **zavírat/zavřít**

clothes **šaty, oblečení**

coach *(long-distance bus)* **(meziměstský) autobus**; *(hire-~)* **autokar**; *(of train)* **vagón**; *~ station, see bus-station*; *~ trip* **zájezd**

coat **kabát**; *~ hanger* **ramínko**

code **kód**; dialling ~ **předčíslí**; post-~ **poštovní směrovací číslo (PSČ)**

coffee **káva**; decaffeinated **k. bez kofeinu**

coin **mince** (f.)

cold (low temperature) **zima**, (indisposition) **rýma**; It's ~ **Je zima**; I'm ~ **Je mi zima**; I have a ~ **Mám rýmu**

colour **barva**

comb **hřeben**

come **přicházet/přijít**; ~ here! **Pojďte sem!**; ~ tomorrow **Přijďte zítra**; ~ back **vracet se/vrátit se**; ~ in **vstupovat/vstoupit**; 'C~ in!' **Dál!**

comfortable **pohodlný**

compartment (in train) **kupé**

complain **stěžovat si**

complaint **stížnost** (-i, f.)

computer **počítač** (m.)

concert **koncert**

concourse **hala, dvorana**

condom **prezervativ, kondom**

Congratulations! **Blahopřeji!**

connection (transport) **spoj** (m.)

constipation **zácpa**

consulate **konzulát**

contact **kontakt**; (vb.) **kontaktovat/s-;** ~ lenses **kontaktní čočky**

cookie **sušenka**

corkscrew **vývrtka**

correct (right) **správný**

cost (n.) **cena**; (vb.) **stát (stojí)**

cotton **bavlna**; ~ wool **vata**

couchette **lehátko**; ~ car **lehátkový vůz**

cough (n.) **kašel**; (vb.) **kašlat (kašle)**

country **země**; ~side **venkov** (-a)

couple **pár, dvojice**; married **manželská d.**

courier **kurýr**

course (of meal) **chod**; race-~ **dostihová dráha**; of ~ **samozřejmě**

cream **smetana**; whipped ~ **šlehačka**; ~ cake **šlehačkový dort**

credit card **kreditní karta**

crisps **lupínky, brambůrky**

crossroads **křižovatka**

crowd **dav**; ~ed **plný lidí**

cup **šálek**

cupboard **skříň** (f.)

curtains **záclony** (f.pl.)

cushion **polštář** (m.)

custom **obyčej, zvyk**

customs **celnice**; ~ duty **clo**

cyclist (m./f.) **cyklista/cyklistka**

Czech (language) **čeština**, to speak ~ **mluvit česky**; (person m./f.) **Čech/Češka**; (adj.) **český**; ~ Republic **Česká republika**

damage (n.) **škody, poškození**; (vb.) **poškozovat/ poškodit**

damp **vlhký**

dance (n.) **tanec**; (vb.) **tancovat**

danger **nebezpečí**; ~ous **nebezpečný**

dark: it's ~ **je tma**

date **datum**; What's the date? **Kolikátého je?**

daughter **dcera** (dat./loc. **dceři**)

day **den**; days of the week see Unit 11

dead **mrtvý**

deaf **hluchý**

decide **rozhodnout se**

deep **hluboký**

delay **zpoždění**

delicatessen **lahůdkařství**

dentist (m./f.) **zubní lékař(ka)**

department **oddělení**; ~ store **obchodní dům**

departure (train, bus) **odjezd**; (plane) **odlet**

design **dizajn, návrhářství**

dessert **dezert, moučník**

destination **cíl(ová stanice)**

diarrhoea **průjem**

diesel (fuel) **(motorová) nafta**; ~ engine **naftový motor**

differen|ce **rozdíl**; ~t **jiný, rozdílný**

difficult **těžký, obtížný**

dining room **jídelna**

dinner **večeře** (f.)

direct (adj.) **přímý**

direction **směr**; ask for directions **zeptat se na směr někam**

dirt **špína**; ~y **špinavý**

disco **diskotéka**

divorced **rozvedený**

do **dělat/u-**

doctor **doktor/-ka**

dog **pes (psa)**

door **dveře** (f. pl.)

double **dvojitý**; ~ bed **manželská postel**; ~ room **pokoj pro dva**

down(wards) **dolů**; ~stairs **dole**

drink **nápoj**; soft ~ **nealkoholický nápoj**; (vbs.) **pít/ vy-, pít/napít se**; something to ~ **něco k pití**; What will you have to drink? **Co si dáte?**

drive **řídit**; driving/driver's licence **ridičský průkaz**

driver **řidič**; (professional) **šofér**

drug (therapeutic) **lék**; ~s (narcotics) **drogy**

drunk **opilý**

dry **suchý**; ~ cleaner's **chemická čistírna**

during **během** + gen.

duvet **peřina**

each **každý**; ~ other **jeden druhého**

ear **ucho** (pl. **uši** f.) (see Unit 13)

early **brzy**

east **východ**

Easter **Velikonoce**; *~ egg* **velikonoční vajíčko**, *(painted)* **kraslice**

easy **snadný, jednoduchý**

eat **jíst/sníst, jíst/najíst se**; *something to ~* **něco k jídlu**

egg **vejce, vajíčko**; *scrambled ~s* **míchaná vejce**

either … or … **buď … nebo …**

elbow **loket (-kte)**

electric **elektrický**; *~ity* **elektřina**

elevator **výtah**

else: someone ~ **někdo jiný**; *someone ~'s* **cizí**; *something ~* **něco jiného**; *somewhere ~* **někde jinde**

embassy **ambasáda, velvyslanectví**

emergency **naléhavý případ**; *accident and ~ (A & E), (US) ~ room* **pohotovost**

empty **prázdný**

end (n.) **konec**; (vb.) **končit/s-**

engaged (toilet, telephone) **obsazeno**

engine **motor**

Eng|land **Anglie**; *~lish* **anglický**; *~lishman/-woman* **Angličan/-ka**

enjoy: We ~ed the play **Hra se nám líbila**; *We ~ed ourselves* **Bavili jsme se dobře**; *~ your meal!* **Dobrou chuť!**

enough **dost**; *That's! ~* **To stačí!**

entrance **vchod**

envelope **obálka**

especially **zejména**

Europe **Evropa**; *~an* **evropský**; *(person)* **Evropan/-ka**

evening **večer**; *this evening* **dnes večer**

every **každý**; *~body* **každý, všichni**; *~thing* **všechno**; *~where* **všude**

excellent **skvělý, výborný**

except **kromě** + *gen.*

exchange rate **devizový kurz**

exciting **vzrušující**

excursion **zájezd**

excuse me (to be let past) **s dovolením, pardón**; *(seeking attention or apologizing)* **promiňte**

exhibition **výstava**

exit **východ**

expensive **drahý**

expired: my passport (visa) has expired **vypršel(o) mi pas (vízum)**

eye **oko** (pl. **oči** f.) *(see Unit 13)*

face **tvář** (f.)

fairly **poměrně**

fall **upadnout, spadnout**; (n. US = UK autumn) **podzim**

family **rodina**

far **daleko**

fare **jízdné**; *What's the fare?* **Kolik to stojí?**

fast **rychlý**

fat (n.) **tuk**; (adj. of person) **tlustý**

father **otec**

faucet (US = UK tap) **kohoutek**

fault **vada, porucha**, (blame) **vina**; *~y* **vadný**

favourite **oblíbený**

fax **fax**

feel **cítit (se)**; *I'm not feeling well* **Necítím se dobře**

ferry (sea) **trajekt**; *(river)* **přívoz**

fetch **jít pro** + *acc.*

fever **horečka**; *hay~* **senná rýma**

few (hardly any) **málo** + *gen.*; *a ~ (at least some)* **několik** + *gen.*

field **pole**

filling (in food, pen) **náplň**, *(in tooth)* **plomba**

film **film**; *develop a ~* **vyvolávat/vyvolat film**

find **najít** (**najde, našel**); *~ out* **zjišťovat/zjistit**

fine (adj., weather) **pěkný**; (n.) **pokuta**

finger **prst**

fire **oheň** (**ohně,** m.); *(conflagration)* **požár**, *Fire!* **Hoří!**

first **první**; *at ~* **napřed, zpočátku, nejdřív**; *~ aid* **první pomoc**; *~ class* **první třída**; *~ name* **jméno**

fish **ryba**

fix (mend) **spravovat/spravit**; *(see to)* **zařizovat/zařídit**

flat (n.) **byt**; *(adj. = level)* **rovný**; *~ tyre* **prázdná pneumatika**

flight **let**

floor **podlaha**, *(storey)* **poschodí, patro**

florist's **květinářství**

flower **květina**; *bunch of ~s* **kytice**

'flu **chřipka**

fly (n.) **moucha**; (vb.) **létat|letět**

food **jídlo, potraviny**

foot **noha, chodidlo**; *on ~* **pěšky**

for: (benefit: he did it ~ me) **pro** + *acc.*; *(to treat: something ~ toothache)* **na** + *acc.*; *(exchange: pay ~ something)* **za** + *acc.*; *(intended duration: come for three weeks)* **na** + *acc.*

foreign **cizí, zahraniční**; *~er (m./f.)* **cizinec/cizinka**

forest **les** (-a)

forget **zapomínat/zapomenout**

fork **vidlička**; *knife and ~* **příbor**

form **formulář**; *fill in a ~* **vyplňovat/vyplnit formulář**

fortnight **čtrnáct dní**

four-wheel drive **pohon na čtyři kola**; *4 x 4 (vehicle)* **terenní auto**

France **Francie**

free (at liberty) **svobodný**; ~ of charge **bezplatný, zadarmo**

freeway (US) **dálnice**

freezer **mraznička**

French **francouzský**; (language) **francouzština**; ~man/woman **Francouz/-ka**; ~ fries **hranolky**

frequent **častý**

fresh **čerstvý**

Friday **pátek** (see Unit 11)

fridge **lednička**

fried **smažený**

friend (m./f.) **přítel/přítelkyně, známý/známá**

from (a place) **z** + gen., (a person) **od** + gen.

front **přední část**; in ~, at the ~ **vpředu**; in ~ of **před** (Unit 12)

fruit **ovoce**; ~ juice **džús, ovocná šťáva**

full **plný**; ~ board **plná penze**

fun **zábava, legrace**

funny (peculiar) **divný**; (ha-ha) **legrační**

further **dál(e)**

future **budoucnost** (-i, f.); in ~ **v budoucnosti, příště**

garage (petrol station) **čerpací stanice**, (coll.) **pumpa**; (for repairs) **opravna aut**; (shelter) **garáž**

garden **zahrada**

garlic **česnek**

gas **plyn**; (US fuel) **benzín**; ~ station (US) **čerpací stanice**

gate **vrata** (nt.pl.); (at airport etc.) **východ**

gate(way) **brána** (inst. **branou**)

gents (toilet) **páni, muži**

German **Němec/Němka**, (adj.) **německý**; Germany **Německo**

get (obtain) **dostávat/dostat**; (fetch) **přinášet/přinést**; ~ to **dostat se do** + gen.; ~ back **vrátit se**; ~ off (bus etc.) **vystupovat/vystoupit**; ~ on **nastupovat/nastoupit**; ~ up **vstávat/vstát**

gift **dárek**; ~ shop **dárkový obchod**

girl **dívka**

give **dávat/dát**

glad (m./f./pl.) **rád/ráda/rádi**

glass (material) **sklo**; (vessel) **sklenice**; ~es (spectacles) **brýle** (f. pl.)

go (on foot) **chodit|jít**; (on wheels, horseback) **jezdit|jet** (for more see Units 9 and 12)

gold **zlato**

good **dobrý**; Good! **Dobře**; ~ bye **Na shledanou**

got: I've ~ to go **musím jít**; have you ~ …? **Máte…?**

grateful **vděčný**

green **zelený**

greengrocer's **zelinářství**

grey **šedý, šedivý**

grilled **grilovaný**

grocer's **potravinářství**

ground **země**; ~ floor **přízemí**

group **skupina**

guest **host**; ~house **penzión**

guide (person and book) **průvodce**, (f.) **průvodkyně**; ~ed tour **turistický zájezd (s průvodcem)**

hair **vlasy** (pl.); have one's ~ cut **dát se ostříhat**

hairdresser's (men's) **holičství**, (ladies') **kadeřnictví**

hairdryer **fén**

half **půl** + gen.; ~ board **polopenze**; ~ = child's (ticket etc.) **dětský**

ham **šunka**

hamburger **hamburger**

hand **ruka**; ~bag **kabelka**; ~ luggage **příruční zavazadla**

hangover **kocovina**

happen **stávat se/stát se** (stane se)

happy **šťastný**

hard (not soft) **tvrdý**, (not easy) **těžký**

hardware shop **železářství**

hat **klobouk**

have **mít**; ~ to (must) **muset**

hayfever **senná rýma**

head **hlava**, (of a workplace) **vedoucí**

headache **bolest hlavy**; I've got a ~ **Bolí mě hlava**

headlight **přední světlo**

hear **slyšet/u-**

heat **horko**; ~ing **topení**

heavy **těžký**

heel (of foot) **pata**, (of shoe) **podpatek**

hello **dobrý den**, (to a familiar) **ahoj**, (on phone) **haló**

help (n.) **pomoc**, (vb.) **pomáhat/pomoct**; Help! **Pomoc!**

herbs **byliny**

her (not him) **ji**, (not his) **její**

here **zde, tady**

hi! **ahoj!**

high **vysoký**

hill **kopec**

him **ho, jeho**

hire **pronajímat/pronajmout**

his **jeho**

hitchhike **stopovat, jezdit|jet stopem**

hole **díra**, (small) **dírka**

holiday **dovolená**, on ~ **na dovolené**; ([school] ~s) **prázdniny**

home: at ~ **doma**; go ~ **jít** or **jet domů**

horse **kůň** (pl. **koně**)

hospital **nemocnice**; maternity ~ **porodnice**

host **hostitel**, ~ess **hostitelka**, (in bar) **hosteska** hostel **noclehárna, ubytovna**; *youth hostel* **(turistická) ubytovna (pro mládež)**

hot **teplý, horký**; ~ *dog* **párek v rohlíku**; *it's ~ (of e.g. food)* **je to moc teplé**, *(of weather)* **je horko**; *I'm ~* **je mi horko**

hotel **hotel**; *4-star ~* **čtyřhvězdičkový h.**

hour **hodina**

house **dům (domu)**

how **jak**; *how much/many?* **kolik?**

hungry: *be ~* **mít hlad**

hurry: *be in a ~* **spěchat, mít naspěch**

hurt **bolet**

husband **manžel**; *~ and wife* **manželé**

I **já**

ice **led**; *~ cream* **zmrzlina**

if **jestli, kdyby** *(see Unit 15)*

ill **nemocný**

immediately **hned**

important **důležitý**

impossible **nemožný**

in **v** *+ loc.*; *Is he ~?* **Je tady?** *or* **Je doma?**; *~ ten minutes* **za deset minut**

including **včetně** *+ gen.*

indigestion **trávicí potíže**

information **informace**

injur|ed **zraněný**; *~y* **úraz**, *(minor)* **rána**

insect(s) **hmyz** *(no pl.)*

instead of **místo** *+ gen.*

interesting **zajímavý**

international **mezinárodní**

interpret **tlumočit**; *~er* **tlumočník**

intersection **křižovatka**

into **do** *+ gen.*

introduce *(oneself)* **představit (se)**

invit|ation **pozvání**; *~e* **zvát/pozvat**

Ireland **Irsko**; *Irish* **irský**; *~man/~woman* **Ir/-ka**

iron *(n.)* **žehlička**, *(vb.)* **žehlit**

jacket **sako**

jeans **džínsy** *(m.pl.)*

jewel **klenot**; *~lery* **šperky**; *~ler's* **klenotnictví**

job **zaměstnání, práce**

jog: *go ~ging* **chodit|jít běhat**

joke **žert**, *(narrated)* **vtip**

journey **cesta**; *Have a good ~!* **Šťastnou cestu!**

juice **šťáva**, *(as beverage)* **džús**

jumper **svetr**

just *(= only)* **jen(om)**; *(adv.)* **právě**

keep **nechávat si/nechat si**

key **klíč** *(m.)*

kilogram **kilo**

kilometre **kilometr**

kind **laskavý, hodný**

kitchen **kuchyně** *(f.)*

knee **koleno** *(see Unit 13)*

knife **nůž**; *~ and fork* **příbor**

knock down/over **srážet/srazit**

know *(a thing, person etc.)* **znát**; *(a fact)* **vědět**

lad|y **dáma, paní**; *~ies' (room)* **dámské záchody** (**Dámy** *or* **ženy** *on the door*)

lager **ležák**

lake **jezero**

lamp **lampa**

language **jazyk**

large **velký**

last **poslední**; *(with week etc.)* **minulý**; *~ night* **včera večer**

late **pozdě**; *~r* **později**

laugh **smát se (směje se)/za-**

launderette, laundromat **veřejná prádelna**

lawyer *(m./f.)* **právník, právnička**

leaflet **leták, brožura**

leak *(n.)* **únik**; *(vb.) (gas)* **unikat**, *(water)* **téct (teče), kapat (kape)**

learn **učit se/na-**

least: *at ~* **alespoň, přinejmenším**

leather **kůže**

leave *(= depart)* **odjíždět/odjet, odcházet/odejít**; *(deposit)* **nechávat/nechat**; *(forget)* **zapomínat/zapomenout**

left **levý**; *~ luggage (office)* **uschovna zavazadel**

leg **noha** *(see Unit 13)*

lemon **citrón**; *~ade* **limonáda**

lend **půjčovat/půjčit**

less **méně**

letter **dopis**; *~box* **poštovní schránka**

lettuce **(hlávkový) salát**

licence **povolení, licence**

lift *(elevator)* **výtah**; *Can you give me a ~?* **Můžete mě svézt?**

light **světlo**; *(not dark)* **světlý**, *(not heavy)* **lehký**; *Do you have a ~?* **Máte oheň?**; *~er* **zapalovač**

like: *I (don't) ~ it* **(ne)líbí se mi to**; *Would you ~ a drink/something to eat?* **Dáte si něco k pití/k jídlu?**; *(adj.)* **podobný**, *What's he/it ~* **Jaký/Jaké je?**; *something ~ this* **něco takového**

line **linka**

lips **rty** *(sg. **ret**)*

list **seznam**

listen **poslouchat**

litre **litr**

little **malý**; *a ~* **trochu** *(+ gen.)*

live **žít**, *(dwell)* **bydlet**

local **místní**

lock *(n.)* **zámek**, *(vb.)* **zamykat/zamknout**

locker: *left-luggage ~* **skříňka na zavazadla**

London **Londýn (-a)**
long *(adj.)* **dlouhý**, *(adv., = a long time)* **dlouho;** ~er **déle**
look *(at)* **dívat se/po- na** + *acc.;* ~ *after* **starat se/po** + *o* + *acc.;* ~ *for* **hledat**
lorry **naklaďák**
lose **ztrácet/ztratit**; ~ *one's way* **zabloudit**
lost property *(office)* **ztráty a nálezy**
lot: *a* ~, ~*s* **spousta** + *gen.*
loud **hlasitý, hlučný**
lounge **salón**
love **milovat**
low **nízký**
luck **štěstí**
luggage **zavazadla** *(n. pl.);* ~ *label* **visačka**
lunch **oběd**; *(vb.)* **obědvat**

magazine **časopis**
mail **pošta, dopisy**; *(vb.)* **posílat/poslat poštou**; ~ *box* **poštovní schránka**
main **hlavní**; ~ *course* **hlavní chod**
make **dělat/u-**
man **muž, člověk**
manager **vedoucí, manažer**
many **mnoho** + *gen.*
map **mapa**; *street-*~ *(of a town)* **orientační plán (města)**
market **trh**
married *(of man)* **ženatý**, *(of woman)* **vdaná**; *a* ~ *couple* **manželé**
match **zápas, utkání**
matches **zápalky, sirky**
matter: *it doesn't* ~ **Nevadí, Na tom nezáleží**; *What's the matter?* **Co je?**
maybe **možná, snad**
meal **jídlo**
mean: *What do you mean?* **Co tím myslíte?** *What does it mean?* **Co to znamená?**
meat **maso**
medicine **lék(y)**
medium **střední**
mend **opravovat/opravit**
men's room **pánské záchody** (**Páni** or **Muži** on the door)
mention: *Don't mention it!* **Není zač. Za málo!**
menu **jídelní lístek**
message **vzkaz**
metre **metr**
midday **poledne**; *at* ~ **v poledne**
middle: *in the* ~ *(of)* **uprostřed** (+ *gen.*)
midnight **půlnoc**; *at* ~ **o půlnoci**
milk **mléko**
mind: *never* ~ **to nevadí**; *Do you mind (noun)?* **Vadí vám ..?**; *Would you mind -ing?* **Vadilo by vám**

+ *inf.*; *Would you mind if I …?* **Vadilo by vám, kdybych ..?**
mineral water **minerálka**
minute **minuta**; *Just a* ~ *!* **Moment!**
mirror **zrcadlo**
Miss **slečna**
missing: *be* ~ **chybět**
mistake **chyba**
mix *(things)* up **plést/s- (plete) si**
mobile *(telephone)* **mobil(ní telefon)**
Monday **pondělí, pondělek** *(see Unit 11, 4)*
money **peníze** *(m. pl.)*
month **měsíc** *(for names of the months see Unit 11)*
more **více** (+ *gen.*)
morning *(early)* **ráno**, *(up to lunchtime)* **dopoledne**; *this* ~ **dnes ráno**
most **nejvíce** (+ *gen.*)
mother **matka**
motorbike **motorka, motocykl**
motorway **dálnice**
mountain **hora**
mouth **ústa** *(nt. pl.)*
movie **film**
Mr **pan**; ~ *and Mrs X* **manželé X-ovi**
Mrs **paní**
Ms – *no equivalent, use* **slečna**
much **mnoho** + *gen.*; ~ + *comp.* **mnohem** + *comp.*; *not* ~ **moc ne**
museum **muzeum**
mushrooms **žampiony**, *(wild)* ~ **houby**
music **hudba**
must **muset**
mustard **hořčice** *(f.)*
my **můj, moje, moje**

name **jméno**; *My name is …* **Jmenuju se …**; *What's your name?* **Jak se jmenujete?**
napkin **ubrousek**
narrow **úzký**
natural *(behaviour etc.)* **přirozený**, *(to do with nature)* **přírodní**
near **blízko, nedaleko;** ~*est* **nejbližší**
nearly **téměř**
necessary **nutný, nezbytný**; *that's not* ~ *to* **není tře**
neck **krk**
need **potřebovat**; *you needn't …* **nemusíte** + *inf.*
neither … nor … **ani … ani …**
never **nikdy**
new **nový**; *the* ~*s* **zprávy**; ~*spaper* **noviny**; ~*sagent's* **prodejna tisku, trafika**
next *(in sequence, time)* **příští**; *('N*~*!', e.g. patient)* **další**; ~ *to* **vedle** + *gen.*
nice **pěkný**, *(of a person)* **milý**

night **noc**; last ~ **včera večer**; during the ~ **v noci**;
'Good ~!' **Dobrou noc!**
no **ne**; (not any) **žádný**
nobody **nikdo**
noisy **hlučný**
non-alcoholic **nealkoholický**
none **žádný**
non-smoking **nekuřácký**
nor **ani**
normal **normální, běžný**
north **sever**; ~ east **severovýchod**; ~ west
severozápad
note (bank~) **bankovka**
nothing **nic**
now **teď, nyní**
number **číslo**
nuts **ořechy**

o'clock: five ~ **pět hodin**; see Units 9, 13
often **často**
oil **olej** (m.)
OK **dobře**
old **starý**
olive **oliva**
omelette **omeleta**
on **na** + loc.; on TV **v televizi**; What's on? **Co dávají?**
once **jednou**; at once **hned**
one **jeden, jedna, jedno**
one-way (street) **jednosměrná (ulice);** ~ (ticket)
jednoduchá (jízdenka)
onion **cibule** (f.)
only **jen(om)**
open (vb.) **otvírat/otevřít**, (adj.) **otevřený**
opposite (prep.) **proti** + dat.; (adv.) **naproti**
or **nebo**
orange **pomeranč**; ~ juice **pomerančová šťáva**
order **objednávat/objednat**
ordinary **obyčejný**
other (different) **jiný**; the ~ ten **druhý**; and ~s **a další**
our(s) **náš, naše, naše**
out: be ~ **nebýt doma, být venku**; go ~ **jít ven**;
~doors **venku**
over (position) **nad** + inst. or acc.; (quantification)
nad, přes + acc.; ~ there **tamhle**
overnight **přes noc**; ~ stay **nocleh**
own (vb.) **vlastnit**, (adj.) **vlastní**

pack(et) **krabice, krabička**; (vb.) **balit/za-**
package **balík**, small ~ **balíček**
pain **bolest** (-i); I have a ~ here **bolí mě tady**; it's
painful **bolí**; ~killers **lék proti bolesti**
pair **pár** + gen.
panties **kalhotky**
pants (under~) **spodky**; (US trousers) **kalhoty**

pantyhose, see tights
paper **papír**; (= news~) **noviny**
parcel **balík**
Pardon (me)? **Prosím?**
parents **rodiče** (m. pl.)
park **park**; (vb.) **parkovat/za-;** car-~, ~ing lot
parkoviště
part **část** (-i)
participate (in) **(z)účastnit se** (+ gen.)
partner **partner/-ka**
party (group) **skupina**; (celebration) **oslava,**
večírek, party (f.)
passport **(cestovní) pas**
pavement **chodník**
pay **platit/za-;** ~ phone **telefon na mince**
pen **pero**; (ballpoint) **propisovačka**
pencil **tužka**
people **lidé**
pepper **pepř**; (green/red as veg.) **paprika**
percentage **procento**; five per cent pět **procent**
perfume **parfém**
perhaps **možná, snad**
person **osoba**
petrol **benzín**; ~ station **čerpací stanice**, (coll.)
pumpa
pharmacy **lékárna**
phone (n.) **telefon**, (vb.) **telefonovat**; ~ book
telefonní seznam; ~box **(telefonní) budka**;
~card **telefonní karta**; ~ number **telefonní číslo**
photo(graph) **fotografie**, (coll.) **fotka**
picture **obraz, obrázek**
piece **kus**
pillow **polštář** (m.)
pink **růžový**
place **místo**
plane **letadlo**
plaster(s) **náplast(i)**
plate **talíř** (m.)
platform (at station) **nástupiště**; Which platform
for Brno? **Z kterého nástupiště jede vlak na**
Brno?
play **hra**, (vb.) **hrát**
pleasant **příjemný**
please **prosím**
plug (elec.) **zásuvka**, (in basin) **zátka**
poison(ous) **jed(ovatý)**
police **policie**; ~man **policista**; ~ station **policejní**
stanice
polluted **znečištěný**
pool: swimming ~ **bazén**
pork **vepřové**
port **přístav**
possible **možný**; Is it possible to ..? **Je možné** + inf.;
as … as possible **co nej-**

post **pošta**, (vb.) **posílat/poslat poštou**; ~box **poštovní schránka**; ~card **pohlednice**; ~ office **pošta**; ~e restante **poste restante**
potato **brambora**; ~ chips (US) **lupínky, brambůrky**
pound **libra**
prefer: I'd prefer … **Chtěl bych radši …**
pregnant **těhotná**
prescription **předpis**
present (gift) **dárek**
pretty **hezký, pěkný**
price **cena**
private **soukromý**
prize **cena**
probably **asi, patrně, nejspíš**
problem **problém**
program(me) **program**
pronounce **vyslovovat/vyslovit**
public **veřejný**; ~ holiday **den pracovního klidu**; ~ lavatories **veřejné záchodky**
puncture: I've had a ~ **píchl jsem**
purse **peněženka**, (US = handbag) **kabelka**
put **dávat/dát**
pyjamas **pyžamo**

quarter **čtvrt**
question **otázka**, (enquiry) **dotaz**
queue **fronta**
quick **rychlý**
quiet **tichý**; ~! **Ticho!**; peace and ~ **klid**
quite **docela**

radiator **radiátor**
radio **rádio, rozhlas**
rail: by ~ **vlakem**
rain **déšť**, (vb.) **pršet**
rape **znásilnění**, (vb.) **znásilňovat/znásilnit**
rare **vzácný**, (of steak) **krvavý**
rather **spíš**; I'd ~ **Radši bych …**
razor **holicí strojek**
read **číst/pře-**
ready **připravený, hotový**
real **skutečný**; ~ly **opravdu**
receipt **bloček, potvrzení**
reception **recepce**; ~ist **recepční**
recommend **doporučovat/doporučit**
recorded: by ~ delivery **doporučeně**
red **červený**
registered: by ~ mail **doporučeně**
remember **pamatovat si/za-, vzpomínat si/vzpomenout si**
rent **nájemné**; (vb.) **najímat si/najmout si**
repair **oprava**; (vb.) **opravovat/opravit**; have/get one's watch ~ed **dát si opravit hodinky**

repeat **opakovat**
reserv|ation **rezervace**, ~e **rezervovat**, ~ed **obsazeno**
restaurant **restaurace**; ~ car **jídelní vůz**
rest room (US = lavatory) **záchod**
return **návrat**; ~ ticket **zpáteční lístek**
reverse **charge** (call) (hovor) **na účet volaného**
rice **rýže** (f.)
right **správný**; (not left, proper) **pravý**; That's right! **Správně!**; You're right! **Máte pravdu!**
ring **prsten**; (vb.) **volat/za-, telefonovat/za-**; ~ back **zavolat zpátky**
river **řeka**
road **silnice**, (in town) **ulice**
rob **okrádat/okrást**
roll: bread ~ **rohlík**; round ~ **houska**
room **pokoj** (m.), single ~ **p. pro jednoho, jednolůžkový p.**; double/twin ~ **p. pro dva, dvoulůžkový p.**; ~ service **(hotelová) obsluha**
rosé (wine) **růžové víno**
round **kulatý**; ~ trip **cesta tam a zpátky**; (US) ~ trip ticket **zpáteční jízdenka**
route **cesta, trasa**; (bus-) **linka**
rubbish **odpadky** (m.pl.); ~ bin/basket **koš na o.**
rucksack **ruksak**
run (person) **běžet|běhat**, (bus etc. service) **jezdit**; (manage) **vést**

safe (n.) **sejf**; (adj.) (not dangerous) **bezpečný**, (in safety) v **bezpečí**
salad **salát**
salt **sůl** (soli)
same: the ~ **to samé**; it's all the ~ (to me) **je (mi) to jedno**
sandwich **sendvič**, open ~ **obložený chlebíček**
sanitary towels (US napkins) **(dámské) vložky**
Saturday **sobota** (see Unit 11, 4)
say **říkat/říci**; How do you ~ this in Czech? **Jak se tohle řekne česky?**
schedule (US = timetable) **jízdní řád**
scissors **nůžky** (f.pl.)
Scot (m./f.) **Skot/-ka**, ~tish **skotský**; ~land **Skotsko**
seat **sedadlo, místo**; Is this ~ taken? **Je tady volno?**; Do take a seat. **Posaďte se, prosím.**
second (n.) **sekunda**; (adj.) **druhý**; travel ~ class **jezdit|jet druhou třídou**
see **vidět/u-**; May I ~ it? **Můžu se na to podívat?**; I ~ **rozumím**; See you! **Nashle**
self-service **samoobsluha**
sell **prodávat/prodat**
send **posílat/poslat (pošle)**
separately (pay, send, travel, live) **zvlášť**
serious **vážný**
service **služba, obsluha**

serviette **ubrousek**

several **několik** + *gen.*

shade **stín**; *~s (sunglasses)* **sluneční brýle**

shampoo **šampón**

share **dělit se/roz-** + *o* + *acc.*

shaver **holicí strojek**

sheet **prostěradlo**

shirt **košile** *(f.)*

shoe **bota**; *~laces* **tkaničky do bot**; *~ polish* **krém na boty**; *~ shop* **prodejna obuvi**; *shoe repairer's* **opravna bot**

shop **obchod, prodejna**

short **krátký**; *~s* **šortky** *(f.pl.)*

shoulder **rameno** *(see Unit 13)*

show (performance) **představení**; *(vb.)* **ukazovat/ ukázat**

shower **sprcha**; *of rain* **přeháňka**

shut **zavírat/zavřít**; *They're/It's shut.* **Mají/Je zavřeno.**

sick **nemocný**; *be ~ (vomit)* **zvracet**; *I feel ~.* **Je mi na zvracení.**

side **strana**; *~walk* **chodník**

sight (eye~) **zrak**; *(tourist attraction)* **pamětihodnost**; *be/go ~seeing* **navštěvovat pamětihodnosti**

silver **stříbro**

since (given that) **když**; *(time prep.)* **od** + *gen.*

single: a ~ ticket **jednoduchá jízdenka**; *I'm ~* **jsem svobod|ný/~ná**; *~ room* **jednolůžkový pokoj**

sister **sestra**

sit (be sitting) **sedět**; *(sit down)* **sednout si**; *Do sit down.* **Posaďte se, prosím.**

size **velikost** *(-i)*

ski **lyže** *(f.)*; *(vb.)* **lyžovat**; *~er* **lyžař**; *~ tow* **(lyžařský) vlek**

skin **kůže** *(f.)*

skirt **sukně** *(f.)*

sky **obloha**

sleep **spát** *(spí)*; *~ing bag* **spací pytel**; *~ing car* **lůžkový vůz**

slow **pomalý**; *~ly* **pomalu**; *~ down* **zpomalovat/ zpomalit**

small **malý**

smell (pleasant) **vůně**, *(neutral)* **zápach**, *(unpleasant)* **smrad**; *There's a smell.* **Smrdí.**

smoke **kouř** *(m.)*, *(vb.)* **kouřit**; *Do you mind ~?* **Vadí vám kouř?** *(non-)* *~r* **(ne)kuřák**

snow **sníh** *(sněhu)*; *it's ~ing* **sněží**

so (+ adj. or advb) **tak**; *(therefore)* **proto**; *So do I* **Já také**

soap **mýdlo**; *~ powder (washing ~)* **prací prostředek/prášek**

sober **střízlivý**

sock **ponožka**

soda water **sodovka**

soft **měkký**; *~ drink* **nealkoholický nápoj**

sole **podrážka**

some (amount) **trochu** + *gen.*, *(number)* **nějaké** *(pl.)*

some|body **někdo**; *~thing* **něco**; *~times* **někdy**; *~where* **někde**

son **syn**

soon **brzy**; *as ~ as possible* **co nejdřív**

sorry: I'm ~ **Promiňte!**; *S~? (I didn't hear/understand)* **Prosím?**

sort **druh**; *this ~ of* **takový**; *What sort of …?* **Jaký …?**

soup **polévka**

south **jih**; *~ east* **jihovýchod**; *~ west* **jihozápad**

souvenir **suvenýr**; *~ shop* **prodejna suvenýrů**

speak **mluvit**

spectacles **brýle** *(f.pl.)*

spend (money) **utrácet/utratit**, *(time)* **trávit/s-**

spirits **tvrdý alkohol**

spoon **lžíce** *(f.)*; *tea~* **lžička**

spring **jaro**; *in ~* **na jaře**

square **náměstí**

stair(s) **schod(y)**

stamp (postage) **známka**; *(rubber-~)* **razítko**

stand **stát** *(stojí)*

start **začátek**; *(vb.)* **začínat/začít** *(začne, začal)*; *The car won't start.* **Auto nestartuje.**

starter (hors d'oeuvres) **předkrm**

stately home **zámek**

station **nádraží**; *bus ~* **autobusové nádraží**

stay (remain) **zůstávat**/*zůstat*, *(dwell)* **bydlet**; *~ overnight* **přenocovat**

steak **biftek**

steal **krást/u-** *(krade, kradl; ukradne, ukradl)*

steep **prudký**

still **ještě**

stomach **žaludek**; *I've got ~ ache* **bolí mě ž.**

stone **kámen**

stop (bus, tram) **zástavka**; *(vb.)* **zastavovat/ zastavit**

straight **rovný**; *~ ahead* **rovně**

strange **divný**; *~r* **cizinec**; *I'm a stranger here* **jsem tu cizí**

street **ulice**

string **provázek**

strong **silný**

stuck (jammed) **zaseklý**; *(glued)* **přilepený**, *(together)* **slepený**

subway (pedestrian) **podchod**, *(US = metro)* **metro**

suddenly **najednou**

sugar **cukr**

suit **oblek**; *~case* **kufr**

summer **léto**, in ~ **v létě**

sun **slunce** (nt.); ~glasses **sluneční brýle**; ~burn
spálení (sluncem); ~stroke **úpal**; ~tan **opalení**,
~tan oil **olej na opalování**

Sunday **neděle** (see Unit 11, 4)

supermarket **supermarket, velká samoobsluha**

supper **večeře** (f.)

supplement **příplatek**

sure: Are you sure? (m./f.) **Jste si tím jist(a)?**

surname **příjmení**

sweater **svetr**

sweet **sladký**; (dessert) **dezert, moučník**; ~s
bonbóny

swim **plavat**; have a ~ **zaplavat si**; ~ming costume,
trunks **plavky**; ~ming pool **bazén**

switch **vypínač**; ~ off (lights) **zhasnout**, (engine,
TV) **vypnout**; ~ on (lights) **rozsvítit**, (engine, TV)
zapnout

table **stůl (stolu)**

take **brát/vzít (bere; vezme, vzal)**

talk **mluvit**

tall **vysoký**

tampon **tampon**

tap **kohoutek**

tape: adhesive, sticky ~ **izolepa**

taste **chuť** (f.)

taxi **taxi, taxík**; ~ driver **taxikář**; ~ rank, stand
stanoviště taxíků

tea **čaj** (m.)

telephone **telefon**; (vb) **telefonovat**; ~ directory
telefonní seznam

television **televize**; on ~ **v televizi**

tell **říkat/říci (řekne, řekl)**

terrible **strašný**

text (message) **esemeska**

than **než**

thank **děkovat/po-**; ~s **díky**; no ~s **děkuji, ne**;
thank you (very much) **děkuju (pěkně)**

that **ten, ta, to** (see Unit 5); (conj.) **že**

theatre **divadlo**

their(s) **jejich**

then **potom**

there **tam**

thick **silný**

thief **zloděj**

thin (of thing) **tenký**, (of person) **hubený**

thing **věc (-i)**

think (that …) **myslet(, že …)**; ~ about **přemýšlet**
o + loc.

thirsty: be ~ **mít žízeň**

this **tenhle, tahle, tohle** (see Unit 5)

throat **hrdlo, krk**

Thursday **čtvrtek** (see Unit 11, 4)

ticket **lístek**; (for travel) **jízdenka**, (for air travel)
letenka; return ~ **zpáteční jízdenka**

tights **punčocháče** (m. pl.)

time **čas**; What's the ~? **Kolik je hodin?**; last ~
minule; for the last ~ **naposled**; next ~ **příště**;
Have a nice ~! **Hezky se bavte!**; ~table **jízdní řád**

tin (of food) **plechovka, konzerva**; ~ opener
otvírák konzerv

tip **spropitné**

tire (US = UK tyre) **pneumatika**

tired (fatigued) **unavený**; (sleepy) **ospalý**

tissue **papírový kapesník**

toast **topinka**

tobacco **tabák**; ~nist's **trafika**

today **dnes**; ~'s paper **dnešní noviny**

toe **prst (na noze)**

together **spolu, společně**

toilet|s **záchod|y**; ~ paper **toaletní papír**

tomorrow **zítra**; the day after ~ **pozítří**

tonic **tonik**

tonight **dnes večer**

too **příliš**; (also) **také**

tooth **zub**; I've got ~ ache **bolí mě zub**; ~brush
kartáček na zuby; ~paste **zubní pasta**

torch **baterka**

tour (of a site) **prohlídka**, (by coach) **zájezd**

tourist (m./f.) **turista/-ka**; ~ information office
turistická (informační) kancelář

towards **(směrem)** k + dat.

towel **ručník**; bath ~ **osuška**

town **město**; ~ centre **centrum**

toy **hračka**; ~shop **hračkářství**

track (US = UK platform) **nástupiště** (nt.)

traffic lights **semafor**

train **vlak**; Is this ~ for …? **Jede tento vlak do …?**

tram **tramvaj** (f.)

translate **překládat/přeložit**

trashcan (US = UK dustbin) **popelnice, koš na**
odpadky

travel **cestovat**; ~ agency **cestovní kancelář**;
~lers' cheque **cestovní šek**

trip **výlet**; How was your trip? **Jaká byla cesta?**

trousers **kalhoty** (f.pl.)

true **skutečný, pravý**

try **snažit se** + inf., (~ on/out) **zkoušet/zkusit si** +
acc.; (attempt) **pokusit se o** + acc.

T-shirt **tričko**

Tuesday **úterý** (see Unit 11, 4)

turn (vb.) **otáčet/otočit**; ~ back **obracet se/**
obrátit se; ~ right/left **zabočovat/zabočit**
doprava/doleva

twice **dvakrát**

twin room **dvoulůžkový pokoj**

tyre **pneumatika**

umbrella **deštník**
under **pod** (Unit 12); ~ground (railway) **metro**;
  ~pants **spodky**; ~wear **spodní prádlo**
understand **rozumět** + dat.
unleaded (petrol) **bezolovnatý (benzín),
  natural**
until **do** + gen.
up (out of bed) **vzhůru**; ~wards **nahoru**; ~ there
  tam nahoře; ~stairs **nahoře**
urgent **naléhavý**
USA **Spojené státy (americké)**
use **používat/použít**
useful **užitečný**

vacation **prázdniny**; on ~ **na dovolené**
valid **platný**
value **hodnota**
veal **telecí (maso)**
vegeta|bles **zelenina**; ~rian (m./f.) **vegetarián/ka**
velcro **suchý zip**
very **velmi, moc**
vinegar **ocet (octa)**
visit **navštěvovat/navštívit**
voice **hlas**

wait **čekat/počkat**
waiter **číšník;** W~! **Pane vrchní!**
wake-up call **buzení telefonem**
walk: go for a ~ **jít se projít**; Is it far to ~? **Je to
  pěšky daleko?**
wallet **náprsní taška, peněženka**
want **chtít** (see Unit 4)
warm **teplý**
wash **mýt/u-;** get ~ed **mýt se/u-;** ~basin
  umyvadlo; ~ing **prádlo**; ~ing machine **pračka**;
  ~ing powder **prášek na praní**
wasp **vosa**
watch **hodinky** (f. pl.); (vb.) **dívat se na** + acc.
water **voda**
way: on the ~ **na cestě**; this ~ **tudy**; that ~
  tamtudy; which ~? **kudy?**
weather **počasí**
Wednesday **středa** (see Unit 11, 4)
week **týden**; for a ~ **na týden**; in a ~('s time) **za
  týden**; last ~ **minulý týden**; next ~ **příští týden**
weight **váha, hmotnost**
welcome **Vítám(e) vás**; You're ~! **Rádo se stalo!**

well: I'm not ~. **Není mi dobře**; as ~ (also) **také**; ~
  done (steak) **dobře propečený**
west **západ**
wet **mokrý**
what? **co?**
wheel **kolo**
when? **kdy?**
where? **kde?;** ~ to? **kam?**
which? **který?**
white **bílý**
who? **kdo?**
whole **celý**
whose? **čí?**
why? **proč?**
wide **široký**
wife **manželka**
wind **vítr (větru)**
wine **víno**; ~ list **nápojový lístek**
winter **zima**; in the ~ **v zimě**
with **s** + inst. (Unit 12)
without **bez** + gen.
woman **žena**
wood **dřevo**; ~en **dřevěný**; (trees) **les(ík), háj**
wool **vlna**
word **slovo**
work (n.) **práce**, (vb.) **pracovat**; It won't ~.
  Nefunguje to.
worr|y: I'm ~ied **mám starost**; Don't ~! **Nedělejte
  si starosti!**
wors|e **horší**; ~t **nejhorší**
wrap **balit/za-**
write **psát/napsat**
wrong **špatný, chybný**; something's ~ **Něco není
  v pořádku**; What's ~? **Co je?, Co se děje?;**
  What's ~ with it? **Co s tím je?**

x-ray **rentgen**, (vb.) **rentgenovat**

year **rok**
yellow **žlutý**
yes **ano**
yesterday **včera**; the day before ~ **předevčírem**
young **mladý**

zero **nula**
zip **zip**
zoo **zoo(logická zahrada)**

Subject index

Numbers in **bold** refer to the units which include the material.

Notes

Notes

Notes

Notes

Notes